THE MANAGEMENT
OF BUSINESS
AND PUBLIC ORGANIZATIONS

McGRAW-HILL SERIES IN MANAGEMENT
Keith Davis and Fred Luthans, Consulting Editors

Allen   Management and Organization
Allen   The Management Profession
Argyris   Management and Organizational Development: The Path from XA to YB
Beckett   Management Dynamics: The New Synthesis
Benton   Supervision and Management
Bergen and Haney   Organizational Relations and Management Action
Blough   International Business: Environment and Adaptation
Bowman   Management: Organization and Planning
Brown   Judgment in Administration
Buchele   The Management of Business and Public Organizations
Campbell, Dunnette, Lawler, and Weick   Managerial Behavior, Performance, and
  Effectiveness
Cleland and King   Management: A Systems Approach
Cleland and King   Systems Analysis and Project Management
Cleland and King   Systems, Organizations, Analysis, Management: A Book of Readings
Dale   Management: Theory and Practice
Dale   Readings in Management: Landmarks and New Frontiers
Davis   Human Behavior at Work: Human Relations and Organizational Behavior
Davis   Organizational Behavior: A Book of Readings
Davis and Blomstrom   Business and Society: Environment and Responsibility
DeGreene   Systems Psychology
Dunn and Rachel   Wage and Salary Administration: Total Compensation Systems
Dunn and Stephens   Management of Personnel: Manpower Management and Organiza-
  tional Behavior
Edmunds and Letey   Environmental Administration
Fiedler   A Theory of Leadership Effectiveness
Finch, Jones, and Litterer   Managing for Organizational Effectiveness: An Experiential
  Approach
Flippo   Principles of Personnel Management
Glueck   Business Policy: Strategy Formation and Management Action
Golembiewski   Men, Management, and Morality
Hampton   Contemporary Management
Hicks and Gullett   The Management of Organizations
Hicks and Gullett   Modern Business Management: A Systems and Environmental Ap-
  proach
Hicks and Gullett   Organizations: Theory and Behavior
Johnson, Kast, and Rosenzweig   The Theory and Management of Systems
Kast and Rosenzweig   Experiential Exercises and Cases in Management
Kast and Rosenzweig   Organization and Management: A Systems Approach

Knudson, Woodworth, and Bell Management: An Experiential Approach

Koontz Toward a Unified Theory of Management

Koontz and O'Donnell Essentials of Management

Koontz and O'Donnell Management: A Book of Readings

Koontz and O'Donnell Management: A Systems and Contingency Analysis of Managerial Functions

Levin, McLaughlin, Lamone, and Kottas Production/Operations Management: Contemporary Policy for Managing Operating Systems

Luthans Contemporary Readings in Organizational Behavior

Luthans Introduction to Management: A Contingency Approach

Luthans Organizational Behavior

McNichols Policy Making and Executive Action

Maier Problem-solving Discussions and Conferences: Leadership Methods and Skills

Margulies and Raia Organizational Development: Values, Process, and Technology

Mayer Production and Operations Management

Miles Theories of Management: Implications for Organizational Behavior and Development

Mundel A Conceptual Framework for the Management Sciences

Newstrom, Reif, and Monczka A Contingency Approach to Management: Readings

Petit The Moral Crisis in Management

Petrof, Carusone, and McDavid Small Business Management: Concepts and Techniques for Improving Decisions

Porter, Lawler, and Hackman Behavior in Organizations

Prasow and Peters Arbitration and Collective Bargaining: Conflict Resolution in Labor Relations

Ready The Administrator's Job

Reddin Managerial Effectiveness

Richman and Copen International Management and Economic Development

Sartain and Baker The Supervisor and His Job

Schrieber, Johnson, Meier, Fischer, and Newell Cases in Manufacturing Management

Shore Operations Management

Shull, Delbecq, and Cummings Organizational Decision Making

Steers and Porter Motivation and Work Behavior

Steiner Managerial Long-Range Planning

Sutermeister People and Productivity

Tannenbaum, Weschler, and Massarik Leadership and Organization

Wofford, Gerloff, and Cummins Organizational Communication: The Keystone to Managerial Effectiveness

THE MANAGEMENT OF BUSINESS AND PUBLIC ORGANIZATIONS

Robert B. Buchele

College of Business Administration
University of Hawaii

McGraw-Hill Book Company

New York St. Louis San Francisco Auckland Düsseldorf
Johannesburg Kuala Lumpur London Mexico Montreal New Delhi
Panama Paris São Paulo Singapore Sydney Tokyo Toronto

Library of Congress Cataloging in Publication Data

Buchele, Robert B
    The management of business and public organizations.

    (McGraw-Hill series in management)
    Includes bibliographical references and indexes.
    1. Management.   2.   Public administration.   I.   Title.
HD31.B7694   658.4   76–13224
ISBN 0–07–008697–4

**THE MANAGEMENT OF BUSINESS AND
PUBLIC ORGANIZATIONS**

                    9 0 DODO 8 9 8 7 6

This book was set in Times Roman by Kingsport Press, Inc. The
editors were William J. Kane and Annette Hall; the cover was
designed by Anne Canevari Green; the production supervisor was
Dennis J. Conroy. The drawings were done by ECL Art Associates, Inc.
R. R. Donnelley & Sons Company was printer and binder.

To LuVerne
and our children

Contents

Preface

This book is designed for persons who are in or headed for managerial careers in business, government, or organizations that are both nonprofit and nongovernment (hospitals, foundations, charities, etc.).

Today it is hardly necessary to argue that the management, or administration,[1] of all these types of organizations should be taught together. First, educational and medical-health organizations as well as government at all three levels already employ vast numbers of people and no doubt will employ an even larger proportion of the work force in the years immediately ahead. For this reason, many undergraduate and graduate students simply cannot predict whether their careers eventually will be in private or public enterprises; even those who are already in their careers may shift from one sector to another. Second, it is obvious that many business and government managers must work intimately together, not only on defense and space programs but also in many other major undertakings such as low-cost housing, air and water pollution control projects, all forms of transportation and road building, medical care projects, the training of underprivileged youths, and even the managing of public schools. Third, business and government managers have a great deal to learn not only *about* one another but also *from* one another. Although there is some validity in the often-heard remark that "Government must become more business-like," it is also true that some government managers have much to teach some business people in such fields as computerization, logistics, and project management.[2]

---

[1] "Management" and "administration" will be used interchangeably in this book. Although some writers apply "management" to business and "administration" to public enterprises, we do have schools of business administration and we do talk about management of the public's business.

[2] David S. Brown (ed.), *Federal Contributions to Management* (Frederick A. Praeger, Inc., New York, 1971), especially chap. 10.

For these reasons, some leading schools of business administration (such as UCLA and Northwestern) have changed their names to "school of management," noting their movement into the teaching of public management too; and Yale University in 1976 launched a new school to award a master's degree in public and private management.[3] These schools recognize that our society has evolved from a collection of small family and work units into one of vast, complex institutions—private, semiprivate, and public—and that the responsibility for making these function effectively rests with their managers.[4]

METHODS OF THIS BOOK

There is debate, however, on *how* to teach these long-separate subjects together. Some teachers favor complete integration—the so-called generic approach, or "management is management is management" wherever it is applied. The danger is that this will produce a generalized, bland mixture that will satisfy no one. Other teachers, feeling that there are significant differences that must not be submerged between types of management in the different settings, favor the opposite extreme—presenting separate side-by-side business and public treatment of each subject. The danger here is that the final product will be long and repetitive.

The way out of this dilemma, which has emerged during the author's nine years of teaching a private-public management course, is the middle way; thus this book gives integrated treatment to some subjects and separate treatment to others that are essentially different in the public as opposed to the private context.

It is impossible for this modest-sized book to cover details for many kinds of business and public organizations; however, this book does cover the main patterns of management—the main trends and the main problems of these fields. Students should concurrently read books and journals from their own particular fields—retail store management, bank management, nursing administration, police management, or any other—so that they will understand the managerial practices current in any particular field in light of the practices, trends, and problems in management generally. Each student will know, then, whether the administration literature in his or her particular field is up to date or behind the times, academic or practical, balanced or heavily slanted toward one approach.

MAIN CHARACTERISTICS OF THIS BOOK

A key aim of this book is to be realistic, to provide a grasp of what actual managerial (administrative) practice is today and how it is changing. To do otherwise—that is, to concentrate either on current practice or on advanced techniques—would be misleading. Much of current practice will soon be outdated; yet to concentrate on

---

[3] For a discussion of the implications of these developments for the universities and for the whole field of management, see Frank Cassell, "The Politics of Public-Private Management," *MSU Business Topics,* September 1972, pp. 7–18.

[4] Peter F. Drucker, *Management: Tasks, Responsibilities, Practices* (Harper & Row, Publishers, Incorporated, New York, 1974), pp. 130–132.

advanced techniques is to mislead students about what they will find today in the real world.

Both teachers and students have been bombarded by powerful literature—Alvin Toffler's *Future Shock*[5] and *The Eco-Spasm Report*[6] and Peter Drucker's *Age of Discontinuity*[7] are examples—indicating that traditional organizational structures and managerial practices are crumbling under the impact of accelerating change in technology, social values, and the amount of knowledge available. These and many other writings make one feel hopelessly outdated unless one concentrates on advanced concepts such as "organic-adaptive" structures, systems analysis, and simulation models. Clearly, these writings are correct about the trend; but they are misleading about the timing. Anyone who has at least one foot in the real world of business and public management knows that actual practice is a "mixed bag" —mostly traditional techniques, some that are fairly new, a few of the most advanced. Accordingly, the first two sections of this book describe managerial practices in a "here's where it is now and here's where it is going" format. That is realistic. Only after that, in Part Three, is it pulled together and boiled down into a theory approach.

Another main aim of this book is to give the reader a balanced, comprehensive grasp of management, which happens to be a complex subject. In this respect this book is different from those that feature just one approach—whether it is the behavioral aspects, the quantitative techniques, the information systems approach, the consideration of social responsibility, or the strategy concept. To overstress or to neglect any one of these approaches is to give students a lopsided framework on which to continue to build their knowledge of management during their careers. On the contrary, once the student has a balanced base, the instructor may add whatever emphasis seems appropriate in the particular situation. The book is short enough that there will be time in a typical semester for the instructor to do just that.

Another characteristic of this book is that it usually, but not always, takes a higher-level-management view of problems rather than a first-level, or supervisor-section-head, view. Some students may feel that they need a lower-level course (supervisory practices, budgeting and production planning, etc.) in addition to or in place of the material covered in this book. Perhaps that is what some do need. But for many students it is best to take a higher-level viewpoint; it gives them material that they may use and grow with throughout their careers rather than only during the first year or two.

THE HOPE UNDERLYING THIS BOOK

The managerial job in either the private or public context

can be full of intellectual challenge or routine plodding.
can be the vehicle for making the lives of subordinates either satisfying or miserable.

---

[5] Random House, New York, 1970.
[6] Bantam Books, New York, 1975.
[7] Harper & Row, Publishers, Incorporated, New York, 1969.

can bring great personal growth for the manager or can be a stunting, frustrating experience.

can call forth analytical brilliance or can be just so much "muddling through."
can be a great adventure or a dull journey.

I hope that this book will help you realize that you have these choices to make by selection of certain work organizations and by how much you put into studying and working at management.

ACKNOWLEDGMENTS

Many students, managers, professors, and others have helped me to gain the experience that underlies this book and to write it. I am indebted to colleagues from various schools at the University of Hawaii who had the idea for an interdisciplinary course in management and who offered me the opportunity to teach it; I am especially indebted to the School of Public Health and Professor Robert Mytinger who made time available for working on this book. And thanks are owed to Professor Sheldon Varney of the School of Education, who has cooperated in teaching the interdisciplinary course. Helpful suggestions on particular parts of the book have been given by colleagues in the College of Business Administration, including Professors Clay Reeser, Lane Kelley, Ralph Sprague, and Marvin Loper. I have not hesitated to "pick the brains" of visitors to Hawaii, notably Professors E. W. Martin, Jr., of Indiana University, and John R. Croxall, of Miami University of Ohio. Special thanks are due Professor Keith Davis of Arizona State University, who contributed an excellent critique of an early draft. Also, Professors Karl Magnusen of Columbia University and Richard Babcock of California Polytechnic State University at San Luis Obispo reviewed the manuscript and offered many helpful suggestions. The research assistance of Jack Karbens, Deborah Carlson, Allan Fujimoto, and Earl Hashimoto has been greatly appreciated. Although all these persons have done their best to help, they have not always been able to make me "see the light." Hence I alone must take responsibility for the contents.

The long-suffering and excellently performing departmental secretaries Mrs. Ruth Takahata and Mrs. Gladys Kuwata are owed a great debt of gratitude—as also is my wife who proved to be not only a fine editor and proofreader but also an expert at the vexing job of indexing.

Robert B. Buchele

THE MANAGEMENT
OF BUSINESS
AND PUBLIC ORGANIZATIONS

Part One

Business Management and Public Administration from Ancient Times into the 1970s

Part One provides a sweeping overview of the subject that will be considered in greater depth in the remainder of this book: management (or administration, as it is sometimes called) of both business and government organizations. This will be accomplished in the following steps:

- Chapter 1 covers the past and the present, giving the history of management theory and practice and a description of where they stand currently.

- Chapter 2 concerns the future, giving a description of the approach to the management theory and practice—"systems management"—that is emerging in the late 1970s as the dominant approach.
- Chapters 1 and 2 are graphically summarized in a chart at the end of Part One.

The purpose of this fast sweep over the past, present, and future of management is to provide perspective, a sense of the whole. These two chapters briefly touch the important subjects in the field of management, indicating when and why each developed. As readers study these subjects in depth in later chapters, they may occasionally want to turn back to Chapters 1 and 2, using them as a basic reference to refresh their memories about how some particular subjects fit into the whole.

1

The History and Current Status of Management Theory and Practice

EARLY MANAGEMENT THOUGHT

From many centuries preceding the Christian era there is evidence that people carried on sizable enterprises, such as building the pyramids, and that they kept tax records.[1] Sometimes pre-Biblical and Biblical persons wrote about management in surprisingly modern-sounding language—such as the advice given to Moses on how to organize and delegate in order to relieve his own burden, or the saying of the Chinese philosopher Lao-Tzu:

> A leader is best
> When people barely know that he exists.
> When his work is done, his aim fulfilled,
> They will all say, "We did this ourselves."[2]

The Greek philosophers had many things to say about leadership, and Alexander the Great reportedly made wise use of staff experts.[3]

Perhaps the most formidable body of ideas for managers formulated before modern times was the writings on leadership of Niccolò Machiavelli in the early sixteenth century. Although Machiavelli's name has become synonymous with cunning and deceit, some of his ideas have the ring of enlightened modern thinking.

3

Both the era of mercantilism and the period of the industrial revolution produced considerable literature on such management subjects as personnel relations and accounting.

In the nineteenth century, a Prussian general named Von Clausewitz wrote on planning and the importance of defining objectives. In America, many persons wrote on business subjects, especially in connection with railroads. The first school of business, the Wharton School at the University of Pennsylvania, was established in 1881, and two more (Chicago and California at Berkeley) were established before the turn of the century.

Mention of these early writings reminds us that some aspects of management are age-old topics that appear throughout the recorded history of government, war, religion, and business. However, the first three major contributions to the modern theory and practice of management appeared roughly between 1900 and 1920. They were the writings of Max Weber, a German sociologist; Frederick W. Taylor, an American engineer; and Henri Fayol, a French industrialist.

THE FIRST MAJOR WRITERS ON MODERN MANAGEMENT THOUGHT

Weber: The Theory of Bureaucracy

Max Weber (1864–1920), a prolific writer and man of many interests, was impressed with the effectiveness of the government offices in Germany in his time, and he sought to draw from them a model for efficient organization of large-scale activities. His theory of bureaucracy abstracts what he believed to be the essential characteristics of large-scale organizations: Official business is conducted according to stipulated rules, through offices whose specialized work is delimited in terms of impersonal criteria; officials cannot appropriate their offices, and official business and private affairs, official revenue and private income are strictly separated; officials are given the authority necessary to carry out assigned functions, but the means of compulsion at their disposal can be used only under clearly defined conditions; the offices are linked functionally in a hierarchy; each office is directed toward common goals; officials are personally free to accept or not accept an appointment to an office; and offices are offered on the basis of technical qualifications, constituting a full-time occupation.

According to Weber, such an organization is technically superior to all other forms of administration, much as machine production is superior to nonmechanical methods. He felt that specialization of duties brought precision, speed, and thorough knowledge of documentary records; other features of his model were assured continuity, a sense of discretion, uniformity of operation, and reduction of friction.

Weber's main writing on this subject was published in Germany in the year after his death, 1920, but found little recognition in the United States until an English translation appeared in 1947.[4] Some writers have used Weber as the basis for their lists of mechanistic principles of management; others, chiefly sociologists, have modified his idealized concept, seeking to make it more realistic. Thus, some have pointed out that leadership by rules can lead to an increase in conformity,[5] impersonality, and ritual, which results in less innovation and initiative. Also, communications that must pass through many hierarchical levels can become stilted and meaningless. Others have pointed out that restricting people to narrowly defined duties does not always lead to the precise meshing of the contributions of specialists; rather, it sometimes leads to frustration, conflict between offices, and substitution of the individual's goals for those of the organization.[6]

Although modifiers of Weber's theory have pointed out that bureaucracy can have serious faults, such was the power of Weber's original analysis that many scholars still use his theory of bureaucracy as the starting point for explaining why and how large-scale organizations, both government and business, function. The term "bureaucracy" is currently used in two ways: (1) technically, as by Weber, and (2) popularly, to characterize the inefficiencies of government administration.

Taylor: Scientific Management[7]

Frederick W. Taylor (1856–1915) eventually became acclaimed as "the Father of Scientific Management," but for most of his life he was simply a production engineer, one of a number of pioneers working toward improved industrial management. After serving a few years as a supervisor in the Midvale Steel Works in Philadelphia, he was immensely frustrated by the futility of the way in which the supervisors of his day tried to motivate workers, commanding and cajoling them by turns. Taylor's common sense told him that greater production was possible. He resolved either to change the basic working relationship radically or to find a new career outside industrial management. What was needed, he decided, was a lot more knowledge about how the job could be done better; he felt that it was management's job to acquire that knowledge.

Taylor convinced the management of the Midvale Works to undertake experiments that then ran in that plant and in other companies for over two decades. He used scientific method in that he gathered precise, exhaustive data and systematically evaluated alternative ways of doing jobs. Although some of the tasks studied were as simple as shoveling coal or carrying pig iron, his experiments produced dramatic increases in productivity. Some of his improvements were as elementary as using different shapes and sizes of shovels for different types of coal, while others brought better work flow, materials handling, materials specification, and inventory control. In later experiments, Taylor devoted the same painstaking care to gathering and analyzing data on the more complex problems of cutting metals. It turned out that management previously really knew little about the best speeds, feeds, angles of cut, tool shapes, or tool materials.[8]

Taylor's main book was published in 1911,[9] but it was another event of that year which earned him national and international fame. Louis Brandeis, later on the U.S. Supreme Court, was representing shippers in hearings on the railroads' petition for rate increases. He argued that the railroads should first apply the ideas of scientific management to see whether these could achieve savings that would make rate increases unnecessary. Taylor and others testified before the Interstate Commerce Commission and later before a committee of the House of Representatives. In January 1911, Brandeis filed a powerful brief claiming that the railroads might save as much as $1 million per day by better management; this brief attracted worldwide attention. Georges Clemenceau, French Minister of War in World War I, directed all factories to use scientific management; Lenin told the Russians they should do the same. In October 1911, the first Scientific Management Conference was held at Dartmouth College; the next year saw the founding of the Society to Promote the Science of Management (which evolved into the Taylor Society and then into the present-day Society for the Advancement of Management).

Taylor's monumental contribution was to demonstrate that scientific method could bring great improvements over the "by-hunch" and "by-intuition" methods then prevailing in industrial production. This lesson has steadily penetrated one area of management effort after another, and it is still doing so.

Fervently trying to achieve what he called a "mental revolution" among both management and labor, Taylor argued repeatedly that scientific management was not a group of efficiency devices or pay schemes but a philosophy whereby management recognizes that its job is to search scientifically for the best methods of doing each job, to plan and organize work, and to train workers so that the best methods could be used. He sought labor's cooperation and a spirit of work harmony that would bring higher wages via higher productivity. He sought to develop each worker's highest level of efficiency.

Despite Taylor's efforts to make scientific management more than efficiency engineering, that is what it became to many people. Although some practitioners expanded his ideas in ways that would have pleased Taylor, many "efficiency experts" of the 1920s and 1930s carried their work to extremes that generated resistance not only from union officials (fearing diminution of their functions) but also from workers (fearing that they would work themselves out of jobs). As personnel managers developed new insights into the "human relations" of work, the efficiency experts were branded as mechanistic and insensitive to human values. Also, as we shall see, experiments in the 1960s indicated that the division of labor can be carried to the point where productivity drops because of sheer boredom (or, conversely, that job enlargement can bring increases in productivity).

Fayol: The Process Theory of Management

Henri Fayol (1841–1925) is seen by many scholars as having written the first complete theory of management. In midcareer, this French mining engineer took control of a nearly bankrupt mining company and made an outstanding success of it. After much reflective thinking about the nature of management, he began speaking and writing a few years before his retirement in 1918. His major work appeared in French in 1916 and was published in English by the International Institute of Management at Geneva in 1929; however, it did not receive wide distribution in America until a new English edition appeared in 1949.[10] His ideas were brought to the United States in the 1920s and 1930s, largely by British scholars; however, they received far more attention in public administration than in business administration.[11]

Fayol's basic theory proved eventually to be the lasting part of his work. He theorized, first, that there is a definable, teachable body of knowledge called "management" (as distinct from the specific techniques unique to production, marketing, or any other specialized parts of a total enterprise). Second, he explained the basic nature of management as consisting of the functions of planning, organizing, commanding, controlling, and coordinating. This list was soon altered by public administration writers to POSDCORB (planning, organizing, staffing, directing, coordinating, reporting, and budgeting), which became the framework for many textbooks. Thus the POSDCORB approach replaced the subject-matter approach (police administration, public health administration, educational administration, etc.), which had been used since Woodrow Wilson gave public administration its first formulation in 1889.[12]

Writers on business administration have produced innumerable variations, including a popular one using five categories: planning, controlling, organizing, staffing, and directing.

Fayol's theory proved powerful because: (1) It identified and focused on the basic processes of management as opposed to the detailed techniques that had previously been stressed. In consequence, planning and controlling came to be better appreciated; many managers greatly improved their organizations' planning and controlling capabilities. (2) Management theory did, indeed, prove teachable. The basic processes, or functions, proved easy to understand, so this approach helped managers grasp the overall nature of the many-faceted job of managing.

Fayol's approach, usually called "process" or "functional" theory, came into widespread use in government in the 1930s and in business in the 1950s. Some recent writers have grouped Fayol with Weber and Taylor (inasmuch as their ideas were mutually compatible), classifying the group as "classical" or "traditional." Also, Fayol's approach is referred to as "universalist" because he contended that it applies to managers of all types (military, government, business, etc.) at all levels of organizations.

Fayol's book also stressed principles of management, but these have proved of less lasting usefulness. His fourteen principles included one on the efficiency of specialization of labor, one on the relationship of authority to responsibility, one on the unity of command (an employee should have only one boss), one that asserted that there should be a chain of command from the highest to the lowest level, one asserting that the optimum degree of centralization depends upon circumstances of each situation, and others.

In the late 1950s and the following decade, as behavioral scientists probed deeply into how organizations actually work, it became clear that in many situations some of these principles (especially on specialization of labor) could be harmful to cooperation. Also, as more highly educated specialists came into the administrative structures of government and business, it became clear that they wanted more discretion than was indicated by the unity-of-command and chain-of-communication principles.

Thus the principles of Fayol and other writers came under heavy attack. Unfortunately, some of the attackers discarded Fayol's basic process theory along with the principles, not realizing the continuing importance of all the processes, especially planning and control, in the managerial job.

Modern writers on public administration refer to the years during which Fayol's theory was predominant as the era of emphasis on process, technique, efficiency, and the view of government administration as totally nonpolitical, simply the execution of policy set by a legislature.[13] As noted later in this chapter, they regard process theory as outmoded because politics and administration are now more intertwined than separate. But the processes are still vital.

1920–1940: BOOM AND DEPRESSION

The booming prosperity of the 1920s saw many financial innovations, including intricate holding companies. The deep Depression of the 1930s, following the 1929 stock market crash, saw new government regulatory agencies established to curb the less desirable financial practices. Thus business managers had to learn many new financial techniques and how to live with new regulations.

Managers had to learn, also, to live with unions and a new body of labor law. The combination of the Depression and Franklin D. Roosevelt's New Deal legislation resulted in unionization of the nation's basic industries.

During these decades the so-called scientific management movement moved forward on many fronts, such as time-and-motion study, work simplification, plant layout, incentive pay schemes, and the physical conditions (lighting, air conditioning, cleanliness) of work.

Another "movement" was building during the 1920s, the so-called personnel management movement. Resulting partly from the use of psychological tests for selection and placement by the government during World War I and partly from the availability of a new type of specialist, the industrial psychologist, the field of personnel management expanded rapidly. New techniques of selection, training, placement, job classification, and compensation were developed in business and government. American industrialists were regarded as far more enlightened as well as efficient in the use of human resources than industrialists in other parts of the world.

The New Deal era not only greatly expanded the ranks of public administration but also changed the nature of higher-ranking administrators' jobs. The nature of legislation changed

> . . . from general, court-enforced prohibitory laws to more specific, administratively executed, positive laws designed to reach public goals rather than just to control private actions. A considerable increase in executive agency discretion to interpret and apply legislation has followed, and interest groups have realized that, in consequence, they must actively relate to the agencies as well as to congressional committees.[14]

Thus, the earlier, nonpolitical executors of preset policy became administrators who not only had to do considerable policy setting but also had to be politically active in order to keep their programs in good standing with legislators, lobbyists, and other interest groups.[15] This affected not only the few hundred administrators described by the Second Hoover Commission in 1953 as "noncareer" administrators but also thousands of "career," or nonpolitical appointment, administrators.[16] Thus process and politics became intertwined in higher-level administrative jobs.

The General Motors–Du Pont Management Ideas

Also taking form in the mid-1920s were important innovations in managerial planning, controlling, and organizing. Apparently without knowledge of Fayol's work, interrelated management groups at the General Motors and Du Pont corporations were developing data gathering for planning and control systems twenty-five years ahead of their time. Their work involved, also, concepts of decentralization with coordinated control, or—as it was sometimes stated—decentralized administration with centralized policy. These innovations in management were given credit for the extraordinary success of General Motors in the memoirs of the man who headed the corporation for many years.[17] And other pioneers, notably J. O. McKinsey at Marshall, Field and Co., a Chicago department store, stressed the need for formulating objectives and annually reviewing achievement against them.[18]

Schools of Business Administration and Schools of Public Administration

The vigor with which the field of management was developing is illustrated by the growth of schools of business administration of college rank. In 1911, the year that Taylor's work burst into prominence, there were 19 such schools or departments; by 1925, there were 183. Some of these concentrated on the older fields of accounting or business economics; others emphasized production (with lots of Taylor), marketing, finance, and transportation. In the mid-1920s, the Harvard Business School turned its attention to top management, preparing "generalists" who could integrate the efforts of specialists in production, marketing, finance, personnel administration, and the other sections of a business. Little attention had been given to general management theory or practice. Weber's analysis of the workings of the total organization had not yet had an impact in the United States; Fayol's approach would not significantly penetrate American business for another two decades. So Harvard took an empirical approach to teaching general management, using as the main instructional device cases taken from actual business situations.

The case method not only helped Harvard become the leading school of business administration but also eventually came to be widely used, sometimes exclusively and sometimes in combination with other methods. Case method and a preoccupation with top, or general, management today still dominate Harvard; however, the cases have changed, first from dealing mostly with specific immediate problems to dealing with some broader planning problems. More recently, problems of corporate strategy and social responsibility have received considerable emphasis. Now the Harvard casebooks have many "notes" containing substantial hunks of theory; also, some faculty members research and write on planning and control systems, thus embracing a good part of process theory. The school has moved, too, into the fields of quantitative methods and the uses of computers in business, now having a computer lab.

The rise of schools of public administration is more difficult to trace because much of the teaching was and still is done within established departments of political science. However, it is clear that the field started with instruction in the management of particular kinds of public agencies (police, welfare, etc.), moved into instruction via the process theory, and has made some use of case method. There are a number of universities where the two subjects are taught in separate departments; but in a few schools (e.g., Cornell), they are in the same departments. A number of schools have become graduate schools of "administration" or "management," denoting an integrated approach (e.g., Northwestern, UCLA, and University of California at Irvine). The Woodrow Wilson School at Princeton and the Maxwell School at Syracuse University are examples of graduate schools of public affairs focusing on the formulation of public policy. A number of noncredit government schools have the same focus.

The Hawthorne Experiments

Perhaps the greatest management changes of the interwar decades arose from the Hawthorne Experiments. This formidable research project began in the mid-1920s as a rather routine study of the effect of different types and amounts of lighting on productivity, but it was expanded to far more basic aspects of managing human beings at work. The Hawthorne Experiments, running until the mid-1930s, led to many new insights basic to modern management. The results were published in the late 1930s, but their major impact was not felt until well into the next decade.[19]

As the lighting experiments at the Hawthorne plant of the Western Electric Company proceeded, it was noted that production of the control and experimental groups was responding to some factor other than the changes in physical conditions. Social scientists, notably Elton Mayo, were brought in to seek an explanation of these results. In time, chiefly by interviewing workers (an innovation!) as to what was happening, it was determined that a number of nonphysical factors were indeed affecting productivity.

The experimental program was expanded to include an elaborate nondirective interviewing program, a sociometric study of group functioning, and another study on the effects of monetary incentives.

Among the factors that appeared to make the workers feel better and to increase their productivity were such social (that is, nonphysical and noneconomic) factors as being set aside in an experimental group that received special recognition, being listened to by management-type people, and being supervised by researchers who took more interest in them as individuals than did the typical supervisors of that day. Although some latter-day writers question the validity of these impressions (seeing monetary incentives as accounting for productivity increases),[20] nevertheless the Hawthorne Experiments greatly stimulated interest in "democratic" or person-centered patterns of supervision as opposed to the autocratic, work-centered supervision then prevalent.

The Hawthorne Experiments produced other insights and stimulations, too. Some dealt with the group influences upon workers, such as their need to belong, their susceptibility to being pressured by the group even to the point of limiting production despite monetary incentives to increase production. The group influences were closely related to additional insights into formal organization and informal leadership—the idea that the real, or truly controlling, communications often come via channels other than those appearing on the formal organization chart and from persons other than those officially designated as supervisors. Still other insights gained at Hawthorne pointed out the therapeutic effect of listening, that is, encouraging employees to have their say about what was going on at the work place.

Experimentation among groups of schoolchildren as well as in a variety of industrial, commercial, and governmental work situations produced evidence linking consultative—or participative—patterns of leadership with greater creativeness and less dependence on the part of workers, better group cohesiveness, and higher productivity in some types of situations.[21]

The ideas coming out of the Hawthorne and other experiments appealed to many persons, some of whom launched a wide variety of experiments. Others simply started preaching the new gospel, sometimes a bit overenthusiastically or indiscriminately, which on occasion led to confusion and negative reactions.

Despite the misapplications and negative reactions, there can be little doubt that a great change in thinking about managerial leadership resulted from the Hawthorne Experiments and the myriad experiments and writings that followed from them. Recently, however, some social scientists have contended that the change was not basic enough. The term "behavioral sciences" has come to replace "human relations." Some observers felt that the Hawthorne insights were being used merely to manipulate workers to get them to accomplish the organization's goals. Thus the earlier advocates of human relations were seen as working within the traditional value system and accordingly were labeled "neoclassical," denoting only a modification, not a basic change, from classical or traditional managerial practice. Some behavioral scientists, as noted later in this chapter, feel that their insights into the human relations of work should be used to bring the goals of the individual and the organization together in ways that lead to greater development of each individual's creative potential.

Chester Barnard—Hawthorne and More

Hard-to-read writing and an emphasis on theory are usually associated with professors; it so happens, however, that a successful businessman wrote what is at once probably the most profound and hardest to read of all books on management.[22] Chester Barnard, while president of the New Jersey Bell Telephone Company, dug deeply into the social sciences, rigorously applying the insights of psychology and sociology to his experiences as an executive.

Barnard was in close touch with the Harvard Business School group that participated in the Hawthorne studies, and some of his ideas were related to those studies. Thus he explained the role of informal organization, how it supplements the communications of the formal organization and helps maintain individual feelings of personal integrity and self-respect. Also, his acceptance theory of authority, indicating that subordinates can frustrate authority that they do not accept, ties closely to Hawthorne revelations of how workers, through their informal organizations, restricted output in defiance of monetary incentives.

Barnard saw the organization as a social system (a system of consciously coordinated activities or forces of two or more persons), and he concluded that the persistence of such a cooperative system depends upon its effectiveness in meeting cooperative goals and its efficiency in satisfying the participants' motives. These concepts can be seen as a statement of the basic social science theory underlying the Hawthorne findings; they can also be seen as going beyond Hawthorne to provide the foundation for much of the work done later by behavioral scientists.

In addition, Barnard's focus on decision making as a key managerial process and his explanation of the noneconomic factors that influence decisions laid the basis for later work by Simon and others, who revolutionized decision theory.[23]

Post-World War II: The 1950s and 1960s

During World War II and the decade of the 1950s, many major developments —including computers and the concept of information systems, powerful quantitative decision techniques, and behavioral sciences ideas that challenged many established management practices—came crashing into the middle of public administration and business management. During the 1960s, while managers were trying to assimilate these revolutionary ideas, they (both public and private) were also faced with an additional pressure. This was a new urgency to solve such huge socioeconomic problems as decay of the cities, mass transportation, air and water pollution, improvement of the educational system, and provision of medical care to all citizens.

This cascade of new ideas and new pressures not only brought many changes in managerial practices but also shook management theory to its foundations. A leading authority in public administration has said that his field suffered a "crisis of identity" (which started to develop before World War II) from which it has not yet emerged;[24] a leading authority on business administration referred to the theory of his field as "a jungle."[25]

The new developments have been so numerous that an integrated chronological account cannot be given in a few pages. Rather, the remainder of this chapter describes the main developments briefly, noting a few of their interrelationships, and summarizes the current status of management practice and theory.

Management Development Programs

A dramatic innovation that will continue indefinitely was the return of significant numbers of mature executives to the classroom. This interest in executive development programs resulted from a sequence of events that started with the depression years, when there were few opportunities for executive development. Then came the World War II years, when business and government were expanding rapidly but most of the younger people who might have been receiving management training were in uniform. After the war came additional rapid expansion of government and business, coupled with a great demand for managerial talent. The resulting shortage of managers spurred educators to devise a variety of programs for developing supervisors, middle-rank managers, and general executives. Dozens of universities and professional associations offered such programs; hundreds of companies and government agencies developed their own programs in house.

Two big lessons have emerged from twenty-five years of experience with many different kinds of management development programs: (1) Administration can be and should be a matter of lifelong learning. It is that complex, that changing, that challenging. Even the best managers always have a lot to learn. (2) To be highly effective, classroom instruction—whether on campus or in house—must be linked to the real problems of the participants' organizations and the day-to-day working relationships between superior and subordinate. Or, put another way, the managerial climate prevailing in an organization can utterly defeat or discourage the lessons taught in the classroom unless those lessons realistically face what is actually happening in that organization.

Behavioral scientists now talk of *organization development* (OD) rather than executive development, and they intervene in an organization's planning and control processes to achieve changes in leadership practices and to make the organization more effective. (OD will be discussed later in this chapter as well as in Chapter 7.)

But the linking of development programs to real problems and real working relationships inevitably involves criticism of the current management methods. Unfortunately, even today, most high-level executives in business and public life are not ready for such criticism and challenge. In government administration the problem is especially difficult, because any criticism of existing management methods can be picked up by politicians, blown up into "a mess that we must clean up," and made into a political issue. For these reasons, the great bulk of both business and governmental management development programs remains today on a safe but rather ineffective classroom-only basis.

Management by Objectives and Planning-Programming-Budgeting System

When Fayol's process theory of management was first used by American business immediately following World War II, the planning and controlling functions enjoyed rapid development. The groundwork for this had been laid by the outstanding success of the General Motors and Du Pont companies, leaders during the 1930s and 1940s in planning techniques and control of decentralized operations via return-on-investment analysis.

The leadership, or direction, function also received intense development during the years following World War II; however, this was done by a different group of teachers and writers, those especially interested in the human relations insights stemming from the Hawthorne Experiments. Somehow the leading process theorists were slow to pick up the new ideas in human relations, so they were criticized for neglecting the human factor. On the other side, the human relations specialists were so engrossed with their own work that they did not appreciate the significance of managerial planning and control, so they were accused of neglecting the core of management in favor of "happiness." In consequence, the two groups spent considerable energy criticizing one another until they were brought together in the management by objectives (MBO—or control by objectives or management by results) approach, largely via a 1954 book entitled *The Practice of Management,* by consultant-teacher Peter Drucker.[26] His practical tone and clever phraseology helped MBO gain wide acceptance among business executives during the 1960s, but the applications were often superficial and ineffective.

As is implied in its name, the management by objectives approach stressed the importance of having well-formulated objectives and plans for the firm as a whole and for its component parts. Also stressed was the use of control reports that would measure achievement against the objectives. Chief among the controls was return-on-investment analysis. The use of human relations insights was tied to productivity in the way that objectives, plans, and controls were developed; thus it was stressed that there should be participation, or two-way communication up and down the line, in their formulation. Managers at each level would have an opportunity to participate in the formulation of objectives for their own units—objectives that would be consistent with those of the company as a whole. And participation was recommended in the designing of controls, that is, in deciding by what criteria progress toward objectives would be measured. Such results-oriented criteria provided a new basis for reviews of performance—or performance appraisals—a chronically ineffectual process in many companies and government organizations. Today, some businesses claim considerable benefits from MBO, but others have given up their attempts to use it.

A parallel but somewhat broader approach in the public sector is PPBS (planning-programming-budgeting system), which calls for budgeting by mission rather than incremental budgeting by organizational unit—the government agencies' time-honored way of budgeting. Budgeting by mission focuses on tasks to be done rather than on maintaining established organizations; also, it provides the basis for measuring results achieved against plans and for systematically considering alternative ways of accomplishing a given mission.

PPBS has twenty-five-year-old roots; however, its rise in importance is usually associated with the regime of Robert McNamara in the Department of Defense in the mid-1960s.[27] On the basis of the Defense Department's experience with it, PPBS was mandated for all departments of the federal government by President Johnson in 1965. Many states, counties, and cities followed Johnson's lead. But implementation problems proved so great that PPBS is no longer mandated on the federal level and only a few states are claiming any success with it.

These experiences with the formidable problems of implementing MBO and PPBS will be discussed at a number of points in later chapters and summarized in Chapter 11.

Managerial Decision Making

Until World War II, managerial decision making was a rather sterile subject. Economics had contributed a few useful decision tools such as marginal analysis, breakeven curves, and investment payback analysis; but the bulk of business economics was not used by managers because it was based on the unfounded assumption that decision makers had complete information and that decisions were determined by ultrarational objectives and analytical processes. The field of logic had contributed John Dewey's steps in problem solving (consisting of defining objectives, searching for alternatives, evaluating alternatives, and selecting and implementing a course of action), but rare was the businessperson who used them. Also, Frederick Taylor and others had demonstrated the value of thorough data gathering and systematic analysis, but these ideas continued to be applied mainly at the shop-floor level. The great bulk of managerial decision making was actually done much less rationally than was indicated by economists, much less formally than was indicated by Dewey, and much less scientifically than was indicated by Taylor.

In the years since World War II, however, the subject of managerial decision making has come alive. Exciting changes have come from many directions—planning and control techniques, especially MBO–PPBS at the objectives level and PERT (program evaluation and review technique) at the project level; new methods of forecasting; the concept of corporate strategy; the increased amount of well-processed data made available to decision makers via computers; and useful insights into the realities of decision processes developed by behavioral scientists. Thus increased use of leadership techniques that bring more persons' talents into the decision-making process has been encouraged. The "operations research" or "management sciences" specialists have brought into management highly developed decision criteria (emerging from the field of statistics) and many new quantitative decision techniques (made practical by the availability of computers).

New concepts in organization structure have also contributed importantly to the improvement of decision making. Thus project structures (a manager with "project authority" overlaying the traditional functional departments in a cross-hatch pattern) utilizing PERT and PERT/Cost techniques can pull together the information needed to give a sharp focus to the decisions involved in managing the project.

On the government side, all these same forces have been at work; however, progress is slower, with certain exceptions, because government decision making is plagued with additional complexities. Rational approaches are often bogged down and obscured by pluralistic politics (the presence of so many sides to be heard on every question and the pressures to cater to special interests and short-run considerations).

While many factors have already contributed to the strengthening of managerial decision making, much more intensive study and rapid change lie ahead. Since this is the area in which today's young managers will probably see the greatest further change before the end of their managerial careers, decision making is considered in greater depth in Chapter 9; and references on many subtopics are supplied there.

Computers and New Organization Structures

The early use of computers in business and government involved changing clerical operations from manual or mechanical operations to much faster electronic operations. The second phase involved automation of some of the simpler forms of decision making, such as inventory reordering in industry or the screening of tax returns against standards in the Internal Revenue Service. The third phase, which is only now beginning, affects managers not only in their decision techniques but also in the way they design their management information systems (MIS).

Project structures, often computer-facilitated, are seen by some writers as a basic departure from the bureaucratic structure that has characterized large-scale organization since Weber's time.[28] They note that project managers communicate across and around the traditional lines; also, their authority is neither staff nor line in the traditional sense. Writers in business and public administration have declared the "coming death of bureaucracy" because the traditional structures are too cumbersome for modern decision making.[29] However, it appears that the death predictions are premature; bureaucracy is still well entrenched in many government and business organizations.

The computer's extraordinary ability to process and transmit data makes it possible either to centralize or to decentralize decision-making authority. It is not yet clear which of these tendencies will predominate; however, it is clear, as is illustrated in some detail in the chapter on organizing, that computers are making practical many new ideas in organization structuring. These new kinds of structures, in turn, facilitate new patterns of superior-subordinate relationships, as is brought out in the immediately following paragraphs.

Technology, Complexity, and New Patterns of Management

Thirty years of war, cold war, and undeclared war plus ten years of space exploration have produced an unprecedented emphasis upon technology. Both government agencies and private businesses now manage large numbers of scientists and engineers developing high-technology products for incredibly complex military, space, and satellite communications programs. Some other government agencies are moving in the same direction, as they take on the complicated problems of urban transportation, ghettos, pollution, and full medical care to the needy. These programs have an R&D (research and development) character too, requiring highly trained specialists in physical, social, and biological sciences plus experts in data processing.

Much of private industry, too, is moving heavily into R&D, because (1) products from paint to cameras to kitchen ranges have become technologically sophisticated and (2) the pace of product obsolescence has become so great. Part of this rapid obsolescence is due to technological change, and part is due to the fact that the United States economy shifted from emphasis on production to emphasis on consumer choice. Many firms made the "marketing concept" paramount in their planning; they stressed market research to discover consumer needs, and they mounted R&D programs to produce new products that serve those needs. In the mid-1970s, the oil price increases and energy shortages indicated that R&D programs might have to shift from catering to consumer needs to saving energy and scarce materials.

Thus many government and business managers have been, and increasingly will be, confronted with learning to manage R&D programs, and in the process they are bringing profound changes to the field of management.[30]

The planning of R&D programs requires coordination of (1) the conceptions of scientists, (2) the developmental capabilities of engineers, and (3) the predicting capabilities of market and economic researchers. The controlling of such projects requires fine judgments that will neither cut off valuable ideas too soon nor permit unproductive projects to absorb vast amounts of money. In short, the managerial functions of planning and control are extended to their limits in the managing of R&D efforts.

The functions of leading and organizing also are changing greatly in the managing of R&D. Learned scientists, working in rapidly changing technologies that require the coordination of many specialists, do not work well under the traditional concepts of narrow job descriptions, unity of command, bureaucratic communications along a chain of command, and top-down leadership; rather, a more flexible structure and a colleague-type leadership are required. So R&D organizations and the R&D parts of other organizations are managed by persons seen as "change agents," and these sections are structured differently from the straight production or "steady-state" departments.

One observer with long experience as a government official sees the same trends at work throughout public administration. He contends that now a public administrator must use a soft voice instead of a command voice and must communicate by "lateral brokerage" among many specialists and peers rather than by communications along the formal lines of the organization structure. As an extreme example, he points out that an infantry officer calling for a supporting air strike is talking to a highly trained person not under his command, and he therefore communicates in a softer voice than did the traditional infantry officer. He further states:

> New appointees to top positions in government are appalled at the way their options are narrowed by lateral brokerage among their professional subordinates before important matters can be brought up for "decision." . . . At every level of government, the complexity of the subject matter widens the circle of executives whose special knowledge is essential or whose oxen are gored . . . every decision is shared with other groups, and every major improvement—a new hospital, a downtown plaza, a poverty program, a community college, a metropolitan water plan, or whatever—involves the creative manipulation of multiple public authorities. . . . In the process of modernization the whole spectrum shifts—away from the more formal, hierarchical, order-giving way of doing business and toward more informal, fluid workways of bargaining, brokerage, advice, and consent.[31]

The same writer goes on to point out the effects of the "process of modernization" on organizational structure:

> The modern public executive thus has to learn to move in a fluid environment. To the beginning student of administration, or the detached observer, if any, the large-scale organizations of our big democracy may still look like square and static diagrams on a two-dimensional chart. But to the practitioner, they feel like chemical reaction in a liquified solution. It must have been a perceptive analyst of modern administration who first said that a task of public management was as difficult as nailing Jello to the trunk of a tree.[32]

In sum, new patterns of management, arising in technology-based operations, are spreading to many government and business organizations that increasingly employ scientists and other specialists. In later chapters the new patterns of management used by NASA (the National Aeronautics and Space Administration) will be studied for clues as to how organizations will be structured and led in the future.

Working Attitude and Productivity

There is a need for new kinds of working relationships at the rank-and-file worker level, too. The effect of technology there has often been to ultrasimplify the production line or clerical job through mechanization and automation. But this has happened at the very time when the typical worker has achieved a much higher level of education than ever before, and the result has been widespread job dissatisfaction. Workers' reactions have included high absenteeism and low productivity; they complain of boredom and the meaninglessness of their jobs. This has come to be known as the "Lordstown syndrome," after a highly mechanized General Motors plant at Lordstown, Ohio, which has experienced many work stoppages and generally poor performance.

The alienation of the work force is aggravated by changing demographics. A large percentage of the rank-and-file group is from racial minorities, which are groups not usually well understood by the majority-type supervisors.

A worrisome aspect of the productivity crisis is its relation to the nation's international trade and the balance of payments. With the United States being outproduced in certain kinds of products by various countries (particularly Germany and Japan) and often running an annual unfavorable balance of payments, the improvement of productivity becomes a high-priority matter. This includes the problem of productivity of government workers; government employment absorbs an increasing percentage of the total work force, yet it contributes little to international trade and the balance of payments.

A National Commission on Productivity has conducted extensive studies of the productivity problem and various ways of combating it in industry and in public administration. The suggested solutions—which include replacement of production lines with work teams, job enlargement,[33] new incentive systems, and new work schedules ("flexi-time" and the four- or three-day week)—will be discussed in Chapters 8 and 11.

Behavioral Sciences and Organizational Behavior

The term "behavioral sciences" has entered this chapter at various points; perhaps it would be good at this point to pull together some behavioral sciences insights into management to get a feel for this particular approach.

In connection with executive development, it was noted that behavioral scientists, using an organizational development approach, seek to remove barriers to organizational effectiveness and to aid the development of individual managers. In connection with decision making, it was noted that behavioral scientists have dissected the decision-making process in great detail.

Also, as noted, behavioral scientists have attacked traditional organization structures and principles as ill suited to today's complex, technology-based enterprises and to many of today's educated workers. Behavioral scientists have sought answers to the productivity problem by redesigning jobs to make them less boring and more conducive to the use of initiative.

Behavioral scientists have done significant research on the relationship between, on the one hand, the nature-technology of the work being done in a particular organization and, on the other, the type of organizational structure that is most appropriate. Viewing the organization as a sociotechnical system, they have found that certain types of structures and certain types of leadership are more effective in certain types of industries. This contingency approach is presented in the chapters on structure and leadership. It is related to the concept of organizational character, a concept that is useful in understanding why certain persons and certain programs succeed in one organizational setting yet fail in another.[34]

Behavioral scientists have also studied managers' value systems, comparing their professed values with the way they actually spend their working time.[35] Still another innovation by behavioral scientists, which is in its early stages of application, is human resource accounting, which focuses on the investment an organization has in its personnel and the return being achieved.[36]

While most of the behavioral sciences work applies equally to public administration, there have been many studies primarily concerned with government organizations. One has contributed the concepts of "bureaupathology" (the creation of anxiety in organization) and "bureausis" (a social disease, with frustration as the key symptom, resulting from inability to adjust to bureaucracy).[37] A study of bureau management concludes:

> The sum of these observations can be quickly stated. The theology of administration is a less satisfactory explanation of what goes on in the bureau form of group life than the sociology of administration. Not structure but people are the stuff of which a bureau is made. And its motive force is dynamics, not mechanics. . . . There is no science of "bureau" administration, narrowly conceived, that is different from the science of group behavior in other forms of administrative groups.[38]

Although they are to an extent direct descendants of the human relations specialists stemming from the Hawthorne Experiments, the behavioral scientists of the 1960s were quite critical of earlier human relations practices. Thus they contended that for two decades, the human relations insights into the psychology and sociology of people at work were used to manipulate workers to achieve management's traditional objectives. The behavioral scientists seek to redirect leadership theory and participative management practices away from manipulation and toward truly joint effort, where goals serve the development needs of the workers and middle-rank managers as well as the needs of top management and the organization as an entity.

In sum, behavioral scientists have probed deeply into organizational behavior in both business and government, studying how people actually behave in work situations with differing structures, technologies, styles of leadership, and the stresses that go with different stages of development. Their work has already contributed to many aspects of management and no doubt will continue to replace some established managerial principles and practices with new insights and a broader range of techniques.

Social Responsibilities of Managers

A few diehards still argue that a firm's overriding responsibility is to profitably satisfy society's needs as evidenced in the marketplace, and that any distraction of energy or finances from that task will result in less service to society.[39] Despite this argument, however, business leaders have increasingly over the past two decades given of their own and their firms' money and talents to community fund drives, park commissions, cultural projects, school and hospital boards, racial integration programs, and many other socially useful enterprises.[40]

Recently, however, the social responsibility issue has shifted; it appears that the public is demanding that business undertake two additional kinds of social responsibilities: first, responsibility for cleaning up its own pollution and the pollution caused by its products, for improving the safety of its products, and for paying much more heed to consumer interests, and second, responsibility for contributing to the solution of some of society's major socioeconomic problems (the ghettos, mass transportation, the improvement of education, and the extension of adequate medical care to all) through its normal process of tackling a job with the anticipation of doing it profitably. As Henry Ford II has put it: "Management should stop thinking about the public's changing expectations as costs . . . [and] start thinking about changes in public values as opportunities for profit by serving new demands."[41]

Can industry effectively reorient its objectives to include some such activities? Can industry effectively apply its engineering, production, marketing, finance, and other skills to these challenges?[42] So far, the evidence is inconclusive. A number of companies have entered the waste-reconversion field, but it appears that failures are outnumbering successes. Some firms have tried contract teaching—that is, contracting with a local school board to operate elementary schools—but early results are discouraging.[43] Some aerospace firms have done systems analysis studies of pollution and transportation for various state and local governments; but after more than five years, these have not been implemented.[44] One banker has won recognition for his "private urban renewal" program.[45] The most profitable of the large lumber companies has been a leader in recycling, which not only controls pollution but also saves considerable amounts of money.[46]

This issue concerns government managers too. If private businesses can do these jobs, then government agencies must learn to work with them. Just as NASA harnessed an array of industrial talents into an effective moon-landing project, so must other agencies organize industrial talents to solve other big projects while avoiding the glaring waste and confusion that have characterized the welfare and medicare programs. If business cannot do these jobs, then government agencies must learn to do them, because it seems clear that the body politic is going to insist on these jobs being done.

OTHER SIGNIFICANT DEVELOPMENTS IN MANAGEMENT

Within the last decade or so, there has been an awakening to the need for the study of management in many professional fields such as hospitals, group medical practices, nursing, libraries, police, schools, universities, social work, and others. For example, there are many graduate schools of hospital administration and many noncredit programs for management development in that field. While some of the other fields have not progressed that far, graduate and undergraduate courses in administration are being offered in these fields, and their professional journals contain many management articles. In the latter part of Chapter 3, management activities specific to some of these fields will be discussed.

Three big topics within the overall field of management will not be considered in this book for reasons of space; however, they should be mentioned here for the sake of completeness.

Multinational and Comparative Management

The study of the contrasting methods of management used in different countries and how to adapt the methods of one country to the economy and culture of another is called *comparative management*. Management of a company that operates in many countries is called *multinational management*.[47]

Many European and Asian companies have over the past two decades been much concerned with learning how to compete with the foreign branches of American firms; some of them are adapting some American methods to their own situations, and some are attempting to surpass American methods.[48] But the learning is not all one-way; American managers have something to learn from managers in other countries, especially since Germany and Japan have been surpassing the United States in productivity. That methods of some foreigners may work well not only in their own countries but also in the United States is hinted at by the early results achieved by Japanese-managed companies in the United States. The main difference appears to be that Japanese managers have greater concern for their worker's ideas and personal problems; they get better communications from the bottom up.[49] There is also an indication that their slow but thorough way of arriving at executive decisions may be more effective participative leadership than is usually secured in this country.

In the last decade, many large American companies have been much concerned with how to organize their multinational operations and how to adapt their leadership methods and marketing practices to the cultural-social-economic requirements of different regions.

As leading American, European, and Asian companies continue to expand their operations to many countries, it becomes clear that sooner or later the truly international company will become a reality. Thus these large firms will change from being American (or British, or German, or French, or Japanese) companies, doing a minor part of their total business in foreign countries, to truly international companies in which no one country is dominant. This problem will present many difficult problems for government administrators, who must devise ways of working with other countries on the accounting, taxation, antitrust, and other regulations of these international companies.[50] The United Nations is studying the advisability of establishing a Commission on Multinational Corporations which would not only promote a series of agreements on these subjects but also would provide enforcement machinery and sanctions. In addition, the new United Nations agency would develop guidelines for investment practices between a multinational company and a government (e.g., can the company lay off workers when the government is attempting to maintain employment?) and guidelines that would encourage developing nations to reduce the bureaucratic and graft hindrances to multinational companies.[51]

Development Administration

Applied to public administration in the so-called developing countries this rather new field of study seeks to fit administrative processes and techniques to a particular country's stage of development (that is, the capability of its political, cultural, and economic institutions) and to its developmental objectives.[52] It is closely related to the concept of comparative management in that it prescribes administrative methods and techniques appropriate to the actual local conditions instead of prescribing the best or most modern management practices of the industrially advanced nations.

Specialists in development administration seek to make economic planners aware of the fact that their plans will fail if they are not administratively feasible; thus the country must have the quality of leadership, the control of taxation, and the strength of administrative procedures to make the economic plans work. Or, in the words of one eminent economic planner, "The administrative implications of planned development have turned out to be deeper and more far-reaching than has been supposed."[53]

Futuristics

Just emerging as an academic discipline is the field known as "futuristics." It looks to the avoidance of future problems and the appreciation of future opportunities; it is concerned with what our current policies should be in order to avoid what might or might not happen in the future if we do not have such policies now.

The futurist Alvin Toffler has not given much consideration to management in his book *Future Shock;* however, to the extent that he has considered management, his ideas are consistent with those of other writers who feel that temporary, flexible types of organization structure are needed to cope with rapidly changing problems. Toffler prescribes the concepts of "adhocracy" and "participatory bureaucracy" as main elements of a new form of management to replace traditional bureaucracy.[54]

Futuristics has as yet hardly penetrated management thinking; however, chances are that it soon will do so. As futuristics develops specific planning, forecasting, and control techniques that prove useful, it will probably find acceptance in business and government management.

SUMMARY AND CONCLUSIONS:
MANAGEMENT THOUGHT TODAY

This introductory chapter has scanned a tremendous number and range of management ideas and techniques. Unfortunately, it leaves the subject rather strung out, not pulled together into a neat statement of the current theory and practice of management. But this is the way it actually is; this is the current state of affairs in both business management and public administration.

New ideas and techniques are being used by many organizations, yet traditional methods are still being practiced by many others. Old theories have been generally discarded, yet no new overall theory of management has been thoroughly developed and generally accepted. It is little wonder, then, that business management theory has been declared "a jungle" and public administration theory has been described as being in "an identity crisis from which it has not yet emerged."[55]

In the literature of *business* management, there was a decade-long (mid-1950s to mid-1960s) debate in which defenders of the "traditionalist," or process, theories fought against such newer approaches as the "social structure" school, the "behaviorist" school, and the "management science" school.[56] Finally, the name-calling and one-sided arguments subsided, and writers began to advocate a "multiple," or "modern," approach that combined some of the old with some of the new.[57] It now appears that the "multiple-modern" approach, strongly influenced by increasing use of computers, is developing into something that is being called *systems management.* Although systems management is as yet neither fully defined nor fully operational, it does appear to be the label under which the field will once again be unified.

The theory and practice of *public* administration appear to be even more pulled apart and even less close to being unified under a single new label. Ever since the New Deal days of the 1930s, government administrators have been managing more and more huge enterprises—defense, space exploration, welfare, equal health care and educational opportunity for everyone, antipollution programs, and many others. In setting up such vast programs, Congress and the state legislatures can legislate only general objectives; much definition of objectives and policy formulation must be left to the administrators. Also, the legislative branch must rely upon administrators for help in preparing legislation, because it is the administrators who have the staffs, the computers, and the organizations to do the necessary information-gathering and analysis. For these reasons, it is necessary to recognize that administrators work in a political environment; politics and administration are inextricably interwoven. The old politics/administration dichotomy is long dead; in fact, there is a strong tendency to scorn, as hopelessly outdated, any writing that mentions efficiency, the administrative processes (POSDCORB), or other elements of the old approach. Yet, who would argue that efficiency in government is not still mightily important, although certainly not as important as purpose? There is a tendency to scorn mention of effectiveness too, on the ground that, since the purposes of any government program are multiple, it is impossible to state precise objectives and to measure results against those objectives. Yet many persons in the field are not willing to give up on the attempt to be reasonably clear about what it is that particular government programs are trying to accomplish.[58] What has been called "the new public administration" is centrally concerned with social justice, but social justice will have to be defined for particular programs if progress is to be made toward it.

Much attention is being given to the "policy sciences," which comprise the analysis of public issues, the setting of objectives, and the formulation of policies by which to achieve those objectives, including social justice.[59] The focus is on problems rather than institutions.

One writer feels that it is through the emphasis on policy analysis that public administration theory will finally bring politics and administration solidly together.[60] This would appear to be a move toward systems thinking—looking at total government, both political and administrative aspects, as a single system for defining and achieving public objectives.

Inasmuch as systems management appears to be the emerging synthesis in both business and government administration, this rather new concept—what it is, its possibilities, its limitations, and its current state of development—will be studied in Chapter 2.

REVIEW QUESTIONS

1 What were the major characteristics of a bureaucracy as put forward by Weber?
2 Outline the major ideas that Taylor advocated for scientific management.
3 Briefly list the major assertions about management processes that Fayol proposed in his theoretical work.
4 Describe some of the major findings and criticisms of the Hawthorne Experiments.
5 Identify some of the new ideas and pressures which had such a strong impact on practice and theory of management in the 1950s and 1960s.
6 How do practices developed five decades ago by General Motors and DuPont relate to the currently popular management by objectives?
7 Why is process theory (POSDCORB) regarded as outdated in public administration? What are some of the current theory issues in public administration?

DISCUSSION QUESTIONS

1 What advantages for business managers and public administrators would accompany the development of a unified theory and practice between the two?
2 Why does the term "bureaucracy" so often carry a negative connotation?
3 Do alternative means of learning management and public administration exist? If so, what are the advantages and disadvantages of the different approaches?
4 In your opinion, what are the important problems, both theoretical and practical, in management and public administration that need early attention and solution?
5 Do socially responsible actions of business firms depend on the values held by their managers?

NOTES

[1] Except as specifically noted, this section will be an abstraction from a much more complete and well-documented account given in chap. 1 of Claude S. George, Jr., *The History of Management Thought,* 2d ed. (Prentice-Hall, Inc., Englewood Cliffs, N.J., 1972).

[2] *The Way of Life,* translated by Witter Bynner (The John Day Company, New York, 1944), saying 17.

[3] Edward C. Bursk, Donald T. Clark, and Ralph Hidy (eds.), *The World of Business* (Simon and Shuster, New York, 1962), vol. III, chap. 3, pp. 1644–1646. This four-volume set of selections from the

literature of business contains many instances of rather modern thought from the pre-Biblical period as well as excerpts from writers of all eras and all cultures on a wide range of business subjects.

[4] *The Theory of Social and Economic Organization,* translated by A. M. Henderson and Talcott Parsons, edited by Talcott Parsons (Oxford University Press, Fair Lawn, N. J., 1947).

[5] R. K. Merton, *Social Theory and Social Structure,* revised and enlarged edition (The Free Press, New York, 1957), pp. 50–54.

[6] Philip Selznick, "Foundations of the Theory of Organization," *American Sociological Review,* February 1948.

[7] Most management textbooks of the past three decades contain sections on Taylor and scientific management, so the present account draws on many sources. George, op. cit., contains a fairly complete account. See also John F. Mee, *Management Thought in a Dynamic Economy* (New York University Press, New York, 1963), pp. 40–46.

[8] Taylor recounted these decades of experimentation in a paper, delivered at Dartmouth College in 1911, entitled "The Principles of Scientific Management." This is reprinted in Harwood Merrill (ed.), *Classics in Management* (American Management Association, New York, 1960).

[9] *Principles of Scientific Management* (Harper & Brothers, New York, 1911).

[10] *General and Industrial Administration* (Sir Isaac Pitman & Sons, Ltd., London, 1949).

[11] Luther Gulick and Lyndall Urwick (ed.), *Papers on the Science of Administration* (Institute of Public Administration, New York, 1937). This volume was the first major recognition in the United States of Fayol's work.

[12] Woodrow Wilson, "The Study of Administration," *Political Science Quarterly 2,* 1887, pp. 197–222.

[13] See, for example, L. C. Gawthrop, "Commentary," in *The Administrative Process and Democratic Theory,* edited by L. C. Gawthrop (Houghton Mifflin Company, Boston, 1970), pp. 105–114.

[14] M. D. Reagan, *The Administration of Public Policy* (Scott, Foresman and Co., Glenview, Ill., 1969), p. 247.

[15] Among the many writers who might be cited are V. O. Key, "Administration as Politics," in *Politics, Parties and Pressure Groups* (Thomas Y. Crowell Company, New York, 1958); and H. Stein, "Introduction," in *Public Administration and Policy Development* (Harcourt, Brace, and World, Inc., New York, 1952).

[16] H. Cleveland, "Executives in the Political Jungle," *The Annals of the American Academy of Political and Social Science,* September 1956, pp. 38–40.

[17] Alfred M. Sloan, Jr., *My Years with General Motors* (Doubleday & Company, Inc., Garden City, N.Y., 1964). There is no mention in this book of Fayol or any other theorist; in fact, on p. 47 Sloan says, in connection with his "Organization Study" report which in 1920–21 set up the new GM structure and policies: " . . . so far as I am aware, this study came out of my experience . . . I had not been much of a book reader."

[18] J. O. McKinsey, *Business Administration* (South-Western Publishing Company, Incorporated, Cincinnati, 1924).

[19] The documentary report was given in Fritz J. Roethlisberger and W. J. Dickson, *Management and the Worker* (Harvard University Press, Cambridge, Mass., 1939). A less technical report, much shorter, by Roethlisberger was *Management and Morale* (Harvard University Press, Cambridge, Mass., 1941). A much broader interpretation of the relevance of the Hawthorne insights to the problems of an industrial society was given by the leading figure in the experiments, Elton Mayo, in *The Human Problems of an Industrial Civilization* (The Macmillan Company, New York, 1933). The latter book was reissued by The Viking Press in 1960.

[20] Alex Cerey, "The Hawthorne Studies: A Radical Criticism," *American Sociological Review,* June 1967.

[21] Early experiments with schoolchildren, headed by Kurt Lewin, are reported in R. Lippitt, "An Experimental Study of the Effects of Democratic and Autocratic Atmospheres," *University of Iowa Studies in Child Welfare,* no. 16, 1940, pp. 45–195. Two decades of research, conducted in many different kinds of work situations by the Institute for Social Research of the University of Michigan, is reported in Rensis Likert, *The Human Organization* (McGraw-Hill Book Company, 1967). Likert favors the term "supportive" rather than "participative," "consultative," or "democratic" leadership.

[22] *The Functions of the Executive* (Harvard University Press, Cambridge, Mass., 1938).

[23] A useful introduction to Barnard as well as an updating is William B. Wolf, *How to Understand Management: An Introduction to Chester I. Barnard* (Lucas Brothers Publishers, Los Angeles, 1968).

[24] Dwight Waldo, "Scope of the Theory of Public Administration," in *Theory and Practice of Public Administration,* monograph 8 (The American Academy of Political and Social Science, Philadelphia, 1968), p. 5.

[25] Harold D. Koontz, "The Management Theory Jungle," *Journal of the Academy of Management,* December 1961, p. 175.

[26] Published by Harper & Brothers, New York. For a later book on the same idea but stressing details of application, see George Odiorne, *Management by Objectives* (Pitman Publishing Corporation, New York, 1965); and his "The Politics of Implementing MBO," *Business Horizons,* June 1974, pp. 13–21. See also, S. J. Carroll, Jr., and H. L. Tosi, Jr., *Management by Objectives: Applications and Research* (The Macmillan Company, New York, 1973).

[27] David Novick, "The Origin and History of Program Budgeting," *California Management Review,* Fall 1968, pp. 7–12.

[28] David I. Cleland and William R. King, *Systems Analysis and Project Management,* 2d ed. (McGraw-Hill Book Company, New York, 1975), pp. 15 and 183–184.

[29] Warren G. Bennis, "The Coming Death of Bureaucracy," *Think Magazine,* December 1966, pp. 30ff. Bennis has since refined and tempered the dramatic death predictions; see his own article in the collection of readings he has edited, *American Bureaucracy* (Aldine Publishing Company, Chicago, 1970).

[30] James R. Bright, *Research, Development and Technological Innovation* (Richard D. Irwin, Inc., Homewood, Ill., 1964). Albert H. Rubenstein, "Organizational Factors Affecting Research and Development Decision-Making in Large Decentralized Companies," *Management Science,* July 1964, pp. 618–633. For more recent work by Rubenstein and his associates, see *Program Summary, 1967–70: Research on the Management of Research and Development.* The Technological Institute, Northwestern University (Northwestern University Press, Evanston, Ill., 1971).

[31] Harlan Cleveland, "The American Public Executive: New Functions, New Style, New Purpose," in *Theory and Practice of Public Administration: Scope Objectives, and Methods,* Monograph 8 (American Academy of Political and Social Science, 1968), p. 171.

[32] Ibid., p. 168.

[33] This technique, which amounts to reversing job specialization in order to restore variety, interest, and challenge to jobs, has secured increased productivity in some industrial production jobs and in the service representative job in telephone companies. See W. J. Paul, Jr., Keith B. Robertson, and Frederick Herzberg, "Job Enrichment Pays Off," *Harvard Business Review,* March–April 1969, pp. 68–78. Also see M. Scott Meyers, "Every Employee a Manager," *California Management Review,* Spring 1968, pp. 9–20.

[34] For citations of leading works on contingency theory and sociotechnical systems, see Chap. 6, footnotes 10 through 15. A system for analyzing problems of organizational change is given in J. A. Seiler, *Systems Analysis and Organizational Behavior* (The Dorsey Press and Richard D. Irwin, Inc., Homewood, Ill., 1967), especially chaps. 1 and 2.

[35] G. W. England, "Managerial Value Systems: A Research Approach," *Ethics and Employment,* Graduate School of Business Administration, University of Minnesota (University of Minnesota Press, Minneapolis, 1967). See also England's "Personal Value Systems of American Managers," *Academy of Management Journal,* March 1966.

[36] For more on this subject, see Chap. 8, pp. 228–229.

[37] Victor Thompson, *Modern Organization* (Alfred A. Knopf, Inc., New York, 1961).

[38] Earl Latham, "Hierarchy and Hieratics—A Note on Bureaus," *Employment Forum,* p. 6, reprinted in Gawthrop, op. cit. This volume contains a number of behavioral sciences articles on public administration.

[39] Theodore Levitt, "The Dangers of Social Responsibility," *Harvard Business Review,* September–October 1958, p. 44.

[40] Keith Davis and Robert L. Blomstrom, *Business and Its Environment,* 2d ed. (McGraw-Hill Book Company, New York, 1971), sec. 4.

[41] "The Contract between Industry and Society," *Harvard Business School Bulletin,* May–June 1970.

[42] Richard S. Rosenbloom, "Social Entrepreneurship," *Harvard Business School Bulletin,* May–June 1969, pp. 23–26.

[43] "The Customers Pass the Test—Or Else," *Business Week,* Sept. 12, 1970, p. 42.

[44] "What Aerospace Sees on the Ground," *Business Week,* Sept. 25, 1965, pp. 87–90; "Aerospace Firms Seek to Apply Talents to Curbing Urban Ills," *The Wall Street Journal,* June 9, 1965, p. 1; R. S. Rosenbloom and J. R. Russell, *New Tools for Urban Management,* Division of Research, Graduate School of Business Administration (Harvard University Press, Cambridge, Mass., 1971), p. 19.

[45] "Atlanta Banker with a Social Conscience," *Business Week,* July 25, 1970, pp. 34–36.

[46] "How Social Responsibility Became Institutionalized," *Business Week,* June 30, 1973, p. 78. This article gives a rundown on many firms' social responsibility actions. For a comprehensive set of views

on the social responsibility issue, see James W. McKie (ed.), *Social Responsibility and the Business Predicament* (The Brookings Institution, Washington, 1975).

[47] Endel J. Kolde, *International Business Enterprise,* 2d ed. (Prentice-Hall, Inc. Englewood Cliffs, N.J., 1973). A four-volume series of readings on all aspects of international operations is S. P. Sethi and J. N. Sethi (eds.), *Multinational Business Operations* (Goodyear Publishing Co., Pacific Palisades, Calif., 1972). Also see, Raymond Vernon, *Manager in the International Economy* (Prentice-Hall, Inc., Englewood Cliffs, N.J., 1972).

[48] J. J. Servan-Schreiber, *The American Challenge* (Atheneum Publishers, New York, 1968).

[49] Richard T. Johnson and William G. Ouchi, "Made in America (under Japanese Management)," *Harvard Business Review,* September–October 1974.

[50] "Servan-Schreiber Updates His Challenge," *Business Week,* Oct. 14, 1972, pp. 63–68. For a different view of this problem, see Mira Wilkins, *The Maturing of Multinational Enterprises* (Harvard University Press, Cambridge, Mass., 1974).

[51] "A U.N. Plan to Monitor the Multinationals," *Business Week,* June 15, 1974, p. 85; also "New Era for the Multinationals," *Business Week,* July 6, 1974, pp. 73–74.

[52] For a set of papers on this subject, see John D. Montgomery and W. J. Siffin (eds.), *Approaches to Development: Politics, Administration and Change* (McGraw-Hill Book Company, New York, 1966). For an article surveying the comparative-developmental administration field and supplying extensive citations, see Keith M. Henderson, "A New Comparative Public Administration?" in *Toward a New Public Administration,* edited by Frank Marini (Chandler Publishing Company, San Francisco, 1971).

[53] Tarlok Singh, "Administrative Implications in the Five Year Plans," *Indian Journal of Public Administration,* July–September 1963, pp. 336–343, cited in a valuable article on this topic: H-B Lee, "An Application of Innovation Theory to the Strategy of Administrative Reform in Developing Countries," *Policy Sciences,* Summer 1970, p. 178.

[54] Chap. 7. A set of articles in *Daedalus,* Winter 1969, applies the futuristic approach to business and business managers.

[55] The condition of public administration theory is perhaps best indicated by a 1971 book of readings entitled *Public Administration in a Time of Turbulence,* edited by Dwight Waldo (Chandler Publishing Company, San Francisco).

[56] Koontz, op. cit.; William H. Scott, "Organizational Theory: An Overview and an Appraisal" *Journal of the Academy of Management,* April 1961, p. 9.

[57] P. J. Gordon, "Transcend the Current Debate on Administrative Theory," *Journal of the Academy of Management,* December 1963.

[58] In fact, some writers feel that unless bureaucracies do become more rational, more effective, and more efficient, it will do no good to set up worthy social objectives and institute ambitious programs to achieve them. See Gawthrop, op. cit., concluding commentary, pp. 437–446. See also Alan K. Campbell "Old and New Public Administration in the 1970's," *Public Administration Review,* July–August 1972, pp. 343–347. Dean Campbell sees two current ambivalencies: first, desires for "responsiveness" to social needs versus desire for efficiency and effectiveness; and second, desire for community participation in decisionmaking versus desire for strong leadership that can make progress toward solving the terribly difficult, major socioeconomic problems.

[59] For a set of papers by proponents of the "new public administration" see Frank Marini (ed.), *Toward New Public Administration* (Chandler Publishing Company, San Francisco, 1971).

[60] Peri E. Arnold, "Reorganization and Politics: A Reflection on the Adequacy of Administrative Theory," *Public Administration Review,* May–June 1974, pp. 205–211.

RECOMMENDED READINGS

Boettinger, Henry M.: "Is Management Really an Art?" *Harvard Business Review,* January–February 1975, pp. 54–64.

Committee for Economic Development, Research and Policy Committee, *Social Responsibilities of Business Corporations* (Committee for Economic Development, New York, 1971).

Miewald, Robert D.: "The Greatly Exaggerated Death of Bureaucracy," *California Management Review,* Winter 1970, pp. 65–69.

Lippett, Gordon L.: "Hospital Organization in the Post-industrial Society," *Hospital Progress,* June 1973, pp. 55–64.

Chapter 2

The Trend to Systems Management

It was suggested in Chapter 1 that a new approach called "systems management" will probably become the dominant way of thinking about and practicing management (or administration). The first purpose of this chapter is to make clear what is meant by "systems management"; this will be done using the following headings:

What Is a System?
Twelve Uses of the Term "Systems" in Government and Business
So, What *Is* Systems Management?
   Definitions
   How Is It Different from "Old" Management?

The second purpose of this chapter is to give some indication of how important systems management potentially is; this will be done via the following headings:

Potential Advantages
Potential Limitations and Dangers
Conclusions: The Importance of Systems Management

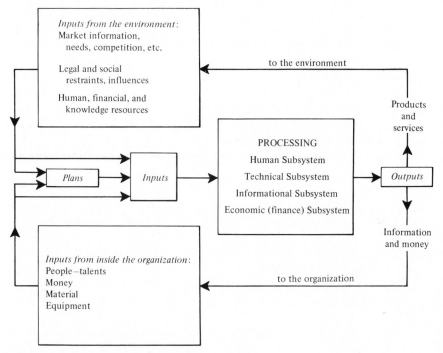

Figure 2-1 An organizational system.

WHAT IS A SYSTEM?

In its simplest form, a system consists of an input, a processing unit, and an output. An organizational system[1] (business or nonbusiness) may be seen as having inputs, processing, and output as shown in Figure 2.1.

Figure 2.1 does not tell much about how systems management actually works; however, it does hint at three ideas that will be encountered often during this chapter, three ideas that are contained in the definition finally formulated: (1) The *holistic view*—emphasis upon the firm as a whole rather than as a collection of separate departments such as manufacturing, sales, engineering, etc.; (2) stress on the organization's *relation to the environment,* which is especially important in these times when rapid changes in the environment force frequent internal changes in products, processes, and other activities; and (3) the key role of *information flow,* which is a hallmark of the computer era.

The label "systems" has in recent years been applied to a variety of managerial activities. A review of twelve of the ways in which this term has been used in business and government administration will give some strong clues as to what basic ideas constitute the essence of systems management.

TWELVE USES OF THE TERM "SYSTEMS" IN GOVERNMENT AND BUSINESS

1 Systems Selling Marketing specialists have used "systems selling" to denote, for example, the selling of an entire production line (or system) as a unit instead of selling the lathes, conveyors, welders, and other equipment separately. Again, industrial salespeople no longer sell nuts and bolts; they sell fastening systems. As another example, office equipment firms now sell "interior systems"—that is, integrated sets of office equipment instead of separate typewriters, file cabinets, desks, and paperwork forms.

Although this is a rather frivolous use of systems terminology, it does emphasize making decisions in a larger context—a step toward the holistic approach mentioned earlier. Also, as production lines and fastening processes become more automated, more complex systems will result. The same thing will happen as more and more offices link computers (files), "word processing" equipment, and display screens.

2 Cross-Department Work Flow Some management consultants now describe their work as "systems analysis" because they study the work flow through an organization, not just isolated problems. For example, one consultant discusses a clothing manufacturer who had warehousing–order filling problems; the basic solution proved, however, to lie in another part of the whole work flow—the way in which the garments were being marketed. A change in marketing brought a change in the size and nature of orders received, and this in turn eliminated the warehousing–order filling problem.[2]

The name "rhocrematics" (denoting flow of materials) has been coined by developers of a similar but more fundamental approach.[3] Traditionally, in manufacturing firms, much decision making was departmentalized (the engineering department making the design decisions, the manufacturing department making the materials-handling decisions, the marketing department making the customer-service decisions, the transportation department making the freight-carrier decisions, etc.). The rhocrematics approach, however, looks at all the steps, from product design through delivery to the customer, as one integrated system. For example, air freight companies have used this approach to argue that many companies could save money by using air freight, despite the higher freight charges, because savings would come in lighter materials and lighter packaging, fewer warehouses, and smaller inventories. In an integrated set of decisions, the higher freight costs would be more than offset by the many other savings made possible by the use of air freight.[4]

3 Social Systems Behavioral scientists studying management see organizations as social systems in which "everything is related to everything else." Accordingly, they too feel that a decision should be made with consideration of its effects throughout the organization. For example, an appliance manufacturer had succeeded partly because of easy credit policies and therefore was able to get by with mediocre product quality; however, when this firm tightened its credit policies, it was found that product quality had to be improved in order to stay competitive. Achieving quality improvement, it turned out, required changes in the training of employees, the pattern of supervision, and the organization structure. In other words, a single change reverberated throughout the system.

In order to illustrate the complexity and magnitude of interrelationships within

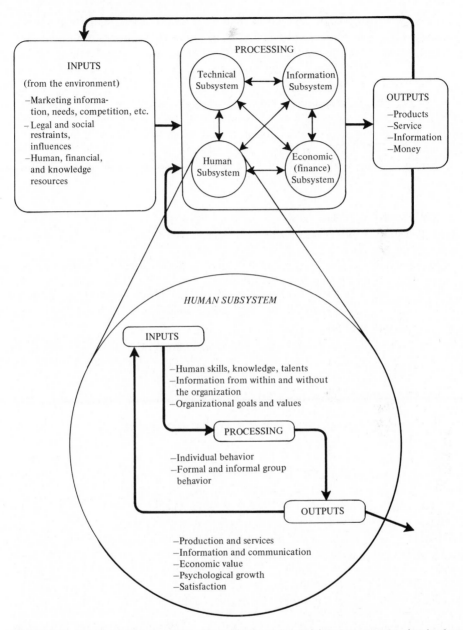

Figure 2-2 An organizational system with emphasis on its social system aspects, showing how a change in any input or in any part of the processing can affect the humans involved and vice versa.

a social system, Figure 2–1 has been recast in Figure 2–2 with the human subsystem amplified.

In teaching how to manage change, one behavioral sciences authority sees the systems approach as a method of achieving a deep rather than a shallow diagnostic view. It provides a means of comprehending multiple-causation, complex interrelationships rather than relying on too simple, single-cause explanations:

> The idea of system, in a sense, frees us from the compulsion to oversimplify by making the complexity that is characteristic of human behavior in organizations conceptually manageable. It also urges us, by insisting that we define the focus of our study before we begin analysis, to clarify our role and to admit to the limits and strengths of our abilities to act.[5]

The computer is a vital element of the systems approaches outlined in points 4–12 and in the definition of systems management that we shall finally develop.

4 Computerized Data and Information Systems   The simplest computer-based data processing system is one that merely substitutes computer for manual operation. A computerized accounts receivable ledger is an example.

More complex systems not only substitute computer for manual processing but also automate a bit of the decision making. An example would be an airline reservation system which decides whether or not to accept a new reservation; another example would be an inventory control system which automatically reorders supplies when stocks are reduced to a predetermined point.

A still more complex system processes data, compares that data to some stored pattern, makes a decision (for example, that a certain danger exists), and feeds that decision to a person who uses it as part of the input for another, larger decision. An example would be an air defense radar-computer network; another would be any management-by-exception control report.

An even more complex data system is what is coming to be called the "management information system" (MIS). Such a system not only does all the things the three foregoing types of systems do but also furnishes managers at various levels with the data and models each needs to plan his or her operation (including projective simulations).

The MIS will be described in Chapter 9, and some of the current debates about it will be discussed there. Here it is necessary to make only one point: A computerized information system is part of a total organizational system. Unfortunately, sometimes the management of a computerized information system is referred to as "systems management." It would be less confusing if it were referred to as "information systems management," leaving the more general term "systems management" to denote management of the organization as a whole, which is how it will be used throughout this book.

5 Automated Operations   The term "automation" usually refers to accomplishment of production without human intervention after the original setup is actuated. In such automated installations as an oil refinery or radio assembly line, a computerized data flow controls automated materials-handling equipment and other machinery that accomplishes the actual production. Quality and quantity of production are controlled by comparing measurements (taken automatically) against preset standards.

In some systems (such as the radio assembly line), the equipment carries out a preset routine; in others (such as the oil refinery), the system has "feedback loops" that can automatically adjust the process if a different grade of crude oil enters the system.

Some progress in linking an automated production line to a fairly extensive information system is being made in the lumber industry. One company reports a production system that can automatically sense what grade and kind of log is entering the mill and can cut it into the products that yield the greatest return. This same company plus another report information systems that bring current information on market conditions (prices and demand) and inventories into a computerized profit-planning (or budget-projecting) system that involves deciding what products to produce.[6] If these two systems can be joined, the use made of each log would be decided automatically on the basis of up-to-the-minute market and inventory conditions. Theoretically, a computerized cost-accounting system could also be tied in; however, computerization of cost accounting is proving quite sticky because of the lumber industry's difficult joint-costing problems.

There are reports, too, of using computerized simulation models in long-range planning by still another lumber company.[7]

If and when a firm integrates all these various systems, that company will be deeply into systems management.

6 Project Management A key element in still another systems approach is the "project-" (or "product-") management structure for effective management of each of a number of projects (or products) within a large overall organization.

Even in precomputer days, many firms had so many products that it was difficult to keep a fresh, clear focus on the problems and opportunities of each one. In consequence, "expediters" and specialists with various titles were established not only to coordinate the decision making for a given product (as in rhocrematics) but also to expedite it through the manufacturing, distribution, and marketing processes.

Large defense firms not only had many products but also faced the problem of coordinating projects (or products) of incredible complexity, often requiring from five to ten years to move from inception to final delivery to the customer. These firms established project managers heading substantial teams; however, they retained the traditional "functional" managers to be sure that, for example, the engineers on one project did not repeat the mistakes (or ignore the good new ideas) of engineers on another project.

Consequently, in both defense and civilian industries crosshatch (or project management or matrix) structures, as illustrated in Figures 2–3, 6–3a and 6–3b, have been developed. Utilizing computer-facilitated techniques such as PERT (program evaluation and review technique) and PERT/Cost for planning and controlling complex projects and utilizing remote pickup equipment to feed in data from all over the company, project managers can run a taut management ship on their own projects. They can draw from the firm's total information system such data as they need, and they can feed to the firm's top management the information required to keep informed about how well the project managers are doing their jobs.

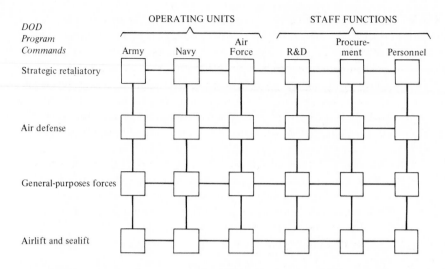

Figure 2-3 Programs and functions in the Department of Defense. The squares in the diagram represent those segments of operating units and staff functions whose mission is a part of a major program listed on the left. For example, each of the three services and associated staff functions has a role to play in the strategic retaliatory capability of the Department of Defense. It is because of its two-dimensional format that this general type of structure is called a "matrix" organization. The diagram is patterned after a diagram in David I. Cleland and William R. King, *Systems Analysis and Project Management,* 2d ed. (McGraw-Hill Book Company, New York, 1975), p. 133.

Project management is seen as part of systems management by some writers because *(a)* it is intimately connected with sophisticated computerized data systems and quantitative decision techniques—both of which are, in turn, seen as integral parts of systems management; *(b)* it is basic to the idea of temporary organizational structures designed especially to accomplish particular missions. Thus it is a technique that can help management cope with rapidly changing missions, which is allegedly one of the strengths of systems management that make it the coming form of management; and *(c)* it can utilize such systems analysis (see point 7, below) procedures as establishing systems objectives and parameters, synthesizing alternative systems configurations, and establishing the conceptual baseline for performance, cost, and schedule.

7 The McNamara-DOD Approach The pattern of management introduced into the Department of Defense during the tenure of Secretary Robert S. McNamara typifies systems management to some writers.[8] It contained most of the systems features we have discussed so far in this chapter plus a number of other features.

There is still a great deal of controversy over the regime of Secretary McNamara. Whatever the merits of each side in that controversy, it is still true that he vigorously introduced an ambitious new pattern of management; some features of it will long survive in the Defense Department as well as in other places. Certainly no one will deny that the logistics planning and control systems developed by this group have been outstandingly successful.

The idea of "keeping the whole in mind while making smaller decisions" was basic in the McNamara pattern. He identified a limited number of big jobs to be done, "key missions" such as a nuclear retaliation mission, a hot-spot response mission, and others. He then developed an organization structure and budgeting procedure that focused sharply on these missions. This tying of budgeting to key missions was the essence of the new PPBS (planning-programming-budgeting system). By keeping the big picture in mind while making detailed budgeting decisions, he hoped to eliminate some air bases, navy yards, and other expenses not essential to the key missions.

The organization structures developed in both the Defense Department and major contractor companies to keep a clear focus on the key missions were project (or program) structures, which used PERT and PERT/Cost extensively for control. With PPBS and PERT computerized, the Defense Department had evolved an extensive MIS (management information system).

Five-year plans, in the form of "mission program packages," identified the sub-missions, or responsibilities, of each of the armed services, comprising each key mission. The spelling out of these five-year plans helped identify imbalances between the armed services and gaps that were not adequately covered. It also helped promote longer-term (than annual) budgeting.

McNamara's program persistently challenged established methods, asking whether the mission might not be better accomplished by a different strategy, a different weapons system, a different operations routine. This was the "seventy-six trombones" program in which seventy-six such challenges were analyzed in written reports. In these studies many computer-facilitated quantitative techniques such as cost-effectiveness analysis and simulation models were used.[9]

Another analytical tool used by the McNamara group was "systems analysis," which also stresses the holistic approach, that is, considering the effect on the whole while making decisions on subsystems or sub-subsystems. The many scientists and engineers who entered management (government and business) ranks during World War II and the cold war years that followed brought into management the systems-analysis viewpoint and techniques that they had used in designing weapons and space equipment.

For example, engineers designing the guidance, gun-control propulsion, and communications systems for a weapons system (such as a fighter plane) must be sure that these subsystems are compatible with one another as to speed of operations, range, power requirements, and other features; also, the subsystems must fit into the space and weight limits of the overall system, the plane. Sometimes subsystem performance is suboptimized in order to optimize overall system performance. Also, the plane can be seen as a subsystem of the larger system, the Strategic Air Command, which can, in turn, be seen as a subsystem of the entire defense system, which, in turn, . . . etc.

Similarly, an organization can be seen as a system consisting of human, technical, economic, and informational subsystems (as in Figure 2-1); however, the organization as a whole can also be seen as a subsystem of the industry, the economy, etc. In the McNamara regime, systems analysis was used not only for selecting from among alternative weapons systems to accomplish a given mission but also for policy questions such as what force posture to choose for certain geographical areas.[10]

Some writers see systems analysis as equivalent to systems management; however, it is clear that it is only one element in the entire McNamara-DOD pattern of management. That pattern as a whole is called "systems management" in this book.

The ideas and techniques discussed so far in this chapter have been used in actual practice; those discussed in the remainder of this chapter have been at best only partially applied in actual practice, existing chiefly in the literature.

8 Integrated Medical Care Systems   A major, urgent socioeconomic problem is presented by the explosive increases in the costs of medical care plus the virtual breakdown of the medicare and medicaid programs designed to defray this expense for the elderly and the indigent. A holistic, systems approach to the delivery of medical care might be a solution to this problem.[11] While no totally integrated medical care system exists at the present time, some organizations have made some progress in this direction, at least enough to indicate that the solution may lie in this direction.

Medical care has traditionally been delivered via a highly fractionated system. General practitioners, specialist M.D.'s, laboratories, hospitals, pharmacies, physical therapists, convalescent homes, long-term-care facilities, and health insurance companies all get into the act; and typically each is a separate business organization with its own record keeping, its own offices, its own overhead, its own profit. Furthermore, the existence of this multitude of small, independent units rendering medical services has greatly complicated the problem of administering the medicare and medicaid payments.

This total problem seems to be a "natural" for a systems approach, that is, a holistic approach to delivering medical care, implemented by a computer-based information system. If some present group medical practices would expand to include a hospital, lab, insurance group, convalescent home, etc., then a few large, efficient data processing systems would replace the multitude of small, inefficient, highly redundant, mostly manual systems. Patients would get more different kinds of treatment per visit, so length of treatment would be shortened. Confined patients could be placed in the most economic type of bed without elaborate moving arrangements, settling old accounts, opening new accounts, etc. Insurance reimbursement could be handled with far less paperwork than is required when several separate organizations are involved. In addition, welfare and medicare agencies could deal efficiently, computer to computer, with a few large suppliers of services rather than with thousands of individual doctors, dentists, optometrists, and labs because the policing or control problem would be greatly simplified.

Inclusion of the insurance function in such large organizations would provide incentive to move toward the practice of preventive medicine—sometimes called the health maintenance approach—which some authorities think is the most important change needed in our system of rendering health care services.

9 Educational Administration   Probably the most frustrating aspect of administering schools and school systems has been the difficulty of formulating generally acceptable objectives. A major research project in educational administration has formulated a systems approach that focuses on the formulation of objectives via a three-dimensional matrix that considers many different types of objectives at various educational levels and for various types of personalities under changing environmental conditions. For planning and controlling educational operations, PPBS is recommended; also, cost-effectiveness studies are suggested for measuring output against input.[12]

The final report on this education project declares:

> . . . public enterprises are being forced to implement more efficient and effective management techniques in an effort to conserve available resources and improve the quantity and quality of public service. . . . Probably the most promising organizational renewal technique involves the use of a systems approach.

At another point the report explains:

> A systems approach to managment focuses upon organization-environment relationships. In addition, relevant input-output relationships are identified, analyzed, and defined in relation to organizational purposes. Management is based upon clearly defined objectives which are specified using verifiable performance terms. Emphasis in management is upon feedback control procedures, which lead to efficiency and effectiveness in performance. Finally, all performance is managed so it will result in desired benefits to society.[13]

While no such integrated system is actually operational in an educational institution, some are moving in this direction. Also, many universities have computerized clerical functions (such as billings and grade reporting) and have automated some simple decisions (such as class scheduling). A few are using PPBS and a few have developed fairly complete MISs. The University of Toronto has in operation a simulation model titled "comprehensive analytical method for planning in the university sphere" (CAMPUS). CAMPUS is made up of computer programs that assess the objective of some segment of the university, compute activity level necessary to sustain the objectives, generate the resource requirement, and combine this into a series of reports that assess the effects of alternative courses of action.[14]

The Western Interstate Commission for Higher Education (now known as the National Center for Higher Education Systems) has developed a planning and management system consisting of a series of computer-based models to help universities with such problems as predicting demand, projecting facilities requirements, managing physical facilities, and apportioning costs to various activities.[15]

Clearly, new patterns of administration are coming to the field of education,

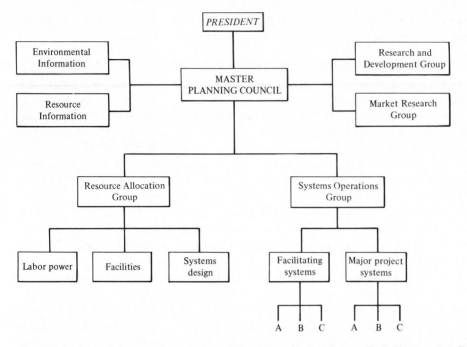

Figure 2-4 Speculative organization chart of the future. R. A. Johnson, F. E. Kast, and J. E. Rosenzweig, *Theory and Management of Systems,* 3d ed. (McGraw-Hill Book Company, New York, 1973), p. 128. The structure is suggested in the book cited; the interpretive comments are the present author's.

and features usually associated with the systems approach will be basic in the new patterns.

10 The Resource Allocation Model It has been suggested that as the role of computers in management enlarges and the systems approach is further developed, firms might be organized as shown in Figure 2–4.

Under this concept the master planning council would have responsibility for grand strategy, for shaping the nature of the firm as a whole, for adding to and subtracting from the package of ventures so that the firm keeps pace with environmental change.

Once it is decided that a new venture is to be undertaken, the resource allocation group would have the responsibility for designing the information and operating systems for that new venture and would also be responsible for changing the established operating system if unsatisfactory results occurred or if the project reached a new stage of growth. This group would contain a high expertise in systems design and analysis. It would know how to translate major policy decisions into operating structure, how to fit structures to task, how and when to restructure, how to supply appropriate data flows to different levels of decision makers, and how to decide which decisions to automate and which to leave to human beings.

The operating section of the organization consists of some facilitating (or service) systems plus the project systems; thus this structure carries out, in a slightly different way, the project management idea that has been discussed earlier in this chapter.

While there has been a definite trend toward greater use of project structures, there is little indication that the other features of the resource allocation model are being put into actual use. Perhaps this model should be regarded as an interesting thought stimulator rather than as a projection of what systems management will look like when it actually arrives.

11 Dynamic Operations Model   Over a decade ago a startlingly innovative book, *Industrial Dynamics* by Professor Jay Forrester, described a new approach to diagnosing an organization's operation.[16] Forrester used an elaborate computerized model of a division of a firm. It was a dynamic model that depicted the flow of orders, material, workforce, capital equipment, money, and information in day-to-day operations. Forrester claimed that by studying the interrelationships (leads, lags, amplifications, etc.) between these flows, he was able to stabilize fluctuations in employment in a division manufacturing and selling an electronic component.

While many other persons have used mathematical simulations to study certain aspects of an organization's operation, Forrester's approach is far more ambitious and difficult in that it seeks to comprehend in fairly realistic detail the dynamics of an organization's operation. That is, it follows the organization's activities continuously, studying the effects of actions in one period on decisions in later periods.

Although it is recognized that Forrester has made a tremendous conceptual contribution to management, numerous competent persons have disputed both his general claims and his specific claims with respect to the one operation in which he applied the technique.[17] Critics feel that many more flows would be needed to yield usable results; they feel, also, that the state of the art of model building simply is inadequate to do the job required by the industrial dynamics concept.

12 Complete Systems Management   Presumably, eventually all the concepts discussed in this chapter and some not yet conceived will be brought to fruition within one organization; then we will have a pattern of management that might be described as complete systems management.

What would such an organization be like?

The information flow (the MIS) would be totally integrated. Any data item (e.g., a customer's name, address, order number, order items, etc.) would be entered only once manually; thereafter it would be reproduced electronically whenever required by the sales, credit, cost accounting, purchasing, industrial engineering, shipping, or any other department. Each department would feed in data, on-line, as orders are received, production is achieved, inventories are depleted and replenished, etc. All data would be available on an up-to-date, real-time basis wherever and whenever needed.

Specialized subsystems (such as an airline reservation system, an inventory control system, a production-control system, or even a fully automated manufacturing operation) would be built into the total data flow; that is, these subsystems would draw information from and feed data into the general system; more important, they would make many programmable-type decisions.

Automation of operations would be carried to the most economical point under the current state of the art.

Computer-generated reports, not only the usual financial reports such as the profit-and-loss statement but also reports needed for control at many points throughout the organization, would flow from a totally integrated information system. Since all internally generated information could be made available to any executive, there would be no need for passing data up and down the chain of command; rather, each executive, with the help of information technology specialists, would be expected to draw from the data flow whatever reports were needed to plan and control any particular part of the organization. There would be complete integration of planning, budgeting, control reporting, and results reporting (encompassing both PERT and MBO-PPBS techniques).

The structure would be designed with primary attention to what decisions need to be made and at what point in the total process they can be made best. Then jobs would be defined at decision points, and the information flow would be designed to give the decision-maker the needed information.

Human decision makers would be relieved of many of their more routine duties, so they would have more time and more information for making innovative and judgmental decisions. Much decision making, especially long-range, would be done with the assistance of many quantitative tools of analysis, systems analysis, and simulation models capable of projecting approximate results of many alternative decisions on a given problem. Conceivably, the firm's data system would be able to tap outside systems for economic, sociological, or technological data needed in connection with the planning process. Day-to-day decisions would often be based on the insights afforded by an "industrial dynamics" type of model.

The specialists in systems design would be specialists not only in information technology but also in human/machine relationships; they would be teamed with behavioral sciences experts who understand that such systems require new personnel selection standards, new kinds of training, and new kinds of jobs (e.g., systems maintainers). They would, one hopes, help line managers apply social systems analysis to the human problems of systems management.

Some persons doubt that such a complete systems approach will ever arrive. But it is not necessary to have the complete system in order to enjoy some of the benefits of systems management.

Before such a millennium arrives, if ever, much more progress will have to be made in the underlying sciences of information theory (about kinds of information and how they are communicated), cybernetics (about human/machine systems of control and communication), and about the kinds of information needed to control systems.[18] While the sciences of information theory and cybernetics have been used by persons who design computers, they are hardly known in the field of management; in time, they will be brought more directly into the construction of models that will help us to understand complex organizations better. So, also, will social scientists' understanding of such properties of systems as entropy (the tendency to run down, or become disorganized) and negentropy (the opposite of entropy which is achieved by storing energy that can counter the entropy process), equifinality (the idea that a system can reach the same final result despite different initial conditions and different pathways), and boundaries (what is included/not included in the system).[19]

SO, WHAT *IS* SYSTEMS MANAGEMENT?
Definitions

This chapter has demonstrated that the term "systems" has been applied to quite a few different ideas, some from actual practice and some hypothetical, in the field of management (administration). In short, the use of systems terminology has not yet settled down; it does not yet denote a specific pattern of management. In such an unsettled situation, a writer seeking to formulate a definition can either: (1) be general, producing a definition that covers everything, but probably is not very tangible[20] or (2) be specific, producing a definition that is more tangible but is so at the cost of arbitrarily emphasizing certain ideas and omitting others. This second option is the basis of the definition offered here:

> *Systems Management:* Management (the process of working with and through other persons to define and achieve the objectives of a formal organization) that is characterized by the following practices: (1) Views the organization both as a system with its own subsystems and as a subsystem of larger environmental systems; (2) takes a holistic approach, using techniques of analysis that emphasize the interrelationships among the component parts of the organization; (3) uses flexible, changing organization structures, served by computerized information flows, to keep structure adjusted to changing tasks; (4) designs information flow and uses quantitative techniques to strengthen decision making; and (5) views the organization as a social structure and as a series of human/machine relationships.

How Is It Different from "Old" Management?
One way to make this definition more meaningful is to review its main concepts, asking about each: "How, if at all, does it relate to older management ideas and practice? To what extent is it either new or not-so-new?"

1 *Systems management views the organization as a subsystem of larger environmental systems* This approach reminds the firm or government agency that it must constantly adjust to the threats and opportunities posed by changes in the environment; that is, it must not be so inner-directed that it fails to keep up with changes in markets, technologies, employee-employer relationships, or public reactions to the organization's actions.

While long-range planners have for four decades made "assessing the environment" their first step, the systems approach makes this step more systematic and more tangible by requiring a planner to consider each major external subsystem and its effect upon the internal subsystems and the whole.

2 *Systems management is holistic, stressing the interrelationships of the compo-*

nent parts of an organization in decision making   This cross-department orientation in decision making is not new. The management field has long recognized the need to train generalists as well as specialists; also, the idea of project expediters working across departmental boundaries is not a new one. However, again, systems management does this more thoroughly and in a variety of ways. The use of simulation models makes clear the effect of a decision at any one point in the system upon other parts of the system. Project management's stress on lateral communications and cross-departmental negotiating is another approach to integration; in fact, some observers see it as a basic departure from traditional principles on structure, authority, and lines of communication.

3 *Systems management views the organization as an integrated social system in which "everything is related to everything else"*   While this concept goes back thirty years to Barnard and others, it has only recently been brought into the heart of the managerial job. For decades, the human relations specialists and behavioral scientists worked on the periphery of management, conducting supervisory training and executive development programs that focused on communications and leadership patterns, but rarely got involved in the firm's major decisions on financing, product line, manufacturing organization, marketing policies or planning and control procedures. That they now relate their social sciences insights to basic activities is a sign of maturity and an advantage for systems management.

4 *Systems management fosters a spirit of constant challenge of established practice*   If scientists and engineers can bring to top managers the spirit of constant challenge via systems analysis, they will have made a great contribution to the furtherance of participative management and executive development, two concepts that predate the systems concept but rarely have been effectively practiced. Participative management and executive development can be effective only in an organizational climate that encourages creativeness and innovation, which unfortunately often border on criticism of the established order. Many top executives' fears of criticism have vitiated these programs.

5 *Systems management is mission-oriented*   The management-by-objectives concept in business and program budgeting in government are long-established. However, the systems-management version (PPBS) adds a great deal by linking MBO to mission-oriented structures and, in turn, linking both to the budget. In addition, the use of computer-facilitated networks (PERT and others) has greatly strengthened the feedback process by which a sharp focus can be kept on progress toward objectives; so, also, has use of project structures.

6 *Systems management uses quantitative methods extensively*   It can be contended that currently available quantitative methods of analysis are simply an extension, accelerated by being computer-facilitated, of older quantitative methods such as breakeven analysis or capital payback analysis; however, it can be more persuasively argued that currently available quantitative methods represent a quantum improvement over the older methods because they are so varied and can be used to solve so many different kinds of problems.

7 *Systems management is dependent upon sophisticated, computer-based information systems*[21]   Some writers argue that systems management can exist without computers; however, that argument is rejected here because neither the project structures nor the quantitative techniques would have much potency if *not* facilitated by computer-based management information systems and computerized calculations.

POTENTIAL ADVANTAGES

1 *Systems management is a new synthesis of managerial thinking that potentially can significantly advance both theory and practice* In the immediately preceding paragraphs we have noted that while there is much in systems management that is not new, there is something that is new. It does bring management (administration) squarely into the computer era, designing better information flows to decision makers; it does encourage the use of quantitative techniques facilitated by computers. Thus it promises to upgrade decision making.

Also, it promises to increase ability to tailor organizational structures and information flows to focus on achievement of objectives. It promises to increase awareness of the need to adjust to environmental change—an increasingly important aspect of management today. It promises, further, to increase openness to challenges of established practices.[22]

2 *Systems management can become a very teachable theory of management* It includes much of traditional management (particularly process theory's emphasis on planning and control) and MBO; yet it also comprehends the newer aspects of management such as computer-based information systems, quantitative decision techniques, and the social structure approach to understanding organizational dynamics. It is, therefore, far more complete than either the old theories or new partial theories (such as a behavioral science approach or a decision-theory approach). This completeness is what will make it highly teachable. Students will have a comprehensive grasp of management into which they may fit whatever ideas they encounter; they will not be confused by partial approaches that they have trouble bringing together.

3 *Systems management potentially can contribute significantly to the solution of complex socioeconomic problems* It has been persuasively argued that our past failure to solve such problems as water pollution, air pollution, the decay of the inner city, urban transportation and high cost of medical care can be explained by the fact that only partial, fragmented attacks have been made on these problems. In other words, a systems approach is required to understand the scope of such problems and to formulate realistic attacks upon them.[23]

An indication of the possible use of systems management in attacking the problem of reducing the cost of medical care has been given earlier in this chapter; also, some applications to current educational problems have been suggested. A number of other applications of systems analysis to major socioeconomic problems have been reported; however, it must be recognized that most of these studies have not been implemented.[24]

POTENTIAL LIMITATIONS AND DANGERS

1 *The technically oriented specialists may overpower the social scientists* If the systems approach can further the integration of our understanding of the human subsystem with the other subsystems, great progress will have been made. If the systems approach fails to do so—that is, if engineers, scientists, and mathematicians so dominate systems management applications that the social system viewpoint is ignored—then the classic mistake made fifty years ago by the scientific management movement will have been repeated. Much of the progress toward participative-consultative forms of leadership will have been lost.

2 *Efficiency may override purpose* Domination by technical specialists may also lead systems analysis to become chiefly a way of achieving greater and greater efficiency. However, with its sensitivity to the environment and its mission orientation, systems management can stress purpose, such as solving major socioeconomic problems.

3 *Rigidity, rather than flexibility, may result* Much has been made of the potentiality of systems management to change project structures and information flows in response to environmental changes and changes in the job to be done. These changes will presumably be designed and implemented by highly qualified specialists in systems design. But the facts of life, at least to date, are that it is exceedingly difficult to get most complex, computer-based information systems to function satisfactorily; in consequence, there is great reluctance to make any change in an established system. Until the arts of systems design and implementation have progressed considerably beyond their present state, there is likely to be more rigidity than flexibility in organizations that make extensive use of computer information flows. We may, as one observer has warned, succumb to "hardware hypnosis" and spend the current generation "computerizing our mistakes."[25]

4 *Loss of accountability of subordinates may occur instead of greater accountability* When interrelatedness of subsystems is stressed, via the "everything is related to everything else" viewpoint, only the person in overall charge can be held responsible for results. While the stress on project management promises greater decentralization of accountability, it might stop at that level if no one below that level carries individual responsibility for results. It will be necessary to learn to make groups responsible, partly through group incentive systems and profit sharing.[26]

5 *Separation of management into distinct levels—highly trained, highly specialized, and each inexperienced in the work of the other levels*—could lead to gross planning errors and to frustrating limitations on many individuals' upward mobility.

CONCLUSIONS: THE IMPORTANCE OF SYSTEMS MANAGEMENT

Systems management is potentially of top importance to most practicing managers and to students of both business and government management. It effectively pulls together the still useful parts of older management theory with the new features of the computer era into a usable, teachable modern theory.

True, systems management is at this point a bit futuristic; it is not yet fully understood or fully applied. However, many features of systems management are already operational throughout business and government administration, and the trend will continue for the simple reason that computerization will increase. We have as yet only scratched the surface of the use of computers in management. Also, we are only beginning to learn to cope with rapid environmental change. If computerized information systems can achieve flexibility, then systems management can cope well with rapid change.

In teaching, it is far better that a textbook be ahead of the times rather than behind the times. Most readers of this book will have from ten to thirty years of working life ahead of them. A nonsystems approach is likely to be completely outdated ten years from now; a systems approach probably will not be outdated until twenty or more years from now.

The chart that follows this chapter summarizes Chapters 1 and 2 graphically. It also provides a bit of speculation about when complete systems management will be achieved and what forces might in time make systems management obsolete.

REVIEW QUESTIONS

1 What are the major components of a system?
2 Distinguish between:
Management of an information system
Systems management
Systems analysis
Automation
3 Review the definition of "systems management" given in the text and use it to describe (*a*) the management of a parts department in an automobile dealership and (*b*) the administration of a police department in a medium-sized city.
4 List the ways systems management differs from older management ideas. Give examples of each.
5 What potential advantages does systems management offer? What are potential limitations and dangers in its use?

DISCUSSION QUESTIONS

1 With reference to the field (trade/profession/industry, etc.) with which you are, have been, or plan to be associated: How prominent is systems management in the literature of that field? Which of the twelve descriptions in this chapter best fits the current state of development, if any, of systems management in that field?
2 With reference to the chart at the end of Part One, what forces will lead to further change in management during the last decade of the century? What effects do you feel these various forces will have?
3 Discuss: "Whether or not systems management prevails generally in the future depends upon the outcome of the struggle between rigidity and flexibility."
4 The text points out certain economies and advantages that might follow the establishment of an integrated medical care system. What factors seem likely to impede the establishment of such a system?
5 Do you believe that the potential advantages of systems management outweigh its potential limitations and dangers? Why?

NOTES

[1] The study of organizational systems can be seen as part of a much larger, highly intellectual subject called "general systems theory," denoting the study of similarities in the theoretical constructions of different disciplines. See K. Boulding, "General Systems Theory—the Skeleton of Science," *Management Science,* April 1956, pp. 197–208; reprinted in P. Schoderbek (ed.), *Management Systems: A Book of Readings* (John Wiley and Sons, Inc., New York, 1967 and 1971). Alternatively, see the foreword, preface, and chap. 1 of P. Schoderbek, A. Kefalas, and C. Schoderbek, *Management Systems: Conceptual Considerations* (Business Publications, Inc., Dallas, Tex., 1975).

[2] Allen Harvey, "Systems Can TOO Be Practical," *Business Horizons,* Summer 1964, pp. 60–61.

[3] Stanley H. Brewer, *Rhocrematics: A Scientific Approach to the Management of Material Flows,* Bureau of Business Research, University of Washington (University of Washington Press, Seattle, 1960).

A chapter is devoted to rhocrematics in R. A. Johnson, F. Kast, and J. E. Rosenzweig, *The Theory and Management of Systems,* 2d ed. (McGraw-Hill Book Company, 1967), chap. 8. In the third edition (1973), it is covered under "Flow Systems" in chap. 11.

[4] Similar arguments have been made with respect to Air Force logistics and supply operations, see B. A. Schriever, "Needed Right Now: A Systems Approach to Real Planning," *Air Transportation,* June 1965, p. 38.

[5] J. A. Seiler, *Systems Analysis in Organizational Behavior* (Richard D. Irwin, Inc., Homewood, Ill., 1967), p. 9.

[6] "Computers Point Way to Profits in Lumber," *Business Week,* Jan. 1, 1966, pp. 80–81; systems being used at Boise-Cascade and Weyerhaeuser Company are described. The latter is described in more detail in Johnson, Kast, and Rosenzweig, op. cit., 3d ed., chaps.7 and 8.

[7] A system in use at Potlatch Forests, Inc., is described in J. Boulden and E. Buffa, "Corporate Models: On-Line, Real-Time Systems," *Harvard Business Review,* July–August 1970, pp. 73–77.

[8] This description of the McNamara management methods relies heavily upon Donald J. Smalter and Rudy L. Ruggles, Jr., "Six Business Lessons from the Pentagon," *Harvard Business Review,* March–April 1966, pp. 64–76.

[9] For an account of how these cost-effectiveness techniques were being used a decade later to evaluate a variety of governmental nondefense programs, see "Are Government Programs Worth the Price?" *Business Week,* June 30, 1975, pp. 114–116.

[10] "Notes on Systems Concepts," *Teaching Notes, EZ-P 432,* copyrighted 1966, for use at the Harvard Business School, p. 1. What is given here is a simplified treatment of systems analysis, which can get quite complicated. One prominent public administration writer stresses that rarely are objectives set clearly and finally in advance; rather, "First, the analyst attempts to solve the problem before he knows a great deal about it. Then he continuously alters his initial solution to get closer to what he intuitively feels ought to be wanted. Means and ends are continuously played off against one another. New objectives are defined, new assumptions are made, new models constructed until a creative amalgam appears that hopefully defines a second best solution, one that is better than others even if not optimal in any sense." Aaron Wildavsky, "The Political Economy of Efficiency," *Public Administration Review,* December, 1966, pp. 303–302. See also Charles J. Hitch, *On the Choice of Objectives in System Studies* (The Rand Corporation, Santa Monica, Calif., 1960), p. 19; E. S. Quade (ed.), *Analysis for Military Decisions,* Report R-387-PR (The Rand Corporation, Santa Monica, Calif., 1964).

[11] T. Purola, "A Systems Approach to Health and Health Policy," *Medical Care,* September 1972, pp. 373–379; D. B. Starkweather, "Beyond the Semantics of Multihospital Aggregations," *Health Services Research,* Spring 1972, pp. 58–61.

[12] Donald R. Miller, *A Systems Approach to Planned Change in Education* (San Mateo County Board of Education, San Mateo, Calif., 1970), vol, I, p. 70; vol. II, pp. 129–152.

[13] Ibid., vol. I, preface; vol, II, p. 101.

[14] Edward Wheatley, "Putting Management Techniques to Work for Education," *College and University Business,* April 1970, pp. 57ff, 58–59. See also R. Brady, "Budget System: Key to Planning," *College Management,* January 1970, pp. 45–47; and V. R. LoCascio, "A Computerized Simulation Model for Colleges and Universities," *Management Controls,* August 1973, pp. 195–200.

[15] Robert Huff, *Focus on MIS: A Report on the WICHE-ACE Higher Education Management Information Systems Seminar* (Western Interstate Commission for Higher Education, Boulder, Colo., 1970).

[16] Jay Forrester, *Industrial Dynamics* (The M.I.T. Press, Cambridge, Mass., 1961); and a reconsideration by Forrester, "Industrial Dynamics after the First Decade," *Management Science,* March 1968. For a brief indication of how industrial dynamics works, see Edward B. Roberts, "Industrial Dynamics and the Design of Management Control Systems," *Management Technology,* December 1963, and reprinted in P. Schoderbek (ed.), *Management Systems: A Book of Readings* (John Wiley & Sons, Inc., New York, 1967 and 1971).

[17] H. I. Ansoff and Dennis P. Slevin, "An Appreciation of Industrial Dynamics," *Management Science,* March 1968. For rejoinders by Forrester and by Ansoff and Slevin, see the May 1968 issue. Professor Forrester has moved on to greater challenges, developing a model of the life cycle of cities to be used in attacking the problem of urban decay; see *Urban Dynamics* (The M.I.T. Press, Cambridge, Mass., 1969). He has also developed a simulation model of the entire world to predict the consequences of current trends in population, production, etc. The first publication issuing from this work is Dennis Meadows, *The Limits to Growth* (Potomac Associates, Washington, D.C., 1972).

[18] For a discussion of these sciences in lay language, see R. C. Weisselberg and J. G. Crowley, *The Executive Strategist* (McGraw-Hill Book Company, New York, 1961), pp. 204–209. For a more

technical discussion, see M. K. Starr, *Management: A Modern Approach* (Harcourt Brace Jovanovich, Inc., New York, 1971), chap. 12; also Sir Stafford Beer, *Cybernetics and Management* (John Wiley and Sons, Inc., New York, 1959).

[19] A classic on this subject is Daniel Katz and Robert Kahn, *The Social Psychology of Organizations* (John Wiley & Sons, Inc., New York, 1966), chapters on open systems theory.

[20] Here are some definitions that have been widely quoted in the literature: (1) "The systems concept or viewpoint is the simple recognition that any organization is a system made up of segments, each of which has its own goals. The manager realizes that he can achieve the overall goals of the organization only by viewing the entire system and seeking to understand and measure the interrelationships and to integrate them in a fashion which enables the organization to efficiently pursue *its* goals." David I. Cleland and William R. King, *Systems Analysis and Project Management,* 2d ed. (McGraw-Hill Book Company, New York, 1975), p. 16. (2) "The systems concept is a way of thinking about the job of managing. It provides a framework for visualizing internal and external environmental factors as an integrated whole. It allows recognition of the function of sub-systems, as well as the complex suprasystems within which businessmen must operate." Johnson, Kast, and Rosenzweig, op. cit., p. 3. (3) In their third edition (1973), p. 19: systems management . . . "involves the application of systems theory to managing organizational systems or subsystems. It can refer to management of a particular function or to projects or programs within a larger organization. An important point is that systems theory is a vital ingredient in the managerial process. It involves recognizing a general model of input-transformation-output with identifiable flows of material, energy, and information. It also emphasizes the interrelationships among subsystems as well as the suprasystem to which a function, project, or organization belongs."

[21] Citing a number of writers to support his viewpoint, John F. Rockart contends that current information systems do not deserve to be called sophisticated because they simply mechanize old, precomputer-era paperwork systems; see "Model-based Systems Analysis: A Methodology and Case Study," *Industrial Management Review,* Winter 1970, pp. 1–12.

[22] In contrast to this optimistic assessment of the potential contribution of systems management, we should note the opinion of the original explorer of the "management jungle," Harold D. Koontz, who is quoted as follows: "It is unfortunate that much of (the systems approach) is not related to reality and, therefore, does not contribute to operational science," William R. Millman, "The History of Management Thought," *Proceedings of the Twenty-ninth Annual Meeting,* The Academy of Management, 1969, p. 188. Surely such an opinion rests on a narrow, highly technical definition of what systems management is.

[23] Richard N. Farmer, *Management in the Future* (Wadsworth Publishing Company, Inc., Belmont, Calif., 1967), chap. 5, also K. B. De Greene, *Socio-Technical Systems* (Prentice-Hall, Inc., Englewood Cliffs, N.J., 1973), chaps. 3 and 8.

[24] Olaf Helmer, "The Application of Cost-Effectiveness to Non-Military Government Problems," (The Rand Corporation, Santa Monica, Calif., 1966), p. 3449. Ida Hoos, "Systems Techniques for Managing Society: A Critique," *Public Administration Review,* March–April 1973, p. 157.

[25] J. A. Beckett, *Management Dynamics: The New Synthesis* (McGraw-Hill Book Company, New York, 1971), p. 210.

[26] L. H. Mantel, "The Systems Approach and Good Management," *Business Horizons,* October 1972, pp. 50–51.

RECOMMENDED READING

Emery, F. E.: *Systems Thinking,* Penguin Modern Management Readings (Penguin Books Inc., Baltimore, 1970).

Henry, Porter: "Manage Your Sales Force as a System," *Harvard Business Review,* March–April 1975, pp. 85–94.

Johnson, Richard, Fremont E. Kast, and James E. Rosenzweig: *The Theory and Management of Systems,* 3d ed. (McGraw-Hill Book Company, New York, 1973).

Sayles, Leonard R. and Margaret Chandler: *Managing Large Systems: Organizations for the Future* (Harper & Row, Publishers, Incorporated, New York, 1971).

Schoderbek, Peter P., Asterios G. Kefalas, and Charles G. Schoderbek: *Management Systems: Conceptual Considerations* (Business Publications, Inc., Dallas Tex., 1975).

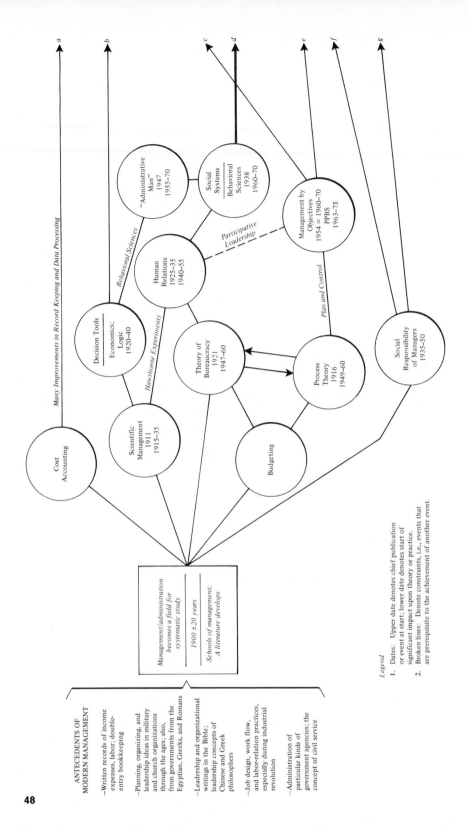

Management/administration becomes a field for systematic study

1900 ± 20 years

Schools of management: A literature develops

Many Improvements in Record Keeping and Data Processing

Cost Accounting

Scientific Management 1911 1915–35

Decision Tools
Economics; Logic 1920–40

Behavioral Sciences

Hawthorne Experiments

"Administrative Man" 1947 1955–70

Social Systems
Behavioral Sciences 1938 1960–70

Human Relations 1925–35 1940–55

Participative Leadership

Management by Objectives 1954 = 1960–70 PPBS 1963–75

Theory of Bureaucracy 1921 1947–60

Budgeting

Process Theory 1916 1949–60

Plan and Control

Social Responsibility of Managers 1935–50

ANTECEDENTS OF MODERN MANAGEMENT

—Written records of income expenses, labor; double-entry bookkeeping

—Planning, organizing, and leadership ideas in military and church organizations through the ages; also, from governments from the Egyptian, Greeks, and Romans

—Leadership and organizational writings in the Bible; leadership concepts of Chinese and Greek philosophers

—Job design, work flow, and labor-relation practices, especially during industrial revolution

—Administration of particular kinds of government agencies; the concept of civil service

Legend

1. Dates: Upper date denotes chief publication or event at start; lower date denotes start of significant impact upon theory or practice.

2. Broken lines: Denote constraints, i.e., events that are prerequisite to the achievement of another event.

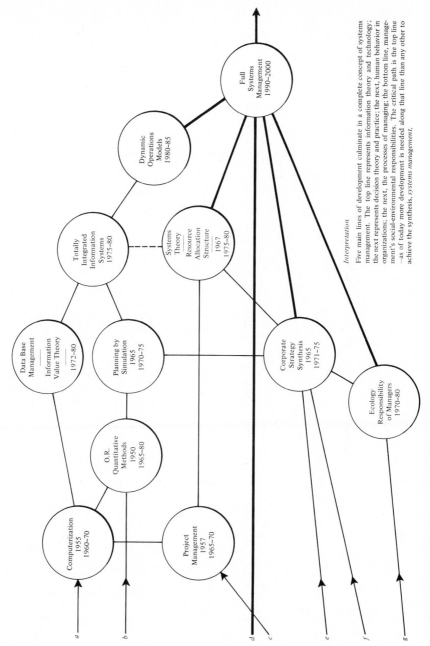

Full Systems Management 1990–2000

Dynamic Operations Models 1980–85

Totally Integrated Information Systems 1975–80

Systems Theory Resource Allocation Structure 1967 1975–80

**Data Base Management
——————
Information Value Theory
1972–80**

Planning by Simulation 1965 1970–75

Corporate Strategy Synthesis 1965 1971–75

Ecology Responsibility of Managers 1970–80

O.R. Quantitative Methods 1950 1965–80

Computerization 1955 1960–70

Project Management 1957 1965–70

a

b

d

c

e

f

g

Interpretation

Five main lines of development culminate in a complete concept of systems management. The top line represents information theory and technology; the next represents decision theory and practice; the next, human behavior in organizations; the next, the processes of managing; the bottom line, management's social-environmental responsibilities. The critical path is the top line —as of today more development is needed along that line than any other to achieve the synthesis, *systems management.*

DIAGRAMMATIC SUMMARY OF PART ONE

49

Part Two

Managerial Practices and How They Are Changing

The reader who has just finished the first two chapters might well ask: "But what is management *really* like, what administrative techniques are actually being used today?"

The purpose of Part Two is to answer this question insofar as it is answerable. But it is not easily answered for three reasons: First, there are many different patterns of management being used today. On the business side, it has long been true that small firms typically are managed quite differently than are large firms; but not all small firms are managed in the same way, nor are all large firms. On the government side, innovative patterns of management prevail in the Defense Department, NASA, and a few other agencies, but traditional patterns persist in most places.

Today the diversity is great because a flood of new techniques, new concepts, and new technologies has rendered the old management theory and practices obsolete; but the new theory and practices are not yet clearly established. In fact, current practices in both business and government range from one extreme that might be described as nineteenth century to what might be described as space age.

Second, there is available little objective, quantifiable information about the true character of managerial practices (as opposed to the formal, or professed, practices); in consequence, the answers given must be somewhat subjective.

Third, the effectiveness of any given type of management is situational. Accordingly, a pattern of management that seems out of date may in fact be quite effective in some situations; similarly, an ultramodern pattern, while effective in some situations, might be quite inappropriate in others.

Still another problem plagues students of administration (management) who try to be entirely practical, who try to present it "the way it really is"—the problem of whether they should concentrate their studies on one specific type of organization or on a broader spectrum of types of organizations. On the one hand, they can be very factual if they study only the management of, say, police departments in medium-sized cities, or the management of large department stores. But the literature of a particular field is sometimes limited or stereotyped; they are likely to miss valuable ideas and techniques. On the other hand, if they study only general principles, it is often hard to link ideas to reality; this causes much of what is studied to be rather meaningless.

Keeping all these problems in mind, Part Two will answer the question of what management is really like in two ways that together should solve most of these problems.

- Chapter 3 will sketch a number of patterns of management typical of various sizes and types of business organizations. This same chapter will also describe some specific new government management programs—attempts to develop a new pattern of management to replace the old bureaucratic practices.
- Chapters 4 through 8 also look at actual management practices, but with a different focus. These chapters will examine how the basic processes (planning, controlling, organizing, leading, and staffing) are currently being performed in government and business; in addition, these chapters will look at how the processes are changing as both business and government move more deeply into computerization and toward systems management. Chapter 9 examines current practices and trends in decision making and the closely related subject of management information systems.

All these chapters aim to attune the student to basic trends as well as to current practices.

Chapter 3

Patterns of Managerial Practices

In order to give some feel for what actual practice is like, this chapter will first describe the patterns of management found in a number of types and sizes of business firms. Although those covered here are only a few of the many types of businesses that exist, this material does indicate the variety of practices in the field of management today.

Unfortunately, it is not possible to describe a similar set of patterns of managerial practice from the public sphere. There simply is not enough descriptive material available in the literature to permit development of a typology. This chapter will describe the one significant new pattern of government management that has appeared in recent years; it will also describe some of the reforms in government management that have been attempted in past years and some of the new ideas that have been tried in recent years.

Accordingly, this chapter will be presented via the following sections:

Business Organizations
    How Small Firms Are Managed
    How Medium-sized and Large, Nondiversified Firms Are Managed

BUSINESS ORGANIZATIONS

How Small Firms Are Managed

The Traditional Small Firm   If "small" is defined as having fewer than 250 employees, then the *traditional* small firm can be described as being managed informally, arbitrarily, planlessly, almost precariously. Such firms are chronically underfinanced; moreover, they do not have organized new-product (or service) development plans. In consequence, mortality among small firms is high. It is especially high in the first year of existence, but data on small business failures indicate significant mortality also among those in business for a number of years.[1]

One study of the origins of successful (that is, surviving) small firms indicates that most of them "just happened" rather than being carefully planned. Thus the founders of these firms "backed into" entrepreneurship because they could find no other solution to their personal-professional problems; they did not calculatingly design a business to exploit some product idea, technical talent, or managerial capability.[2] Their success is due to hard work, sacrifice, and/or some outstanding personal capability (such as product design or manufacturing ability) rather than to a well-planned and executed competitive strategy.

The typical small firm operates with a minimum of data, making little or no use of computers or of quantitative tools of analysis (even of the old ones like breakeven analysis). Such data as are available are gathered for tax reporting purposes; thus they are in a form that is not very useful for managerial control. In addition, they usually are out of date (from a control standpoint) before they are received. Decisions are made on a "feel" rather than a factual basis.

For example, a twenty-eight-employee firm distributing industrial equipment, parts and supplies simply did not know its costs by product line; once the costs were determined, it was clear that one line was losing more than the profits of nine other lines.

Another example is that of a forty-employee wholesale laundry that did not know its cost structure. Once a breakeven chart was done, however, it was clear that the owner had been following precisely the wrong strategy. Despite the fact that he actually had high fixed costs and unused capacity, he was doing no advertising or promotion and was refusing to set special prices for volume accounts.

Finally, there is the example of a baby-equipment manufacturer with ninety employees who was making the reverse error. A breakeven study showed that his directly variable costs were extremely high. Yet he was promoting and advertising heavily and offering many price reductions for volume sales.

In all these cases, the key executives did not know the basic facts about the cost structures of their businesses that a simple breakeven chart would reveal—despite the fact that they had lived with these situations full time for many years. In consequence, decisions were just plain wrong.

Leadership in these informally managed small firms varies from the purely "go it alone" autocratic type, through the paternalistic-family type, all the way to a close-knit, friendly type of participative pattern. The autocratic pattern appears to be most common, probably because many people who start businesses want to do all the decision making, often being unable to work effectively with others. The autocrats keep information to themselves, trusting no one; they are not open to help from employees or from outsiders. They tend to have only close relatives and dependent employees on the board of directors and rarely develop capable successors.

The Technology-based Small Firm The combination of rapidly advancing technology (especially in electronics) and continuing high military-space expenditures for many years presented opportunities for new, small, technology-based companies. Usually an individual, a pair, or a trio of scientist-engineer(s) sensed an opportunity for some new product. Inasmuch as some advanced products, at least initially, are not mass produced, substantial capital is not usually required to enter business. Design capability is crucial. Sometimes the scientist-engineers realize that their talents should be supplemented by market research and marketing capability; but that, often, is the limit of their grasp of management. The result is a new small firm strong in product development capability, based on market needs of that moment, and with some marketing capability; however, such a firm lacks financial knowledge, does not realize the data flow needed to make intelligent management decisions, and is utterly lacking in any sense of leadership or human relations (except among the scientist-engineers preoccupied with technical achievement). While such a firm may succeed for a time, it sooner or later fails, especially when the time comes that additional new products are needed.

During the stock market booms of 1959–1961 and 1967–1969, many such technology-based small companies went public—that is, their stocks were sold to the public via the stock market—amidst great ballyhoo about their amazing technological breakthroughs. While a few such companies did prosper, the vast majority were spectacular failures. Many investors and investment-advisers paid dearly for their naïveté about management.[3]

An outstanding success story is that of the Hewlett-Packard Company, which started in a garage and has grown steadily and profitably for over twenty-five years; it is today a giant multinational company. Hewlett-Packard's success appears to be rooted in willingness regularly to invest a large part of its resources in new-product research and development (R&D). The firm's outstanding new-product performance has been coupled with conservative financial management and aggressive marketing.[4]

The Aggressively Managed Small Firm   There are not many small firms that could be described as aggressively managed, simply because the few firms that could be so described usually quickly become large firms or are acquired by large firms. It is quite possible, however, that there will be more small firms that are managed aggressively, because in recent years an increasing proportion of the persons coming out of graduate schools of business administration are entering small business.[5] (Apparently they feel that small business offers greater opportunity to use their talents and to be well rewarded; also, this may be part of the younger generation's disillusionment with all large organizations.)

Although there may be many different bases for success in small business, it can be said as a generalization that the successful firm is cognizant of the need for (1) a competitive strategy based on product development, operational (manufacturing or service-rendering) and marketing capabilities, and a sound knowledge of the competitive situation and (2) an organizational survival plan for being alert to and coping with those "key crises" that often prove fatal to small firms at their various stages of development:

     1   *The starting crisis* covers the mistakes most commonly made by new firms, such as lack of rounded managerial experience, inadequate accounting data, and undercapitalization. Frequently these mistakes hurt a firm later on in its growth rather than at the start.

     2   *The cash crisis,* which cripples some firms that do not do careful cash-flow planning.

     3   The *delegation crisis,* which occurs at that point at which a firm becomes too large for one-person management.

     4   *The leadership crisis,* which occurs at that point at which a firm needs a full management team and complete formal controls.

     5   *The finance crisis,* which occurs when a firm outgrows its original-plus-plowback financial base.

     6   *The prosperity crisis,* which can take the form of either the extreme of complacency or the opposite extreme of too-fast growth.

     7   *The succession crisis,* caused by neglect of those long-in-advance moves that not only provide an able successor but also solve the control and liquidity problems that can occur upon the death of an owner.[6]

The few small firms that are prepared in all such matters are open to help, lots of help, in understanding their own strengths and weaknesses vis-à-vis this series of key crises. Realizing that management of a small firm is a many-faceted, demanding task and that even the best managers need help, they seek help from employees, financial sources, a strong board of directors, consultants, and suppliers.

     Aggressively managed small firms are increasingly using computers for much of their routine clerical work (payroll, billings, and accounts receivable), sales analysis, inventory control, and their profit-and-loss (P&L) statements and balance sheets. The availability now of good "canned" programs has made it feasible for small firms to computerize these activities via service bureaus, time-sharing arrangements, or their own minicomputers.[7]

How Medium-sized and Large, Nondiversified Firms Are Managed

Definition A medium-sized firm can be defined roughly as one having between 250 and 1,000 employees; usually it has worked its way past the key crises that often destroy young, growing firms. Its financial and organizational affairs are more stabilized than those of small firms, so its management must be analyzed by different criteria.

Medium-sized and large, nondiversified firms are discussed together here because they have quite similar situations to manage. In both cases their dominating characteristic is that they are essentially in a single-product and/or single-service field, however broad that field may be (such as the giant steel companies, IBM in business machines, Continental Can in containers, a copper-mining company, or a chain of large department stores). Also, even the small companies are large enough to require reasonably full management staffs and programs and their own computers, and most are publicly financed.

Management Patterns Found in This Grouping The widest possible range of patterns is found in this grouping. At one extreme, some firms in this category—including some of the very large ones—are poorly managed, showing erratic earnings over the years. At the other extreme, some of these firms (such as IBM and Continental Can and a few of the smaller ones) are among the most effectively managed and consistently profitable firms in the world.

Probably the single factor making for excellence rather than poor performance in this category is the quality of the firm's tomorrow-mindedness, which consists primarily of a strong competitive strategy and a new-product program adequate for executing that strategy. As has just been noted with reference to the Hewlett-Packard Company, successful execution of a strong competitive strategy demands regular commitment of major funds to the new-product program. But funds alone are not enough; they must be supported by capability in assessing market changes, in product R&D, in manufacturing new products of quality, and in marketing new products.

Another big part of a firm's tomorrow-mindedness is its achievement of an organizational climate that attracts and nurtures a steady supply of talented technical and managerial personnel, people whose new ideas will keep all these key capabilities sharp no matter what changes occur in the environment. Usually such a climate is achieved by an open and participative type of leadership, possibly practicing the management by objectives (MBO) concept, plus a substantial executive development program; however, sometimes it can be achieved by nonparticipative-type leaders who possess exceptional technical or sales ability. Many but not all the successful firms in this category have done a thorough job of applying the MBO concept. And some of the less successful ones will be found to have abandoned their MBO effort because it was producing meaningless paperwork rather than meaningful two-way communications or because the objectives formulated were too unrealistic to spur unusual innovation and effort.

Another distinguishing mark of the more successful firms in this category is that, usually, they have progressed into the third stage of computer usage. Thus these companies will have computerized management information systems that help executives know how their units are progressing vis-à-vis their plans and objectives. These same organizations will be making some use of computer-facilitated quantitative tools of analysis in decision making about investments in new facilities, new processes, and new products. They are progressing toward systems management.

While it is possible for a firm to move ahead too rapidly and too uneconomically in the use of computers and sophisticated tools of analysis, progress on these matters is usually a sign of effective management. When it is combined with positive indications on the other criteria discussed in this section, such progress is a solid sign of effectiveness.

How Diversified Majors Are Managed[8]

Definition   A diversified major may be defined as a large company that has become established in a wide variety of product areas over a long period of time, primarily through internal expansion into related areas. Examples of such companies are General Motors, General Electric, Bendix, Borg-Warner, and Ingersoll-Rand. While they are quite diversified, they diversified more slowly and less radically than did the conglomerates.

Range of Management Patterns Found in This Grouping   The diversified majors show the most uniform management patterns found among any of our groupings. With few exceptions they could be described as professionally managed, steadily profitable, financially sound companies.[9] Rarely does one of these companies slip into a private depression brought on by mismanagement; rarely is one of these companies forced into a distress merger.

Typical Management Pattern in This Grouping   The pattern of management that is dominant among these firms derives from the GM–Du Pont practice, started in the 1920s, of combining decentralized operation with centralized policy coordination. Since the early 1950s, this pattern has further developed as *management by objectives* or *control by results*.

These organizations are characterized by a high degree of decentralization into profit centers along product lines and by large, expert corporate staffs in such areas as R&D, marketing, manufacturing, and purchasing (as well as in those areas in which all large firms have corporate staffs: financial controls, long-range planning, and personnel management).

The concept of decentralization with centralized policy coordination is made to work by a strong framework of communications between the corporate staffs and the divisional executives. Long before Peter Drucker and other advocates of MBO stressed the need for participative management in the setting of objectives and the design of control measurements, General Motors executives were required to subject their ideas to rigorous discussion up and down the line and with corporate staff before they were brought to top management.[10] Although such discussion may not be participative management as it is seen by some writers, it is a form of participative management that has done much to develop executives. This practice—plus more formal educational efforts (of which the GM Institute and the management school operated by General Electric Company are outstanding examples)—has assured these firms of adequate supplies of capable executives at all levels. In these firms, top executives do not stay on past retirement age; rarely do these firms go into deep declines.

Certainly the diversified majors have not completely escaped the red tape–delay–frustration–bureaucracy syndrome that affects all large organizations; neither have they kept the middle and lower levels of management as open to challenge and as stimulating as are the higher ranks. Indeed, some middle managers and first-line supervisors in these companies might find it hard to believe the description given here of the management pattern prevailing at the diversified majors.

These companies are leaders in applying the fairly new concept of corporate strategy. In commenting on the appointment of Reginald H. Jones as president of General Electric, *Business Week* asserted:[11]

> He was vaulted into GE's top spot largely because of his identification with "strategic business planning"—a technique that treats the company's vast array of ventures as an investment portfolio, sorting out the winners and losers through systematic analysis. . . . Strategic business planning has become GE's route to faster growth. . . . The concept . . . involves a continuing in-depth analysis of market share, growth prospects, profitability, and cash generating power of each venture. The probing goes far deeper than any planning operation GE has conducted before.

Are the diversified majors moving toward systems management? Although only a few of these firms use this terminology,[12] the answer to this question must be affirmative. First, the diversified majors are using computers extensively in manufacturing operations, project planning and control, and sales reporting and analysis. For example, a recent report tells how the automobile companies have cut time lost due to model changeovers from weeks to days or hours and goes on to say:[13]

> At most Ford plants, '73 production ends on Friday, cleanup crews work over the weekend, and '74 models start rolling on Mondays. At several plants, the change is being accomplished in one day. . . . The Ford system uses a massive computer that keeps track of every component from the time it is ordered until it is installed in a car. "If we didn't have that computer control, we couldn't have done this," says [vice president Marvin] Runyon.

They are increasingly automating both physical operations and programmable decisions. Second, they are increasingly strengthening and expanding their management information systems to improve control at all levels of management. Third, with their powerful corporate staffs focusing hard on R&D, employing systems analysis and many sophisticated quantitative techniques of analysis, they are eminently aware of the environmental changes posing challenges to them (thus meeting three of the basic elements of systems management as defined in Chapter 2).

How Conglomerates Are Managed

Definition   The indelicate term "conglomerate," which to some people has connotations of congealed oatmeal, is now well-established as the designation for firms that have become diversified rapidly, via acquisitions and mergers, in more or less unrelated fields. While each geographical area has its local miniconglomerates, the concern here is with large national and international conglomerates.

Management Patterns Found among Conglomerates   Between their inception some twenty or more years ago until 1969–1970, when many of them ran into deep trouble, conglomerates developed a fairly uniform set of distinguishing characteristics. The most prominent feature was use of the financial device of achieving a high price-earnings multiplier[14] for the firm's stock, using that stock to acquire firms with lower price-earnings multipliers and thereby automatically achieving a boost in current earnings per share for the conglomerate.[15] This stimulates still higher prices for the conglomerates' stock, putting the entire cycle in motion once again.

Also prominent was this management pattern: emphasizing decentralization of responsibility to aggressive division heads while motivating them with low-priced options on the firm's booming stock. Because the conglomerate was in so many different kinds of business, it could not closely supervise the division heads. In consequence, "tiger" division managers were given great independence as long as they achieved a good return-on-investment. Since such simplified supervision required little corporate staff, a "lean" corporate office became part of the conglomerates' pattern of management. Both the independence of the supercharged division head and the leanness of the corporate staff were hailed as great virtues.

As is now well known, once the stock market lost its momentum and the conglomerates lost their high multipliers and their ability to make favorable acquisitions, many of them were in serious trouble. As one journal put it, their shining images were shattered.[16] Their new financial and managerial concepts, heretofore so appealing, suddenly appeared to have serious flaws.

However, not all the conglomerates fell into deep trouble; also, within a few years, some of the troubled conglomerates regained good health. What can be learned from the total conglomerate experience? What ideas of lasting value came out of it? Do conglomerates have something of long-run value to offer?

Distinguishing between Effective and Ineffective Management Patterns   The financial wizardry of conglomerates proved to be poor financial management. In order to preserve their cash for fast-growth working capital and in order to increase earnings per share as much as possible, the conglomerators used debt—often convertible debentures—in combination with common stock to make their acquisitions. This caught some of them with exceedingly heavy debt loads when the stock market declined. Since some of this debt had to be refinanced in 1970 and early 1971 at high interest rates, earnings were badly hurt by interest charges. One of the few big conglomerates that was not badly hurt was Textron, which made its acquisitions chiefly for cash. A by-product of using cash was that Textron moved more slowly and selectively, and these factors helped too.[17]

Some conglomerates described their way of working with division heads (tigers) as the "managing of managers." Presumably, if one knew the art of managing managers, one could have great success with a lean corporate office and a minimum of paperwork controls. But problems developed. First, the tigers concentrated so intensely on current return-on-investment that they neglected investments such as R&D; this, in turn, caused firms that boasted of their technological strengths to find themselves with outdated products and technologies.[18] The lean corporate offices did not have the controls to spot these problems in advance;[19] neither did they have the reserve talent in the lean corporate office to move in fast to bolster sagging divisions. Another conglomerate that escaped the depression relatively unscathed was IT&T, Inc., which was atypical in that the corporate office exercised close control over its divisions, largely through the almost superhuman efforts of its top man, Harold Geneen.[20] (However, in 1972–1973, the firm ran into multiple serious problems which were related more to its political activities—illegal donations, improper influence in legal proceedings, attempts to undermine foreign governments, etc.—than to its operations.)

A problem that plagued the most glamorous conglomerate, Litton Industries, was a dangerously high exodus among its division managers. The tigers were tempted to leave the firm so that they could cash in their options, become wealthy, and move on to become heads of newer aspiring conglomerates.[21] (For readers unfamiliar with business, it should be explained that there are inhibitions, legal and ethical, against sales of a company's stock by an officer of that company. Accordingly, when a company officer holds a large paper profit in a firm's stock, there is a temptation to leave the company and sell the stock, turning the paper profit into cash!)

Some of the conglomerates claimed that having the combination of talented, aggressive division managers and a wide variety of high-technology business fields would result in great synergy, that is, technological breakthroughs or new combinations of products and processes that would yield profits. But these breakthroughs failed to materialize, probably because, in the lean corporate offices, there was no structure, no process, no staff responsible for bringing ideas together effectively.

Despite these problems, there appears to be some value in the conglomerate concept. One aspect of this is the idea of a group of businesses balanced as to high versus low risk, stability versus cyclical nature, and new-growing versus stabilized versus declining businesses. The concept of having an organization's basic strength in the ability to manage managers has considerable appeal, and a few firms are making it work. The concept of producing new products by technological synergy between divisions is one that might be made to work too. But ideas will probably be brought to fruition only where the pace is slowed down, the financing is more conservative, and more is learned about how to manage managers, probably through a strong corporate staff.[22]

Summary

The discussion so far in this chapter has been based on size-complexity categories, and there has been a tendency to assume a manufacturing-type enterprise. Utilities, banks, retail stores, and other types of enterprises, each of which has some unique management practices, have been neglected. Nevertheless, enough different types of business organizations have been discussed to make the main points that need to be made: (1) Actual managerial practice is quite varied, not only as between types of businesses but also within any one type; (2) therefore, there is little validity to such often-heard remarks as "In business they do so-and-so" or "Government should be run *the* way businesses are run."

GOVERNMENT AND NONPROFIT ORGANIZATIONS

Public Administration: A Vast Subject

That the field of public administration is vast in sheer numbers of persons employed no one will deny. In February 1975, federal civilian employment was 2,727,000 persons; state, local, and county governments employed about 11,900,000 persons.[23] Thus total direct public employment exceeded 14 million without counting military personnel (over 2 million). Over one-sixth of all employed persons worked for some level of government; in additon, several million more persons were employed under government contracts.[24] Clearly, government is not only our greatest industry but also our greatest growth industry, showing a 58 percent increase in the decade 1963–1973 and a 4 percent increase in the depression year 1974, when private employment was decreasing.

As obvious as the size of public administration is the difficulty of its management problems. The almost impossible problems of managing the federal government have been authoritatively documented by top-level commissions from early days, and in modern times from the 1937 President's Commission on Administrative Management (the Brownlow Commission), the two Hoover Commissions (1949 and 1953), and President Johnson's Task Force on Government Organization to the Advisory Council on Executive Organization (the Ash Committee), which reported its findings and recommendations from 1970 through 1972.

The first Hoover Commission study reported so many serious administrative problems that the prospects for ever achieving efficiency and effectiveness in government looked dim indeed.[25] Yet in the two decades following that report, the federal government became ever more huge and complex, taking on about a hundred major new activities. Grant-in-aid programs to state and local governments jumped from a handful to more than 160 (managed by 21 agencies, 150 bureaus, and 400 regional and field offices). Further, by 1969, there were 57 federal programs in job training, 35 in housing, 20 in transportation, 62 in community facilities, 32 in land use, 28 in recreation and cultural facilities, 65 in health, and almost 100 in education.[26]

In view of this vastness and variety, how can one answer the question: What is management really like in public administration?

One way to answer it would be to repeat the age-old description of fumbling, bumbling bureaucracy drowning in red tape and cumbersome communications. But that would be much too simple an answer for today. While there is still much traditional-type bureaucracy (in the bad sense of the term) in government, many formidable improvements have been made and are being made.

What will be done in the following pages is to describe some of the main problems of government administration, some of the attempts to solve those problems, some of the big changes currently taking place, and some of the managerial practices found in specific types of government and nonprofit organizations such as education, medicine, and police. It is hoped that this material will help readers better understand the literature and actual practices in those particular sectors of public administration that interest them.

The "Big Reports" and Responses to Them

The Brownlow Commission told President Franklin D. Roosevelt that he needed help, and this advice resulted in the establishment of the Executive Office and its high-level aides "with a passion for anonymity." Also, in 1939, Roosevelt moved budgeting from the Treasury Department to the Executive Office. These moves were first steps in a process that continued through many administrations—the process of giving the President stronger help in managing the bureaucracy, especially enabling him to use the budget to effectuate policy.

The first Hoover report (1949) presented discouraging conclusions about the splintering of authority among various executive branch agencies dealing with parts of a single problem, about lack of authority to match the responsibility assigned agency heads, about the pervasive need for developing capable administrators, and about the tendency of Congress to write unadministrable provisions into legislation. It led to the consolidation of previously separate departments into the new Department of Defense and of various widespread activities into the new Department of Health, Education, and Welfare. In the same year that the report appeared, an Executive Order established the Advisory Committee on Management Improvement; also, the Order required agency heads to make periodic and systematic appraisals of their operations. Between 1952 and 1959, the Advisory Committee's recommendations resulted in twenty-five major management studies.

The second Hoover Commission (1953–1955), like the earlier one, studied government structure and the functioning of agencies; however, it also studied the wisdom of policies. It submitted nineteen reports on such topics as personnel and civil service, paperwork management, federal medical services, lending agencies, transportation, real property management, budget and accounting, intelligence activities, and others. The reports approached efficiency on the most detailed level, presenting a picture of "sprawling and voracious bureaucracy, of monumental waste, excesses and extravagances, of red tape, confusion and disheartening frustrations, of loose management, of regulatory irresponsibilities and colossal largesse to special segments of the public, of enormous incompetence in foreign economic operations, and of huge appropriations frequently spent for purposes never intended by the Congress."[27] Estimated potential savings via the 314 recommendations ran to a few billions of dollars per year;[28] however, few of the recommendations were ever enacted, perhaps because the commission scattered its shots so widely.

The movement toward stronger presidential control via the budget was continued by the Budgeting and Accounting Procedures Act of 1950. Following this act, the Bureau of the Budget (BOB) developed plans for the organization, coordination, and management of the executive branch with a view to efficient service.[29] This responsibility was later strengthened by the creation in 1959 of an Interagency Advisory Council on Management Improvement to advise BOB and in 1960 by creation of a Management Services Branch in BOB to meet the needs expressed by top administrative personnel of the agencies for leadership and assistance. The PPBS experience was another move in this direction. Another great step toward presidential power was the establishment in 1970 of the Office of Management and Budget (OMB), the superagency operating out of the White House, whose head has been called the chief manager or executive vice president of the federal government.[30] This move was a recommendation of the Ash Committee, appointed by President Nixon. Following the revelation of the Nixon scandals, Congress sought to reclaim from the President some power over the budget; it established its own staff group and built more discipline over total spending into its budgeting procedures.[31]

Another topic that has received continuing attention through the years is productivity in government operations. The Management Services Branch worked on measurements of productivity during the Johnson administration. More recently, the OMB has joined in the work of the National Commission on Productivity to develop a productivity index and better work measurement systems for all federal agencies.[32] However, this work has been hampered by the lack of an adequate management information system.[33] In December 1975 President Ford signed legislation establishing a Center for Productivity and Quality of Working Life. The legislation requires the Comptroller General to evaluate the effectiveness of the Center by the end of 1978.

The decades of the 1950s and 1960s also saw extensive executive development efforts in many federal agencies, government schools, and university programs designed especially for government administrators (which are also discussed later in this chapter.)

The OMB is also overseeing a program of annual management improvement plans generated in each Cabinet department and federal agency, a series of management improvement workshops conducted by the Civil Service Commission, and periodic conferences by two high-level groups (the Executive Officers Group, or EOG, composed of the assistant secretary for administration in each department and equivalent officers from other agencies, and the Agency Management Analysis Officers Group, composed of management officials one level down from the EOG members).[34]

The Ash Committee's report also criticized the executive branch for having a tortuous process of federal grant-in-aid programs calling for too much detail, too much paperwork, and too much reporting.[35] The response to this criticism has been twofold: (1) creation of ten regional federal offices to serve as one-spigot conduits for a broad variety of federal programs and (2) the "New Federalism," which lumps seventy narrowly targeted grant programs into four general programs of special revenue sharing with local governments.[36] One indication of how paperwork can be cut is given in an account of the decentralization of twenty-nine Health, Education, and Welfare Department programs in which the annual state plans for each were changed from 300-page documents to 20-page preprinted agreements. This modification alone eliminated 400,000 pages that state officials had to write and federal officials had to read each year—about 800 man-years of work.[37]

Finally, the Ash Committee has recommended folding seven domestic Cabinet departments into four to improve the "creaking machinery of the Presidential Office." But these recommendations were not immediately implemented.

Despite these many efforts at management improvement throughout the two decades following the issuance of the 1949 Hoover report, one authoritative writer in 1971 stated flatly: "The same indictment could be written today."[38] Apparently the improvements made during these years were balanced, or even overbalanced, by the inefficiencies inevitable in the great proliferation of activities during the same years.

Other Problems in Government Management

To this recital of the problems of the federal government must be added the woes of the federal regulatory agencies. These have not only become bastions of delay and red tape but have also been widely accused of becoming captives of the industries they are supposed to regulate rather than protectors of the public interest.[39] In the mid-1970s, largely as a result of efforts of consumerist groups, considerable pressure was building up for reform of various regulatory agencies. The reforms include restructuring to replace five-member commissions with single heads bearing full responsibility; using stricter ethics and more open proceedings; speeding up administrative procedures; and reducing the need for resorting to the courts to settle disputes.

So far, this chapter has dealt with the management problems of the federal government only; but similar problems exist in most, if not all, state and local governments, which collectively employ four times as many persons as does the federal government.

One critic has written: "State governments are mostly feeble. City government is archaic."[40] Although the person making these charges is quite knowledgeable and there is some validity to his charges, it should be quickly pointed out that on neither level is the situation completely hopeless. As will be brought out later, some state governments are succeeding with PPBS where the federal government has failed. Another experienced observer points out that state governments should not be our scapegoats but rather the object of our hopes; he feels that the "one person, one vote" decision by the U.S. Supreme Court will enhance the quality of state governments by reducing the power of the rural demagogues in many states.[41] He points out that some states have achieved high-quality universities and new levels of public sanitation; also, they have broken ground in social policy in such fields as abortion, doing away with the death penalty, land-use laws to preserve the quality of life, and no-fault auto insurance.

Most states and large cities are actively training professional managers in a variety of management internship and executive development programs. Also, as noted in the discussion of productivity programs in Chapter 8, a number of cities have made significant contributions to that program and the ideas generated are regularly disseminated through the International City Management Association.[42]

Major Changes in Management Practice

PPBS (Planning-Programming-Budgeting System) The attempt, starting in 1965, to install PPBS in all federal agencies and departments and in many state and local governments represented a major effort to improve administration.

This technique involves, first, the definition of the "missions" to be accomplished by an organization after consideration of possible alternatives. The process then calls for a definition of a program structure—that is, a set of projects for accomplishing each defined mission. Again, this is decided after evaluation by objective analytical techniques of alternative ways of approaching each mission. Then plans (usually five-year) are formulated for each program, and they are translated into budget and results expected terms. Control reports are designed to monitor both the expenditures and the results for comparison with plans.[43]

One key aim of PPBS is the linking of the budgeting process to objectives, that is, to missions to be accomplished. If achieved, this linkage would be a radical departure in two respects: (1) It would emphasize the *purpose* of expenditures rather than, as under traditional budgeting, the *objects* or things for which money is being spent, and (2) it would require a new look at each period's expenditures (that is, consideration of what old programs should be discontinued, which programs could be afforded at any one time, and similar questions). This would be a major change from the traditional incremental approach in which each new budget merely adds or subtracts a bit from the previous period's budget, thus perpetuating established programs and the bureaucracies attached to them. The difficulty of discontinuing government activities has been noted by Peter Drucker: "Indeed the inability to stop doing anything is the central degenerative disease of government and a major reason why government is sick today.[44]

Another key hope for PPBS is to fix personal responsibility for results to be achieved by expenditures. Still another hope is that it would encourage participation by lower-level managers in the formulation of objectives, since the basic input on each program element originates with the person in charge of that element.

After six years' experience, PPBS in the federal government was officially terminated in June 1971, when agencies were relieved of the requirement for submitting the various program memoranda, special studies, and five-year plans that had become the standard PPBS paperwork. On the state and local level, PPBS is also having difficulty, although it is still operative in numerous places and is even enjoying some success in a few states.[45]

A highly qualified observer with long experience as a financial specialist in federal agencies stated in early 1971:

> Lip service is still sometimes paid to PPBS, but even in DOD [the Department of Defense] it is my understanding that the theory has fallen before the practical limitations of the approach. Incidentally, in a technical sense PPBS is less "budgeting" by mission and more "planning" by mission; nowhere, as far as I know, has an agency's Federal

budget system been changed. Indeed, the attempts to apply PPBS have resulted in separate organizations to handle the system, and its output has been supplemental to the budget.[46]

Another authority agrees that the tie-in with budgeting was the key aim and the key failure of federal PPBS, pointing out that in those states where the technique has succeeded, the tie-in with budgeting has been achieved.[47] Still others see the furthering of analysis as the heart of PPBS; they feel that it has succeeded, and that the improved analyses will continue even though the detailed paperwork aspects of PPBS are discontinued.[48]

Still others feel that PPBS failed because it ran roughshod over some important American political values.[49] Thus incrementalists argue that traditional budgeting gave more scope to bargaining by diverse political interests; they see the big role of expert analysts in PPBS as violative of this tradition.

Finally, another explanation of the difficulties with PPBS stresses the administrative errors made in its implementation, as illustrated by the experiences of one state:

In this particular situation, the State Legislature enthusiastically decided that PPBS was to be adopted. The administration's first step was to appoint a two-man "analysis group" to head the effort. The second step was to launch a training program in which former DOD experts were brought in to lecture on PPBS to the department heads of the State Government. The third step was to design new budget forms, and the fourth step was to issue the forms along with a call to all departments to submit PPBS-style budgets and plans for all their programs.

With benefit of marvelous hindsight, it is now clear that many mistakes were made. First, the analysis group was too small. Second, the training was given by the wrong persons (too sophisticated, too removed from the local situation) to the wrong persons (the department heads bucked the work down the line, so the people two and three levels down who actually did the work had had no training). Third, the new process should *not* have been started in all parts of all departments for two big reasons: (*a*) The training job required was too big; and (*b*) the computerized data system, which was in deep trouble even before PPBS, was totally inadequate to provide the planning data or control reports needed to make PPBS work.

The people who actually did the work were in most cases long-time employees who never before had been called upon to think in terms of objectives or in terms of alternative programs for accomplishing objectives—to say nothing of quantitative methods of evaluating the alternative programs. The response of these frightened persons was a classic in bureaucratic behavior. They simply wrote volumes of rather meaningless prose. One department, of the total of sixteen, alone made a first PPBS presentation of over 3,000 pages on 130 programs! Most were submitted with no substantive review by the department heads. Clearly the two-man analysis group could not cope with this flood, so that the first year the Governor had no input from the PPBS process. Since they had had no feedback from their great efforts of the first year, many persons resisted the process the second year. So, again, the Governor had no PPBS input on which to base his annual budget message. The third year, a more realistic training program was undertaken, so there was a small amount, but only a small amount, of useful output from PPBS to the Governor.

In sum, for some combination of these reasons, PPBS has failed at the federal level, although it may have left some legacy of improved program planning and analysis. Some states are succeeding in tying it in with the budgeting process, and some states and cities are giving it a new trial in a simplified, less "paperworky" form.[50] One federal department claims success with an MBO approach.[51]

PPBS has spotlighted the weaknesses of traditional incremental budgeting. Even if PPBS is finally swallowed up without trace by the great bureaucratic process on all three levels of government, sooner or later the rising cost of government will demand greater rationality in governmental budgeting with respect to:

1 *Purpose*—concern with what clients are to be served and what is to be done for them. This requires new initiatives, breaks with the past; it is rarely accomplished via incrementalism.
2 *Strategy*—conceptual thinking about the priorities among purposes and the merits of alternative ways of accomplishing a purpose; this, too, is rarely accomplished by incrementalism.
3 *Measurement*—of results achieved by expenditures, so that managers can learn from their experiences, successful and unsuccessful.

The Use of Computers   As early as 1962, one writer observed: "There is hardly a self-respecting federal agency that does not have its payroll on a computer or else has plans to put it on."[52] Thus, since the early 1960s, making more effective use of computers has been a big challenge facing public managers at many levels of almost every organization. It no doubt will continue to be a big challenge for at least another decade as continuing progress is made along three lines: (1) replacement of older computers with new, more powerful ones that can do bigger and more complex jobs, (2) movement from the first phase of computer usage (mechanizing clerical operations) into the second phase (automation of some programmable operations) [one development of this type is the linking of computer memories (electronic files) to word processing equipment (chiefly text-editing typewriters) and TV display screens to automate parts of many clerical operations[53]], and (3) increasing third-phase use of computers (in managerial decision making).

It was reported that the federal government owned or leased 5,900 general-purpose computers by late 1971, with over three thousand of them being used by the Armed Forces. The total number was increasing by almost 600 per year, and almost 100 per year were being replaced by new machines.[54] If that rate of increase continues (and it probably will because in the mid-1970s minicomputers are finding many applications), the federal government will by 1980 have 12,000 computers in service, and well over half of them will be less than ten years old.

The Armed Forces alone have—usually under contractual arrangements with think tanks and defense industries—pioneered many new types of computers and new computer programs. They have used computers not only in combat situations and for early warning systems but also for weapons research. And in many instances their managerial usage, especially in equipment maintenance and material control logistics systems, has been ahead of private business's.[55]

Managerial use of computers has been made by agencies as diverse as the

Veterans Administration, the Census Bureau, the General Accounting Office, and the Federal Reserve System.[56] Perhaps the outstanding managerial decision-making use has been by the Internal Revenue Service, which employs its computers in deciding who shall be audited. The machine examines each return, evaluates a number of weighted factors against established norms, and comes up with a score that indicates the likelihood that the individual's tax liability will increase if the return is audited.[57] It is possible that had the IRS been less successful or slower in its computerization, the entire United States tax collection system might now be badly bogged down and ineffectual as a result of the rapidly increasing workload that it has had to carry (81 million individual returns and 50 million refund checks in 1974).

The Social Security Administration manages to keep its huge clerical task under control despite frequent changes in tax and benefit rates and regulations. Also, computer-generated data have contributed greatly to the decision making behind these changes. Having fifty-one computers (in 1971), the Social Security Administration's installation has been called "the most advanced technology in the country," including business applications.[58]

State and Local   In the 1960s, state and local governments lagged far behind the federal government in computer usage; however, they began to make progress toward the end of that decade and in the early years of the 1970s. It is likely that in the mid-1970s, the state and local usage amounts to about one-fifth of the federal usage, or about 1,200 computers.[59] Clerical usages include not only the usual payroll and accounts payable processing but also voter registration, elections, property records, cost accounting, budgetary reporting, and vital statistics records. Nonclerical applications include numerous law-enforcement activities such as mobile terminals in patrol cars that give quick access to information on stolen vehicles and wanted persons and a system for matching crime data to patterns of known criminals. Some local transit authorities are using computers in their operations, and both state and local governments use computerized PERT systems to plan and control complex construction projects.[60]

Many state and local governments suffer from inability to afford a sufficient number of highly qualified computer experts. A federally subsidized program is showing some signs of helping states and cities with one of their most difficult problems, the administration of social welfare programs:

> With subsidy from the federal Health, Education and Welfare Department, the city of Chattanooga, Tenn., has developed a system that has eliminated a great deal of duplication of records and has reduced the amount of time spent by counselors going out into the field. The computer-based system has integrated the counseling and record-keeping of the city's 90 public and private welfare agencies.
>
> In most cities welfare recipients fill out forms and undergo interviews for each service they receive, and for some individuals this can involve separate agencies for food stamps, aid-to-dependent-children, dental care, medical care, legal aid and psychological consultation. But in Chattanooga this can all be accomplished via one counselor and one form. Today 60 employees make all house calls and in-office surveys formerly done by hundreds of counselors.

Further benefits of integration are illustrated by the case of a 42-year-old woman who had been on welfare for 20 years, shuffling from one agency to another but never undergoing a medical examination. When the computer discovered this fact, it scheduled her for an examination which revealed an easily-correctible minor brain disease. Now on medication, she is able to earn her own living.[61]

But not all experiences are so happy. Consider the following case which the author has had an opportunity to observe firsthand:

In this state government a seven year effort to achieve a comprehensive, integrated computerized system for all state agencies finally was abandoned. A completely new approach, in which the big job is broken into a number of smaller pieces, is being substituted for it. Clearly the key mistake was in trying to do the job all at once. Being totally integrated, if one part failed, all parts failed. Also, the state's accounting system was simply not good enough to proceed with computerization. In addition, the state was unable to pay the salaries needed to attract enough top-flight computer talent.

In sum, government administration at federal, state, and local levels is midstream in computerization. Gains have been made, and even greater gains are in prospect in both clerical productivity and in the quality of managerial decision making. Perhaps the greatest possibilities lie in the use of simulations—computerized dynamic models—to solve some of the vexing socioeconomic problems with which all levels of government are struggling.[62]

Managerial Patterns for Handling Huge Public Projects—NASA   The National Aeronautics and Space Administration (NASA) moon-shot program is the outstanding example of successful mobilization of the national will, talents, and resources to achieve a major public objective. In fact, it was so successful that it has urgently raised such questions as these:

If we can put a man on the moon, why can't we build enough houses to eliminate slums?

If NASA can effectively integrate the capabilities of 20,000 separate business and government organizations, why can't we eliminate the overlapping, ineffectiveness and confusion of the 300 different local, state, federal and private groups trying to deal with social problems in Milwaukee?[63]

Clearly, similar questions could be asked about mass transportation, air pollution, the costs of medical care, or other problems.

While the moon-shot program was as huge, expensive, and technically complex as any of these other problems, it did have some special characteristics that may partly explain why it has been solved whereas the others have not: (1) Inspirational leadership was supplied by President Kennedy to meet the competitive challenge of the Soviet Union's Sputnik. This generated a willingness to spend unlimited billions of dollars. (2) The moon-shot program was an entirely new thing that did not threaten entrenched positions of the building trades unions or certain social work professionals or the highway lobby or the American Medical Association or anyone else.

While such factors as these may have had much to do with NASA's success, a unique pattern of managerial organizing, planning, leadership, and control also had much to do with it. In consequence, this pattern of management is being hailed as the answer to traditional bureaucracy, the pattern of management that will prevail as bureaucracy dies because it is too cumbersome and inflexible to cope with today's problems. *Fortune* has suggested that ultimately the management lessons learned may prove to be the greatest payoff from the moon-shot project.[64]

The NASA Managerial Techniques[65]   Structurally, the Apollo moon-shot project consisted of a relatively small group of NASA personnel who provided overall management to a federation of thousands of contractor organizations grouped by projects. At the Kennedy Space Center, only 3,000 of the total of 23,500 employees belonged to NASA.

This program required much innovation and experimentation to solve wholly new technical problems; yet it also required precise integration of all subsystems and close schedule coordination, inasmuch as only one contractor at a time could work in the launch tower. The great paradox of the NASA experience is that these problems were solved by a combination of highly flexible methods (collegial leadership and a planning process that allowed much reassessment and redirection) with tight schedule and quality controls.

The federation of contractors was more horizontal, less formally structured than the typical vertical hierarchies in business or government. Only NASA could give orders; one contractor could not give orders to another. The absence of hierarchy (and the accompanying need to secure umpteen approvals of every expenditure) did much to encourage initiative and experimentation. The face-to-face communication needed in solving technical problems flowed freely, uninhibited by formal channels of communication and superior-subordinate relationships. Frequently special task forces were established to improvise answers to problems.

Yet there was close cooperation in solving technical problems and there was disciplined schedule control. One key to the cooperation was the fact that contractors did not simply deliver their products, leaving the use of them to NASA personnel; rather, contractors operated their own equipment during the space flights.

Also, top NASA executives made a big thing of what they called "visibility" —an extensive chart-room approach to control in which all contractors were kept informed of the progress and problems of other contractors. Under this FAME (forecasts and appraisals for management evaluation) program, contractors were urged not to hide incipient problems but to report them at the first inkling of possible schedule slippage or design change. Further, trends on the charts were regularly projected by computer so that developing dangers could be anticipated.

The visibility program combined with complete openness (all contractors were welcome at all reporting and evaluation sessions) did much to build a team spirit and a sense of responsibility on the part of each contractor organization.

The precision required in the final product was achieved by a combination of techniques in addition to the chart-room meetings. One was the practice of careful review by top NASA management of each key source selection decision. Another was the use of a contractor specifically and solely charged with monitoring the integration of parts and subsystems. A third technique was insistence on thorough documentation every step of the way—so-called configuration control—under a strong Change Control Board.

Another feature that is given much of the credit for NASA's success is that the government scientists were as competent as the business scientists or the university scientists serving on advisory review boards. Thus the program avoided the problems that occur when some scientists ignore and work around government officials whom they do not respect.

Still another fateful feature was the combination of scientists and nonscientists in management, with a nonscientist at the top. This helped achieve a balance between too much scientific inquiry and too much "let's get on with production."

Is This the Pattern of the Future?   In sum, the most ambitious of all government-business undertakings was successful under a rather different pattern of management. Is this, then, the answer to bureaucracy—the combination of management practices that will enable systems management to solve today's big public tasks?

One writer has recently argued persuasively that schools of business administration must reorganize their offerings radically, not only to teach a systems management approach (such as the NASA pattern) but also to teach both business people and government managers to understand one another and the problems of working together effectively.[66] Yet another writer, reviewing the first ten years of experience with systems analytic techniques in the public sector, is not so convinced. Granting that NASA scored "an undisputed triumph for the management of gigantic undertakings," this writer nevertheless finds that no other major systems analysis studies (including industry-government efforts in waste disposal, education, and mass transportation) have been implemented.[67] Apparently the *systems analysis* was so academic that the studies could not be implemented, so they never got to the point of using *systems management.*

Improving the Quality of Public Executives   The need for managerial training was stressed by the 1949 Hoover Commission and by the Committee for Economic Development, a prestigious business-sponsored research group.[68] They urged the federal government to match the all-out executive development efforts being made by large businesses during the 1950s and 1960s. And these urgings stimulated many new programs in executive recruitment, establishment of "super-grades" in the Civil Service, two-way temporary exchanges of executives between government agencies and business firms,[69] and a seminar sponsored by the Brookings Institution at which business executives and government managers exchanged know-how. But the biggest development has been the creation of many executive training programs both within the government and at universities.

Within the federal government, every Cabinet department and many agencies have at least one continuing program. For example, the Internal Revenue Service has a six-month course designed to train managers as part of its Executive Selection and Training Program; also, it sends senior executives to the Harvard Advanced Management Program. The Armed Forces have a whole series of schools, including the Commmand and General Staff College at an intermediate management level, the Industrial College of the Armed Forces for senior officers of all services, and at the top level a War College for each service. Many military commands have their own local management training programs. Overall, on an interagency basis, the Civil Service Commission provides management training for middle-level civilians at two Executive Seminar Centers, one on each coast. In 1968 the Federal Executive Institute (FEI) was established on the University of Virginia campus to provide an eight-week program for the topmost members of the civil service. In addition, there are a number of government-sponsored programs, credit and noncredit, at universities.

Most of these courses provide classroom instruction in communications, human relations, types of leadership, organization and delegation of responsibility and authority; when PPBS was being instituted, considerable effort was devoted to it. Another subject given considerable emphasis is program management with a heavy systems flavor (i.e., definition of objectives and constraints, systems analysis, etc.). The higher-level programs feature appearances by leading government figures who recount their experiences and views.

While it is clear that a sizable effort is being made within the federal government, it is not clear how effective that effort is. One critic has described it as "a vast, uncatalogued, uncoordinated series of conferences, seminars, meetings, training sessions, and, quite frankly 'boondoggle' types of activities." Further, he accuses the Civil Service Commission of dominating the content, imposing its "personnel" view, and he recommends that the interagency programs be placed under the Office of Management and Budget.[70]

The Intergovernmental Personnel Act of 1970 provides for grants to states and localities to upgrade public service through training programs and through temporary interchange of employees between federal, state, and local governments and institutions of higher education.

Training in Public Policy Analysis In recent years there has been increasing concern at the FEI and at universities with public policy analysis training for high-level public executives and for younger persons of high potential. The Woodrow Wilson School of Public and International Affairs at Princeton offers a year-long program, combining administrative techniques and policy analysis, for "a select group of Federal Government employees who have demonstrated high competence and unusual promise." Both the FEI and Woodrow Wilson School curricula feature broad-scope reading lists on sociopolitical problems and seminars with experienced public executives who present their "slice of life" materials. Degree and nondegree programs are offered at such long-established graduate schools of public administration as the Maxwell School at Syracuse University and the Center for International and Public Affairs at the University of Southern California; in addition, a number of leading schools of business administration—including Northwestern, Stanford, Chicago, and UCLA—have programs in the management of public enterprises which focus, at least in part, on policy analysis in the solution of major socioeconomic problems.

Possibly the most ambitious of all these programs is that undertaken by the Kennedy School of Government at Harvard University, which seeks to integrate

the talents of various disciplines within that university. In announcing the program
the then-president of Harvard stated:

> There goes among us . . . a deeply-held conviction that it is not sufficient to pursue
> knowledge for itself, but that somehow knowledge must be put to work for moral, social,
> and political ends. What is wanted is an education which will recognize this and help
> to make it possible.
>
> Perhaps the most vivid single example at Harvard of this force now at work here
> and everywhere in higher education is a new program developed last year in the
> Kennedy School of Government. The faculty of this School is made up of scholars from
> a number of fields many of whom have at one time or another been involved in the
> practical work of government. In thinking about their function in recent years they
> appear to have come to the conclusion first, that we now have neither the men in public
> life, nor the knowledge required, to solve the many frightfully complicated problems
> of race, poverty, pollution, decay of cities, inadequate medical care, educational defi-
> ciency, law enforcement and all the rest that enfeeble and oppress our society; and
> second, that the nation lacks a program of education likely to produce the men required
> to formulate and administer government policies to cope with such problems.
>
> The School's new program in Public Policy has been designed to try to produce
> such men. It is founded in the recognition that, if intelligent public policy is to be
> formulated, we must now have at the highest levels of government men who combine
> specialized knowledge in some professional or academic discipline with mastery of the
> sophisticated new methods recently developed for policy analysis—men who will bring
> to their work a new professional ability as well as desire to relate knowledge to moral
> and political purposes. This last is the chief point of all.[71]

Originally heavy on quantitative methods of decision making and on economic
analysis, the Kennedy School program appears to be moving toward emphasis on
case studies of actual government programs that stress problems of implementation
and the actual outcomes—economic, sociological, political—of those programs.[72]

The surge of interest in the "policy sciences" appears to be based on recognition
of (1) the role of the administrator as an initiator and shaper, as well as an executor,
of public policy and (2) the fact that at present we do not know a great deal about
how to solve major problems or how to make complex organizations work effectively
in a turbulent environment. Exactly what comprises training in this new field has
not yet been definitively determined. As one writer notes: "Policy sciences, however
perceived, do represent a new endeavor which is only now entering the experimental
stage and just starting on its learning curve.[73] "Policy sciences" may be defined as
a new interdisciplinary field rooted in the fact that we now have some choice among
alternative futures. Policy analysis appears to require training in (1) the processes
of consultation, consensus, compromise and confrontation; (2) the identification of
the many groups interested in any significant public policy issue and the measurement of the views of those groups, which calls for a solid grounding in sociology,
psychology, and statistics; (3) the possibilities and limitations of the many analytical
techniques now available, both quantitative and nonquantitative; (4) program planning and implementation; (5) macroeconomics, public finance, and the incidence
of various forms of taxation; (6) systems analysis, especially the economic reactions

of various markets—domestic and international—to governmental stimuli, restraints, and taxation; and (7) technology assessment, the ability to foresee long-run impacts of technological changes. Points 2, 5, 6, and 7 are vital to understanding the second- and third-order consequences of public policy decisions; much more must be learned about how to teach all this before there will be real progress in avoiding the misfirings, frustrations, and failures that have plagued so many major reform programs.

How Specific Types of Public Organizations Are Managed

Education (Public School Systems)   Public school enrollment in the United States has been estimated at over 46 million, and there are estimated to be over 2 million teachers and about 135,000 administrators.[74] Although the relationship between levels is certainly not the typical hierarchical relationship found in large business organizations, nevertheless there is some validity in depicting the structure as follows:

Federal U.S. Office of Education (USOE)
↓
State educational agency (SEA) (all states)
↓
Intermediate units (some states)
↓
Local school districts (almost 20,000)
↓
Schools

A continuing managerial problem is the definition of the power and functions of each of these levels. At the top, the USOE has no line authority over the lower levels, but it exerts some influence via its staff of experts and via funding of programs carried out at lower levels. In the middle of the structure, there is an ongoing struggle for influence between the SEAs and the intermediate and local offices. While SEAs traditionally have been quite powerless, being chiefly keepers of records and inspectors (as to attendance, facilities, etc.), they have gained power over the last three decades by building staffs of specialists who influence educational and administrative policy.[75] However, the lower two levels (districts and schools) continue to be the heart of the system, and they receive the greatest attention in educational administration literature.

Thus, there is a continuing centralization versus decentralization debate on a number of levels—where should the power and the bulk of the administrative personnel be located? One troublesome aspect of this struggle is that the higher levels tend to be inhabited by highly specialized staff experts turning out sophisticated academic studies that people at the lower levels cannot or will not use.[76]

To this multilevel power struggle within the administrative structure, there must be added the desires for influence of three other groups:

1 Boards of education, whether elective or appointive.

2 Community groups seeking participation in shaping curriculum and other matters.

3 Unions, which have recently become an important part of the public school scene, sometimes emphasize local power and sometimes regional or national power. A union may or may not be the means whereby teachers exercise some influence on decision making.

Far and away the most difficult managerial problem in public education is the defining of objectives. In its most simplified form this is a debate over "The three R's versus social adjustment"; however, it is actually much more complex than that, involving such goals as the Jeffersonian idea that schools should help make democracy work as well as such ideas as that schools should help to prepare people for the world of work, to make the best use of leisure time, to work with other peoples of the world for human betterment, to discover and nurture creative talent, to make intelligent use of resources, and to deal constructively with psychological tensions.[77] While few people would disagree with such broad goals as these, it is the translation of them into a priority list of measurable missions that is so exceedingly difficult and controversial.

When it is realized that these difficult conceptual problems in determining objectives and educational missions must somehow be solved amid multilevel, multigroup power struggles, it is not surprising that in most places they have not been resolved.

There have been numerous attempts to set objectives via experiments in systems management, e.g., the PEP experimental program in San Mateo, California, (mentioned in Chapter 2), PPBS, and MBO programs.[78] Usually funded by USOE, these experimental programs have run head-on into the objectives-setting problems just described. They have also run into the problem of moving from traditional budgeting categories (such as instruction, administration, operations, etc.) into PPBS mission categories (such as learning intellectual skills, developing the individual, preparation for employment, etc.).[79] And they have run into many of the other difficulties (inadequate training, insufficient staff assistance, resistance to innovation, etc.).[80] It is still too early to know what, if anything, the long-run impact of these experiments will be; however, one must be skeptical in view of the unpromising results achieved by PPBS in other fields.

With such formidable problems besetting the determination of educational objectives and missions, it is clear that not much can be accomplished on the measurement of results achieved—that is, on the control function—in school systems. In fact, some writers contend that the basic flaw in the educational system is that there is no separate group which assumes the evaluating role:

> . . . the system presupposes the validity and appropriateness and worthwhileness of any curricular experience. Nobody has to prove anything to anyone. . . . The real crux of the educational problem lies in the fact that the same people who are responsible for planning policy or effecting plans also assume the evaluation role. . . . In education being professional is equated to being loyal, being dependable and studying for additional

degrees. . . . Competence in other professions is not measured by someone higher up "on the line of authority" ladder . . . the educational system must be changed. We dare not presume that "good" men are enough to make educational effort effective. . . . The educational system is inadequate. It lacks integrity, is incomplete. No formalized process uses feed-back data systematically and effectively to enable the system to improve. . . .[81]

The difficulty of setting educational objectives and missions also blocks the use of computers for important managerial decision making. Theoretically, a computerized set of educational records could be used to measure the effectiveness of alternative curricula, of individual teachers or teams of teachers, of teaching materials, and even of patterns of leadership at the principal or supervisor level. But these measurements would have to be made in terms of results achieved with students, and the results would have to be in terms of objectives.

There have been a number of rather radical attempts to measure results achieved and to link them with funds expended. One approach that has been tried in a number of school districts is so-called performance contracting, whereby a school system subcontracts teaching a whole school, or a number of grades, or certain subjects to an outside agency. Results are defined in terms of students' scores at the end of a semester in subject-matter tests. In one case the contractor guaranteed certain results, agreeing, that is, to forego the fee per student for those individuals who did not achieve specified test scores; in other cases the amount of compensation received by the contractor varied with the test scores received. Most contractors relied on programmed (and sometimes mechanized) methods. One contractor has achieved improved scores (relative to control groups under the old methods) at 10 percent less cost per student. Despite this, however, results with performance contracting have been disappointing.[82] The main problem has been that the contractor's teachers taught specifically to the test; they sacrificed a rounded curriculum to highly specific cramming of facts for tests.[83] One of the more successful programs involved small groups of students for single subjects rather than an entire school; this program also had enough planning time to do a careful job of teacher selection.[84]

Another plan for achieving accountability for results in educational programs is the voucher system, a free-market approach in which each child's parents are given vouchers exchangeable for a certain number of dollars in tuition payments and are free to choose whatever school they prefer. Presumably this free choice would force the schools to produce or fail. While the experiments are still too new to show definite results, it is clear that the plan faces at least two big problems: (1) its susceptibility to use by people seeking to preserve racial segregation and (2) the fact that it enables the affluent to procure better schooling for their children by supplementing the voucher payments.[85]

At the operating level, educational administration appears to face about the same managerial problems and issues as does any other type of organization. Thus there are many studies of types of leadership and decentralization of authority. One study of high school principals has identified four patterns of leadership behavior and six types of organizational climate generated by them, depending upon the types of teacher behavior encountered.[86] Another study of six urban school districts has found that innovation (in matters of curriculum and administration) is associated with administrative decentralization and high levels of public participation.[87]

The nature and range of administrative problems in a large school system (200,000 students, 12,500 employees, 200 schools) may be seen in the critical findings of a legislative auditor's study:[88]

1 The department is top-heavy.
2 There is a great deal of buck-passing.
3 The schools lack direction from the top, which often doesn't really know what's going on in the middle.
4 The department's curricular planning implementation and evaluation are nothing to brag about.
5 The department has little or no systematic training, recruitment, or promotion programs.
6 There is in-house fighting over who is in charge of what.
7 The Board of Education, according to its minutes, spends almost 90 percent of its time on decisions on managing and controlling departmental operations rather than on formulating policies and overall strategies—the main duties officially charged to it.
8 The public accountability of the elected school board is questionable because of the legal powers of the State's chief executive. For all practical purposes, the Department of Budget and Finance has become the effective program manager for education.
9 District school advisory councils do little in terms of the job charged them.

Education (Universities)   Higher education in the United States has been estimated as having over 7 million students and employing over 800,000 teachers and about 90,000 administrators at 2,300 schools.[89] After many years of expanding budgets, expanding enrollment, expanding facilities, and expanding organizational structures, this large higher-education establishment in the mid-1970s came upon an era characterized by the following:

1.   *Financial austerity* resulting from cost inflation coincident with a cutback in federal spending on research and education; in some states sharp cutbacks in appropriations for state colleges and universities have added to the stress.[90]

2.   *A competitive market* in which some schools have unused capacity (because of smaller numbers in that age group and because a degree is no longer regarded as a guarantee of a job) has developed rather abruptly; for private schools, except the most famous, a seller's market has changed to a buyer's market. Thus there is pressure to offer a more attractive product.

3.   *Pressures for participation in management* have resulted from student unrest and from financial austerity. Thus activist students clamor for some influence in decision making. Legislators are quite concerned both with the administrators' handling of student protests and with the ever-expanding budgets. Faculty groups, feeling threatened by the financial pressures, are demanding a greater voice in decision making and in some cases are electing to be represented by a union.

Some of the pressure for some influence in the decision making has taken the form of legal actions, and administrators find themselves as defendants in a flood of lawsuits ranging from one flunked-out student's plea for reinstatement to a faculty member's resistance to being retired at age sixty-five.

Without pretending to cover all these developments, the following pages will discuss them under three headings: (1) the new concern for purposes and goals; (2) new teaching and administrative efficiencies; and (3) new developments in governance and leadership.

Concern for Purpose and Goals   Under financial strain, managers of public universities have been forced to reconsider what basic purposes the university should serve. One aspect of this question is the issue of open versus restricted admissions— should the public university's limited resources be stretched to serve everyone with a high school diploma who wants to go to college (even though some are not promising college material), or should the resources be used to do a better job of educating a smaller, more select group?

Managers of private universities are confronted with a different question brought on by financial austerity: Should they, and can they, maintain their standards in the face of unused capacity and reduced revenue?

Administrators of both private and public institutions are reexamining the incredible profusion of activities that have grown up at every large institution, asking: Which are purposes we should be serving with our limited resources, and which are the less worthy?[91] A variant of this question is: What are we doing that is being done as well or better by someone else? Or, from a different perspective: Should this university or college concentrate on selected areas of distinctive competence, or should it try to maintain all the activities undertaken during expansionist times? For schools in urban areas this can mean arrangements for accepting credits from one another. For example, why should four schools in the Chicago area offer advanced Russian; or why should three universities in New York City maintain expensive drama departments when one of the schools is clearly doing a far better job than the other two? In order to face up to a multitude of questions such as these, twenty-seven states have set up planning boards for higher education, and the federal government stipulated that, in 1973, $2 billion would no longer be parceled out to individual institutions but would go to state planning boards for allocation to the schools.[92] The message to top managers of individual schools is clear: Strengthen your planning as to exactly what purposes, what goals, your institution should serve, and institute economic cooperation with other schools.

Efficiency   Financial tightness has also placed a premium on efficiency in both administration and teaching. Potential efficiency improvements lie in the use of computers (which most universities have for academic purposes) for record keeping, class scheduling, and planning utilization of facilities. Computers can help, too, in financial planning and controlling; thus a cost simulation model can project costs of programs and combinations of programs under various possible conditions. Also, computerizing the budgeting process can not only relieve the drudgery of budget work but also give decision makers good views of their alternatives.[93] Such procedures can also help meet legislators' demands for greater accountability for results achieved by funds expended.[94] But this requires a level of expertise in computerized information systems not usually found in abundance in the business management staffs of universities or, in fact, anywhere in most state governments. For this reason, interuniversity organizations, as mentioned in Chapter 2, have taken on the job of developing computerized systems that may be used on all campuses. Also, a number of foundations and professional organizations have funded special seminars designed to teach these skills to university management personnel.

On the teaching side, legislators have in some cases demanded that faculties carry heavier teaching loads. (Sometimes this demand is made by legislators who simply do not understand how faculties work; sometimes it is made by legislators who understand exactly how faculty members work, how faculty administrators work, and how soft administration can lead to abuses by faculty members of their traditional autonomy and the tenure system.) But, again, solution of this problem calls for a discipline in administration down the line of command—a concept antithetical to the traditional concept of weak academic deans and department heads as colleagues who do the bothersome paperwork details for a company of self-governing scholars.

Almost all colleges and universities are increasingly using programmed learning, and some smaller schools are making savings via independent studies supervised by faculty members.[95]

Governance and Leadership   It is clear, then, that today's college or university presidents are working under a number of extraordinary pressures. As one president puts the problem: "How do you get everybody in on the act and still get some action?"[96] Solving this difficult problem requires professional management of the highest order; perhaps something related to the NASA pattern that combines informal collegial relationships with tight overall control. But, unfortunately, university administrators traditionally have been trained as scholars and teachers, not as administrators. Professor Herbert A. Simon has noted:

> The college president is an executive. Like every executive, his responsibilities are varied and unbounded. His organization's product—new and transplanted knowledge and skill—may seem a bit unusual when compared with the products of an automobile manufacturer . . . but comparing colleges with other organizations in our society, one sees that their most striking peculiarity is not their product, but the extent to which they are operated by amateurs. They are institutions run by amateurs to train professionals.[97]

The top executive must be not only an intellectual leader and an excellent money-raiser but also a decisive saint—that is, a person who can patiently solicit and use the participation of many different groups yet make the hard decisions about which purposes the university will serve and which it will not serve. Little wonder, then, that the position has been described as an impossible job and that at one point almost 300 presidencies were vacant in the United States.[98]

Administration of a large university today calls not only for extraordinary talents in the president but also for a number of other highly capable specialists, including at least an academic vice president who can recruit and retain (partly by securing research grants) a top-notch faculty; an administration vice president who can handle housing, construction, contract administration, and myriad other business affairs including the computerization discussed earlier; a financial vice president who can raise and invest funds; an external relations vice president who can handle alumni and community affairs; and a planning vice president. But it is rare that such an array of talent is welded into an effective, nonbureaucratic campus administration. Rather, as one observer notes:

> The president and other top officers are frequently not of the highest caliber, the organization of authority on many campuses is ragged, out-of-date, or inept. And the ranks of the administration are woefully thin, considering the rapidly expanding work load that universities are being asked to undertake.[99]

Health Care Services   The huge health care services industry, which already amounts to about 7 percent of the total gross national product (GNP) in the United States, is expected to expand by 1980 to about 10 percent of GNP or an expenditure of $160 billion with almost 5 million employees.[100] This vast industry has management problems on many fronts.

Perhaps the most formidable management challenge is to halt the soaring cost of medical care. It was suggested in Chapter 2 that the highly fractionated medical care delivery system (many kinds of physicians, nurses, paraprofessionals, therapists, laboratories, hospitals, pharmacies, private medical insurance carriers, government insurers, extended care facilities, and others) might be more efficient if it were reformed along systems management lines—i.e., into fewer, more comprehensive, highly computerized organizations.

Also needing stronger management are the many public health departments throughout the country, which are confronted not only with the usual problems of a public bureaucracy but also with the difficult task of managing staffs that include some medical doctors—the greatest of all individualists. In addition, the functions of these departments have expanded steadily, especially since they are playing a key role in water- and air-pollution control. Clearly, in many situations these departments have outgrown the managerial abilities of physician-administrators. Most public health officers are M.D.'s who hold an additional degree in public health, but that additional degree usually focuses on such topics as epidemiology, immunization, sanitation, and medical statistics rather than management.[101] Thus these difficult managerial jobs are being handled by managerial amateurs, so it is not surprising that their departments are typically characterized by poor communications, poor public relations, and poor contract administration (on research projects).

Medical Research   Interestingly and sadly, this same combination of problems (managing the medical doctor and bureaucratic organization) has plagued major medical research programs. One authority in the field has said: "Bureaucratic inefficiency within the National Institutes of Health has, over the years, seriously retarded and impeded cancer research. I suspect that it has similarly retarded and impeded other research as well."[102] Also, apparently, political ambitions caused the program to be expanded too rapidly for the limited number of scientists available. Since these charges were made, the matter has received extensive discussion in Congress, and the cancer program has been restructured to give it substantial independence from the National Institutes of Health (which, in turn, is embedded in the Department of Health, Education, and Welfare).[103]

Health Services Difficulties in administering health care services have developed in connection with the medicare (federal) and medicaid (some states) programs. Partly because difficult-to-administer provisions (about doctor-patient relations) were written into the legislation, partly because some private physicians have abused the system, partly because governmental organizations simply have not had adequate control systems, and partly because more people are being given more medical care than ever before—for all these reasons—costs of medical care have skyrocketed since the advent of these programs. One jurisdiction has contracted the management of its federal-state medicaid program to a private firm.[104]

Clearly, the traditional method of delivering medical care service is in deep trouble. Whatever solution is finally attempted—whether national health insurance, expansion of existing hospitals into community health centers, or expansion of current prepaid group medical plans into "health maintenance organizations"—will call for managerial skills of a high order.[105]

Unfortunately, space limitations prevent us from delving into all the managerial practices and problems of each of the different types of medical service organizations. But a few pages can be devoted to examining managerial practices in the single most important type of medical service organization, the general hospital. And a few pages will be devoted to a key group in hospitals—the nurses—who have begun to give considerable thought to the managerial aspects of their profession.

Hospital Administration The professionalization of hospital administration has progressed rather rapidly in recent years. Today the chief administrator and often an assistant or two hold graduate degrees in hospital administration.

For over a decade and continuing today, the MBO format, including the participative leadership side of it, has been the dominant approach among these graduate programs in hospital administration. Consultants in the hospital field have been stressing MBO, too. In consequence, there is widespread application of the MBO concept.[106]

There appears to be general agreement that the chief objective of a hospital is to improve steadily the quality of care and cure given ill persons. There is agreement, too, that the control of costs is an urgent objective. And there is recognition and acceptance of the fact that most hospitals have responsibilities in the education of medical and paramedical personnel and in medical research. While there is agreement on these objectives, nurses often complain that in practice the quality-care objective is neglected by hospital administrators who are preoccupied with financial performance. A number of measurements against the quality-care objective (such as average length of stay, cure rate, and customer complaints) are in common use; also, the nursing profession has developed more sophisticated approaches to measuring quality of care.[107] Considerable data on actual costs of certain services, as well as standardized cost accounting systems, are available through hospital industry associations.

The cost pressures of recent years have caused individual hospitals to reexamine their objectives with respect to what services they should and should not render. Like universities, hospitals have been forced to look closely at the duplication of services in a given geographical area. Since some extremely expensive diagnostic and therapeutic equipment is used on only a small percentage of patients, it simply does not make economic sense for every hospital to have all the latest and finest equipment and specialists to operate it. Accordingly, hospitals have increasingly been participating in regional planning groups that decide how much of each kind of medical facility is needed in an area. Such planning has been made a condition for receiving federal funds.

The idea of cooperation among hospitals in a given area has been extended to include the sharing of such services as laundering and supplies purchasing; substantial savings have resulted.[108]

Structurally, the classical hospital problem—having one chain of authority for the medical doctors (most of whom are not employees of the hospital) and a separate chain of authority for all other personnel—continues to be a problem; however, it is not as great a problem as it has been in the past. The main device for handling this situation has been to have the board of directors (or trustees) play an active role in hospital governance. With both the medical chief of staff and the administrator reporting to the board (which includes medical and nonmedical persons), problems may be brought there for resolution. As hospital administrators have become more and more professional, they have gained the confidence of their boards, especially when the medical doctors on the board have been chosen because they have shown some understanding of and sympathy for the process of management. Also, the administrators have learned something about how to gain the cooperation of doctors; and, as doctors increasingly practice in groups rather than individually, they have acquired some respect for the role of managers.[109]

Computerization is another area in which hospital management is currently changing. Improvement in time-sharing equipment and the advent of the minicomputer undoubtedly have pushed the percentage of hospitals using computers far above the 50 percent figure recorded in 1970.[110] Over 80 percent of the applications were for accounting and financial purposes, although thirteen other basic applications (patient record systems, patient scheduling and order systems, patient diagnosis and treatment systems, personnel scheduling systems, etc.) have been made.

Because most computer installations have been piecemeal developments, hospital managers are now struggling, and will for years continue to struggle, with redesign of their systems to make them more comprehensive. Only when the computer system has an integrated data base and can serve a number of nonbusiness management functions will it be able to make a substantial contribution to cost reduction.

Through the years, two forces have steadily increased the size and complexity of hospitals: (1) the increasing technological sophistication of medical science and (2) the ever-expanding role of the general hospital, which is becoming a community health service center.[111] The resulting situation is described in one study:

> To do its work, the hospital relies on an extensive division of labor among its members, upon a complex organizational structure which encompasses many different departments, staffs, offices, and positions, and upon an elaborate system of coordination of tasks, functions, and social interaction.[112]

In addition to the general administrators and a variety of types of medical doctors, the hospital encompasses graduate professional nurses (in supervisory and nonsupervisory positions and in a number of postgraduate specializations), practical nurses, nurses aides, laboratory technicians, dietitians, pharmacists, physical therapists, x-ray specialists, housekeepers, maintenance personnel, social workers, and finally, the computer specialists who, it is hoped, will help develop systems that help achieve coordination and integration of all these different persons. It is, then, not surprising that one leading textbook concludes its chapter on hospital administration in this way: "The managerial system is difficult to define. The diversity of the authority structure creates a dispersal of the planning and control functions."[113]

Clearly, professionally trained managers using MBO and the information systems specialists—both now heavily engaged in hospital administration—are meeting a severe test in attempting to integrate all these specialists into an efficient and effective whole.

Nursing Administration   In the middle of the large general hospital, playing a key role, are the graduate professional nurses who:

1   Are full-time hospital employees, a part of the formal organizational structure, but must also take direction from outsiders, the doctors
2   Are trained to focus on the quality of patient care but have been kept from doing that by the bureaucratic structure and the paperwork requirements
3   Are increasingly acquiring advanced degrees and specialist qualifications (in anesthesiology, psychiatry, surgery, etc.) but have been unable to achieve organizational status that enables them to use these new capabilities fully

Faced with these frustrations, nurses and teachers of nursing have in recent years taken an increasing interest in administration, as evidenced by the start, in 1971, of the *Journal of Nursing Administration* and the addition of administration courses to the nursing curricula in some schools.

Nurses reason that administrators tend to be preoccupied with financial results and that medical doctors are too specialized and/or too rushed to consider the patient's total care needs; it is the nurse, they contend, who is trained to bring cure and care together, who has considerable direct contact time with the patient, and who is, therefore, the one who should be in charge of the team of paramedics, practical nurses, and others who provide patient care. The trouble is, however, that traditional organization structures have not been conducive to such practice; rather, the tall hierarchical structures, division of responsibility into many bits, and formidable sets of rules and regulations for all activities have been suitable to a philosophy of following the doctor's orders (the "handmaiden of the physician" concept) and abiding by the rules and regulations of the institution. But in recent years the more highly educated nurse has pushed for—and in some cases secured—flatter and more decentralized structures that give nurses in the lower organizational levels more chance to plan and control patient care. Thus, in some decentralized structures the director of nursing reports directly to the hospital administrator rather than to an assistant administrator; also, one level has been eliminated between assistant nursing director and head nurse, to yield the structure shown in Figure 3–1.

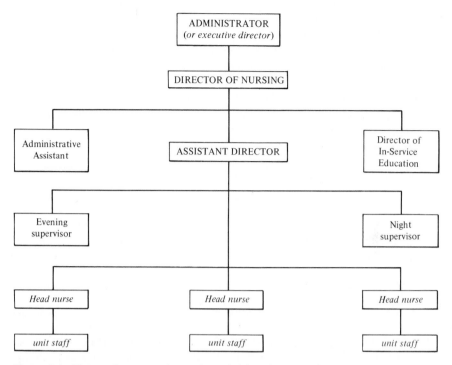

Figure 3-1 Flattened structure for nursing administration.

To this flattened structure is added, in some cases, the idea of decentralizing staff authority (and, therefore, budget control) to the head nurse, a function formerly performed at a higher level.[114] Also, under the primary-nurse concept, the first-level professional nurse has control over a patient's care from admission to discharge—again, a function that has in the past been located higher in the structure.[115] In addition, there has been some experimentation with a matrix, or crosshatch, type of structure, with line nursing units (surgery, cardiopulmonary, medicine, musculoskeletal, etc.) supported by staff, or resource units (logistics, environmental services, personnel, training and professional services).[116]

The other factor keeping nurses from delivering nursing services of the type they have been trained to deliver has been the paperwork burden, and that is being attacked in some hospitals via computerized record keeping and use of nonnurse "ward managers" for nonnursing tasks.[117]

Another organization problem is presented by the advent of the nurse clinical specialist holding an advanced degree—a nurse who may be highly trained in anesthesiology, psychiatry, surgery, or other specialized types of nursing. These nurses hope to have the freedom to respond, to go where they are needed, when other nurses call for their advice. They would thus have more freedom of movement and discretion in recommending care procedures than nurses have had in the past.

Consistent with the trend in the hospital administration field, there is a great interest in MBO in the literature and in textbooks of nursing administration too.

However, attempted applications are running into difficulty, especially in getting the more senior nurses (that is, those in high-level positions) to use the open two-way communications that are a vital part of MBO.[118] Another point of resistance to change has been in changing performance reviews into the constructive format envisioned in the MBO concept.[119]

Tying in with the MBO trend is a strong interest in newer styles of leadership. As in business, there is some experimental evidence linking participative leadership with increased productivity.[120]

In response to the pressure for cost reduction and to the much-publicized shortage of nurses, there have been some systems-type studies looking to better utilization of the nursing talent that is available, especially reducing the time spent in clerical work, such as record keeping and medication ordering and checking.[121]

Police Administration

The management of crime control is fragmented among federal, state, and local police; prosecutors; judges; detention officials; parole boards and parole officers; and social workers. Accordingly, a local police department should be viewed as a subsystem of a subsystem of a large crime-control system. In view of the fact that the parts of this system—especially the judges, parole officers, and police officers—seem to be working at cross purposes much of the time, the need for systemswide objectives and policies is apparent. In fact, perhaps the most frustrating and discouraging current feature of police work is the freeing of obviously guilty criminals by judges on technical legal grounds and the placing on parole of convicts who return to crime, sometimes shooting it out with police. Yet at this point it is not clear how this working at cross purposes can be eliminated, that is, how systemswide objectives and policies can be achieved among these separate units, despite the fact that the problem has been studied extensively by a presidential commission.[122]

Systems Analysis at the Departmental Level   Even when only the local police department is considered, police work appears to be suffering from inadequate systems analysis. Thus, one writer contends that a major problem in police work is adherence to a single systems analysis—an analysis that sees crime as a function of desire plus opportunity; it relies predominantly on repressing desire (temporarily) by foreclosing opportunity via omnipresence (high visibility of patrols), aggressive patrol, rapid response, and follow-up investigation.[123] (This is sometimes called the DDA approach—deter, detect, apprehend.) It is felt that if the systems analysis put more emphasis on minimizing opportunities (through cooperation between police and community organizations and individuals to improve security measures) or on lessening desire (through study of criminal motivation and cooperation with social workers in those sectors of the population most prone to become criminals), more effective strategies could be developed.[124] In this context the police administrator's problems are quite similar to those of the business executive who must analyze the consumer's motivations in order to formulate the firm's basic strategy.

Prior to the study of the President's Commission on Law Enforcement and Administration of Justice (in 1967), less than 1 percent of police department budgets was devoted to research and development.[125] Since then, there has been considerable federally funded technical assistance; however, most of it has gone to the support of the DDA strategy. For example, operations research techniques have been used to improve the development of personnel, new communications centers have been developed to reduce response time (i.e., the time taken for police to respond to a call), and computers have been used to supply information useful for apprehension purposes (such as names and descriptions of wanted persons or license numbers of stolen vehicles).[126] This emphasis on detection and apprehension is questionable inasmuch as the Commission's own studies showed that, in a large city, a patrolling police officer's chances of encountering a robbery in progress are once in fourteen years.[127]

One example of how less tradition-bound operations research and systems analysis might help is a study that has found that the narrow bottleneck in the burglary-robbery system is the fencing of stolen merchandise. It would, then, appear that a likely strategy would be to concentrate on upsetting the retail outlets, taking the profit out of some types of burglaries and lessening the desire to commit them.[128] Again, use of simulation models of police operations can not only improve allocation of resources (e.g., how many cars to use at any given time) but also improve the training of dispatchers and operations planners.[129]

The Generation Gap The conservative character of police organizations is noted not only in the limiting of R&D efforts to the traditional DDA approach but also in a serious generation gap between higher-level managers (sergeants, lieutenants, captains) and the rank-and-file police personnel. The former are almost exclusively older people who have been trained only in the technical details of police work and who have been long conditioned to a semimilitary type of leadership; rarely have they had any managerial training or education in sociology.[130] It is not surprising, then, that they resist new theories and new strategies that would change their methods of working (especially reducing time spent in patrol and clerical duties in order to have more time to work with community organizations and social workers on preventive methods).[131] The latter group, the rank-and-file police personnel, are predominantly young, and they are increasingly acquiring college educations while working full time.[132] This generation gap between conservatives and persons attuned to new conditions and new approaches has led to demands for "lateral entry," that is, opening the middle and higher ranks of police departments to persons who have not come up through the police ranks.[133] It is hoped that such outsiders would be more likely to develop new philosphies of law enforcement, new systems analyses, and new strategies and techniques.

Organizational Structure Problems The conservatism of police departments is reflected in their organizational structures too. Thus, most are still structured along functional lines (the main departments being patrol, traffic, investigation, detention, and the like). However, if more emphasis is to be put on eliciting community help, as some systems analyses indicate should be done, the primary structural division should be by geographical areas. Specialists from the different functions would be formed into teams to work permanently in a given area, so that they could become thoroughly familiar with the individuals and groups of the area. Also, project teams should be used for special projects.

Control Measures   If new analyses lead to new objectives and new plans, there must also be new control measurements fitted to those plans and objectives. Presumably, the new approaches would be mostly preventive in nature. One writer states that current practice is to conduct criminal investigation on a case-method basis and to direct intelligence activities at individual offenders or groups. Success in police work is measured, he reports, by the arrest of a burglary group and the clearance of a number of cases. He contends that this is a futile process, given the volume of crime in relation to control resources.[134]

CONCLUSIONS

The foregoing review of a few administrative activities in police administration reveals problems parallel to those found in hospital-nursing administration: the need for a systems approach to the larger systems (crime control and medical care services), the generation gap between higher levels of supervision and the first-line professionals (police officers and nurses), the struggle to change traditional organizational structures into forms more suited to modern conditions, the need for new kinds of control measures, and the need to make more effective use of computers. Some of these same problems were also noted in the description of educational administration—especially those having to do with structures, control measures, and the use of computers.

Reviews of other public institutions such as libraries, courts,[135] prisons,[136] welfare departments, and others would reveal some similar managerial problems in each field. Certainly military management is a huge subject covering every known pattern of management, from the most sophisticated (in logistics management) to the most traditional. The fact is that in recent years, many fields have become more and more aware of management and are making efforts to increase their managerial competence.

This chapter has also reviewed some of the management programs currently important in public organizations and the different patterns of management found in business organizations.

The overall aim of this chapter has been to give the reader some feel for what current managerial practice actually is and some idea of the main problems and main lines of development.

A secondary objective was to demonstrate to the reader that the field of management is turbulent, dynamic, changing. That is a big part of the reality of management today. While there is a general direction to this change—toward systems management—it is at times not easy to discern.

Another aim has been to impress upon the reader that many different styles of management are in use today, sometimes even within the same type of organization. Variety, too, is a big part of the reality of management.

Still another objective has been to demonstrate that although there is much variety in managerial practice, there is much similarity too. A manager in any given field can often learn a great deal from studying managerial practice in other fields, because often, as all these fields move toward professional management, others have grappled with very similar problems.

REVIEW QUESTIONS

1 List the main features of MBO. Which of these features derive from management patterns of the 1920s? Which are central to the new trend toward systems management?
2 List the five main factors that distinguish well-managed firms of the medium to large, nondiversified type from poorly managed firms in the same category.
3 What makes the diversified-major–type firms the best managed?
4 Why did the recommendations of the Brownlow Commission and two Hoover Commissions fail to result in a generally well-managed federal bureaucracy?
5 What three things do all levels of government need in order to achieve increased rationality in their budgeting?

DISCUSSION QUESTIONS

1 Of all the patterns of managerial practice described in this chapter, which most closely matches that in the organization with which you are, have been, or hope to be associated? In what ways is the pattern in your organization different?
2 Why have MBO programs sometimes failed?
3 In what respects can it be said that PPBS did not fail?
4 Discuss similarities you find in current administrative problems facing police, medical, and educational administrators.

NOTES

[1] *The Failure Record through 1973* (Dun and Bradstreet Publications, New York, 1974).

[2] Orvis F. Collins and David G. Moore, *The Enterprising Man* (Bureau of Business and Economic Research, Michigan State University, 1964), pp. 243–244. A revised version of this book is *The Organization Makers* (Appleton-Century-Crofts, Inc., New York, 1970).

[3] "The Go-Go Is Gone but Not Forgotten," *Business Week,* Apr. 24, 1971, p. 71.

[4] "Hewlett-Packard: Where Slower Growth Is Smarter Management," *Business Week,* June 9, 1975, pp. 50–58.

[5] *The Young Businessman: Small Company or Larger?* (Hobbs, Dorman and Company, New York, 1968). This key finding has been reported in *Generation,* vol. 1, no. 4, p. 34. *Business Week,* Dec. 16, 1972, p. 73, reported that in recent years, from 12 to 14 percent of all new MBAs entered firms of fewer than fifty employees; however, in 1972 the percentage fell to 10.6 percent.

[6] For details about how these crises develop and what can be done to avoid or solve them, see Robert B. Buchele, *Business Policy in Growing Firms* (Chandler Publishing–International Textbook Co., Scranton, Pa., 1967), part I.

[7] "A Minicomputer Tempest," *Business Week,* Jan. 27, 1975, pp. 79–82.

[8] This classification title, its definition, and some of the ideas in this section come from Norman Berg, "What's Different about Conglomerate Management?" *Harvard Business Review,* November–December 1969, p. 112.

[9] According to as yet unpublished studies, diversified, decentralized large firms have proved more profitable than single-product large firms. In consequence, single-product large firms have steadily come to represent a smaller portion of the United States economy. Some clues as to the reasons for this may be found in the research of Alfred D. Chandler, Jr., as presented in his *Strategy and Structure* (M.I.T. Press, Cambridge, Mass., 1962). Large firms that did not diversify became locked in with respect to both capital investment and management talent, industries which became less and less profitable as they

matured. In the case of steel, countries that were bombed out during World War II built entirely new plants that have proved more efficient than older American plants.

[10] Alfred P. Sloan, Jr., *My Years with General Motors* (Doubleday & Company, Inc., Garden City, N.Y., 1964), p. 435.

[11] "GE's New Strategy for Faster Growth," July 8, 1972, p. 52. See also, in the same magazine, "Mead's Technique to Sort Out the Losers," Mar. 11, 1972, pp. 124–130.

[12] An account of how a newly appointed general manager of the Chevrolet Division of General Motors went about eliminating three levels of manufacturing management and ferreting out each department's problems by use of a systems analysis team is given in "A Swinger Tries to Cure Chevrolet's Ills," *Business Week,* Sept. 18, 1971, p. 62. The team of 340 persons is described as the "largest systems-development operation in the automobile business. They study and analyze the controls of the business. The objective is to improve our response time."

[13] "Shifting Faster to the '74s," *Business Week,* June 30, 1973, p. 19.

[14] For the uninitiated, if a company earns $2 per share after taxes and its stock sells at $18 per share, the multiplier is 9.

[15] For an excellent study of many aspects of conglomerates which describes this process and other aspects of conglomerate management, see Harry H. Lynch, *Financial Performance of Conglomerates* (Harvard Business School, Division of Research, Boston, 1971). Also J. T. Hackett, "Corporate Growth Revisited," *Business Horizons,* February 1974, pp. 25–31.

[16] "The Shattered Image of Litton Industries," *Forbes Magazine,* Dec. 1, 1969, pp. 26–38.

[17] "Royal Little Looks at Conglomerates," *Dun's Review,* May 1968, pp. 25–26; also "Is Textron Ready for a Take-off?" *Business Week,* Oct. 7, 1972, pp. 66–71.

[18] *Forbes Magazine,* op. cit., pp. 27–28.

[19] In a 1970 announcement of its new management information system, a Litton executive is quoted: "If today's MIS had evolved a couple of years earlier, probably 1968 (the earnings drop) would never have happened." *Business Week,* Mar. 28, 1970, p. 180.

[20] Stanley H. Brown, "How One Man Can Move a Corporate Mountain," *Fortune,* July 1, 1966, p. 81. See also "ITT Takes the Profit Path to Europe," *Business Week,* May 9, 1970, pp. 61–62; Anthony Sampson, *The Sovereign State of ITT* (Stein and Day, Incorporated, New York, 1974).

[21] "Litton: B-School for Conglomerates," *Business Week,* Dec. 2, 1967, pp. 88–90.

[22] Textron has succeeded with a lean corporate staff; apparently this firm was strong enough on the other factors mentioned here, especially in selecting healthy businesses for acquisition, that a large corporate staff was not needed.

[23] U.S. Department of Commerce, *Survey of Current Business,* March 1975, table 1 and pp. 2-13 and S-14.

[24] The number employed on contract was estimated at almost 5 million in 1961 by Victor K. Heyman in "Government by Contract: Boon or Boner?" *Public Administration Review,* Spring 1961, p. 59.

[25] *General Management of the Executive Branch,* a February 1949 report of the Commission on Organization of the Executive Branch of the Government.

[26] Reported by the editors of *Business Week* in "Washington Outlook," Jan. 4, 1969, p. 28. In another estimate, President Johnson's chief aide on domestic affairs, Joseph A. Califano, Jr., states that purely domestic programs multiplied tenfold between 1961 and 1968 (see *Business Week,* June 21, 1969, p. 164).

[27] Neil Macneil and Harold W. Metz, *The Hoover Report 1953–1955,* The Macmillan Company, New York, 1956), p. 299.

[28] *Digests and Analyses of the Nineteen Hoover Commission Reports,* Citizens Committee for the Hoover Report, 1955, p. 243.

[29] This account of the period from 1949–1965 relies heavily on Gordon T. Yamada, "Improving Management Effectiveness in the Federal Government," *Public Administration Review,* November–December 1972, pp. 764–765.

[30] "Nixon Puts the Accent on Management," *Business Week,* Dec. 2, 1972, pp. 29–32.

[31] "The New Economic Braintrusters in Congress," *Business Week,* May 5, 1975, pp. 70–71.

[32] Yamada, op. cit., pp. 765–769.

[33] "Nixon Likes Litton's System," *Business Week,* Mar. 28, 1970, p. 162.

[34] Yamada, op. cit.

[35] "Industry Lends Its Know-How," *Business Week,* Feb. 21, 1970, p. 141. This judgment is confirmed by the *Thirteenth Annual Report of the Advisory Commission on Inter-governmental Relations* (U. S. Government Printing Office, 1972). Entitling its report "The Crisis Continues," this Commission,

which studies the relations of federal, state, and local governments, finds that "the multiplication of Federal assistance programs, with a parallel proliferation of management difficulties" poses a "real challenge to statesmanship at all levels."

[36] "Nixon's New Federalism Shapes the '74 Budget," *Business Week,* Feb. 3, 1973, pp. 58–62.

[37] Frederic V. Malek, "Management Improvement in the Federal Government," *Business Horizons,* August 1971, p. 17.

[38] George A. Steiner, *Business and Society* (Random House, Inc., New York, 1971), chap. 23.

[39] For a few examples, see the following articles from *Business Week:* "An Entrenched ICC Fights Off the Reformers," Oct. 9, 1971, pp. 48–49; "Now, Economists as Advocates," Jan. 20, 1973, p. 58; "Taking Pressure off the Agencies," June 23, 1973, p. 30; "Regulating Federal Regulators," Jan. 13, 1968, pp. 24–25; "The Opening Shot to Reform the CAB," July 7, 1975; and an editorial, "Clean Up the CAB," July 14, 1975. See also two symposia on this subject: "Regulatory Administration: Are We Getting Anywhere?" *Public Administration Review,* July–August 1972, and a set of three articles—D. H. Fenn, Jr., "Dilemmas for the Regulator," L. M. Pellerzi, "A Conceptual View of the Regulatory Process," and L. M. Kohlmeier, "Effective Regulation in the Public Interest" all in *California Management Review,* Spring 1974.

[40] John W. Gardner, in a newsletter dated June 1971 for the organization Common Cause, Washington, D. C., points out that New York City is on the verge of bankruptcy and that many other cities are not far behind. "New York: It's Time to Face the Music," *Business Week,* May 5, 1975, pp. 68ff. and "The Underwriters Grow Wary of City Issues," *Business Week,* July 7, 1975, p. 56.

[41] Ira Sharkansky, *The Maligned States* (McGraw-Hill Book Company, New York, 1972).

[42] Richard S. Rosenbloom and John R. Russell, *New Tools for Urban Management* (Harvard Business School, Division of Research, Boston, 1971). See also "Symposium on the American Manager: An Urban Administrator in a Complex and Evolving Situation," *Public Administration Review,* January–February 1971; and "Symposium on Governing Megacentropoles," *Public Administration Review,* September–October 1970.

[43] For a detailed discussion of PPBS, see D. I. Cleland and W. R. King, *Systems Analysis and Project Management,* 2d ed. (McGraw-Hill Book Company, New York, 1975).

[44] *The Age of Discontinuity* (Harper & Row, Publishers, Incorporated, New York, 1969), p. 194.

[45] Allen Schick, "A Death in The Bureacracy: The Demise of Federal PPBS," *Public Administration Review,* March–April 1973, especially pp. 146–147. See also O. Poland, "Why Does Public Administration Ignore Evaluation?" *Public Administration Review,* March–April 1971. See also Stanley B. Botner, "Four Years of PPBS," *Public Administration Review,* July–August 1970, pp. 425–431.

[46] John R. Croxall, Ph.D., in correspondence to the author dated April 1971.

[47] Schick, op. cit.

[48] This was the view of a panel of PPB practitioners who gathered in Washington, D.C., on Mar. 2, 1972, under the auspices of the Association of Public Program Analysis to discuss "Is PPB Dead?" as reported by Schick, op. cit., p. 146.

[49] Aaron Wildavsky, "The Political Economy of Efficiency: Cost-Benefit Analysis, Systems Analysis, and Program Budgeting," *Public Administration Review,* December 1966, pp. 835–852.

[50] H. P. Hatry, "Status of PPBS in Local and State Governments in the United States," *Policy Sciences,* June 1971, footnote, p. 189. New York State did move in this direction in its 1970 edition of "Guidelines for Program Analysis and Review" (Division of the Budget and Office of Planning Coordinator). Also, the city-county government of Honolulu uses a simplified MAPS (monthly actions programs summary) plan involving monthly review of progress against major goals. See also Rosenbloom and Russell, op. cit., pp. 78–80, and J. A. Worthly, "PPB: Dead or Alive?" *Public Administration Review,* July–August 1974, pp. 392–393.

[51] Rodney H. Brady, "MBO Goes to Work in the Public Sector," *Harvard Business Review,* March–April 1973, pp. 65–74. Although Mr. Brady gives a fairly detailed account of his application of MBO in the Department of Health, Education, and Welfare during 1970–1973, he makes no mention of HEW's experiences with PPBS or of the key problem of tying in the objectives with the budgeting process.

[52] Frank W. Reilly, "Policy Decisions and EDP Decisions in the Federal Government," *Public Administration Review,* September 1962, p. 130.

[53] It has been estimated that by the end of 1973 a wide variety of federal organizations employed 22,500 word processors and that by 1980 the number will have increased to 81,500. "The Office of the Future," *Business Week,* June 30, 1975, p. 50.

[54] "Washington Cracks Down on Computer Costs," *Business Week,* Oct. 23, 1971, p. 73.

[55] "Problem Solver, Problem Maker," *Business Week,* Oct. 17, 1970, p. 185.

[56] The contributions to computer development and computer usage by the Armed Forces and many other parts of the federal government are described in David S. Brown (ed.), *Federal Contributions to Management* (Frederick A. Praeger, Inc., New York, 1971), chaps. 10, 11, and 12.

[57] Alan F. Westin and Michael A. Baker, *Databanks in a Free Society* (Quadrangle Books, Inc., Chicago, 1973). This volume contains fourteen detailed profiles of computerized organizations in business and government.

[58] "For Social Security, It Works Like a Dream," *Business Week,* June 5, 1971, p. 110. The Social Security Administration is also one of the organizations described in the Westin-Baker book noted in the immediately foregoing footnote.

[59] Estimate by Henry L. Willis reported in C. Y. Cornog (ed.), *EDP Systems in Public Management* (Rand McNally & Company, Chicago, 1968), p. 7.

[60] Every issue of *Government Data Systems* contains reports of new computer applications at the state and local levels; similar reports are found in many issues of *State Government Administration* from 1972 through 1974.

[61] "A Computer Simplifies Welfare," *Business Week,* Nov. 4, 1972, pp. 87–88.

[62] See, for example, Edward I. Friedland, "Turbulence and Technology: Public Administration and the Role of Information-processing Technology," in Dwight Waldo (ed.), *Public Administration in a Time of Turbulence* (Chandler Publishing Company and Intext Publishers, Scranton, Pa., 1971), pp. 134–150.

[63] *The New York Times,* Mar. 24, 1968, p. 28, as cited by Leonard Sayles and Margaret Chandler, *Managing Large Systems: Organizations for the Future* (Harper & Row, Publishers, Incorporated, New York, 1971), p. 6.

[64] Tom Alexander, "The Unexpected Payoff of Project Apollo," *Fortune,* July 1966, p. 114ff.

[65] This section relies primarily on three sources: The *Fortune* article cited immediately above; a book-length study by Sayles and Chandler, op. cit.; and James E. Webb, *Space Age Management* (McGraw-Hill Book Company, New York 1969). Mr. Webb was head of NASA at the time of the Apollo moon-shot program.

[66] Frank H. Cassell, "The Politics of Public-Private Management," *MSU Business Topics,* September 1972, pp. 14–16. See also S. Ramo, "Needed: A New Kind of Government Program Manager," *Harvard Business Review,* July–August 1965, pp. 6–14.

[67] Ida R. Hoos, "Systems Techniques for Managing Society: A Critique," *Public Administration Review,* March–April 1973, pp. 157–158.

[68] *Improving Executive Management in the Federal Government,* The Committee for Economic Development (New York, 1964), pp. 35–42.

[69] H. L. Weiss, "Why Business and Government Exchange Executives," *Harvard Business Review,* July–August 1974, pp. 129–140.

[70] Bob L. Wynia, "Executive Development in the Federal Government," *Public Administration Review,* July–August 1972, pp. 315 and 316.

[71] *The President's Report, 1968–69* (Harvard University Press, Cambridge, Mass., 1969), p. 7. These ideas have been elaborated by Derek C. Bok, the current president of Harvard, in his 1973–74 *Report,* which provides considerable detail about the program.

[72] Richard W. Benka, "The Public Policy Program of the Kennedy School of Government: A Student's View," *Policy Sciences,* March 1971.

[73] Yehezkel Dror, in a prologue to "Universities and the Teaching of Policy Sciences," a symposium covering the December 1970 and March 1971 issues of *Policy Sciences,* December 1970, p. 401.

[74] These estimates were reported by the editors of *The Saturday Review* on the basis of the then latest available estimates from the U.S. Office of Education and the National Education Association, Sept. 19, 1970, p. 67.

[75] Roald Campbell et al., *Strengthening State Departments of Education* (Midwest Administration Center, Chicago, 1967), p. 8.

[76] For three articles on aspects of this problem, see "Symposium on Education and Public Policy," *Public Administration Review,* July–August 1970.

[77] As summarized from Stephen J. Knezevich, *Administration of Public Education,* 2d ed. (Harper & Row, Publishers, Incorporated, New York, 1969).

[78] For a list of forty school districts that in 1971 were trying PPBS, see Harry P. Hatry, "PPBS: A Status Report with Operational Suggestions," *Educational Technology,* April 1972, pp. 19–22.

[79] J. A. Dei Rossi, *Program Budgeting for Improved School District Planning,* Report RM-6116-RC (The Rand Corporation, Santa Monica, Calif., 1961), pp. 46, 59, and 60.

[80] Hatry, op. cit. See also G. L. Immegart and F. J. Pileki, *An Introduction to Systems for the Educational Administrator* (Addison-Wesley Publishing Company, Inc., Reading, Mass., 1973); and

R. A. Nielsen and J. A. Perkins, Jr., "The Public School District: Managing School Dollars," *Management Controls,* May 1973.

[81] Jack Frymier, *Fostering Educational Change* (Charles E. Merrill Publishing Co., Columbus, Ohio, 1968).

[82] "An 'F' for Most Performance Contracting," *Business Week,* Mar. 25, 1972, pp. 84–85.

[83] J. D. C. Welsh, "Perspectives on Performance Contracting," *Educational Researcher,* October 1970.

[84] James A. Mecklenburger and John A. Wilson, "The Performance Contracts in Grand Rapids," *Phi Delta Kappan,* June 1971, pp. 590–594.

[85] Office of Economic Opportunity, *A Proposed Experiment in Educational Vouchers* (U.S. Government Printing Office, 1971), pp. 1–5.

[86] A. W. Halpin and D. B. Croft, *The Organizational Climate of Schools* (U.S. Office of Education, 1962).

[87] Marilyn Gittell and T. Edward Hollander, *Six Urban School Districts: A Comparative Study of Institutional Response* (Frederick A. Praeger, Inc., New York, 1968). For critical comments of the Gittell-Hollander study by a writer who basically agrees with their conclusions, see Bruce C. Ekland, "Public Participation, Innovation, and School Bureaucracies," *Public Administration Review,* March–April 1969, pp. 218–225.

[88] *Report on the Department of Education* (Office of the Legislative Auditor, State of Hawaii, 1973).

[89] *The Saturday Review,* op. cit.

[90] Martin Mayer, "Everything Is Shrinking in Higher Education," *Fortune,* November 1974, pp. 122ff.

[91] For an excellent account of the multitudinous ways in which large universities have been diverted from the original purposes, see Jacques Barzun, "The New University," *Columbia Forum,* Fall 1968, pp. 14–22. See also "How NYU Got into Such a Financial Mess," *Business Week,* July 1, 1972, pp. 32–34.

[92] "The States Try out Master Planning," *Business Week,* Mar. 10, 1973, p. 80.

[93] Jack W. Coleman, "Some Practicalities of Improving Academic Management," *AACSB Bulletin,* January 1975, pp. 11–17.

[94] "Stanford's Business Approach to Budgeting," *Business Week,* Aug. 4, 1973, pp. 63–64.

[95] "Two Schools Innovate to Stay in the Black," *Business Week,* Oct. 30, 1971, pp. 100–102.

[96] Harlan Cleveland, "Seven Everyday Collisions in American Higher Education," an address to the Asian–U.S. Educators Conference, Chiegmai, Thailand, July 1973, p. 23.

[97] In an address to the President's Institute of the American Council on Education at Princeton University, 1966. For a plea for strong leadership, see T. A. Graves, Jr., "Crisis in University Governance," *HBS Bulletin,* September–October 1971, pp. 13–14. This article appeared originally in *Collegiate News and Views,* March 1971. See also B. Richman, *Leadership, Goals and Power in Higher Education* (Jossey-Bass Publishers, San Francisco, 1974).

[98] Bernard Barber, "Professors, Authority, and Change," *Columbia College Today,* Winter 1967–68, p. 40. For seven cogent articles, see "The American University: A Public Administration Perspective," *Public Administration Review,* March–April 1970.

[99] Barber, op. cit. Barber gives an insightful account of the way the need for many specialist talents has developed in university administration. See also Vernon R. Alden, "The Once and Future Decision-Maker," *Business Week,* July 15, 1972, p. 11; and James R. Surface, "Universities Aren't Corporations: Why Corporate Management Won't Work," *Business Horizons,* July 1971, pp. 75–80.

[100] Estimates extrapolated from figures given by Dr. Alan P. Sheldon, director of the Harvard Business School's Program for Health Systems Management, in "High Marks for Health Systems Management," *HBS Bulletin,* November–December 1972, p. 17.

[101] *Official Register, Department of Health Services Administration,* School of Public Health, Harvard University, 1966–67, p. 111.

[102] Solomon Garb, M.D., Medical Director, American Medical Center at Denver, in personal correspondence to the author, dated Oct. 22, 1971.

[103] S. P. Strickland, "Integration of Medical Research and Health Policies," *Science,* September 1971, especially pp. 1101–1102.

[104] "A Private Manager for Medicaid," *Business Week,* May 19, 1975, pp. 45–46.

[105] For coverage of some of these subjects, see "Symposium on the Crises in Health Care: Problems of Policy and Administration," *Public Administration Review,* September–October 1971.

[106] H. H. Hand and A. T. Hollingsworth, "Tailoring MBO to Hospitals," *Business Horizons,* February 1975, pp. 45–56.

[107] G. Pardee et al., "Patient Care Evaluation Is Every Nurse's Job," *American Journal of Nursing,* October 1971.

108 "Performing Major Surgery on Hospital Costs," *Business Week,* May 19, 1975.

109 Some observers see the relationship between board, administrator, and doctors somewhat differently; they feel that it is a triangle, troika, or three-way struggle for power. However, they agree that the administrator's position is gradually gaining power. See F. Kast, and J. E. Rosenzweig, *Organization and Management: A Systems Approach,* 2d ed. (McGraw-Hill Book Company, New York, 1974), pp. 528–529.

110 Marion Ball, Stanley Jacobs, and Frank Colavecchio, "HIS: A Status Report," *Hospitals,* December 1972, pp. 48–52. About one-third of the users had their own computers, the others procured out-of-house services. See also T. T. Thibodaux, "Computer Based Information System," *Hospitals,* March 1973, pp. 57–60.

111 R. M. Sigmond, "Professional Education for Tomorrow's Hospital Administrators: As Viewed by a Hospital Planner," *Hospital Administration,* Summer 1966, p. 28.

112 B. S. Georgopoulos and Floyd C. Mann, "The Hospital as an Organization," *Hospital Administration,* Fall 1962, p. 51.

113 Kast and Rosenzweig, op. cit., p. 536.

114 M. McKillop, "Decentralized Nursing Service," *Canadian Nurse,* June 1970, p. 37.

115 M. Mathey and M. Kramer, "A Dialogue on Primary Nursing," *Nursing Forum,* no. 4, 1970, pp. 357–359.

116 C. Marciniszyn, "Decentralization of Nursing Service," *Journal of Nursing Administration,* July–August 1971, p. 52.

117 E. E. Hilgar, "Unit Management Systems," *Journal of Nursing Administration,* January–February 1972, p. 40.

118 Charles Russell, "Nursing Service Administrator and the Report of NCSNNE," *Journal of Nursing Administration,* January–February 1971, p. 15; H. H. Graves, "Can Nursing Shed Bureaucracy?" *American Journal of Nursing,* March 1971, p. 491; Jean Barrett, *The Head Nurse* (Appleton-Century-Crofts, New York, 1968), pp. 17–19; and T. R. O'Donovan, "Can the Participative Approach to Management Help Decision-Makers?" *Hospital Management,* July 1971, pp. 16–17.

119 Leth Davidson and Arthur Highmen, "How Management Techniques Change," *Modern Hospital,* December 1971, p. 61; Graves, op. cit., p. 494.

120 Harold Oaklander and Edwin A. Fleishman, "Patterns of Leadership Related to Organizational Stress in Hospital Settings," *Administrative Sciences Quarterly,* p. 520; Harold White, "Perceptions of Leadership Styles by Nurses in Supervisory Positions," *Journal of Nursing Administration,* March–April 1971, p. 44.

121 Charles Goshen, "Your Automated Future," *American Journal of Nursing,* January 1972, pp. 62–64.

122 President's Commission on Law Enforcement and Administration of Justice, *The Challenge of Crime in a Free Society* (U.S. Government Printing Office, 1967).

123 T. A. Repetto, "Crime Control Management and the Police," *Sloan Management Review,* Winter 1972–73, pp. 46–47.

124 Ibid., pp. 50–51. See also "A Data System for Policemen," *Business Week,* Jan. 29, 1972, p. 48.

125 Richard Larson, "Decision-aiding Tools in Urban Public Safety Systems," *Sloan Management Review,* Winter 1972–1973, p. 56.

126 Repetto, op. cit., p. 47. The January–February issue of *Government Data Systems* is devoted entirely to "Systems in Law Enforcement."

127 President's Commission on Law Enforcement and Administration of Justice, *Science and Technology* (U.S. Government Printing Office, 1967), p. 12.

128 Repetto, op. cit., p. 52.

129 Larson, op. cit., pp. 61–71, tells of such a simulation in use in Boston and being prepared for use in a number of other cities.

130 Ibid., p. 57.

131 It has been estimated that detectives, whose pay is at least double that of secretaries, spend a large part of their time typing reports, President's Commission on Law Enforcement and Administration of Justice, *Police Task Force Report* (U.S. Government Printing Office, 1967), p. 49.

132 Although police professionals may be found in every big-city university (especially in prelaw, business administration, or sociology curricula), an especially interesting development is the program at John Jay College of the City Univeristy of New York, giving a bachelor's degree in police science or criminal justice. See "Don't Call It 'Pig U,' " *Change,* May 1972, pp. 20–21. Eighty percent of the students' time is spent *not* on technical police courses but on liberal arts courses designed to help them understand the urban forces engulfing their jurisdiction.

[133] V. A. Leonard, *Police Personnel Administration* (Charles C Thomas Publisher, Springfield, Ill., 1970), p. 53. Also, Richard Chackerian, "Police Professionalism and Citizen Evaluation: A Preliminary Look," *Public Administration Review,* March–April 1974, pp. 141–148.

[134] Larsen, op. cit. p. 52.

[135] Edward C. Gallas and Nesta M. Gallas (eds.), "Symposium on Judicial Administration," *Public Administration Review,* March–April 1971, pp. 111–149.

[136] L. T. Wilkins (ed.), "Symposium: Five Pieces on Penology," *Public Administration Review,* November–December 1971, pp. 595–636.

RECOMMENDED READINGS

Benka, Richard W.: "The Public Policy Program of the Kennedy School of Government: A Student's View," *Policy Sciences,* vol. 2, no. 1, March 1971, pp. 67–81.

Churchman, C. West: "Business Education: Preparation for Uncertainty," *Organizational Dynamics,* vol. 1, no. 1, Summer 1972, pp. 12–20.

Hoos, Ida R.: "Systems Techniques for Managing Society: A Critique," *Public Administration Review,* vol. 33, no. 2, March–April 1973, pp. 157–164.

Mintzberg, Henry: "Strategy-Making in Three Modes," *California Management Review,* vol. 16, no. 2, Winter 1973, pp. 44–53.

Staats, Elmer B.: "Measuring and Enhancing Federal Productivity," *Sloan Management Review,* vol. 15, no. 1, Fall 1973, pp. 1–9.

Weiss, Herman L.: "Why Business and Government Exchange Executives," *Harvard Business Review,* vol. 52, no. 4, July–August 1974, pp. 129–140.

The Managerial Processes

Chapter 4 is the first of five chapters describing managerial activity by looking at the basic functions of managers.

Utilizing the process theory, the essence of management (at any level of an organization) can be summarized:

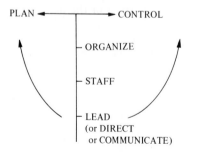

Thus management consists of *planning* what that organization (or part of it) is expected to accomplish and then *controlling* operations (getting reports) so that the plans are actually achieved (a two-way arrow is shown between "plan" and "control" because it is often necessary to replan on the basis of what the control reports reveal). Because it takes people to operate an organization, there must be some *staffing* activities to fill the jobs with people, *organizing* activities to establish who does what, and some leadership (or *directing* or communicating) activity to get action, motivate, inform, coordinate, and supervise the people involved. Arrows extend from "lead" to "plan" and "control" to denote that leadership is expressed in large part in planning and control activities. The way a leader plans and controls (autocratically, or bureaucratically, or participatively, etc.) goes far to establish what type of leader that manager is.

This way of describing the managerial job emphasizes planning and control; some people feel that these two processes should be emphasized because they involve the bulk of managerial decision making. Others object to this emphasis because they feel that the leadership activities should be given the greatest emphasis, since people are any organization's greatest asset. Still others feel that decision making (Chapter 9) should be the central focus in the study of management.

There is little point in taking sides in this argument. All these subjects are vital to effective management; they are best understood as intimately interrelated, with the effectiveness of each depending upon the effectiveness of the others.

While studying these "process" chapters, the reader should keep two thoughts in mind:

1 *Each process is, in fact, discussed quite briefly.* Each of the five processes often is the sole subject of an entire semester's work or a full-sized book. There is a great body of techniques and know-how attached to each of these processes. This book only introduces you to these processes, stressing how they fit together into the whole—management.

2 *Today each process is in transition.* Just as the whole field of management is changing rapidly, so also is each of these processes. In the real world, managers do not suddenly or radically change their ways of working; they do not discard an entire pattern of management, replacing it with a wholly new pattern. Rather, they change bit by bit, trying a new procedure here, hiring a new type of staff person there, installing some new equipment in one section of the business, adding a new product line that uses some old processes and some new ones, asking a consultant to develop and try out a new method of controlling some aspect of the operation, or restructuring some part of the organization. Even when a big change is made, such as taking on the first computer, typically the old methods are retained but are mechanized; it is only later that truly new methods are devised and instituted, and then it is usually done bit by bit.

Accordingly, a realistic description of management must depict each process as a mixture of the old, the not so old, and the new; that is exactly what these chapters do. In time, the new parts will add up to a basically new approach, systems management.

Business Planning and Government Policy Setting

Unbelievable as it may be to today's younger students of management, it is nevertheless a fact that until about thirty years or so ago, the World War II era, most businesses were run without explicitly stated objectives or written long-range plans. Business planning was confined to the lower organizational levels, being short-run planning concerned with machine loading and production scheduling, materials ordering and receiving, and labor recruitment and hiring. In public administration, managerial planning was confined to one-year budgeting and operations schedules; managers of government agencies were seen as executors of plans set by other persons, such as legislators or elected officials.

Since World War II, however, higher-level, longer-range planning has come on strong in business. Today it is rare to find a large firm that does not have a formal long-range planning unit, that does not have written objectives and sets of plans, and that is not using numerous planning tools and techniques. This great change has come about because, by and large, the planners have been winners and the nonplanners have been losers in the competitive struggle.

It is difficult to document fully the sweeping assertion that the planners have been the winners. There is some solid research that supports it;[1] in addition, there is a strong logical explanation of why planning, once implemented by a few firms, developed so powerfully and so rapidly. The first point in this logical explanation is that planned action is generally more effective than unplanned action. While there are such things as too much planning ("paralysis by analysis") and too rigid planning, systematic forethought usually helps to clarify matters and to prevent mistakes that would be made if action were taken impulsively. Second, the management team that has carefully developed its objectives is able to concentrate all its members' efforts on the "success imperatives" needed to achieve those objectives, avoiding diversions that may temporarily appear attractive. Third, and perhaps most vital, there is the point stated long ago by Sir Francis Bacon, "Truth comes more readily out of error than out of confusion." Thus the firm that plans and measures its progress against those plans will learn from its experiences, including its mistakes; the nonplanner will not necessarily learn but is likely to perpetuate confusion. The organization that plans, especially if there is meaningful participation by various levels of managers in that planning, tends to develop a climate of strength; it attracts and holds managers who are professionals, that is, persons who have acquired the confidence and planning skills needed to stay in command of events rather than be their victims. Or, as has long been understood by the military, "Plans may sometimes be useless, but the planning process is always indispensable."

In public administration there has been some, but probably less, development of planning technique and capability. Efforts to link budget decisions to definition of an organization's missions and to take a longer-run approach (i.e., longer than one year) to budgeting have been noted in earlier chapters. So also have efforts to train higher-level public administrators in policy analysis, in recognition of the fact that they do have vital input into the legislative process and do set policy by administrative action.

Inasmuch as the planning process in business and in government is quite different, this chapter will be presented under the following headings:

Business Planning
> What It Is—The Main Planning Instruments
> Planning at Different Organizational Levels
> The Planning Side of MBO
> The Main Lessons That Have Been Learned about Planning
> How Planning Is Changing
> Summary

Government Planning and Policy Analysis
> The Nature of Public Policy Issues and the Policy-setting Process
> New Decision Techniques in Policy Planning
> Implementation Problems
> The State of the Art in Policy Analysis and Government Planning

BUSINESS PLANNING

What It Is—The Main Planning Instruments

Managerial planning in a business organization can be summarized by considering the following five main elements:

1 *Objectives,* which set forth *what* is to be ⎫
accomplished over a certain period   ⎪
2 *Basic policies,* which establish guidelines ⎬ which together con-
for *how* (values, ethics, principles, which fields ⎪ stitute the organiza-
to avoid, which to emphasize, etc.) and *why*   ⎪ tion's *strategy*
(in an intention sense)   ⎭

3 *Long-range plans,* which deal with programs that take a number of years (more than five, as a rough rule), such as an overall research and development program; the development of executives; major capital investments such as conception, location, design and construction of facilities; an acquisition or divestment plan to get into or out of certain fields

4 *Short-range plans,* which require a few months or a few years to accomplish and may take the form of:

    PERT networks for projects such as a model changeover in an automobile company, or conversion of a manual assembly line to an automated line, or fulfillment of a contract to design and manufacture a new missile

    Budgets, the most used of all planning tools, often incorporating a "profit-improvement plan"; this is where all other plans, short-range and long-range, become tangible commitments

    Bar charts, for less detailed project planning

    Operations schedules, etc.

5 *Minor policies, procedures, and rules* pertaining to all parts of the firm

Ideally, a firm does thorough planning that integrates all the types of plans on this list. While some *large* companies actually do all this, some do only part of it. While some *small* firms have carefully thought out strategies and do budgeting regularly, most small firms do only spasmodic, vague planning, rarely putting any of these types of plans into writing.

A graphic presentation of these types of plans, somewhat more detailed, is presented in Figure 4–1. The following section provides further detail by relating how the various plans are used at different organizational levels. And the later sections explain many "how-to" aspects of the process by which these plans are developed and used.

Planning at Different Organizational Levels

In a professionally managed large firm, all managers plan. First-level managers (assistant supervisors or supervisors) will do chiefly short-range planning about next week's or next month's job scheduling and work assignments, but they do some slightly longer-range planning about their own personal development, about the development of their subordinates, and about the way their sections (or units or groups) can be improved. The next level (supervisors or superintendents) will do some longer-range planning about details of new plant layouts, changes in work methods and equipment, or details of new facilities; however, they will also do some budgeting (for a quarter or a year) and short-range planning of operations. Executives at the department-head level will plan annual and biennial budgets and make the main recommendations about new facilities to higher levels. Executives at the division-head or executive-vice-president level will spend considerable time discuss-

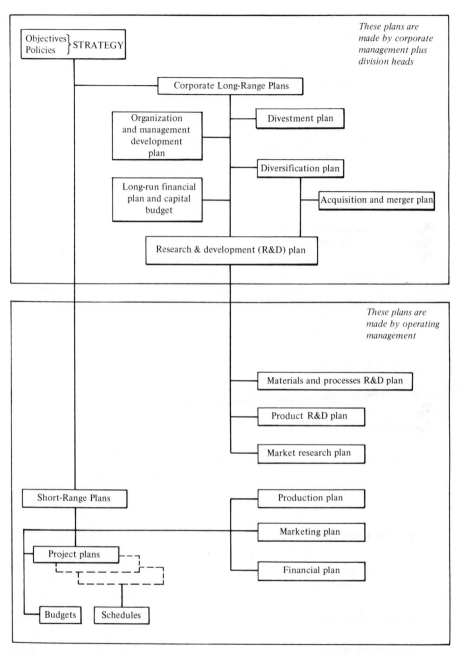

Figure 4-1 The planning process. *(Adapted from a chart originally prepared by Stanford Research Institute and published in* Business Week, *June 1, 1963, p. 54.)*

ing budgets and other plans with the department heads, sending consolidated budgets and product plans upward. They will work, too, on the financial and organizational planning needed to facilitate these plans. The top-level executives in large firms will be chiefly concerned with planning major changes in the nature of the business, with periodically revising the firm's overall objectives, basic policies, and long-range plans. Putting together a great deal of information and expert opinions on environmental change and developing patterns of competition, they are (or ideally should be) concerned chiefly with strategy for the future and only occasionally with current operations or budgets for the next year or two.

The statement that all managers plan means that every manager at whatever level (that is, every person in charge of subordinates) is responsible for giving some thought to the unit's objectives and to the future actions needed to achieve those objectives—no matter how long-range or short-range those objectives may be. Thus planning is an inherent part of every manager's job. Or, put another way, all managers should take a bifocal approach to their jobs—looking sometimes through the upper lens (planning) to focus on future matters and sometimes through the lower lens (supervising) to be sure that operations are running as planned. The proportion of time spent looking through each lens changes from level to level, so that the top executives spend the great bulk, but not all, of their time looking through the upper lens and lower-level managers spend most, but not all, of their time supervising.

The Planning Side of MBO

The MBO approach to management has become perhaps the most widely applied method of planning; accordingly, a discussion of the planning side of MBO will indicate the way many firms go about doing their planning.

Meaningful Participation   A main feature of MBO is that it calls for two-way communications at all levels in the setting of objectives, policies, and plans. These are the most meaningful subjects on which to practice participative management—what does the firm aim to accomplish, how best to go about it, and what will be the roles of various individuals and groups? True participation in the determination of these matters can do a great deal toward making use of all the managerial talent; also, it can do a great deal toward building subordinate managers' self-esteem, professional capabilities, and motivation. One chief executive, who worked regularly for six months with his vice presidents to determine the organization's objectives, remarked that the process made his vice presidents "2 feet taller per man." In contrast, in another large organization, three-fourths of the vice presidents stated, via an anonymous questionnaire, that they did not know what objectives they were supposed to be pursuing beyond the general goals of growth and profit. Incredible as this may seem, it is believable when one realizes that that organization had diversified rapidly, that the chief executive had kept planning in his own hands, and that the chief executive's health problems had limited his time for communicating with his vice presidents just when the organization was becoming much larger and engaging in many more types of businesses. Under such conditions, it is indeed possible for expensive vice presidents not to know what they are supposed to be doing.

The MBO format calls for two-way, give-and-take discussions on objectives and plans; ideally, this will occur at all levels and will yield an integrated set of objectives that all managers understand and accept with some enthusiasm of authorship. Although the lower levels of supervision and the rank-and-file workers may not have a chance to do much about overall company objectives, under MBO they would have a chance to know how their own work fits into the big picture and to discuss with their own bosses the objectives of their own group. Realistically, this type of communication is exceptionally difficult because it takes time, because some line managers are natural hoarders of information rather than sharers, and because still others are poor communicators even though they want to have two-way communications with their subordinates. In some firms, by the time MBO reaches the lower levels, it has become just another meaningless paperwork requirement. In one situation the present author found that to the lower levels of supervision, MBO took the form of a memo (with hard-to-read manual attached) requesting that a form about objectives be filled out and sent to a staff planner. After completing the form, a supervisor received no reaction or feedback of any kind, but the next year the same memo, forms, and manual were distributed to be filled out anew.

Few of the many firms that have attempted to apply MBO have achieved participation in planning by more than three levels of management; nevertheless, it can be a valuable technique at those higher levels.

Multiple Objectives   Another big feature of MBO is that an organization that works hard on setting objectives soon realizes that narrow, single-focus objectives are impractical in today's business world. First, overconcentration on a single measure of achievement—even the single most important one, return-on-investment—can lead to serious distortions. This has been demonstrated in the celebrated electrical industry price-fixing cases in which division heads of a leading firm complained that an all-out push on return-on-investment virtually forced them into illegal collusion on prices.[2] It has been demonstrated in Russia, where strongly pushed production goals have led to such ridiculous practices as producing shoes of only a few sizes.

Peter Drucker recommends having objectives in the following areas: market standing, innovation, productivity, physical and financial resources, profitability, manager performance and development, worker performance and attitudes, and public responsibility.[3]

Flexible Objectives   Objectives are also harmfully narrow or rigid when they limit an organization's awareness of the need to make basic changes in the nature of the business in order to adjust to changes in the environment. In a classic article, Professor Theodore Levitt pointed out that those firms which defined themselves as in the railroad business and set objectives strictly within that context slid downhill with the railroad industry; however, those who defined themselves as in the transportation business saw the need for having policies that would enable them to "periodically evaluate the basic changes taking place in the transportation industry" and "invest in new and coming forms of transportation in order to be a leader in whatever new forms become dominant."[4]

Another big reason for keeping objectives flexible, especially in the sense of being subjected to periodic reevaluation, is that some may simply prove impractical, too difficult, or too easy. A big advantage of having written objectives is that they are in such tangible form that they can readily be reviewed and modified if accumulated experience indicates such action.

Concentration on Success Imperatives   Another strong feature of the MBO approach is that it helps a firm concentrate on what have been called the "success imperatives." Thus, once an organization has defined its main objective in a particular field, the next step is to ask these questions: What are the imperatives for success? What are the few things an organization must do well in this particular field to accomplish its objectives? What is the basis of success of the leading firms in the field? Should we develop the same strengths, or are the leaders vulnerable to competition via a different strategy, a different set of strengths?

Once a management team has worked out the answers to these questions, it can concentrate its efforts on the success imperatives, which then become the subobjectives. A common mistake is to try to do everything well, for organizations trying that usually end up spending energy and limited managerial ability on matters of minor importance and on product lines that should be abandoned.

The Main Lessons That Have Been Learned about Planning

As managerial planning has developed over the years, a number of basic lessons, in addition to those mentioned in the MBO discussion, have been learned:

1 *Planning requires a combination of line and staff effort.* Although planning is (or at least should be) a part of every line manager's job, in large organizations it requires staff specialists to handle the research into environmental changes, making projections of economic, technological and sociological conditions.

In the early days of long-range planning, staff specialists dominated the process. Their finished plans were usually adopted in toto by the line executives. However, these staff-written statements of objectives and plans too often failed to gain true line support even though they were formally accepted by line managers. Instead of becoming the documents which actually guided the firm's activities, these plans gathered dust in the line executives' desk drawers while the disillusioned staff specialists became more and more frustrated.

Much of the same thing often happened in budgeting, especially in firms that did not have a strong follow-up process to enforce budget discipline. Thus, division heads in some organizations would pay little attention to budget formulation, turning it over to their divisional accountants, who put some figures together and sent them up to the corporate accountants. In this way budgets could become mere paperwork or sets of spending restrictions; in either case they reflected little of the real planning of the division head.

The lesson is clear: Line executives should be deeply involved in planning decisions long before the final prettily bound package of objectives, policies, plans, and budgets is presented. If they are not so involved, a responsibility gap can develop. If budgets are not met, the line managers say that the accountants budgeted poorly; the accountants say the budgets were sound and blame the line managers for poor performance. Under such conditions, line managers are not fully committed to accomplishment of the plans.

2 *Plans must balance stability with flexibility.* Many early long-range plans were one-track blueprints that managers were expected to follow to completion. This type of plan often fell of its own weight. Forecasting is so difficult, although excellent techniques have been developed,[5] that one rarely can prescribe detailed actions to be taken a number of years hence. For this reason, line executives found such plans unusable because they were "impractical," "rigid," or "unrealistic."

Plans should have enough stability, or firmness, to provide continuing, consistent guidance; they should help managers to know what jobs lie ahead and to avoid going off onto momentarily tempting tangents. But they should not keep an organization committed to a course of action after it has become apparent that it is wrong.

Techniques have been developed to give planning a balance between rigidity and flexibility. One is multitrack contingency planning, which charts various courses of action to be taken when and if certain major events occur.[6] Other techniques, including network planning and decision trees (which are discussed later), focus on the decisions that must be made at major branches in the road, working out the sequence of events that might flow from each alternative decision. These techniques help managers see the total picture, thus helping them realize when the trend of events calls for changing longer-range plans and when it is wise to stick with these plans. For short-range planning, some firms used the so-called "flexible budget," which sets forth spending plans to be used if, for example, early sales reports run 10 percent or 20 percent above or below projections. Having such plans worked out in advance enables a manager to adjust rapidly to changing conditions. In some businesses, even a brief lag in adjusting to a drop off in sales can cause heavy losses.

Conditions prevailing in the mid-1970s place a greater-than-usual value on planning flexibility and fast adjustment. First, the long-term outlook—for slow growth because of materials scarcity, chronic national and international inflation, dried-up equity markets, and high interest rates—is so different from what it has traditionally been that it is virtually impossible to forecast what the world is going to be like. Second, the pace of events—as demonstrated by the Arabs' oil maneuvers —is so radical that plans are not long valid. Such turbulence requires more planning, not less. Many firms are seeking to cope with these conditions by using computerized models and projecting many different scenarios so that they will be somewhat prepared for whatever happens.[7]

3 *The hard part of planning is forecasting the changes.* In the early days of planning, it was common practice simply to extend known trends (in population, company sales, prices, cost improvements, etc.) to determine what physical facilities, staff, and financing would be needed five or ten years hence. Such straight-line projections often were quite misleading, indicating unrealistically high growth and profit improvement and leading to overexpansion.

Life is not straight-line simple; rarely does a firm actually experience uninterrupted straight-line growth for many consecutive years. Realistically, firms typically have difficult adjustments to make every few years, and one or two such setbacks produce far different ten-year results than does a straight-line projection compounding a certain percentage annual growth rate.

These difficult adjustments may be required by events external to the firm (as discussed in the immediately preceding point) or by events internal to the firm (as discussed in the immediately following point).

4 *Organizational diagnosis is essential to sound planning.* Internal changes can render an organization incapable of carrying out the actions called for by an ambitious set of plans. An organization can get into trouble as readily by failing to recognize and cope with internal changes as by failing to recognize and cope with external changes.

Growth inevitably produces stresses and strains in an organization; lack of growth, or complacency, can produce deterioration of an organization's capabilities. Therefore a firm should, in any case, provide for systematic, periodic diagnosis of the state of its organizational health or, in other terms, a statement of the firm's strengths and weaknesses. Detecting internal problems is difficult because: (*a*) They grow slowly, day by day, and there are no published warning signals such as the economic indicators that warn about external changes, and (*b*) the individual managers are intimately involved, so they often cannot see their own changing ways. Fortunately, management literature now provides some help in detecting internal problems; some writings have defined stages of organizational growth and the problems that often accompany them.[8]

Undoubtedly the most vital consideration in assessing a firm's strengths and weaknesses is what might be called its tomorrow-mindedness, which in turn consists of (*a*) having such market research and ability to assess the environment that it knows when new products are needed and what characteristics those new products should have and (*b*) having the product R&D capability to come forth with those new products.

5 *Interest in social indicators is growing.* As business people have become increasingly concerned with issues of social responsibility, they have felt a need to forecast social indicators just as they now forecast economic and technological conditions. These firms want to be able to forecast, or acquire forecasts of, such social indicators as the public's views on work versus leisure, measures of pollution, and measures of health conditions.[9]

6 *Budgets can be strong planning instruments,* or they may have no planning value. It all depends upon two aspects of the way in which budgets are formulated and used: (*a*) Expenditures and progress against long-range plans should be built into current operations budgets. If this is not done, the long-range plans may never get off the ground. Traditionally, budgets contain only numerical data on the current year's operation, and line managers are rewarded or censured on their performance for the year. That practice inhibits managers from spending money toward long-range accomplishments because such expenditures show no return in the current period. If, however, the budget provides for expenditures against long-range plans and contains some narrative statements of what steps on long-range plans are to be accomplished during the current period, then line managers will be measured each period on the bifocal approach mentioned earlier. (*b*) If, as was the old practice, the budget is formulated by controllers, the restrictive aspects of budgets may dominate; line managers resent such budgets, and they learn many ways of getting around them. However, as has been noted, if line managers participate in the planning and budgeting, they will be motivated to accept responsibility for the results called for in the budgets. Thus positive motivation will replace the negative motivation of restrictive budgets.[10]

It is for these reasons that budgets have been included in the list of main planning instruments rather than relegated to the chapter on control.

7 *Long-range plans should be evaluated by their impact on learning.* They should *not* be judged by the amount of data or number of impressive charts presented, or on the bold growth rate envisioned for the company, or even on the quality of the leather binding in which they are contained. Rather, an evaluator should ask: Have the plans helped the company better to understand its own capabilities vis-à-vis the opportunities and threats facing it? What does a comparison of past plans with past actual results show? Has the organization learned?

An organization cannot be expected to attain the goals set forth in its first or even its second set of plans. However, over time, plans and actual events should come closer together. If a firm is actually achieving its stated goals or even coming close, a great deal of learning has taken place.

How Planning Is Changing

In recent years, as the field of management has moved toward the systems approach, new ideas and practices have come into managerial planning. At least the following three points should be added to the seven older "lessons" already described.

8 *The concept of strategy is increasingly prominent.* Just as the art of management advanced significantly when firms learned to formulate objectives, so another advance is being achieved currently as firms learn to extend their objectives into corporate strategies. Strategy planning helps an organization think incisively about competition and about opportunities and threats arising from environmental change. An organization with a strategy takes the initiative in making the important changes rather than carrying on established routines until it is forced to react to the initiatives of competitors.

At the start of this chapter, strategy was defined as the combination of objectives (*what* is to be accomplished) with major policies (guidelines for *how* and *why* the objectives are to be accomplished; guidelines on which an integrated set of specific long-range plans may be built). The process of formulating strategy has been described as balancing four categories of decisions: first, what a corporation *might* do (alternative objectives in view of environmental opportunities and threats); second, what it *could* do (in view of its capabilities and limitations); third, what it *wants* to do (in view of the risks the decision makers wish to take and other personal values); and fourth, what it *should* do (in view of its social responsibilities).[11]

One writer sets forth six criteria for evaluating a firm's strategy, that is, for deciding whether the strategy is right for the firm: (1) internal consistency, (2) consistency with environment, (3) appropriateness in light of available resources, (4) satisfactory degree of risk, (5) appropriate time horizon, and (6) workability.[12]

Other authors claim that strategy planning pays off, explaining the conditions under which particular strategies are especially effective.[13] In order to make these considerations more tangible, the kinds of decisions involved in determining the strategy of a large firm, a medium-sized firm, and a small firm will be examined.

Large-Firm Strategy A large manufacturing firm, one mainly identified with the farm equipment industry, for example, might formulate its strategy around such issues as these: Should it compete across the board (that is, in all major products and a variety of size and price classes) or should it concentrate on products of its greatest relative strength? To what extent should it invest in foreign manufacture and/or sales versus domestic? Or, perhaps, the relevant question is whether it should compete across the board in foreign markets or choose certain areas particularly favorable to its product strengths. Should the firm increase, decrease, or hold constant its degree of diversification from its major industry? Should the diversification take the form of invasion of industries that use similar skills and facilities (e.g., road-building equipment or trucks), the form of forward integration (toward the customer, toward distributing its own products), or backward integration (toward producing its own parts and raw materials)? If diversifying, should it be done from within, or by merger, or by acquisition? And, in view of the decisions made on the foregoing questions, should the research and development program continue as is or be redirected, increased, or decreased?[14] A set of policies on these and many related questions in marketing, finance, and social responsibility can turn a statement of objectives into a statement of strategy which, in turn, provides the base for specific long-range plans and programs.

Medium-sized-Firm Strategy A medium-sized firm in the same industry, perhaps one manufacturing accessories and parts for the majors, might formulate its strategy around such issues as these: To what extent should it seek to build its own labels (requiring strong marketing) versus manufacturing for others' labels (requiring all-out concentration on production efficiency)? Is it in a position to profitably expand its product lines, or would its profitability be increased by eliminating some lines? What strengths does it have that might enable it to diversify profitably, thus reducing its dependence upon a few customers (and, at the same time, increasing its bargaining power with them)? If it is diversifying, should it be by internal development, merger, or acquisition? And, in view of the answers to the foregoing questions, should its research and development program continue as is or be redirected, reduced, or enlarged? A medium-sized firm is often limited in its strategies by its distribution and production capabilities. Firms of this size must have a strategy involving advertising-promotional and financing (types of financing and amount of leverage) plans consistent with their basic distribution and production capabilities.

Small-Firm Strategy   The essence of strategy lies in getting into a position of competing from strength rather than from weakness, or competing on grounds of your own choosing rather than grounds chosen by your competitors. Nowhere is that more evident or more important than in connection with small firms. Simply because it does not have the raw power or reserve strength to fight larger firms across the board, the small firm must choose some sector of the market (a price range, a size range, a geographical area, a full-service or a no-service approach) in which it can do a better job than the large firm. Also, being especially vulnerable to sudden invasion of its special field by a larger firm, it should diversify; often diversification by merger is best for the small firm if the merger brings the added advantages of more depth in management and added financial reserve. An inherent advantage of smallness is the ability to move fast; hence, small-firm strategy should involve a constant searching for those new ideas that can be exploited quickly without massive risk. Another important element of small-firm strategy is that it should be appropriate in view of the firm's cost structure, its basic nature. Here breakeven curves (illustrated in the next chapter) can help managers realize which strategies make sense for their firms and which do not.

The concept of corporate strategy is entirely consistent with systems management in its concern with adjusting the organization to the threats and opportunities of environmental change—economic, technological, competitive, etc. The two concepts may be expected to advance together. It has already been noted that some writers on systems management anticipate an organization structure that separates strategies from the systems designers and the operations managers, so that the strategists can be cold, hard calculators who allocate the firm's resources among alternative possible uses, unhampered by past loyalties to any section of the business.

9   *The use of the newer decision-making techniques is increasing.* It is in the process of planning that a large part of managerial decision making takes place; accordingly, it is here that the newer decision-making techniques (mostly, but not entirely, quantitative and computer-facilitated) have their impact. In addition to such traditional decision techniques as matrices, capital investment payback analyses, marginal return analysis, breakeven charts, and brainstorming, planners now have available many newer techniques including the following:

PERT   Over the past fifteen years or so, the program evaluation and review technique (PERT) has brought dramatic improvement in the capability of managers to plan large, complex, one-time projects. It has been widely used by both business and government managers on such projects as major construction jobs; research and development programs running a number of years and involving various processes and perhaps a whole family of new products; moving a missile from the original design stage through breadboarding, testing, production designing, retesting, and into production; or coordinating a new-product launching through test marketing, possible redesign, into production, advertising, promotion, original distribution, and the decision to make it a regular part of the product line.

Such projects typically span more than a year, often a number of years, so PERT is usually a longer-range form of planning than budgeting or operations scheduling. It is done before the project starts and is therefore able to consider alternative ways of doing parts of the project, alternative ways to sequence it, and alternative plans for how much equipment or how much manpower to devote to each phase of the total project. Insights into how such problems might best be solved are gained by laying out the project (as in Figure 4-2) in considerable detail that shows how some phases of it might be pursued simultaneously, how certain activities must wait upon the completion of other parts, how long each phase takes (the length of the tails of the arrows), and when each phase is completed (that is, when the "events" are completed as noted by the location of the circles).

The critical path is the sequence of events that determines how long it will take to complete the project; all other paths have some slack in them, but there is no slack in the critical path.

The so-called critical path method (CPM) simply determines the critical path; however, PERT is more complex, and it does more. PERT derives its time estimates (t_e in the diagram) by combining optimistic, most likely (given extra weight), and pessimistic estimates. The spread between these estimates determines the variance (V, which is based on the previous event also), which may be used in normal frequency statistics to calculate the probability that the job will underrun or overrun its estimated time of completion.[15] When these probabilities are substantial, they constitute a warning that a dangerous situation exists; the manager must then

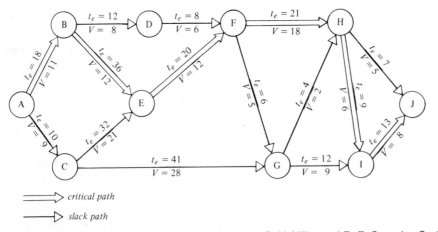

Figure 4-2 Simplified PERT network. [*Adapted from C. McMillan and R. F. Gonzales,* Systems Analysis: A Computer Approach to Decision Models, *3d ed. (Richard D. Irwin, Inc., Homewood, Ill., 1973), p. 294.*]

consider other ways of doing the project, ways that will yield more dependable estimates of time to complete.

Most PERT networks involve hundreds or even thousands of events; hence they require computerization to be usable. When computerized, the PERT network provides an excellent set of control points, or milestones, against which actual progress may be reported.[16] When viewed in this way, it is clear that PERT is essentially a computer-age elaboration and refinement of such earlier planning-control devices as bar charts or milestone budgets.[17]

A PERT network also provides a basis for replanning in case something (such as a strike, fire, flood, or unexpected freeing up of other company equipment) upsets the original planning. The biggest advantage, however, is in calling forth detailed consideration of the interrelationships of the various phases of the total project. Such consideration facilitates thinking about better ways to do a project, trade-offs between using more assets to save time along the critical path or using fewer assets along the slack paths.

Detailed planning can also be the biggest danger of PERT. Thus, if the planning is done in such detail that big strategy decisions cannot be identified or main control points cannot be recognized, PERT becomes an expensive computer and paperwork exercise without major benefits.

One early problem with PERT was that it dealt in *time* rather than in *money;* in consequence, it was not useful for cost estimating or cost control where there was not a linear relationship between time and cost. However, PERT/ Cost has been developed to handle these problems. Although some complex problems are involved (e.g., allocating overhead costs to phases of a project), PERT/Cost is being effectively used, especially by government agencies evaluating their contractors' cost estimates.[18]

Mathematical Techniques In planning it is often necessary to choose between alternative ways of solving a problem such as how to launch a new product, or how many new products to launch at a certain time, or where to build warehouses and how many of them to have, and many other problems that can be partly or wholly quantified. Today's planners, especially those in large organizations with computers and staffs of specialists, have at their disposal a variety of well-developed quantitative techniques for helping solve such problems. (These techniques will be described and discussed in Chapter 9 on decision making.)

Long-Range Planning Techniques At the long-range planning level, a number of methods having great promise have come into use in recent years.

The technique of *simulation* requires building a computerized mathematical model of an organization's total operation or some major part of it, such as the marketing subsystem. While building models is a complex and difficult task, such models are potentially powerful planning tools in the hands of managers capable of using them fully. Indications are that a fairly substantial minority of large firms are using simulation models, and that use of them is increasing under today's unpredictable conditions. Nonetheless, some knowledgeable persons advise caution, as does a company president who states:

> After spending five years, endless management and consultant effort, and a great deal of money, our company still has not developed a reliably predictive computerized model of a middling-sized gas distribution utility.[19]

Models may be used to provide insights into a wide variety of planning problems. One use is simply to project trends to see what financial stresses and strains lie five years ahead or what scale of facilities will be needed. Thus, related models of the operating statement and balance sheet may, on the basis of trends for the past five years, be projected for a number of years into the future. However, a far more powerful use of models is the asking of "what if" type questions; thus the financial model just discussed could be asked to project answers to such questions as: What if we shift one-fifth of our debt to equity? What if we increase inventories (by adding new products to our lines) but do not increase our capital structure?[20] A model of the marketing subsystem may be asked "what if" questions about pricing strategies, increasing or decreasing the number of items in the product line, or other questions about basic marketing actions.[21] An advertising agency has designed a new-product model based on case studies of nearly 120 new-product introductions, to predict within 5 percent the initial purchase levels during the first thirteen weeks of a product's introduction.[22] An overall model of a business can deal with "what if" questions comparing different strategies, each involving different combinations of marketing, production, and financing actions.[23]

One nonquantitative technique promises to help planners determine when major changes will occur. The general name for this approach is the *scenario technique* (wherein a number of planners write out their descriptions of what they think will happen, then explore one another's thinking, then arrive at a final "scenario" or set of them); one specific scenario technique is the *Delphi* method.[24] Delphi involves the use of a number of experts in fields related to the question being estimated—such as when flat television will be a commercial reality, or when there will be a single national building code, or when the desalination of sea water will become economically feasible. The experts give not only their estimate on the question but also their reasoning, including estimates about when other developments essential to this one will occur. The first estimates are interchanged anonymously so that no one will be identified with a certain position and thereby inclined to spend his or her energies defending that position instead of thinking analytically. The process is repeated until a useful consensus develops or until it becomes clear why a useful consensus cannot be developed.

These techniques have been applied to describing the world of some future date and to making more specific forecasts by highly sophisticated "think tank" consulting groups whose client lists include some of the largest companies.[25] Some laboratory-type research has indicated that the Delphi technique and variations of it are more effective decision-making processes than the traditional group conference.[26]

The chapter on systems management has discussed the use of *cost-effectiveness* or *cost-benefit* analysis by Defense Department analysts to weigh the merits of alternative weapons systems or even the relative benefits of alternative missions to a total military program. Potentially this technique has almost endless uses in the long- and short-range planning of civilian businesses; however, it is a rather complex technique, and not many practical applications have been reported.

Still another potentially potent planning technique is the use of so-called *input-output analysis.* This technique involves use of complex tables and formulas that chart the supplier and customer relationships between industries; thus the technique can predict the impact upon a given industry of assumptions about overall economic conditions and about specific other industries. It can also illuminate the effects of new products and processes on specific industries.[27]

10   *The importance of information to planning is increasingly recognized.* In recent years many managers have come to realize that plans are only as good as the information on which they are based. Accordingly, there is today a great emphasis on designing the internal management information system (MIS)—discussed in Chapter 9—that will bring managers the information they need to plan effectively. External information is needed in planning, too, and managers need a flow of such information that will enable them to plan at least as well as their competitors are planning. Today, the internal information flow is often in large part computerized; it is quite possible that at some future date, external information flows also will be computerized.

Summary

In the decades since World War II, business firms have greatly developed the planning function, and this trend continues. The reason is that, in general, organizations that plan have been the winners over the nonplanners. And individual managers have learned that planning helps them continue to learn more and more about the profession of management. Planning helps them to be in control of events rather than being controlled by them.

Planning is a vital interest of managers at all levels of all sizes and all kinds of organizations; however, the nature of planning does vary with the individual's organizational level and with the size of the organization.

This chapter has reviewed why planning works, how it works, some of the do's and don'ts of planning, and some planning techniques. Although it is easy to be misled by academic journals and textbooks that imply that almost all these techniques are in widespread use, it is nevertheless true that some are well established, and the trend is toward greater use of quantitative techniques in planning. Accordingly, line managers in large organizations need to know enough about models and other techniques to understand their contributions and limitations in planning.

Middle-level manufacturing, marketing, and financial executives will increasingly use these techniques in their planning. Higher-level executives, whose main job is planning, will increasingly be at a serious disadvantage if they cannot use these techniques. What these techniques can do for these managers has been well stated by one writer:

Systems analysis and the use of logical models will not eliminate uncertainty or insure correctness; will not foresee all major problem goals, contingencies, and alternatives;

will not eliminate the necessity of judgment or the effect of bias and preconception. Hopefully, however, they will tend to increase the influence of the "best," most informed judgments, both on component matters and in the final weighing of decisions; they can provide choice and a market of ideas. They can discover problems, stimulate relevant questions, and encourage people to face complexity and uncertainty explicitly and honestly.[28]

Even more vital are the nature and quality of the strategies that they develop; these strategies will influence not only the competitive success but also the character of their organizations.

GOVERNMENT PLANNING AND POLICY ANALYSIS

In answer to the question "What is your most difficult administrative problem?" the mayor of a small but growing community recently replied (paraphrased):

> Planning. Look at any major American city, including the one in my own state. God-awful things have been allowed to happen. No one planned these developments.
>
> We can't let such things continue to happen. Even though it's unconstitutional to forbid United States citizens to move into our community, we must devise some sort of plan that will control our growth and will, in the long run, preserve the desirable features of our community.
>
> Such planning involves much searching for ideas, much experimentation, much hard work. Whatever the obstacles, however, we must devise such a plan and we must make it work.
>
> Unfortunately, we politicians and public administrators simply have not yet learned to define what kind of communities, what kind of life-style we want, and then to lay plans to achieve that kind of community.[29]

One point to note in the mayor's statement is that, although he is an elected official, he sees planning as an administrative problem. He knows that he and the legislators of his community must rely heavily upon appointed administrators for analytical studies of public issues, for proposing legislation (and shaping it so that it will be administrable), for interpreting enacted legislation via administrative rulings, and for securing continuing public support for the program that results from the legislation. It is the administrators, having continuing direct contact with the clientele of a program, who can twist, turn, weaken, and defeat programs that they do not understand, are incompetent to administer, or simply do not like. For these reasons, administrators have been called the "fourth branch" in our system of government,[30] a branch that may have as much or more influence on planning and decision making as does the executive, the legislative, or the judicial.

The second point to note in the mayor's statement is his assertion that public administrators have not learned to plan and implement plans effectively. This judgment is shared by many writers who have noted failures of one major national program after another. One of the young academics concludes "the record is dismal." Even one of the older, less "radical" public administration writers admits that

"Old problems remain (or reappear) while new ones are spawned; the pace of change quickens and everything seems intractable, imponderable, or threatening."[31]

Why have public administrators not been able to plan and to carry out plans effectively?

Before answering this question, the point should be made that the problem is *not* with operational-level planning, where government agencies use PERT, budgets, production planning programs, and other planning techniques as much and as well as does private business. In fact, in government, budgeting is virtually an art form; many government administrators are virtuosos in budgeting who could teach business managers much about technique.[32] Also, mathematical decision techniques are used effectively in planning a variety of governmental operations. For one example, the Federal Trade Commission (FTC) plans the use of its limited enforcement resources "to get more bang for the enforcement buck." The FTC uses a model of twenty-four weighted key statistical measures to direct its efforts toward those cases offering a combination of the greatest possibility of successful prosecution and the greatest benefit to society.[33] Many similar examples could be cited to demonstrate that operational-level planning in government is often just as competently done as in business.

The problem is at the higher levels of governmental planning—the levels at which public policy analysis and decision making cope with today's major socioeconomic challenges. "Public policy" may be defined here—slightly differently from the business policy definition given earlier in this chapter—as "The body of attitudes, intentions and values—some explicitly stated and some implied—on which the important programs of a government are based."

The policy-making process is diffuse, sometimes being formal (as in the enactment of legislation containing policy statements) and sometimes informal (as in the implementation of legislation). Policy making occurs in many decisions made during the formulation, enactment, and implementation of legislation.[34]

Why, in actual practice, have legislators and the agencies' administrators that they create so often been unsuccessful (with the NASA moon-landing program being the leading exception) in coping with today's challenges? The answer to this question will be sought via examination of, first, the nature of public policy issues, then the nature of the policy-setting process, then the analytical tools available, and finally some of the problems of implementing policy decisions. Then the current state of the art of public policy analysis and high-level governmental planning can be summarized and some suggestions for improvement considered.

The Nature of Public Policy Issues and the Policy-setting Process

Major public policy issues are so complex and so enmeshed in political pressures that they are exceedingly difficult to understand. Under our system of checks and balances, all branches of government are involved in policy decisions. Also, there are typically many special-interest groups outside government involved in a substantial policy issue, and they bombard administrators and legislators through many channels of communication. One writer has observed, only half facetiously, that there are on the average 5.3 sides to every public issue.[35] In any case, the task of identifying the "leverage points" (individuals, groups, and even procedures such as budgeting) and the influences of each is formidable. Considerable knowledge of how public opinion is formed, measured, and interpreted is required.[36] Formidable also is the problem of knowing how much information to gather from these many parties at interest and when, finally, to stop hearings and get on with decision making.

The policy analysis process is a combination of social and intellectual processes. On the social side, there can be little doubt that a large part of the process involves negotiation, bargaining, and persuasion—in one writer's terms, "building a minimum winning coalition."[37] On the intellectual side, there is great need to reckon the consequences of major legislative or administrative decisions. Such analysis requires understanding of subjects such as the incidence of various kinds of taxes, the reactions of markets to the cost increases involved in an increase in minimum wages, the effects on different industries of particular pollution controls, or the sociological consequences of a particular kind of housing program.[38] There is an almost endless list of such problems, and for many of these problems it takes a great deal of knowledge of the particular subject plus considerable capability in analysis in order to anticipate the second- and third-order consequences—often contrary to the intention of the policy makers—of policy decisions.

Further complicating the task of public policy analysis is the fact that today one must consider the international reactions to policy actions. With strong international competition in many product markets and an unstable international monetary system, actions in the United States affecting commerce, inflation, or national fiscal matters have serious international repercussions. Cranking in the international considerations is now a difficult but necessary part of many public policy analyses.

Many more complicating factors could be added to this account: the unresponsiveness of some legislators and legislatures (especially the seniority system in committee chairmanships), the tendency of bureaucratic administrative structures to drain the life out of programs with excessive paperwork and delays, the "bureaupathic" behavior of ensconced administrators who cannot be held accountable or disciplined, the overwhelming power of giant industrial organizations and of the military establishment, and the near impossibility of discontinuing an established activity.[39]

New Decision Techniques in Policy Planning

One could easily get the impression from public administration literature (especially the part that is most academic and "think tank" oriented) that sophisticated decision-making techniques are being widely used to improve the quality of higher-level governmental planning. Many cost-effectiveness studies, simulations, and Delphi planning efforts are reported, often written by staff specialists or consultants working for the Office of Education, Public Health Service, or some other federal agency. Also, writers have demonstrated the application of many sophisticated tools of economic analysis (such as welfare economics, the Pareto criterion, Arrow's impossibility theorem, the Von Neumann–Morgenstern utility analysis, and discounting techniques) to various public policy issues.[40]

These reports have little effect on actual government policy decisions, however, for two reasons: (1) There is still a big gap between the staff specialists and the line administrator and politicians. The staff specialists' work often is not understood by the persons who are supposed to use it. The same gap exists in business administration, but to a lesser extent because there is less tendency to keep unused staff specialists on the payroll. (2) The rational analysis gets lost in the endless shuffling of proposed legislation among the various branches, the innumerable legislative hearings, the lobbying and political maneuvering in the legislatures. In short, while the complexity of public policy issues demands the highest expertise using the strongest techniques of analysis, the political-bureaucratic processes run roughshod over them. A dramatic example of this occurred when the Department of Defense, in the McNamara era, using systems analysis techniques, identified over 100 military installations as surplus; elected representatives complained so vigorously and log-rolled so effectively to retain the money-spending facilities in their own areas that in the end only a few were closed.

Implementation Problems

Even when a wise policy decision is made on some issue, political pressures often produce unwise decisions on the scope of implementation. Thus programs are immediately launched on a nationwide or worldwide basis (or a statewide basis in the case of state governments). An extensive organization structure is established and staffed—only to become hopelessly entangled in paperwork, confusion, and frustration.

The temptation is great for politicians to move rapidly and massively against serious problems; they want to be able to take credit for an all-out attack, quoting the amount of money appropriated and other indications of the bold scale of their actions. Unfortunately, such implementation is rarely effective because there simply are not enough competent program managers and key staff to solve the problems involved in such massive efforts. However, long before the poor results become evident, the politicians and their key administrators will have moved on to new great challenges, other bold decisions.

The proposal for fostering minority-owned business enterprises (sometimes called "black capitalism" because blacks are the largest minority involved) appears to be a perfect example of unrealistic scope of implementation.

> The recommended program calls for establishment of 100 local "delivery centers" through which financing, management advice, legal help and other forms of assistance, costing $200,000,000 per year, will be delivered to new, minority-owned small businesses. However, the sad fact is that there are probably not enough competent people—of any race or races—available to the program to man three such centers. Exceptionally talented and dedicated persons are required for the key jobs in such centers because it is very difficult to select and train from among the underprivileged persons those who will succeed as business owners-operators. Instead of being spread over 100 centers, the best selection and training specialists available should be concentrated on a small number—perhaps three or four—of carefully nurtured and solidly successful centers. The expansion in numbers should come later when the chances of success are

better. The black community sorely needs some "success models" upon which it can build the confidence of its people in themselves; the last thing the blacks need is a large number of poorly managed centers producing poorly managed businesses doomed to failure.

But programs that start modestly have little political appeal; the idea of 100 centers starting thousands of new minority-owned businesses has much political appeal.[41]

In government, the implementation problems are made extra difficult by the need for integrating federal, state, regional, and local jurisdictions in order to execute a major program.[42]

The State of the Art in Policy Analysis and Government Planning

Clearly, policy analysis, deciding, and implementing are exceedingly difficult. Government planning simply does not have the well-defined objectives (return-on-investment, market share, asset growth, etc.) that corporate planning uses; rather, government planning must work with less tangible social indicators and concepts of social justice. Often public policy issues concern programs that have never been tried before—one-of-a-kind programs for which there are no proved methods or established measures of progress. Further, government planners must cope with many conflicting interests, and they must coordinate numerous large organizations. As a consequence of all these factors, government policy planning has not progressed nearly as far as has business long-range planning with such ideas as corporate strategy or with such techniques as simulation models or Delphi forecasting.

It is true that in particular fields of public activity progress has been made in the art of policy and planning.[43] For example, the field of urban planning has evolved from considering only physical (land-use and architectural) factors to a comprehensive approach (that reckons also with demographic issues, the sociology of the area, the economic impact on the area, and pollution considerations) and then to a dynamic approach (using a computerized model for simulating city growth-decay cycles and their ramifications). Also, much has been learned about the advantages of different methods of preserving land (compensatory zoning versus regulation with compensation to the owner versus outright purchase, etc.). For another example, in the field of medical care services, progress has been made in the regional planning of facilities to avoid the costly duplication and underutilization of expensive medical facilities; also, in some areas, progress has been made toward larger units for delivery of medical care—units capable of planning more preventive medical practice which should in the long run reduce the amount of curative work to be done. Military planning has long been a highly developed field using sophisticated techniques on logistics (linear programming) and strategy (games and other simulations).

There has not been much progress in general public policy planning, that is, technique that can be applied to many kinds of government planning. The main effort at improving all governmental policy planning has been the attempt at federal, state, and local levels to make PPBS work but that, as noted, has not been successful.

The poor results achieved by so many national programs aimed at correcting major socioeconomic problems have caused some observers to reject what they have called "grand design"[44] or "comprehensive"[45] planning or, as in the following quotation, "detailed planning ahead":

> Detailed planning ahead was highly popular for a time. But we have already had too many examples of detailed and systematic plans to go in the wrong direction. The McNamara Pentagon laid down men and equipment in Vietnam more efficiently than this had ever been done before in military history—but it turned out that, on reflection, we did not want them to be there. . . . But in dealing with the assessment of the future results of science and technology, for which more and more public executives find themselves responsible, the quantifiable parts of the analysis often turn out to be the less important parts. That is why detailed planning ahead is no longer so much in vogue.[46]

What alternative planning methods do the critics suggest? Their suggestions appear to borrow philosophically from the "satisficing" (as opposed to ultrarational, optimizing) decision approach and from the "muddling-through" concept. They, too, want to move toward objectives in short steps separately devised rather than steps that are part of a grand design. Or, in the words of the writer last quoted, "The future executive will need a new definition of planning: *Improvisation on a general sense of direction.*"[47]

Another approach is called *advocacy planning*. This is based on the concept that there is no unitary public interest in so complex a field as, for example, urban planning. Rather, there are many different interests, with partly overlapping and partly competing objectives. Thus, it is contended, realistic planning emerges from the "structured competition" of many different advocate plans; in contrast, it is felt, comprehensive urban planning that is centrally coordinated breaks down because it cannot cope with the diversity of interests or the diversity of knowledge brought to the problem by the many advocacy planners.[48]

But a university president argues that advocacy planning is exactly what universities do not need. He feels that having faculty, students, university administration, taxpayers, and professional groups associated with certain professional graduate departments, and other groups each pushing for its own narrow interests, can result only in the stronger groups reaping special advantages at the expense of the weaker groups. And the rule of special advantages is not viable in the long run. He prefers to try to improve the consultative and collegial type of planning that the university has always had. Such planning can focus on a holistic approach to shaping the university, and that should be more long-run viable.[49]

Returning to government planning, it is indeed difficult to see how either advocacy planning (with its heavy burden of special advantages) or incrementalism (with its heavy burden of outdated programs) can provide, within viable budget limits, the new policy initiatives needed to find solutions to great socioeconomic problems. Perhaps the fact that there has been so much advocacy planning and "disjointed incrementalism" in government explains the lack of success in great reform programs.[50]

Clearly, policy planning is *the* area of turbulence in the not-too-well-defined "new public administration." It is an area where know-how lags behind need. One hopes that some of the lessons contained in the unsuccessful PPBS experience will be applied to devising a less complicated planning technique with a new name that will accomplish what PPBS aimed to accomplish. Perhaps some of the managers attending the programs in policy analysis (discussed in Chapter 3) will solve this problem. If the new technique is truly less complicated, it can escape the dangers of "grand design" planning and "escape into technique" planning.[51] If it uses Anthony's suggestion of a system of dual classification of expenditures, perhaps it can succeed in linking expenditures to results.[52] It should be greatly assisted by the procedures and staff created by Congress in 1974 (to enforce upon itself greater discipline in controlling the total of expenditures) if those procedures eventually become fully effective. And the new technique should be implemented via a strategy far more practical than was the PPBS implementation program.

REVIEW QUESTIONS

1   Why is it that firms which plan are more successful than firms which do not?
2   Explain: "Plans may sometimes be useless, but the planning process is always indispensable."
3   Briefly describe the differences in planning that occur at different organizational levels of the firm.
4   What planning instruments comprise the "hierarchy" of integrated plans of a large firm with a thoroughly developed planning function?
5   Explain the difference between budgets which have planning value and budgets which have none.
6   What factors complicate the public policy setting process?

DISCUSSION QUESTIONS

1   With reference to the business or government organization with which you are, have been, or hope to be associated, what type of planning is done by managers at each of the levels to which you have access?
2   Present pro and con arguments about the assertion that an organization should be so structured that people responsible for strategic planning are separated from the system designers and operations managers.
3   Discuss advantages and disadvantages of using a PERT/Cost planning procedure in connection with the establishment of a new county hospital.
4   Why might elected officials and career public administrators differ in their approaches to governmental planning? Discuss methods you can think of to overcome these differences.

NOTES

[1] One research study that makes this link is Robert B. Young, "Keys to Corporate Growth," *Harvard Business Review,* November–December 1961. Young's data relate long-range planning to higher growth rates and higher profitability. Also S. Thune and R. House, "Where Long-Range Planning Pays Off," *Business Horizons,* August 1970; and David M. Herold, "Long-Range Planning and Organizational Performance: A Cross-Valuation Study," *Journal of the Academy of Management,* March 1972. Thune

and House related formal long-range planning, especially in the more rapidly changing industries, with earnings on common equity and earnings on total capital employed. Their work was confirmed, and strengthened in some respects, by Herold. For examples of successful long-range planning by individual firms, see "How American Standard Cured Its Conglomeritis," *Business Week,* Sept. 28, 1974, pp. 88–90; and "Raytheon's Five-Year Plans That Work," *Business Week,* July 14, 1975, pp. 113–116.

[2] Clarence Walton and Frederick W. Cleveland, Jr., *Corporations on Trial: The Electric Cases* (Wadsworth Publishing Company Inc., Belmont, Calif., 1964), pp. 84–91.

[3] Peter F. Drucker, *The Practice of Management,* (Harper & Row, Publishers Incorporated, 1954), chap. 7. Drucker elaborates on the many considerations involved in setting objectives in each area.

[4] "Marketing Myopia," *Harvard Business Review,* July–August 1960, pp. 45–57. Reprinted in the September–October 1975 issue as an "HBR classic."

[5] John C. Chambers, Satinder K. Mullick, and Donald Smith, "How to Choose the Right Forecasting Technique," *Harvard Business Review,* July–August 1971, pp. 45–74. Also, for an explanation of the main terms and concepts used by forecasters, see Robert S. Sobeck, "A Manager's Primer on Forecasting," *Harvard Business Review,* May–June 1973, pp. 6ff.

[6] For an article that explores this problem as well as the line-staff problem, see James S. Hekimian and Henry Mintzberg, "The Planning Dilemma: There Is a Way Out," *Management Review,* May 1968, pp. 4–15.

[7] "Corporate Planning: Piercing Future Fog in the Executive Suite," a *Business Week* Special Report, Apr. 28, 1975, pp. 46–54.

[8] Stages of growth and the problems accompanying them can be fairly definitely identified for growing small firms; see Robert B. Buchele, *Business Policy in Growing Firms* (Chandler Publishing–International Textbook Co., San Francisco, 1967), part I. Stages of growth of larger firms are difficult to identify and categorize; however, growth always produces strains of one type or another in every firm. For a categorization by types of problems that arise, see Gordon Lippitt and Warren Schmidt, "Crises in a Developing Organization," *Harvard Business Review,* November–December 1961, pp. 102–112. For a view of a crisis arising at a particular size, see "The Crisis of the $100–Million Companies," *Dun's Review,* 1966, pp. 49–54. For a discussion of how managerial actions to solve one type of problem often lead to a reaction-type problem, see Larry E. Greiner, "Evolution and Revolution as Organizations Grow," *Harvard Business Review,* July–August 1972, pp. 37–46.

[9] George A. Steiner, "Changing Managerial Philosophies," *Business Horizons,* June 1971, p. 8.

[10] Chris Argyris' early work on the behavioral effects of budget pressures has led to a considerable amount of work on the subject. See Chris Argyris, *The Impact of Budgets upon People* (Controllership Foundation, New York, 1952); D. Decoster and T. Fertakis, "Budget-induced Pressure and Its Relationship to Supervisory Behavior," *Journal of Accounting Research,* Autumn 1968; and W. Daugherty and D. Harvey, "Some Behavioral Implications of Budget Systems," *Arizona Business,* April 1973.

[11] C. R. Christensen, K. Andrews, and J. J. Bower, *Business Policy: Text and Cases,* 3d ed. (Richard D. Irwin, Inc., Homewood, Ill., 1973), p. 110.

[12] S. Tilles, "How to Evaluate Corporate Strategy," *Harvard Business Review,* July–August 1963, p. 114.

[13] L. V. Gerstner, Jr., "Can Strategic Planning Pay Off?" *Business Horizons,* December 1972, pp. 5–16; Sidney Schoeffler, Robert D. Buzzel, and Donald F. Heaney, "Impact of Strategic Planning on Profit Performance," *Harvard Business Review,* March–April 1974, pp. 137–145.

[14] The sizable literature on strategies includes, in addition to those already cited, H. I. Ansoff, *Corporate Strategy* (McGraw-Hill Book Company, New York 1965); J. T. Cannon, *Business Strategy and Policy* (Harcourt, Brace & World, Inc., New York, 1968); and Hugo Uyterhoeven, R. W. Ackerman, and J. W. Rosenblum, *Strategy and Organization: Text and Cases in General Management* (Richard D. Irwin, Inc., Homewood, Ill., 1973), chaps. 1–9.

[15] Methods of calculating the estimated time and variation are given in many textbooks on decision techniques, including C. McMillan and R. F. Gonzalez, *Systems Analysis: A Computer Approach to Decision Models,* 3d ed. (Richard D. Irwin, Inc., Homewood, Ill., 1973), pp. 293–298.

[16] The mechanics for computerizing a PERT network are given in ibid., pp. 299–313.

[17] A graphic portrayal of the derivation of PERT from Gantt charts and milestones budgeting is given by Harold D. Koontz and Cyril O'Donnell, *Principles of Management,* 5th ed. (McGraw-Hill Book Company, New York, 1972).

[18] For a description and evaluation of this technique, see Peter Schoderbek, "PERT/Cost: Its Values and Limitations," *Management Services,* January–February 1966, pp. 29–34.

[19] Eli Goldstone, in *Business Week,* July 21, 1973, p. 10. Skepticism about the practicality of simulation models is also expressed by R. H. Hayes and R. L. Nolan in "What Kind of Corporate Modeling Functions Best?" *Harvard Business Review,* May–June 1974, p. 105.

20 J. Boulden and E. Buffa, "Corporate Models: On-Line, Real-Time Systems," *Harvard Business Review,* July–August 1970, pp. 73–77.

21 Philip Kotler, "Corporate Models: Better Marketing Plans," *Harvard Business Review,* July–August 1970, pp. 135–149.

22 New Products: The Push Is on Marketing," *Business Week,* Mar. 4, 1972, p. 77.

23 Boulden and Buffa, op. cit., pp. 68–70. This article and the previously cited Kotler article are extensively illustrated. So also is Curtis Jones's "At Last: Real Computer Power for Decisionmakers," *Harvard Business Review,* September–October 1970, pp. 75–89. Also very helpful is an article by John S. Hammond III, "Do's and Don'ts of Computer Models for Planning," *Harvard Business Review,* March–April 1974, pp. 110–123.

24 Articles describing variations on the early Delphi technique are A. R. Fursfeld and R. N. Foster, "The Delphi Technique: Survey and Comment," *Business Horizons,* June 1971, pp. 63–74; and "A Think Tank That Helps Companies Plan," *Business Week,* Aug. 25, 1973. For an earlier description of the technique, see "Forecasters Turn to Group Guesswork," *Business Week,* Mar. 14, 1970, pp. 130–134.

25 "A Think Tank That Helps Companies Plan," op. cit.

26 A. H. Van De Ven and Andre L. Delbecq, "The Effectiveness of Nominal, Delphi, and Interacting Group Decision-making Processes," *Academy of Management Journal,* December 1974, pp. 605–621.

27 "Planners Put Big Picture on a Grid," *Business Week,* Sept. 23, 1967, pp. 62–67; "What Input-Output Tells Industry," *Business Week,* Dec. 9, 1967, pp. 88–95.

28 R. D. Specht, "The Nature of Models," in *Systems Analysis and Policy Planning,* edited by E. S. Quade and R. Boucher (American Elsevier Publishing Company, Inc., New York, 1968), pp. 211–227.

29 Shunichi Kimura, Mayor of Hawaii County, a community of 66,000 persons. Hawaii County comprises the entire island of Hawaii, geographically the largest of the Hawaiian Islands but having one-tenth the population of the island of Oahu, where Honolulu is located. Remarks made April 17, 1972 at the Public Leadership Workshop held at the East-West Center, Honolulu.

30 Ira Sharkansky, *Public Administration: Policy Making in Government Agencies,* 2d ed. (Markham Publishing Co., Chicago, 1972), p. 12. See also James W. Davis, Jr., *An Introduction to Public Administration* (The Free Press, New York, 1974), pp. 9–10.

31 The "younger" writer is Peter Savage, "Contemporary Public Administration: The Changing Environment and Agenda," and the latter writer is Dwight Waldo, "Some Thoughts on Alternatives, Dilemmas, and Paradoxes in a Time of Turbulence," both in *Public Administration in a Time of Turbulence,* edited by Dwight Waldo (Chandler Publishing Company, San Francisco, 1971).

32 Allen Schick, "Systems for Analysis: PPB and Its Alternatives," in *The Analysis and Evaluation of Public Expenditures,* Joint Economic Committee, Subcommittee on Economy in Government (U.S. Government Printing Office, 1969), p. 825.

33 "The FTC Builds a Model Informer," *Business Week,* Mar. 11, 1972, p. 94.

34 These definitions are the author's adaptation of those used by Sharkansky, op. cit., chap. 6.

35 Harlan Cleveland, *The Future Executive* (Harper & Row, Publishers, Incorporated, 1972), chap. 6.

36 K. J. Gergen, "Assessing the Leverage Points in the Process of Policy Formulation," in *The Study of Policy Formation* edited by R. A. Bauer and K. J. Gergen (The Free Press, New York, 1968), especially pp. 194–200.

37 R. A. Bauer, "The Study of Policy Formulation: An Introduction," in *The Study of Policy Formation,* edited by R. A. Bauer and K. J. Gergen (The Free Press, New York, 1968), especially p. 14.

38 Or, in Diesing's terms, governmental decision makers must appreciate many rationalities—technical, social, economic, and legal as well as political. Paul Diesing, *Reason in Society* (University of Illinois Press. Urbana, Ill., 1962).

39 For a more extensive treatment of some of these factors and citations of still more detailed sources, see Sharkansky, op. cit, chap. 3; also, Davis, op. cit., chap. 3. Davis identifies interest group participants at each stage of the process, such as deciding that there is a problem, deciding whether or not anything can be done about it, etc., through enactment and implementation.

40 R. Zeckhauser and Elmer Schaefer, "Public Policy and Normative Economic Theory," in *The Study of Policy Formation,* edited by R. A. Bauer and K. J. Gergen (The Free Press, New York, 1968), pp. 27–97.

41 *Minority Enterprise and Expanded Ownership: Blueprint for the 70's,* report of the President's Advisory Council on Minority Business and Enterprise (U.S. Government Printing Office, June 1971), chap. 5.

123

[42] For a study of these problems, see Douglas R. Bunker, "Policy Sciences Perspectives on Implementation Processes," *Policy Sciences,* March 1972, pp. 71–80.

[43] Herman Mertins, Jr., and Bertram M. Gross (eds.), "Special Symposium: Changing Styles of Planning in Post-Industrial America," *Public Administration Review,* May–June 1971. Included are articles on urban planning, fiscal planning, educational planning, national transportation planning, science planning, and health planning.

[44] John W. Dyckman, "New Normative Styles in Urban Studies," in "Special Symposium: Changing Styles of Planning in Post-Industrial America," in *Public Administration Review,* May–June 1971, pp. 327–334. See also J. J. Kirlin and S. P. Erie, "The Study of City Governance and Policy Making: A Critical Appraisal," *Public Administration Review,* March–April 1972, pp. 173–184.

[45] John Friedman, "The Future of Comprehensive Urban Planning," in "Special Symposium: Changing Styles in Planning in Post-Industrial America," *Public Administration Review,* March–April 1972, pp. 315–326.

[46] Cleveland, op. cit., chap. 2.

[47] Ibid.

[48] Dyckman, op. cit.; Friedman, op. cit.

[49] William J. McGill, "From the President," *Columbia Reports,* Winter 1975, p. 2.

[50] Enid C. B. Schoettle regards "disjointed incrementalism" as the most useful description of how the policy-making process operates in the United States system of democracy. See her "The State of the Art in Policy Studies," in *The Study of Policy Formation,* edited by R. A. Bauer and K. J. Gergen (The Free Press, New York, 1968), pp. 150–151. Schoettle takes the term and her description of it from D. Baybrooke and C. E. Lindblom, *A Strategy of Decision* (The Free Press, New York, 1963), chap. 5.

[51] The latter phrase is borrowed from Yehezkel Dror, "Planning in the United States—Some Reactions of a Foreign Observer," a critique of the papers in the planning symposium, *Public Administration Review,* May–June 1971, p. 1.

[52] Professor Robert Anthony, drawing upon his experiences in government as well as his academic work, recommends designation of responsibility centers, a system of dual classification of expenditures, and development of an accounting system in program terms for both operations and appropriations budgets. See his "Closing the Loop between Planning and Performance," *Public Administration Review,* May–June 1971, pp. 388–398. See also Orville Poland, "Why Does Public Administration Ignore Evaluation?" *Public Administration Review,* March–Apil 1971.

RECOMMENDED READINGS

Bunker, Douglas, R.: "Policy Sciences Perspectives on Implementation Processes," *Policy Sciences,* vol. 3, no. 1, March 1972, pp. 71–80.

Schick, Allen: "A Death in the Bureaucracy: The Demise of Federal PPB," *Public Administration Review,* vol. 33, no. 2, March–April 1973, pp. 146–156.

Schoeffler, Sidney, Robert D. Buzzell, and Donald F. Heany: "Impact of Strategic Planning on Profit Performance," *Harvard Business Review,* vol. 52, no. 2, March–April 1974, pp. 137–148.

Sharkansky, Ira: *Public Administration: Policy Making in Government Agencies,* 2d ed. (Markham Publishing Co., Chicago, 1972).

Warren, Kirby: *Long-Range Planning* (Prentice-Hall, Inc., Englewood Cliffs, N.J., 1966).

Chapter 5

Controlling

To a person who has not studied management, the words "control," "controller," and "controlling" may still evoke visions of a penny-pinching accountant wearing a green eyeshade, strictly enforcing budgetary spending limits. Or, perhaps the vision may be of a stack of accounting reports telling how each section of the organization performed during some past period.

Such visions represent the control process as practiced generally some three to four decades ago but in only a few situations today. The process of control has changed dramatically in the past few decades, becoming a powerful influence in the increasing professionalization of management. With continued computerization, control probably will advance more than any other managerial process in the next decade.

As planning improved in the years following World War II, so also did control, because the two processes are so closely related. Each plan provides the basis for control reports, as can be seen especially clearly in the cases of budgets and PERT charts. In these as well as in many other kinds of plans, the main entries serve also as road markers, or control points, at which measurements may be taken to see if actual performance is behind, even with, or ahead of plans. Tied in with plans in this way, control reports serve to help managers make adjustments in their operations; that is, they replan so that objectives will be achieved.

In this way, control became a constructive, forward-looking process focused on helping managers make plans work out successfully. This is in sharp contrast to the old type of controls that used accounting-type reports designed mainly for tax reporting purposes. These old-style reports were precise and complete (as tax reports should be), but it takes time to develop such reports, so they could not be issued until long after the end of the accounting period. Thus the old-style reports were too out of date to be helpful to a manager in the diagnosis and correction of operating problems; they were used, however, as "report cards" by which managers could be complimented or scolded for past performance.

The shift to a forward-looking concept of control has been less well worked out in public administration. Some of the agencies and departments that have made effective use of computers in planning are using them in control too, especially the Armed Forces and organizations using PERT. Except for such instances, however, budget enforcement remains the main control device in government, and attempts to make budgeting more forward-looking by making it more results-oriented have generally not succeeded. Program evaluation, a newer approach to control that is more long-range and "researchy" than budgeting, has made little progress.

Since the subject of managerial control is not too different in the business and government settings, those fields will be handled together in this chapter, with a brief section near the end pointing up some of the unique features in government. The structure is this:

Definition of Control

Control Practices at Different Levels in Large Organizations

Controls in Small Organizations

The Control Side of MBO

Control Lessons Learned in the Precomputer Era

Control Improvements and Problems in the Computer Era

Human Problems of Control

Some Control Problems in Public Administration

Summary

DEFINITION OF CONTROL

Control is the process of measuring actual results, comparing those results to plans (or some standard), diagnosing the reason for deviations of actual from desired result, and taking corrective action when necessary. (Corrective action usually means a change in the way plans are being implemented; sometimes it means changing the plans or, in extreme cases, changing the objectives.)

Because of this continuing feedback between planning and controlling, in the process diagram presented earlier a two-way arrow was used:

Plan↔Control

This idea may be expanded diagrammatically as follows:

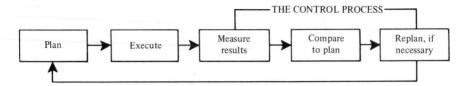

This chapter will deal with written controls. However, it should be remembered that managers get much of their understanding of what has happened and what is going on via verbal communications and inspections. But neither verbal nor written communication alone is adequate. Verbal communications alone can be general and imprecise; they often fail to convey basic trends in what is happening. Written communications alone can, on the other hand, be misleadingly precise unless the manager knows the individual and the situation from which the data come.

CONTROL PRACTICES AT DIFFERENT LEVELS IN LARGE ORGANIZATIONS

Like planning, control is an inherent part of the managerial job; every manager is responsible for control of his or her unit. Just as a pilot of an airliner needs the indicators on the instrument panel and the reports of the navigator to know what is happening, so a manager needs control reports to know exactly what is happening in an operation.

At the Top

Chief executive officers in large business organizations (the chairperson or president), being concerned mainly with objectives and long-range plans, need control reports that will let them know (1) Whether the existing objectives are still adequate or need to be changed in response to new developments in the competitive environment; (2) whether or not key actions pursuant to long-range plans (such as acquisitions, divestments, executive development, new facilities building, major financings, and new-product development) are being taken on schedule and are proving effective; and (3) whether or not current operations are being kept healthy by subordinates.

Pursuant to the first question, the chief executive officer requires periodic reports from outside the organization for an up-to-date assessment of new strategies being tried by competitors; new products, materials, or technologies being developed; forecasts of economic conditions, and projections of how people will be living and working at some future date (say ten or twenty years hence). In connection with the long-range programs, the chief executive needs status reports and frequently revised projections of the ultimate impact of each program on the total corporate position. On the current health of the organization, both return-on-investment and growth reports are needed, as well as periodic outsider evaluations of the motivational tone (or the climate or character) of the organization. Clearly, most of these control reports needed by the chief executive are special, qualitative-type reports rather than data-type reports that flow regularly from the accounting system.

The second-in-command in large businesses, often called the chief operating officer (with the title of president or executive vice president), uses more data reports flowing from inside the operation. This person is likely to be most concerned with monthly chart-room sessions in which each division's performance is reviewed with the division or group managers. For example, AMF, Inc., a large company with nine diversified product groups, has:

> . . . a war room to provide "early warning" of any operational disaster in a product division. The room contains elaborate charts of each profit center's monthly perform- ance against its budget. These charts cover 11 items ranging from orders, sales, and profits to such factors as prices, product mix, shipping costs, manufacturing costs, and inventory turnover. "The charts suggest areas that bear investigation," says W. Thomas York, AMF's comptroller. For example, they point out inventory buildups or cases where production costs are getting out of line. "Give me an explanation of these figures," says (President) Tullis, "and I'll know if the division is in trouble or not."[1]

The best-known chart-room approach is the Du Pont return-on-investment (ROI) analysis illustrated in Figure 5–1.

Although an old system, the Du Pont ROI analysis is so basically sound that many large companies still use it or something very much like it. Focusing on return-on-investment, a measurement of performance by which different types of divisions may be compared, it provides a means of diagnosing the cause of trouble by tracing back through the steps in the chart to the origin of some unfavorable figure. In addition, the chief operating officer would want, at the monthly chart- room sessions, reports from various staff officers, particularly from the financial specialists on current cash position and projected capital needs over the next two years or so.

A similar and closely related (to ROI analysis) diagnostic system is based on variances from budget. The second-in-command is usually concerned with develop- ing an integrated budget for a total operation and, then, analyzing variances from that budget to reveal the location and cause of unsatisfactory performance. A variance in overall profit at the top-management level may be traced to a particular division, then at the next level to a particular department within that plant, and possibly, finally, to a particular operation within that department. Used in this way, budgets become helpful rather than purely restrictive.

Still another way of locating the source of difficulties is ratio analysis. Key ratios are published for many different types of businesses, sometimes broken down by the average in the top quartile, the median, and the average in the bottom quartile, as in Figure 5–2. These ratios are especially useful for top executives in medium-sized and smaller firms who do not have the staffs to prepare thorough chart-room displays.

Top-level government executives (such as federal cabinet members or agency heads or department heads in state government and their top civil service assistants)

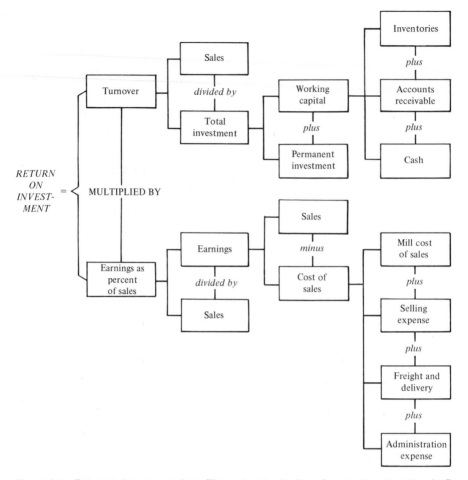

Figure 5-1 Return-on-investment chart. [From How the Du Pont Organization Appraises Its Performance, *Financial Management Series, no. 94 (American Management Association, New York, 1950).*]

also need reports against objectives. However, theirs is a much more difficult problem. Their objectives, which are set partly by legislation and partly by administrative action, are typically not as tangibly stated or as measurable as are return-on-investment and other business objectives. Nor do government officials often have available published ratios, because in most cases there are no other organizations with closely comparable ratios. Hence, they must rely upon comparisons with their own past performance.

In connection with some state and local activities, it is possible to compare performance of one jurisdiction with another; but often the conditions are so different that the comparisons are not highly useful. Also, some research indicates that most localities simply are not managerially sophisticated enough to give much attention to defining objectives or measuring performance against them.[2]

Ratios similar to business ratios are published by professional associations in such fields as hospital administration and charity fund raising.

Figure 5-2 Ratios for Three Types of Manufacturing Businesses from among the Dozens of Manufacturing, Retailing, Wholesaling, and Construction Industries Reported Regularly in Dun and Bradstreet's *Key Business Ratios.*

Line of business (and number of concerns reporting)	Current assets to current debt	Net profits on net sales	Net profits on tangible net worth	Net profits on net working capital	Net sales to tangible net worth	Net sales to net working capital	Collection period	Net sales to inventory	Fixed assets to tangible net worth	Current debt to tangible net worth	Total debt to tangible net worth	Inventory to net working capital	Current debt to inventory	Funded debts to net working capital
	Times	Percent	Percent	Percent	Times	Times	Days	Times	Percent	Percent	Percent	Percent	Percent	Percent
2871–72–79 Agricultural chemicals (40)	6.09	4.11	8.29	17.01	3.90	10.69	43	17.2	25.0	16.0	63.5	19.5	80.5	19.2
	1.86	**1.45**	**5.30**	**7.69**	**2.78**	**4.78**	**57**	**6.6**	**43.8**	**53.2**	**123.3**	**76.5**	**146.3**	**74.9**
	1.25	0.69	1.20	2.31	1.72	2.86	85	5.0	76.7	101.4	178.4	157.9	341.1	130.7
3722–23–29 Airplane parts and accessories (58)	3.52	5.22	12.95	24.78	3.71	5.62	28	7.9	36.4	22.3	25.5	67.2	67.9	28.0
	2.16	**3.04**	**9.06**	**13.32**	**2.92**	**4.57**	**51**	**5.2**	**53.6**	**45.6**	**72.4**	**86.6**	**92.6**	**54.4**
	1.62	1.65	3.19	4.67	2.12	3.41	71	3.8	73.5	75.7	113.7	124.8	117.2	96.2
2051–52 Bakery products (84)	2.50	4.25	12.97	66.78	5.69	23.38	16	39.6	64.2	18.0	34.6	34.2	152.8	23.7
	1.88	**2.54**	**8.70**	**41.57**	**4.08**	**14.45**	**22**	**28.9**	**80.8**	**24.9**	**49.6**	**57.9**	**201.9**	**74.8**
	1.46	0.90	5.43	19.36	2.76	10.37	27	21.9	101.5	42.1	99.0	82.6	287.0	150.7

Still another area of control vital to top-level government executives is the control of public opinion; they must be especially sensitive to how their programs are regarded by client groups, the press, and the public because discontent by these groups can feed back to them through legislators. Accordingly, they need frequent soundings of opinion—somewhat the counterpart of market research.

Budgeting—Important at All Levels

Budget making and enforcement are, of course, priority matters for all levels of government administrators simply because budgets are a necessary step to appropriations. The annual federal budget requires a twenty-eight-month process that keeps legislators, executives, and administrators[3] almost continuously busy and in working relationship with one another. The process starts with initiation by administrators of the agencies and departments, then involves review by higher administrators, review by the executive budget staff (OMB), review and appropriation by the legislature, allocation by the OMB, execution by administrators, audit by the General Accounting Office (GAO), and review by the OMB. The GAO can stop illegal expenditures and can publicize inefficient use of funds. The OMB can exert pressure for compliance with presidential policy by withholding, or threatening to withhold, further allocations. As has been noted, Congress has enacted procedures that impose on itself greater pressure to set and adhere to overall spending limits; the same legislation also provided for a high-powered budget staff that should improve the quality, especially the purpose orientation, of Congress's budgeting efforts.

Government budgeting still is, however, primarily an incremental process; that is, the budget is built on the base of the previous budget, with most deliberations concerning the increments (positive or negative). Government budgeting is also oriented toward object of expenditure rather than purpose. This method of budgeting is not only deeply rooted in the bureaucracy but also simpler than suggested reforms such as PPBS or zero budgeting (which starts with a clean slate each new budget cycle). These features, plus the fact that some government managers are uneasy at the idea of having a control that focuses on their achievements, make it exceedingly difficult to bring about more meaningful budgeting.

Upper-Middle Level

Business managers at the group- or division-head level are concerned with both future-oriented and current operations reports. Their control reports to some extent overlap those used by top executives (especially budget variance analysis and ratio analysis). But they can be in more detail because each middle-level manager needs reports on only a sector of the total organization for which the chief operations officer is responsible.

Group or division heads must be sure that they are making progress on their parts of the corporation's overall change plan (growth, diversification, profit improvement, etc.). To do this they must have reports, at least quarterly and probably monthly, on acquisition programs, product-development programs, future capital requirements, and other long-range matters. And they must have much more detail, at least monthly and sometimes weekly, on current operations matters such as sales, prices and margins by product lines, production, production costs by products, marketing costs, indirect and overhead ratios, cash position, and total inventories. These reports often take the form of a looseleaf book of charts drawn from regular accounting reports, as illustrated in Figure 5–3. Armed with a book of perhaps ten or fifteen charts such as these, the group or division head is prepared to answer the questions of the chief operations officer at the monthly chart-room meetings at which return-on-investment charts for each main section of the business are reviewed. Often, these charts are on transparent materials so that they may be used as overlays to show, for example, the relation of prices to sales or the relationship between sales, inventories, and cash position.

In some types of business as well as in the military, high-ranking executives use computer-fed chart rooms to direct daily operations. Thus divisional vice presi-

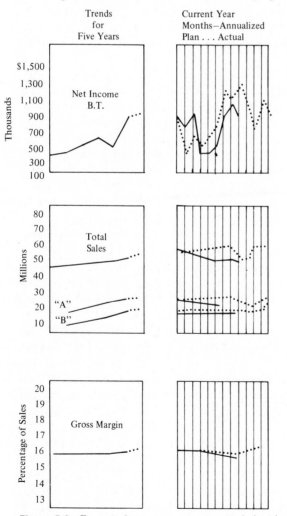

Figure 5-3 Excerpts from management control chart book.

dents at major airlines hold daily operations briefings in so-called war rooms that contain up-to-the-minute information on reservations and flight operations as well as a summary of the previous day's record on passenger loads, schedule adherence, and similar key control reports. After the daily briefing by the vice president, lower-level managers use the war rooms for making decisions such as scheduling or canceling of flights and smaller decisions such as assignment of flight crews and ordering of inflight meals. While the airlines are natural leaders in the use of command centers for daily operations, somewhat similar operations controls are being used by many other types of companies.[4] An installation by one insurance company, used for frequent executive meetings as well as formal monthly reviews, provides for each executive a TV screen that displays videotape, typewritten and graphic material, and material from the company's main bank of computers. What each participant writes on his or her screen with an electronic pen is immediately displayed to the others. This setup gets away from the usual speaker-and-audience arrangement, and executives of the insurance firm claim that it secures excellent participation in decision making.[5]

Upper-middle-level government executives, such as bureau chiefs, are also concerned with a combination of long-range and current operations; however, the latter probably occupy most of their time. And, of course, their reports will be in budget and cost-reduction terms rather than in profit-improvement terms. At this level there is still an attempt to focus on results against objectives; but in some agencies the bulk of the reports are, unfortunately, only in terms of activities carried out, without consideration of whether or not those activities are contributing to the achievement of objectives.

Lower-Middle Level

In both business and government, the lower-middle-level managers (department heads in business or section heads in government) are concerned with a particular sector (production, marketing, engineering, field operations, finance, etc.) rather than with the overall activities of a complete business unit or government agency. Accordingly, their controls are confined to those areas. They probably maintain some of the same monthly charts that their bosses maintain, but most of theirs will be on a weekly basis and a few may be on a daily basis. These may be in the form of wall charts, chart books, accounting reports, or a combination of these three forms.

A production executive, for example, might maintain charts on two or three major long-range projects for which he or she is responsible; these might be complex PERT charts, as illustrated in the chapter on planning, or simple Gantt charts, as illustrated in Figure 5–4.

On the current operations side, the production manager seeks to maintain a relatively steady level of production despite fluctuations in sales. This manager must balance the benefits of a steady production level against the costs of carrying too much inventory or of disappointing customers on delivery dates. Thus the production schedule must be planned with these considerations in mind. The production manager's controls are usually computerized "by exception" reports, sometimes

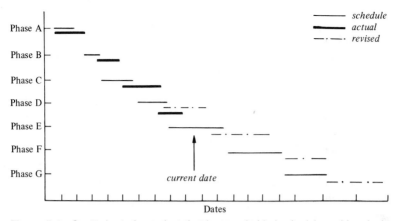

Figure 5-4   Gantt chart of a project that has run behind schedule and has been rescheduled.

charted, that show planned and actual for all of these factors, plus costs and quality.

The inventory controls—vital to production, sales and finance—have been more highly developed than any other type of control and often are even automated in computerized situations. Inventory controls are developed through study of records of past rate of usage, delivery lead time, economic order quantity, the costs of stockouts, and the costs of carrying inventory. Once reorder points and quantities have been determined, the control process may be made automatic for as long as the factors remain unchanged.

Marketing managers, too, require a combination of long-range and short-range controls. They might have long-run control reports, in the form of Gantt charts, on plans to achieve diversification (by types of customers, geographical areas, or product lines.) Or they might keep a PERT chart covering all the different moves to be made over a four-year period to achieve a certain penetration or share of market in a new area. Probably their main long-run control is that concerned with the life cycles (composite and individual) of their products and product lines, as illustrated in Figure 5–5; the main purpose of such controls is to assure that the line as a whole stays healthy via timely replacement of dying products.

Marketing managers' short-range, or operational, controls will probably be mostly computerized "by exception" reports focusing on sales, prices, and margins by products and product lines. Other reports will keep a sharp focus on share of the market by product, too. And they will keep overall measures of the effectiveness of sales management (sales and margins per salesperson and per promotional dollar). The sales manager and production manager, subordinates of the marketing manager, will keep much more detailed control reports—such as sales and margins by in-dividual salespeople, results of particular advertising and promotional efforts, etc.

The marketing managers will keep an eye on inventories even though they may not have the prime responsibility for them; after all, inadequate inventories can do great harm to customer relations.

Marketing managers get periodic control reports on such matters as the con-sumers' and dealers' reaction to their corporate name (that is, the image as seen by

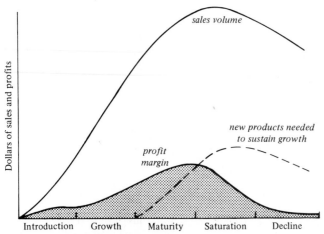

Figure 5-5 Life-cycle curve for a single product or group. Composite curves show when it is necessary to introduce new products to maintain profitability of the line as a whole. [*From Harold Koontz and Cyril O'Donnell,* Principles of Management, *5th ed. (McGraw-Hill Book Company, New York, 1972), p. 362.*]

the consumer), labels, quality, and service. They will get regular expenditure-against-budget reports, not so much for compliance reasons as to be informed as to whether they are getting results commensurate with expenditures and whether greater or perhaps lesser expenditures are needed to accomplish goals.

Similarly, all other lower-middle-level managers—engineering, accounting, finance, personnel, transportation, insurance, or whatever departmentation is used in a particular government agency—will need and will rely upon a combination of long-range and short-range control reports focusing on the selected matters most vital to that type executive at that level. The focus is on his or her particular "success imperatives," the things he or she must do well to succeed.

Lower-Level Managers

Section heads in business or supervisors in government are, of course, chiefly concerned with short-run controls; however, they usually do maintain one or two slightly longer-run reports on the status of some change (new equipment, new process, new materials) whose introduction might take a number of weeks or a few months.

Their main concern is with the same indicators that their bosses are following—production against schedule and against cost and quality standards. At the lower level, some of these reports are daily, some hourly, and some continuous; they are used immediately upon receipt and then compiled into the same weekly or monthly charts that the higher levels watch. The best-known example of a continuous control is statistical quality control, in which frequent samples are tested or inspected and results posted on a control chart. If the results keep within predetermined tolerances, the quality is considered under control; as soon as the results move steadily toward the tolerance limits or exceed them, action is required.

In operations subject to quick changes in activity level, a useful control tool is the "flexible budget." Such a budget lays out in advance what changes need to be made (in direct labor, indirect labor, supporting services, etc.) in the event of a change in level of operations of 15 or 20 percent or more. Having these adjustments worked out in advance enables the section head to adjust to changes much more rapidly than would be possible if the pattern and amounts of changes had to be determined from scratch each time they occurred. Most government operations do not have such flexibility in laying off or hiring help; however, government operations are usually quite stable and hence do not need such flexibility.

Lower-level supervisors also keep control reports on their employees, individually and as a group. They keep running records not only of productivity but also of such matters as training received, accidents suffered, and absenteeism.

Another main area of control records is on equipment, that is, its utilization, maintenance, downtime, and replacement.

And first-line supervisors, like all other managers, must keep records of expenditures against budgets, which usually are more restrictively applied at this level than at any other.

Variations in the Controls in Large Organizations

The foregoing account of controls exercised by managers at various levels of large organizations has been illustrative rather than definitive. Thus, control is far more centralized in some organizations than in others, and in those cases the higher levels would probably receive more detailed reports at shorter time intervals than have been indicated here. Conversely, the higher levels in more decentralized organizations might receive less detailed reports at greater time intervals than have been indicated here. But one point should be made forcefully: Decentralization of decision-making authority does not mean lack of control. In fact, in order to decentralize safely, one must have good controls that will indicate when that decentralized authority is not being used effectively. That does not mean checking on details; but it does mean having controls that tell reasonably promptly when the pattern of decisions—not any single decision—made by a subordinate is not effective.

The focus of these controls should vary also with the nature of the organization's activities; each kind of business or government activity has its own "success imperatives," and they are the things on which controls should report. A firm's strategy also will influence the placement and nature of its controls. And the particular control measurements that are possible (profit and loss, return-on-investment, comparison with standard costs, or contribution margin) will depend upon the organization's structure.[6]

There is an almost endless variety of charting, graphing, and other display techniques that managers may use to put data into a form that they can grasp easily. And there is an almost endless variety of ways of grouping data and of emphasizing particular insights that managers may use to keep control of their responsibilities.[7]

In business and in most government agencies, both objectives and controls tend to be hierarchical and interlocking; controls at each level tie in with controls at the next higher level but are more detailed and on shorter time intervals. This is not to say that there is no room for an individual's objectives but merely that the overall organizational objectives must not be neglected. An individual has the best opportunity to accomplish personal goals when they are compatible with, or at least not in conflict with, the overall goals. In some government activities there is a movement toward less hierarchical objectives, especially toward local autonomy in deciding how federal funds will be used. If revenue sharing and the "new federalism" (decentralization of programs) succeed, such controls as higher government levels have will have to be against broad policies and objectives rather than the specific requirements (for example, that a convalescent home receiving medicare payments must have a graduate dietitian on its staff) that have characterized so many federal grant-in-aid programs.

CONTROLS IN SMALL ORGANIZATIONS

Small-business owners are generally allergic to paperwork controls. Being closely in touch with all operations, they feel that they "know what's going on without a lot of expensive paperwork." Although this is partly true, it is also partly untrue. And the untrue part can prove disastrous.

One danger is that the small firm can lose control of its cash position until the situation has already deteriorated beyond the point of easy correction. Small-business owners, with so many duties to perform, often do not keep close watch on inventories, receivables, and the forward commitments that they have made on equipment leases and rents; suddenly these types of things seem to have soaked up the cash, and the owner is in deep trouble although the business may be growing vigorously and profitably. For these reasons, a monthly cash-flow analysis—projected and actual—is a must for every small business.[8]

Another area in which the small firm should not rely on informal controls is in keeping track of its costs so that it knows exactly what its cost structure is. Comparison with published ratios can help on this problem. Also, costs change over time as the volume of operations grows, processes are changed a bit, the product mix changes, or the customer mix and pricing deals change. Even if the owner of a small business knows at one point in time exactly what costs are, the current cost structure is likely to be seriously inaccurate six months or a year later. Then the owner may well make unwise decisions on bidding for big jobs, pricing special deals to fill in lull periods in the operations, or bonus and commission arrangements with employees.

Wishing to minimize paperwork costs, the small business head often contracts for only the absolutely essential services from the company's certified public accountant—which means an annual profit-and-loss statement and balance sheet that may be used as the basis for the firm's income tax report. Such a report is, unfortunately, not useful for management control purposes. Rather, the CPA should be required to formulate a report that (1) provides a complete listing of all costs, so that bidding and pricing will not neglect some costs; (2) separates fixed from variable costs; and (3) can be rendered without audit at least quarterly and preferably monthly.

The separation of costs into variable and fixed (that is, those that do and those that do not change with changes in sales or production volume) is something that accountants normally do not do because (1) it is easier to lump all direct labor (or all indirect labor, all supplies, all transportation, etc.) into a single account and (2) the separation into variable/fixed is partly judgmental and needs to be reexamined from time to time. Accountants shy away from such decisions. Yet the fact is that such costs as those just mentioned are usually partly variable and partly fixed, and unless the small business owner understands this fact thoroughly, he or she is likely to make foolish decisions, as in the two actual cases illustrated in Figures 5–6 and 5–7. In both these situations the consultant, upon drawing the breakeven curves, discovered that the small firm was following a wrong strategy simply because the owner did not understand how the cost structure had changed over time.

In addition to a cash-flow analysis and a breakeven analysis that depict the basic cost structure,[9] the small firm should also maintain one or two objective measurements on whatever factor (customer service, complete stock, price, quality, or whatever) is considered the success imperative of that particular business. Thus, one successful tire dealer, whose business is based on the idea that most customers know very little about tires but do appreciate good service, periodically does stopwatch studies of how many seconds elapse between the time a customer crosses the threshold and when a salesperson offers to help the customer. A second control is a carefully timed follow-up letter with return postcard inquiring about how the customer's tires are wearing and whether the salesperson's advice and service had been satisfactory.

As the small firm grows and becomes departmentalized, it is essential that

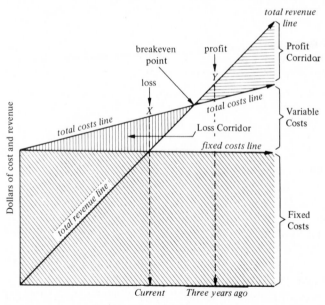

Figure 5-6 Breakeven chart for a firm with high fixed costs. This wholesale laundry had become a high-fixed-cost business when it installed large and highly automated washing and ironing equipment. Such a business must go for volume—that is, advertise heavily and be highly promotional; however, the owner continued to advertise very little in the belief that "quality will sell itself," a policy that had proved successful in earlier years when he had used chiefly hand labor, a variable cost.

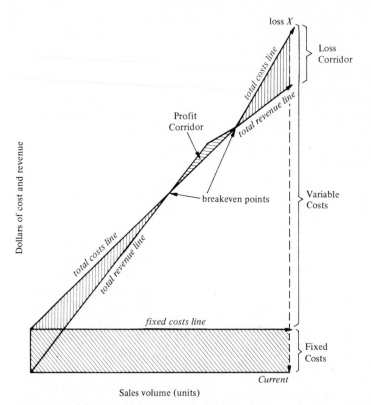

Figure 5-7 Breakeven chart for a firm with high directly variable cost. This toy manufacturer's costs shifted gradually from fixed to variable as he let his plant grow old and kept his product designs unchanged; but his labor, repair and maintenance, spoilage, and materials costs became very high. Instead of launching a program to reduce these variable costs, the owner tried to solve his problem by sales campaigns and price reductions—a chasing-your-own-tail strategy that put him in a loss position at a higher sales volume.

controls be developed for each delegated responsibility. In this way a growing firm gradually acquires the complex of controls employed by large firms.[10]

THE CONTROL SIDE OF MBO

When a manager and a subordinate (at whatever level) using MBO jointly work out that subordinate's objectives and plans for some future period, they have an opportunity at the same time to set up control points. If the objectives and plans are reasonably specific, they will also represent a good statement of the results to be achieved and provide a definition of the units in which those results are to be measured. These are, by nature, positive controls—guideposts that focus on what is to be accomplished—rather than restrictive controls such as budgetary spending limits. These are also controls that the subordinate understands, having had some chance to help make them realistic statements of the results that can fairly be expected. If this is true, it provides an objective basis on which the superior can base a subsequent performance review of the subordinate. The superior then no longer has to "play God" when doing a performance review; rather, this type of control can be exercised on objective, previously agreed-upon criteria. In addition, under this procedure the subordinate can, to some extent, do some self-evaluation and "self-control."

But such an ideal application is, as has been noted in earlier chapters, rarely achieved across many levels of a business organization because the communications task involved is simply too difficult. In addition, there is the problem of keeping job conditions and assignments stable for six months or a year. Too often it is necessary to change a person's assignment temporarily or to alter the amount of help that is given in order to take care of some emergency or some unforeseen opportunity. Such actions play havoc with the idea of holding a person responsible for results defined at the start of the period. Another great control problem arises from the fact that many programs require the participation of various units within a large organization; in such cases it is difficult to hold persons at lower organizational levels responsible for results. For all of these reasons, the control values of MBO have been realized more at higher organizational levels than at lower levels.

Another factor making the control side of MBO difficult is that businesses require multiple objectives and, therefore, multiple controls. But it is difficult to integrate multiple controls; some invariably have more impact than others. Overemphasis of a single control can lead to short-run results (such as in current return-on-investment) but long-run disaster because either long-run investments or social responsibilities have been neglected.

In government, the PPBS experience revealed that all these same problems and more exist. The many hierarchical levels make the assignment of responsibility for results especially difficult. Typically, there are so many adjustments in a budget proposal as it works its way up the channels that no one in the lower levels will accept responsibility for it as finally passed. Also, in the public sphere there is the problem of holding conditions stable long enough to be able to measure results; thus the author's university worked long and hard on its PPBS five-year plans only to have a severe budget cut imposed within a few months of completion of the PPBS effort. Obviously, all assumption of responsibility down the line disappeared.

In theory, MBO and PPBS constitute almost perfect applications of control and participative leadership theory. In practice, however, the application presents many difficulties. While some business firms have surmounted some of these difficulties, the results in government have been discouraging.

Some observers of the government scene note that even in the PODSCORB days, there was no "control" in the formula, only "reporting" of activities and "budgeting" (the CO standing for "coordination"). They feel that the factors discussed here explain why PPBS had little chance of changing this long-standing condition.

CONTROL LESSONS LEARNED IN THE PRECOMPUTER ERA

Between the end of World War II and the time when computers became important in business and government operations, many important lessons were learned about both planning and control (both within and outside the MBO context). These lessons are still valid in the computer era.

1 *Control is a line function that requires staff help.* Just as all managers should decide their own plans, so should they select their own controls against those plans. Only in this way can a responsibility gap ("I laid good plans but the controller gave me poor control reports") be avoided.

Under the modern concept, then, the controller is a staff helper, a specialist in informations systems, who *helps* the line manager get the feedback—that is, the flow of information on actual results—that the manager needs in order to be in full control of the operation and to bear full responsibility for it.

2 *It is in the interaction between planning and control that much managerial learning and growth takes place.* There is such continuous interaction between them that it is impossible to say where planning stops and control starts; in consequence, some teachers feel that planning and control cannot be taught separately. So they teach "plantrol."

Just as budgets and PERT networks are clearly at once plans and controls, so other types of plans, too, should have control points built prominently into them. This applies even to narrative plans.

When control measurements are compared to plans in an ongoing organization, the manager's job is to diagnose the cause of any deviations. It is at this point that a great deal of managerial learning takes place. As managers learn from poor results, they must replan, and in doing so they learn more about planning.

3 *Controls should be selective and strategically placed.* Every written control report costs money to generate. Also, the manager who receives too much data not only wastes time reading but also becomes confused, attempts to control everything and ends up controlling nothing.

For these reasons, selectivity is vital in deciding what reports to create. Like the designer of an airplane's cockpit, a manager should create only as many reports as can be effectively watched and used. These selected reports should be strategically placed in two senses: (*a*) They should be at key checkpoints rather than at every point and (*b*) they should be at those points where costs of controlling are reasonable. Thus, quality control reports on a complex, sealed mechanism should be made before it is sealed to avoid the expense of having to unseal defective units. While this principle is easy to understand with respect to a mechanism, it is much more difficult to understand with respect to the overall health of a business organization. Thus, what are the key indicators of organizational health? What are the sensitive early-warning indicators that the character and vitality of an organization are deteriorating? What are the success imperatives—the limited number of things that must be done well—in a particular type of business? And how can these matters be measured and presented in control reports?

It is especially difficult in government organizations rendering an intangible service (such as education) or a staff unit in a business organization (such as the public relations department) to define specific objectives and strategic results measurements. In consequence, much control in such organizations is still done by budgets that simply restrict spending and by "soft data"—measures of activity (pamphlets produced, classes held, degrees granted, etc.)—that may or may not be related to ultimate objectives.

Another task in control is the elimination of no-longer-needed control reports. Often a periodic control report will be established to spotlight a current problem and will be continued after that problem has been solved. Or sometimes an established report will become unnecessary because a more comprehensive report has been created. Because these kinds of things happen regularly, it is advisable in almost every organization to prune the structure of control reports periodically. A favorite technique for doing this pruning is to assemble all current reports into a "chamber of horrors" exhibit in which overlapping or unnecessary reports are identified by—what else?—red tapes. Another technique is to stop a report to see if anyone really needs it enough to come looking for it.

4   *The ideal control gives the earliest possible reliable, economical indicator not only of what is happening but also of what will happen later.* Because the purpose of control reports is to help managers achieve their objectives, it is vital that indications of trouble or needed corrective action be given as early as possible. However, these indications must be reliable; that is, they must not give false guidance to the manager. And they must be economical; that is, they must not cost more than they are worth.

As the importance of quick-responding controls became recognized, some accounting-type reports were replaced by types of data that could give reliable warnings more quickly. Thus, for example, statistical sampling of sales from selected districts in the early stages of a major sales promotion campaign or product promotion could provide an early indicator of ultimate success or failure of the campaign or promotion. This type of reporting is similar to the familiar election night predictions of final results on the basis of selected early returns.

On election night, it is possible to predict final results on the basis of a few early returns only because a model of the entire system has been put into the computer. The model is based on established relationships between results in certain early-reporting locations and results in larger areas such as states. Similarly, models of operating organizations can predict later effects of certain events such as an increase or decrease in level of production or of financing by one method versus another. Also, PERT networks are models of projects that can predict the longer-range effects of such events as the breakdown of equipment or late delivery of supplies or other schedule upsets. As managers learn to build better and better computer-based models, they will be able to make their controls more and more forward-looking—to use "feedforward control," in the terminology of one pair of writers on the subject.[11]

Sometimes nonquantitative reports give the fastest-acting reliable warnings. Thus, in connection with a research program, a review by experts can sense ultimate failure at a time when the accounting reports still show the program in control. Or, again, a consulting report on organizational health can project the ultimate effects of friction between executives (excessive turnover, poorer decisions, reduced profit) long before it shows up in quantitative reports.

5 *The tools and techniques of control are many and varied.* Many control tools and techniques have already been mentioned in this chapter: budgets and budget variance reports, PERT networks, Gantt charts, statistical samples of quality measurements, ratio analysis, breakeven curves, chart books and chart rooms, ROI charts, cash-flow analyses, periodic consultant studies, product life-cycle charts, and employee performance reviews. But even this long list is not complete; in fact, the number of important control tools and techniques is limited only by the variety of work situations and man's imagination on how to measure results in those situations.

For example, the Armed Forces face a unique control problem in that they cannot fight an actual war to test their capability. To meet this problem, they have long used war games to simulate the real thing. Another technique is the operational readiness inspection, in which a unit is subjected to an unexpected demand that it get a certain number of fully equipped planes into the air in a certain amount of time, or that it move certain equipment a given distance in a given amount of time, or that it counter a certain simulated emergency.

Still another type of control report is the anonymous poll of employee opinion. Thus a periodic poll on a series of questions concerning jobs, pay, working conditions, and working relationships can provide a quick indication of the state of employee morale in general and on the specific topics. When areas of discontent are plotted on a chart (identifying the work unit on one axis and the topic on the other), the result is called a "fever chart" or "measles chart" (when poor ratings are marked in red), which indicates those units and/or topics where trouble may be brewing.

An almost infinite number of control tools and techniques may be used by administrators at all levels of all kinds of organizations to keep informed about what is actually happening; however, they must make wise strategic choices of the limited number to be used in any one organization.

6 *Control of time is essential to all other control.* Undoubtedly the greatest resistance to planning (and, therefore, to any meaningful control) comes from the line executive's feeling that there is not enough time to sit back and think about long-run objectives and long-run plans. This executive often tries to cover over this failure by such remarks as: "I know my objective—it's to make a profit." Or "There won't be a long-run to worry about if I don't stay on the ball and keep this outfit running."

Such executives will never have time to plan unless they first control their usage of time. And the first step to such control is to gather information on how time is actually being used. This information can then be analyzed so that priorities can be set and the misuse of time controlled.

Even though many management authorities have warned that effective time utilization is a prerequisite to effective management, rare is the manager, in large or small organizations, who periodically records and analyzes data on how time is actually spent. (For more on time utilization, including citations, see Chapter 12, plank 13.)

CONTROL IMPROVEMENTS AND PROBLEMS IN THE COMPUTER ERA

Control techniques have advanced rapidly as more and more computers have come into use. Obviously, modern data technology can collect great amounts of data, process it thoroughly and rapidly, and present many different printed (or display screen) reports to exactly the persons needing them. Although some of these capabilities are clearly desirable advances, others may be misused. A few of these issues are examined in the following two points.

7 *Is it managerially desirable to push all systems to their technical limits?* For some years now some managerial controls (such as inventory controls) have been automated (that is, the computer automatically reorders when inventory on hand reaches a predetermined point). Such automation relieves the manager from monitoring details; however, it is still necessary periodically to determine that the program is still valid.

Another way in which computers can provide highly efficient controls is by applying with great proficiency the old management-by-exception principle. Thus, computers can compare measurements of current results against preset programs (budgets, quality control standards, production rates, etc.), demanding the manager's attention only when an exception occurs. Thus, the manager need not read voluminous reports to find the exceptions, since only the exceptions are reported.

The military services have had considerable success with computerized control-by-exception systems in their logistics and equipment (especially aircraft) maintenance activities.

A newer development is the elimination of written reports (and the bulky files that go with them) by providing managers with television screens on which they can call up any part of the vast amount of information contained in the computer's memory.[12] But this development is controversial because many executives cannot (or fear that they cannot) grasp transitory data on a screen as well as they can grasp information in written reports that they may keep in their possession.

The biggest current controversy, however, surrounds the theoretically perfect control system, that is, one that uses a totally integrated information system that is on line and yields real-time reports. "On line" denotes the acquisition of data automatically, as, for example, products are produced or sales are recorded. "Real time" denotes the instantaneous updating of reports as operations events occur. A real-time system might yield not only up-to-the-minute inventory reports but also daily profit-and-loss statements or daily measurements of a department's performance against plan.

The desirability of such control reporting is seriously questioned on both "can" and "should" grounds. The "can" questions concern the technical and economic feasibility of totally integrated information systems. Some authorities contend that the organization that attempts such systems is asking for big trouble because accounting and programming know-how simply are not adequate to accomplish the task. Other authorities contend that at least the larger, more capable organizations are capable of moving effectively in this direction. The "should" questions ask whether daily profit-and-loss statements might not be so unstable, so lacking in perspective as to be misleading rather than helpful to the manager who receives them. The answers to these questions differ, as is demonstrated in the chapter on information systems, from situation to situation.

8 *What are the potentialities and limitations of control centers?* The already described usage by a number of large firms of control (or command or how-goes-it?) chart rooms, sometimes employing the latest information technology, makes clear that such centers have some obvious advantages. They can display large amounts of information and do so expertly; also, they encourage team management by enabling many managers in large companies to interact more effectively and efficiently than they could without such rooms. Also, the NASA control-room technique made it possible to keep very large numbers of projects well coordinated.

Some observers, however, see dangers in such centers. The greatest objection is that they could encourage centralization of control and decision making because the person in charge of such a setup feels all-powerful. Another objection is that staff personnel, the information technologists, can dominate the decision-making process by shaping and interpreting the data. Lower-level managers may feel overwhelmed and dispossessed; they may then neglect their control responsibilities.

In one firm, the author observed the development of an intense resentment by line managers of the staff people, whose influence increased greatly after the control center was created. The resentment erupted into physical combat and culminated in open revolt by the line managers. They forced the resignation of the leading staff people.

Still another objection to the command center idea is that the decision makers tend to become "ivory towerish"; that is, because they become infatuated with their sophisticated data systems, they neglect firsthand observation and face-to-face discussions.

Although the control center is usually found in large and highly computerized organizations, one successful retail organization with fewer than twenty employees also has a "war room." Here the two partners maintain a display of all the advertising done by their competitors and of the competitors' sales (as established by market research studies). An analysis of these displays provides the basis for formulation of their own competitive strategy, which has been exceptionally successful.

HUMAN PROBLEMS OF CONTROL

The eruptions in human relations that have occurred in command centers are only one type of emotional problem to which the control function is vulnerable. Some people are subconsciously afraid of having their performance measured precisely and objectively. Such people seek refuge in organizations where the objectives are vague, the control process is lax, and the performance review process is ineffectual. And if an organization has through the years attracted such persons, it is virtually impossible to change quickly into an organization that sets clear and challenging goals and that systematically and objectively measures performance against them.

Another human problem is that many persons have an innate dislike of being controlled by someone or something else. They resist the pressures of control with counterpressures. One evidence of this is the extensive playing of "budget games" —ingenious ways of getting around budgetary restrictions. Veteran bureaucrats are skilled in playing such games, even to the extent of sometimes reversing the explicit intent of the budget.

Evidence of the resistance to being controlled is found in the widespread sabotage of another kind of control report, the performance appraisal, in which a manager grades the performance of subordinates. In many instances, superiors and subordinates cooperate to produce "down the middle" ratings for everyone—meaningless paperwork that contributes nothing but that satisfies the formal requirement for a periodic rating of employee performance.

As noted earlier, it is hoped that participative methods of planning and control can reduce some of the resistance and resentment generated by traditional control methods in public and private bureaucracies. In any event, managers should not naïvely accept a performance appraisal or a budget or any other formal control report at face value; rather, they should strive to understand the motivations and methods of those who build the budget and of those "controlled" by it. (For citations, see Chapter 4, footnote 10.)

Still another type of human problem of control reporting is illustrated by the Navy's experience with a new type of ship in World War II. With far more communications equipment than any other type of ship had ever had, the then new Amphibious Force Flagships featured an elaborate central command room where all the communications were summarized. Here the commanding admiral was to have, summarized neatly on screens and display boards, current information on how all aspects of an invasion were progressing. Unfortunately, such an elaborate facility was necessarily located below decks in an enclosed part of the ship. But admirals found it impossible to remain seated below decks as soon as a battle started! After all, they were older men whose long training had been to command from the flying bridge, watching the action firsthand. Result: In the first invasion using these ships, the commanding admiral abandoned the fine new control room for the flying bridge. He got his information by a single telephone line from the command room. Immediately after the first battle, the ships were moved into shipyards for many millions of dollars of alterations in which as much equipment as possible was moved to the flying bridge. Moral of the story: Control reports must be fitted to the habits and capabilities of the key persons; or, conversely, the users must be carefully retrained to use new types of control reports. Clearly, a large retraining program faces organizations when they move to computer-generated control reports and command centers quite different from their old styles of controlling.

SOME CONTROL PROBLEMS IN PUBLIC ADMINISTRATION

Many of the impediments to the use of a forward-looking and facilitative type of managerial control in government have already been discussed in this chapter: the long budgeting tradition that focuses on compliance rather than on results achieved, the hierarchical structure that so fractionates responsibility that it is hard to apply responsibility controls, and the difficulty of measuring output in many types of government activity. In addition to these there are a few other aspects of managerial control in government that deserve mention.

One is the matter of the administrability of legislation. In many instances legislators, often at the behest of some special interest, put into legislation certain provisions that make it impossible to control to the objectives of the legislation. One hopes that professional managers will one day gain enough respect in the various levels of government that provisions will be made for task forces of them to evaluate and suggest improvements to the administrability/controllability of major proposed legislation.

Still another difficulty in achieving effective control in government is pointed up by a recent study of administrative feedback—that is, the monitoring of subordinates behavior—in nine federal bureaus. The study finds that "it is virtually certain that a great deal of subordinate non-compliance goes undetected." However, according to the study, the cause of failure to detect noncompliance does not lie in any breakdown of administrative feedback or in the fact that such patterns are inherently undetectable at headquarters; rather, it lies in an incentive structure that encourages superiors not to see the failures. The recommended solution is to change the incentive system under which superiors work. Thus the study urges that superiors be held strictly responsible for the actions of their subordinates; also, much more use of outside audits and of survey research techniques—both to find out and to publicize what is really going on—is also recommended.[13]

A final topic that has received some attention in connection with government control is "program evaluation," which may be defined as determining whether the goals of a program are being met and how well.[14] Presumably the "determining" is done systematically at least and, at best, in a research mode. Presumably too, this approach is on a one-time basis rather than on a continuing basis, as is the case with managerial controls. These features should make it possible for program evaluation to secure evaluative data and material not secured via the flow of operational information, as in the case of typical managerial reports.

Program evaluations are distinguishable from managerial reports in that they are done by outsiders, possibly persons working on a foundation or government grant or on university research. It has been pointed out by one pair of authors that "there have been but a handful of respectable evaluation studies of social action programs."[15]

After reviewing literature on the subject, one writer notes such problems as the fact that the in-government administrators and the politicians concerned with programs often do not share the efficiency, economy, and rationality values of the researchers. He concludes that evaluative research "commonly has little impact on what does or doesn't happen."[16]

SUMMARY

The control process, equipped with a strong philosophy of helping managers accomplish their objectives and with many new techniques, has earned a key place in modern management. For more than a decade, control has been the most rapidly developing part of management; over the next decade that progress will probably be even more dramatic, as further computerization opens up many new possibilities. Undoubtedly, even faster-acting controls will be developed as the pace of change accelerates in all aspects of business.

With continued movement toward systems management, some observers suggest that the term "manager of information systems" replace "controller" where the person has the broad responsibility for helping line managers get the control reports that they need and simply "accountant" where the duties are narrow.

On the government side, only relatively few organizations—those most advanced in computer use—practice a forward-oriented, constructive approach to control; the bulk of control practice continues to be based on traditional-style budgeting. Yet there have been and there will no doubt continue to be efforts to make government organizations more conscious of objectives and of the relationship of control to objectives.

REVIEW QUESTIONS

1 What are the four major steps in the control process?
2 Explain the statement, "Budgeting at all governmental levels is still primarily an incremental process. . . ."
3 What minimal control data are needed by a small firm?
4 How does it happen that budget compliance becomes the actual control in most governmental situations, rather than performance evaluation in terms of results achieved?
5 What are arguments for and against a theoretically perfect control system?

DISCUSSION QUESTIONS

1 With reference to the organization with which you are, have been, or plan to be associated, what main types of control reports are used? What reports are used at your particular level?
2 In what ways can top-level governmental administrators obtain soundings of public opinion about programs under their direction?
3 It is especially difficult in some situations, like educational institutions and staff units, to define specific objectives and strategic measurements of performance. As a consequence, poor controls, such as restriction-of-spending budgets and unrelated activity reports, come into use. Comment on methods or mechanisms which would solve this problem.
4 Discuss the criteria a manager or administrator might use in deciding which controls to install and where to place them strategically.

NOTES

[1] "AMF Rides the Booming Leisure Market," *Business Week*, Sept, 16, 1972, p. 79. See also "Business Says It Can Handle Bigness," *Business Week*, Oct. 17, 1970, pp. 108ff.

[2] C. David Baron, "Program Performance Reporting in Arizona Local Government," *Arizona Business,* April 1975, p. 8.

[3] This section relies upon Ira Sharkansky, *Public Administration: Policy Making in Government Agencies,* 2d ed. (Markham Publishing Co., Chicago, 1972), pp. 243–267, which contains excellent flow charts of the budget determination and execution processes which are, in turn, taken from Aaron Wildavsky, *Politics of the Budgetary Process* (Little, Brown and Company, Boston, 1964), pp. 194–199. In discussing the budgetary process, it is helpful to distinguish between "the executive" (office of the President, particularly the OMB) and "administrators" (agency and department managers).

[4] "Where Airlines Must Pioneer," *Business Week,* Mar. 7, 1970, pp. 86–94.

[5] "Where Electronics Speeds Executive Decisions," *Business Week,* Aug. 10, 1974, pp. 94–98.

[6] For a carefully reasoned and fairly detailed explanation of what types of financial responsibility controls are feasible in various types (as to strategy and organization structure) of businesses, see Richard F. Vancil, "What Kind of Management Control Do You Need?" *Harvard Business Review,* March–April 1975, pp. 75–85.

[7] For a few recommendations from among the great number of books available, see Jack S. Gray and K. S. Johnson, *Accounting and Management Action* (McGraw-Hill Book Company, New York, 1973); Robert N. Anthony and Glenn A. Welsch, *Fundamentals of Management Accounting* (Richard D. Irwin, Inc., Homewood, Ill., 1974); Robert N. Anthony and Regina E. Herzlinger, *Management Control in Non-Profit Organizations* (Richard D. Irwin, Inc., Homewood, Ill., 1975); E. Lynn and R. Freeman, *Fund Accounting,* a revision of the 4th ed. of *Municipal and Government Accounting* (Prentice-Hall, Inc., Englewood Cliffs, N.J., 1975); W. H. Horton, *Data Display Systems* (Business Books, Ltd., London, 1972); T. S. Dudick, *Profiles for Profitability* (John Wiley and Sons, New York, 1972).

[8] Virtually every textbook on elementary accounting or elementary finance provides forms for cash-flow analysis. A number of forms especially tailored for different types of businesses are provided in Joseph C. Schabacker, *Cash Planning in Small Manufacturing Companies* (Small Business Administration, Department of Commerce, 1960).

[9] Despite the complicated treatment given breakeven curves in most accounting or small-business-management textbooks, the present author is convinced that breakeven curves are simple to construct. The important point is either to have the firm's chart of accounts so set up that it separates fixed and variable costs or to learn how to separate them. Then it is necessary only to add up the two kinds of costs and put them in charts such as those illustrated herein. The charts need not be precise in order to convey important insights for decision makers. Once a chart has been drawn for the current level of operations, the small business manager should sketch out how fixed and variable costs would change if certain moves such as expanding, adding new equipment, or dropping a product or service, were to be made. For a book explaining not only the mechanics but also many uses of breakeven curves, see Fred V. Gardner, *Profit Management and Control* (McGraw-Hill Book Company, New York, 1955).

[10] For a description of the various controls used by growing small firms, see Dale Henning, *Non-Financial Controls in Smaller Enterprises,* Bureau of Business Research (University of Washington, Seattle, 1964).

[11] Harold Koontz and Robert W. Bradspies, "Managing through Feedforward Control," *Business Horizons,* June 1972, pp. 25–26.

[12] For a description of how one firm has applied this approach, see "TV Replaces Stacks of Paperwork," *Business Week,* Jan. 30, 1971, pp. 48–50.

[13] Herbert Kaufman, *Administrative Feedback* (The Brookings Institution, Washington, 1973), pp. 62, 63–68.

[14] James W. Davis, Jr., *An Introduction to Public Administration* (The Free Press, New York, 1974), p. 272.

[15] Eleanor B. Sheldon and Howard E. Freeman, "Notes on Social Indicators: Promises and Potential," in *Evaluating Action Programs: Readings in Social Action and Education,* edited by Carol H. Weiss (Allyn and Bacon, Inc., Boston, 1972), p. 170.

[16] J. Davis, op. cit., p. 286. Equally discouraging conclusions are reached by Joseph Wholey in *Federal Evaluation Policy* (The Urban Institute, Washington, 1970), p. 46. See also the "Symposium on Program Evaluation," *Public Administration Review,* July–August 1974.

RECOMMENDED READINGS

Child, John: "Strategies of Control and Organizational Behavior," *Administrative Science Quarterly,* March 1973, pp. 1–17.

Lorange, Peter: "A Framework for Management Control Systems," *Sloan Management Review,* Fall 1974, pp. 41–55.

Sayles, Leonard: "The Many Dimensions of Control," *Organizational Dynamics,* Summer 1972.

Turcotte, William E.: "Control Systems, Performance, and Satisfaction in Two State Agencies," *Administrative Science Quarterly,* March 1974, pp. 60–73.

Chapter 6

Organizing

WHAT IS ORGANIZING?

Every manager, at whatever level of whatever type of organization, somehow organizes his or her subordinates to accomplish the group's tasks. In traditional management thinking, the organizing function consists of determining who reports to whom (the chain of command) and who has what duties, authorities, and responsibilities. This is done in its simplest form by drawing boxes on organization charts and writing job descriptions.

However, today the organizing process is rarely seen in its simplest form. Rather, the subject has become complicated because much has been learned about designing structures to fit particular situations; much has been learned, also, about diagnosing organizational stresses and strains, about how to improve organizational effectiveness by reducing the obstacles to cooperation between units, and about the process of reorganizing.

In addition to all these complications, the subject of organizing is changing as a result of increasing computerization and use of the systems management concept. The indication is that, in the long run, these forces will radically change the organizing process and the shapes of organization structures. In theory at least, systems organizing starts with determining what decisions need to be made in order to accomplish the organization's missions; then determining the information flow and communications needed for making those decisions; and, last, establishing positions for making the necessary decisions. The resultant structures probably will bear little resemblance to traditional hierarchical, departmentalized structures.

Today actual practices in many business and public organizations hang somewhere between the traditional process and the systems process of organizing. Although a few of today's structures are traditional, many have adopted newer-type structures and many are showing some changes under the impact of computerization; yet few, if any, have gone completely to a systems organization structure.

To aid comprehension of this confusing state of affairs, this section will first describe traditional types of business structures, explaining how and why they came into being. Then some of the changes that have occurred in organizing will be discussed. A modern approach to theory will be presented. Then possible future changes will be considered. Finally, the impacts of these same influences upon governmental structures will be studied.

Although many aspects of how organizations actually work are not reflected in the charts, a discussion focusing on charts provides a good starting place. The nonchart aspects of organizing will be added later. Specifically, this section is outlined as follows:

Business Organizations
    The Traditional Functional Structure
    Changes from the Traditional Functional Structure
    Informal Organization, Communications, and "Flat" Structures
    Other Ideas on Organizing
    The Basic Trend in Organizing Theory and Practice: A Situational (or Contingency) Approach
    Clouding of the Staff/Line Concept
    Understanding Organizations and Keeping Them Healthy
    The Impact of Computerization and Systems Management

Government Organizations
    Is Bureaucracy Dying?
    The NASA Structure
    Decentralization
    Computerization and Government Structure
    Reorganizations

Summary and Conclusions

BUSINESS ORGANIZATIONS

The Traditional Functional Structure

As a small firm prospers and grows, it is quite natural for the owner-manager at some point to hire assistance in the form of a person especially competent in some

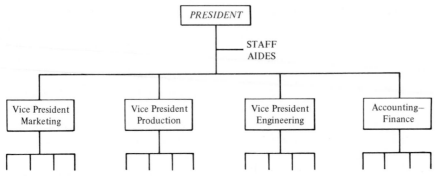

Figure 6-1 Functional organization structure.

function (such as accounting, sales, manufacturing, or engineering), usually the one that the owner enjoys least. As growth continues, this process of organization building continues until the structure looks like Figure 6–1.

It was probably by this process that the so-called functional structure came to be the traditional, almost universal form for businesses in the early days of industrialized society.

Changes from the Traditional Functional Structure

Decentralized Structure   As industrialization progressed and businesses became larger and more complex (that is, having various product lines and serving various markets), leading large organizations shifted to a decentralized structure, as illustrated in Figure 6–2.

This type of structure (quite simplified here) made it possible to break up the

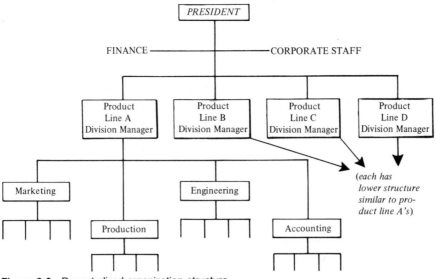

Figure 6-2 Decentralized organization structure.

total management job (which may have been growing impossible!) into a number of smaller pieces. Presumably, the smaller, more homogeneous divisions are more manageable. Also, having a number of smaller entities provides more opportunities for executives to take major responsibilities and to prepare for the top job. This was especially true where the divisions were complete profit centers; that is, where they comprised all the functions so that the division manager had real profit-and-loss responsibility. In such organizations there could be a full delegation of authority (except, usually, for some financial control by the corporate office), so the division head's performance could be measured in part by the return on investment.

In some cases, however, it is not possible to decentralize all major functions. For example, the tin can manufacturers have decentralized manufacturing (empty cans cannot economically be transported, so the manufacturers have many small plants located near the products to be canned) but centralized selling (since most sales are to large food-processing or brewing firms where the corporate office contracts for cans for many plants). In such cases the division managers cannot be held responsible for profit and loss because they do not control sales, so they are evaluated by a "contribution to overhead" measurement or by a comparison to "standard cost" or a synthetic profit-and-loss figure derived by allocating income on some basis. (This type of structure has been called "simulated decentralization" by Peter Drucker.[1])

Companies shift from functional to decentralized structures at various growth points, depending upon the complexity of the firm's product line and markets and the desire to delegate authority. Although most firms decentralize before they reach the $100 million sales level, news accounts tell of much larger firms finally abandoning the functional structure.[2]

Product (Matrix) Structure   In some cases it is not possible to decentralize an organization because many products use the same equipment; in other cases, many products may be sold by the same salespeople or may be distributed through the same warehouse-distribution structure. In such cases it has been possible to achieve concentrated effort and to delegate responsibility for particular products by the so-called product-manager matrix-type structure shown in Figure 6–3a.

In some cases product managers work across the entire structure; they do not have line authority over the persons in the sales, production, and engineering departments with whom they must work to get their jobs done. If they try to issue orders, these might be in conflict not only with orders given by the functional vice president but also with orders given by other product managers. Lacking authority, they persuade upward sometimes, downward sometimes, but most often laterally.

In other situations the product manager (sometimes called a "brand manager") works within the marketing department, coordinating advertising, market research, promotion, planning, and other marketing activities for some particular product or brand. The Procter and Gamble Company, originator of the concept in 1927, has fifty product managers; for many years most other companies selling a large, diversified line of products have been similarly organized. However, a number of large companies have abandoned or modified the concept. As a General Mills executive

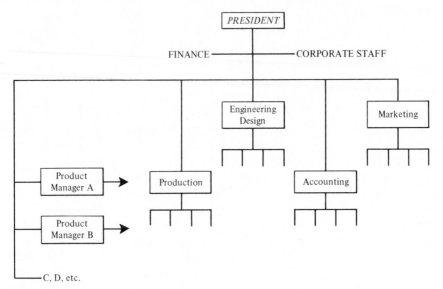

Figure 6-3a   The product-manager structure.

puts it: "Because of market segmentation and other pressures, the product manager cannot be the see-all expert anymore. Our philosophy is that the product manager, while important, is no longer king."[3] In order to get closer to the different segments of the market, emphasis is being placed on persons who specialize in selling a number of products to a particular market segment rather than on product managers.

Project Structures   The project structure, which has enjoyed considerable popularity in the last decade or so, can take many forms. In its matrix (or crosshatch) form, it is similar to the product structure just discussed (Figure 6–3a) in that both are designed to have a manager give full attention to the progress of that project or product and have high visibility as the person responsible for it. However, there are three major differences between product and project structures:

   1   Whereas product structures are usually permanent, project structures are usually temporary, even though they may last as long as ten years.
   2   Product structures usually do not change fundamentally over time, but project structures do. Thus the talents and organization structure required during the design phase of a missile are very different from those required during the

production stage. Flexibility is a key feature of project structures; they are preferred in situations that must cope with rapid change.

   3   While a product manager's office usually comprises only a few persons coordinating the efforts of line departments, a project manager may have anywhere from one to hundreds of persons reporting to him or her. The larger offices are responsible not only for the coordinating of the project but also for the actual work.

   Of the many matrix forms that project structures can take, one is shown in Figure 6-3b. In this illustration, two of the project managers have employees assigned to their projects for as long as the projects need them; the third project manager does not yet have any subordinates and therefore must get work done through employees who actually report to others. In either case—using temporarily assigned workers or getting work done through other persons' workers—it is a form of management that demands considerable skill in coordination, tact, and persuasion. It is this different kind of authority relationship that makes some writers see project management as a radical departure from the traditional bureaucratic structure.[4]

   In some project situations, not only will workers in each department be physically set aside, working exclusively for the project manager during the life of the project, but facilities and space will also be set aside by some type of marking. In other project management situations, a given production worker (or design worker or marketing worker) will be working on various projects.

   Still other project situations do not use the matrix structure but have the entire work force, physically, assigned to the project as a unit; these resemble structures that are decentralized by product except that the projects are temporary. And the NASA structure, Figure 6–6, is another type of project structure, with government offices and contractor companies comprising the projects.

   Management literature abounds in endorsements of the project structure in situations as disparate as that of an international engineering construction company to that of consultants instituting new methods in a large city welfare department.[5]

   Conglomerate Structure   A relatively recent arrival on the business scene has been the conglomerate, a company containing a number of quite unrelated types of businesses, as illustrated in Figure 6–4. Conglomerates have typically been created relatively rapidly and chiefly by acquisition rather than by development of new businesses from within the existing corporation. Since conglomerates place great emphasis on strong motivation and strong performance at the division-manager level, they delegate profit-and-loss authority to that level. This practice carries with it the concept of a "lean" corporate office that is chiefly concerned with overall planning, financing, public relations, and new acquisitions. (At least, this type of decentralization has been the mode of organizing followed by most conglomerates. It is quite possible that this approach may be modified since so many conglomerates have experienced sharp reversals of fortune.) One huge company reports good results from a structure with 4 "subholding companies" divided into 20 operating groups broken down into 1,000 profit centers.[6]

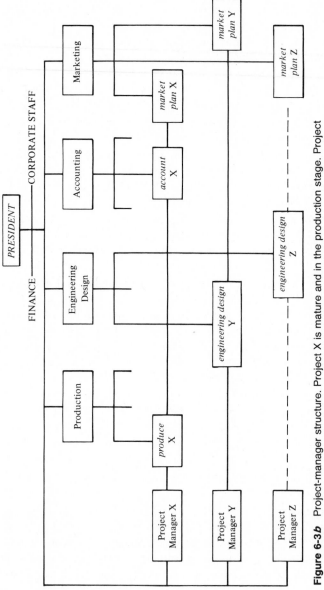

Figure 6-3b Project-manager structure. Project X is mature and in the production stage. Project Y is somewhat younger and still in the design stage; however, marketing planning is taking place in anticipation of the production phase of Project Y. Project Z is the newest of all and, as yet, only a project manager has been added to the structure. The manager of Project Z must rely on the cooperation of the engineering, design, marketing, and other departments for the accomplishment of necessary project work.

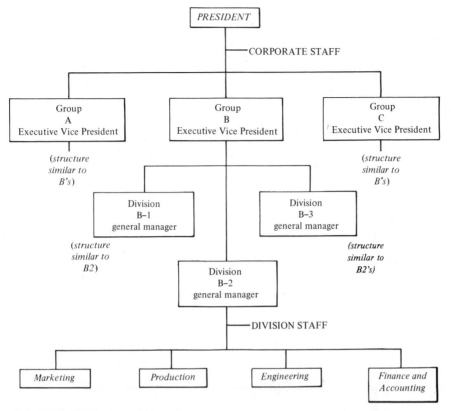

Figure 6-4   Conglomerate structure.

Informal Organization, Communications, and "Flat" Structures

The idea of "flat" structures, a major change from the traditional hierarchies, flowed in part from a lesson learned by the decentralizers: Executives who delegate substantial amounts of authority do not have to supervise subordinates closely; therefore they can supervise more subordinates. The idea of flat structures also derived in part from a lesson learned in the study of the informal arrangements that develop in every formal structure: Every level in an organization presents a potential barrier to full and accurate communications. Thus unofficial channels of communication develop to compensate for persons in the chain of command who cannot or will not communicate effectively.

Putting these two lessons together, some companies decided to experiment with flat structures that spread the span of control far beyond the traditional practice, as shown in Figure 6–5.

Use of this type of structure is sometimes called "delegation by overload." The executive is so overloaded with subordinates that he or she simply cannot supervise them closely; they are therefore permitted to exercise substantial authority and responsibility. Also, managers may get help from the staff specialists without having to go through hierarchical channels. In addition, communication lines are shorter.

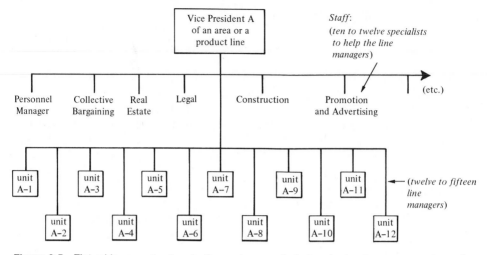

Figure 6-5   Flat, wide-span structure (units can be manufacturing plants, stores, or groupings of stores).

It should be noted, however, that this type of structure appears to have been most effective in companies that have extensive control reports flowing in to the superior. In such situations, a manager can safely delegate authority because control reports would promptly show when someone down the line was not performing well. Thus Sears, Roebuck and Company, one of the leaders in this approach, can judge the performance of any group of stores, any single store, or any department within a store by comparing its results data with those of many other units.[7] Success for this type of structure also depends on having a corps of stable, experienced managers at all levels; in other words, the persons to whom authority is to be delegated should have been proved capable in that company. Substantial delegation in a less stabilized situation can be quite risky.

Other Ideas on Organizing

Structure and the MBO Concept   The easier it is to identify the objectives of a unit and to measure performance against them, the easier it is to apply MBO. Accordingly, structures (such as decentralized or conglomerate or project structures) that delegate full profit-and-loss responsibility to subunits are particularly compatible with MBO.

On the contrary, where two or more units share responsibility for achievement of a goal, the MBO processes—participation in goal setting, determination of measurements, and performance evaluation—must be carried out on a group basis. While this is somewhat more difficult than working on an individual basis, it can be done.

Structure and Leadership   The foregoing sections of this chapter should have made clear the fact that there are basic ties between organizational structure and leadership. Clearly, the main features of the flat structure—heavy delegation, light supervision, and short lines of communication—make it highly conducive to a participative-consultative pattern of leadership. So, also, is the decentralized structure conducive to MBO type participation.

Behavioral scientists have established other ties, too, between leadership and structure. For example, in searching for answers to the productivity problem, which will be discussed in a later chapter, they have found that workers who respond poorly to assembly-line operations are sometimes much more productive under a form of participative leadership that permits teams considerable discretion in organizing their own work layout and job assignments—so-called free-form structuring.

With research and development becoming an ever-greater part of our industrial life, behavioral scientists have given considerable study to what types of structure and leadership are most productive in those activities. It appears that a flat project structure with collegial leadership is best for coping with R&D and other talent-intensive and change-intensive organizations that do not utilize heavy equipment or unique buildings (i.e., businesses in which making changes involves mainly moving people). In capital-intensive businesses, however, it appears that the better solution is a dual structure, involving an "innovation" structure and a "steady-state" structure.[8] Under this approach, new ventures are kept in the innovation structure until they are thoroughly established and ready to be inserted into the regular, or steady-state, structure. Presumably the managers in the innovation structure are selected and trained for less structured, more fluid work. They are expert in the conceptualization, planning, and control of R&D operations and the launching of new ventures; being in a special smaller structure, they can achieve coordination among these activities. Also, their performance is measured by the economics of innovation rather than by traditional manufacturing-distribution efficiency. On the other hand, the performance of the steady-state managers is not confused by inclusion of not-yet-mature ventures in their responsibilities.

The Behavioral Scientist and the Traditional Principles of Organization   The foregoing insights into structuring have been supported by a considerable amount of study by behavioral scientists of the traditional principles of organizing. Their studies have led to attacks on many principles that were once widely accepted.

Probably the most often quoted of these traditional principles of organizing was that having to do with the span of control, that is, how many persons should be reporting to a given superior. At the top echelons, the number was usually between five and eight, and at the lowest level it was usually from fifteen to twenty. Many arguments, including mathematical demonstrations of how adding one or two subordinates multiplied the number of interpersonal relationships the superior had to control, supported this narrow-span doctrine. In recent years, however, this principle has been upset by the flat structures, including some project structures, that necessarily have wide spans of control.

Traditional organization principles also called for precisely drawn job descriptions all along the structure and for frequent updating of the descriptions. Operative, or nonsupervisory, jobs were subjected to job simplification studies so that the one best method of performing the job could be determined and written into the job description. This idea, too, has been shaken up, particularly by those theorists and managers who claim that sometimes less structured groups, in which workers set their own methods, are achieving productivity improvements. These experiments are closely akin to the concept of job enlargement; both approaches seek to instill variety, flexibility, and scope for creativity into formerly rigid, narrow job descriptions.

Another of the traditional principles called for a single, clear chain of command from top to bottom; dual subordination was unacceptable. This principle has been challenged in high-technology organizations in which a line manager or a project manager must follow the instructions of a number of specialists or experts; in effect, such managers report to a number of superiors. Similar multiple subordination exists in all the matrix, or crosshatch, organization structures.

These various departures from traditional principles of organizing have been encouraged and demonstrated by behavioral scientists who have declared obsolete such principles as unity of command, scalar chain of command, and span of control. They find the traditional structures, based on these principles, "inhuman" and "dehumanizing" and totally inadequate for today's educated workers and supervisors and today's fast changing problems. Flexible "organic-adaptive" or "adhocracy" or "free form" structures are prescribed by these writers.[9] Such structures would be accompanied by nonrestrictive job descriptions and participative forms of managerial leadership.

The Basic Trend in Organizing Theory and Practice:
A Situational (or Contingency) Approach

Thirty years ago executives confronted with the problem of structuring an organization had a limited kit of established tools and concepts with which to work. They could use a basically functional structure or a basically decentralized structure, with a few variations in detail. Doctrine on span of control, chain of command, and staff/line relationships was quite fixed. So also was the assumption that jobs should be as simplified (or rationalized) as possible. It was further assumed that both jobs and lines of authority should be clearly defined in an organization manual.

Today's executive has a far greater variety of structures to work with and a far more flexible attitude toward principles of organizing. Clearly there has been a strong movement away from the traditional practices and toward such new practices as flat structures, project structures, product structures, conglomerate structures, free-form structures, and even more than one type of structuring in different parts of a large organization. But what is the basic trend? Which, if any, of these types is the organization structure of the future?

The answer appears to be that, despite claims made by some highly persuasive writers on behalf of free-form structures, no one form represents the wave of the future. Rather, the basic trend in actual practice is toward variety, toward using each of these approaches, new and old alike, in the particular situation to which it is most appropriate. In short, a situational or contingency approach is now dominant. Conclusions along this line have been stated by two well-known management authorities:

> . . . different environments require different organizational relationships for optimum effectiveness. No longer is there a "one best way" whether it is classical or behavioral.[10]

> The true lesson of the organization crisis is . . . that the traditional quest for the one right answer—a quest pursued as wholeheartedly by the new "heretics" of free-form organization as by the most orthodox classicists—pursues the wrong quarry. It misconceives an organization as something in itself rather than as a means to an end. But now we can see that liberation and mobilization of human energies—rather than symmetry, harmony, or consistency—are the purpose of organization. Human performance is both its goal and its test.[11]

The latter writer points out in the course of his article that even today the functional structure is usually the most effective way to organize a small company, that the GM model of federal decentralization is still the most effective way to organize a large manufacturing company, and that it is not clear what is the best way to organize a multinational operation, a multitechnology organization, a multimarket company, or a large government agency.[12]

Strong support for the situational/contingency approach is found in the work of a British research group that studied the determinants of the structural differences among 100 firms. They found, first, that firms with certain types of operating technology (the main types being unit or custom, mass, and continuous process) tended to have certain types of structures. There was a strong tendency for the first and third types to have more humanistic structures; there was a less pronounced tendency for the second type to have a classical structure. They found, second and more importantly, that firms employing structures most appropriate to their technologies were more successful than those whose structures were not the type appropriate to their operations technologies.[13]

The situational/contingency approach is further supported by a formidable and still growing body of research, going off in many directions, which can be summarized as follows as far as structure is concerned: The appropriate structure for any given organization is a function of the interaction of the nature of the work being done, the type of leadership, the characteristics of the subordinates, and the environment.[14]

Clouding of the Staff/Line Concept

Another attitude in the traditional organizing doctrine that is undergoing change is that toward staff/line relationships. Traditionally, staff positions were established when it became advisable to take some bit of authority away from the line (in order to centralize it to secure uniform practice throughout the company, or in order to put it into the hands of a highly qualified specialist, or for some other reason). A number of different kinds of staff (or functional) authority were identified: specialist authority over a particular subject or set of activities, or investigate-and-report authority, or temporary "act in place of the boss" authority. It was felt that the authority of each staff position should be carefully defined and tightly controlled lest the staff person usurp too much authority from the line. And the communications patterns of staff personnel were tightly defined, usually requiring that all communications be routed through the line bosses. It was feared that if these principles were not followed strictly, harmful misunderstandings would develop between staff and line and that, possibly, the all-important "integrity of the line" would thus be compromised.

The influx of highly trained specialists into the management of some organizations has clouded established doctrine about line/staff relationships. Today, some of these specialists are so highly expert in technical fields that they cannot truly be supervised by generalist line managers, much less be held to a strict one-boss reporting relationship and formal lines of communication.[15] For example, in NASA, the space exploration organization, any one of seven persons may abort a space vehicle launch. In such a case, who is the line executive in charge and who are the specialist staff advisers? Or again, the story is told of the project manager in a large defense firm who, conscious of the fact that he had to please a number of different high-powered specialists, remarked to his secretary, "If my boss calls while I'm out, be sure to get his name and phone number."

The term "collegial" has been used to describe such working groups in which various talents cooperate in loosely defined relationships, with freedom of communication upward, downward, and laterally; in these groups the locus of authority to decide a particular question may depend more upon the nature of the question than upon job titles and job descriptions of any staff/line distinction.

Understanding Organizations and Keeping Them Healthy

Once established, an organization structure needs maintenance, improvement, and—in time—alteration to cope with new conditions. It takes continuing, conscious effort to understand the many things going on in an organization that the chart does not show. There are the informal channels of communication which are sometimes more important, for good or for bad, than the formal ones; there are the informal leaders and social groupings that have powerful influences on how an organization actually works as opposed to how the chart indicates it works. The chart does not tell how much authority flows down the lines connecting superior with subordinates or how much feedback flows up the line; neither does it show the quality of those communications. And it does not show changing relationships such as those which occur when certain subordinates are moving closer to the boss while others are becoming more isolated.[16]

Many kinds of changes in the ways an organization actually works are usually taking place, especially when the organization is growing rapidly.

Communications problems change as organizations grow, partly because of sheer size increase and partly because growth often involves new kinds of businesses and new technologies, and there are always new personalities entering the picture. All such changes produce organizational stresses and strains, barriers to effective, cooperative work.

Organizational Development   A technique for keeping aware of what is actually going on in an organization and for working to remove the barriers to effective, cooperative work is what has come to be known as *organizational development* (OD). Behavioral scientists apply OD to help managers consciously recognize, analyze, and cope with any interpersonal relationships or structural conditions that limit organizational effectiveness. The "intervention agents" work with managers in problem-solving meetings built around their planning, controlling, supervising, and other normal managerial processes; sometimes, however, they employ such techniques as sensitivity training, attitude surveys, psychological counseling, and project syndicates to help them better understand one another, to appreciate the talents possessed by others, to better understand the impact of their own actions upon their associates, and to work out whatever changes in structure are needed. (Here again, the subjects of structure and leadership are intertwined; OD, which helps on both, will be discussed further in Chapter 7, on leadership, and citations will be provided there.)

Reorganizing   The time of reorganizing is especially threatening, a time of maximum stress on the group effectiveness of any organization. A going organization can be brought to a virtual standstill if word leaks out that a major reorganization is about to be announced. People's insecurities increase dramatically, and they become so preoccupied with what might happen that they are unable to work. Many a firm has been virtually torn apart by a poorly conceived and poorly executed reorganization. Little wonder, then, that management literature contains articles with titles like "Reorganizing for Results"[17] and "How to Reorganize without Chaos."[18] These articles stress (1) that the firm have clearly in mind the objectives sought in the reorganization, especially that the objectives be geared to the requirements for competitive success in that field and to the firm's objectives and plans; (2) that the relevant principles of organizing be carefully adapted to the present situational factors; and (3) that early reassurance be given those persons who will not be hurt by the change as well as that prompt action be taken to provide for those who will be hurt by it. Obviously, a firm with an ongoing OD program should be able to achieve reorganization with a minimum of trauma.

The Impact of Computerization and Systems Management

On top of all the complexities of the organizing function already discussed in this chapter, a number of other factors will be affecting future structures.

Change in Shape of the Pyramid   The overall shape of organizational structures has traditionally been depicted as a pyramid with a single head and a larger number of persons at each successive lower level.

The top of the pyramid has in some large corporations become blunt in shape; some firms have from three to five top general executives (perhaps a chairperson, a president, and from one to three executive vice presidents or group presidents). Some firms have an office of the president consisting of as many as ten executives, and still others are run by executive councils with as many as twelve members (with any one member holding the top title for only three or four years.)[19] Such arrangements reflect not only the increasing complexity of management but also a deemphasis of one-person rule. In addition, these arrangements provide for orderly succession in top positions. Under a full systems management concept, it is quite likely that the top group will be further enlarged—and the pyramid further blunted—by the inclusion of the long-range planners, systems analysts, and scientists as full members of the top command rather than as staff advisers.

There is controversy as to what will happen in the middle-management ranks as computerization advances.[20] Some observers foresee that these ranks will be greatly reduced in number via the automation of programmable types of decisions. Also, some observers reason that when computers make needed data quickly and easily available to any person at any level, managers will be relieved of many communications chores and will have excellent control reports on activities of subordinates. Under such conditions, supervisors should be able to control operations without so much help from subordinate levels of managers. This would mean fewer middle-level managers, giving an hourglass appearance to the structure.

However, other observers feel that the numbers of middle managers will not be reduced because (1) new types of middle-management jobs will be created (e.g., systems maintainers, systems designers, etc.) and (2) supervisors will do more change planning and more development coaching of their subordinates—in short, they will do a more truly managerial job—once the computer frees them of detail duties. But evidence to date indicates some elimination of levels.

With respect to the lower ranks—first-line supervisors and rank-and-file workers—the prognostication varies industry by industry. Some kinds of operations will be highly automated, drastically reducing the numbers in these ranks and thereby making the base of the pyramid less broad. Other kinds of operations will experience little automation of lower-level activities.

Depending upon how one combines these various prognostications, the typical organization structure of the future can be projected as:

a figure eight with a small bulge at the top loop and a larger bulge at the bottom; or

a football atop a church spire, not very wide even at the base; or

a football atop a flattened pyramid.

Recentralization versus Decentralization   Some observers see the advanced stages of computerization bringing a strong recentralization of authority. They argue that tomorrow's management information system can, in many organizations, bring such excellently processed data to a centralized super decision maker that it will be economical to recentralize much of the authority that has previously been decentralized. However, there are those who see just the opposite development, arguing that even greater decentralization will be possible because (1) lower-level managers will have fresher, better-processed, and more complete data, and therefore they can be trusted with more decision-making authority, and (2) higher-level managers will have better control reports to let them know how well the decentralized authority is being used.

It is quite possible that there will be both recentralization and further decentralization, depending upon the nature of a particular organization's operations and the philosophy of its key people. Sophisticated information technology will be able to do a good job of implementing either centralization or decentralization. To date, however, recentralization has been the usual result when computerization has had any effect at all on structures.

GOVERNMENT ORGANIZATIONS

Is Bureaucracy Dying?

The traditional bureaucratic structure—with its narrow span of control, many levels, hierarchical chain of command, and tightly defined, impersonal job descriptions —is the government counterpart of the traditional functional organization structure of business. And it, too, has come under heavy criticism in the post-World War II era. In fact, attacks on the traditional organizing principles appeared in public administration literature earlier than in business management literature, and for much the same reasons.[21] It has been argued that the many-level structures are simply too cumbersome for today's rapid pace of change and today's complex tasks; also, it has been claimed that bureaucratic channels of communication are too frustrating to the modern, well-educated government worker. For these and other reasons, it has been suggested that the death of bureaucracy is coming, that the old structures must give way to "adaptive, temporary systems of diverse specialists, solving problems, linked together by coordinating and task-evaluative specialists in organic flux."[22] And in the best-selling book *Future Shock,* this vision of the future is carried forward to "adhocracy."

Although the declaration of the coming death of bureaucracy was made in the early 1960s and has been repeated in various modifications many times since, there is little evidence that it is actually happening. In fact, in a 1973 symposium entitled "Organizations of the Future," a number of leading public administration scholars saw nothing of the sort happening; rather, most of them stressed the barriers to structural change in government organizations and predicted little change.[23] Attempts to enlarge jobs or flatten structures run into established (often legislated) procedures, into seniority and the other rigidities of civil service job classifications, and—increasingly—into the rigidities of collective bargaining contracts.

The NASA Structure

The one government organization that is pointed to as a shining example of the newer approaches to organizing is the NASA structure for the moon-landing project. Although neither the director[24] nor others writing extensively on the subject[25] have attempted to sketch the structure, it apparently resembled the diagram shown in Figure 6-6.

Although the director describes it as "a kind of participative and collaborative judgment forming process, with up to four levels of hierarchical authority involved, frequently in simultaneous effort, to draw valid conclusions from a large body of complex incoming information," it is indeed a project structure and a very flat structure for an organization of 32,000 civil service employees (the top 400 were exempt from civil service), and a peak total employment of 420,000. Clearly it had collegial, nonrestrictive patterns of communications. Apparently it lived up to the director's hope: "We have sought patterns of organization and administration that facilitate fast reaction time to signals of incipient failure or emerging opportunity."[26] And clearly it was a successful organization.

Another writer sees the NASA organization as a herald of the future because he sees combination government-business organizations, what he calls "third sector organizations," as the structures for tackling big challenges.[27] He points also to the success of Comsat, the communications satellite company, and he hopes that Amtrak, the railroad corporation, will one day be successful too.

Decentralization

There has been considerable changing of governmental organization structures with respect to decentralization. In a number of fields, the movement to decentralization has almost exactly paralleled that in business, the objective being to delegate responsibility down the line—to break it up into a number of smaller pieces. Thus, instead of one centralized general manager coordinating the centralized functional experts, a number of geographically decentralized general managers are given responsibility for their areas. In the public health field, this choice can be depicted as in Figure 6–7 for a state or city public health office.

The virtues of centralization versus decentralization in public health organizations have long been argued in state, county, and city organizations.[28] The arguments are fairly conventional. Thus centralization makes possible control by highly qualified experts in each functional field. Decentralization creates a number of centers of responsibility, develops more initiative, develops more executives, and provides for closer superior/subordinate relationships.

In large metropolitan areas, police administration has faced a similar choice (see Figure 6–8). Here there is an additional argument that it is important for the police to work closely with leaders in the smaller communities within the metropolis.[29]

Decentralizing to Secure Community Participation   It has just been noted that proponents of decentralization in police administration argue that it is important that a responsible official, and the entire team, work closely with key persons

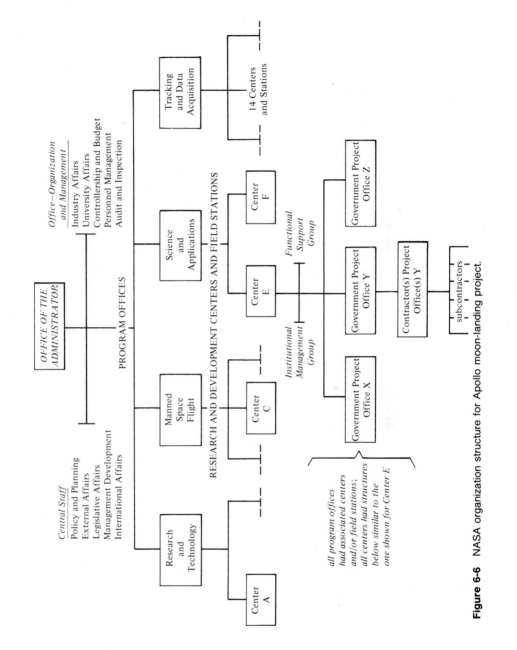

Figure 6-6 NASA organization structure for Apollo moon-landing project.

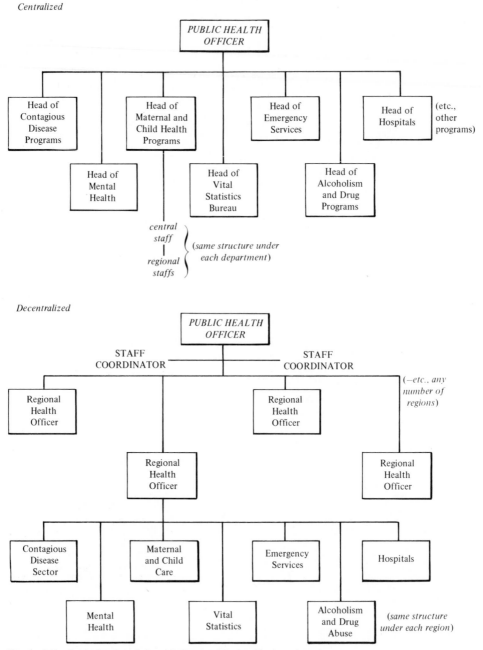

Figure 6-7 Centralized and decentralized public health departments.

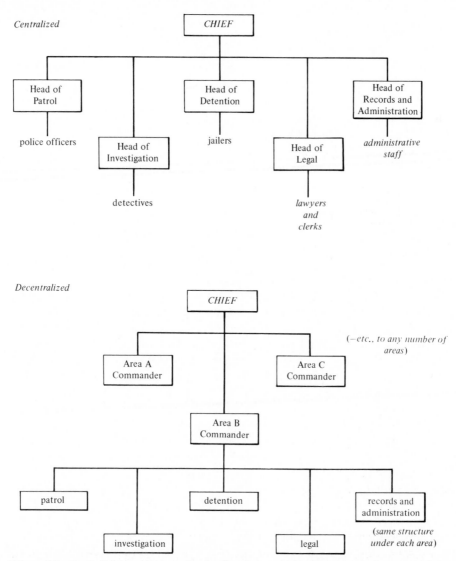

Figure 6-8 Centralized and decentralized police departments. Although the decentralized chart is *not* found in standard textbooks on police administration, it is implied in the writings of sociologists concerned with police-community relations, such as A. J. Reiss, Jr., and David Bordua, "Environment and Organization: A Perspective on Police," in David Bordua (ed.), *The Police: Six Sociological Essays* (John Wiley & Sons, Inc., New York, 1967), pp. 43–45.

in a local area. This feature has been deemed so vital in many federally funded but locally administered programs (housing, urban renewal, etc.) that the structuring of projects for such participation has been mandated.

Argument over local community control has been especially heated in educational administration in some places.[30] There have been major disturbances in New York City on this issue. Also, some states have many school districts (well over 900 in California), some a few, and there is one small state (Hawaii) that is completely centralized into one school district.

Computerization and Government Structure

Although some federal government departments with large clerical operations have made effective managerial use of computers, little impact upon structures was reported in a 1969 study.[31] However, since this study there have been at least two cases of elimination of levels in military organizations. One was the computerization of Air Force personnel records that, by putting status changes directly through the entire system on first entry, eliminated two levels of personnel record-keeping; the other was the computerization of the SAGE early warning radar system which eliminated one command level.[32] Probably many such reductions remain unreported in management literature.

It is predicted that, in government, eventual "streamlining and reorganization" will produce "organizations structured in accordance with the flow of information and the points of decision," in contrast to today's structures, which "are still compartmentalized by artificial functional areas."[33] However, before such reorganization can take place, there must be basic systems studies and data inventories for particular kinds of government activity (e.g., scientific, financial, etc.), and these seem as far off as they were in 1969 when only committees (e.g., the Committee on Scientific and Technical Information and the Interagency Committee on Oceanography) were working on the problem of achieving interdepartmental coordination.

Reorganizations

The great bulk of reorganization recommendations made by presidential commissions have never been effectuated. As noted in Chapter 3, it has been possible to create the Office of Management and Budget and to make progress on such ideas as regional centers to coordinate the action of federal agencies or to decentralize and standardize decision making on grants-in-aid; however, there has been little progress on the big reorganizations needed.

One upsetting feature of our rapid-change society is that new problems refuse to fit into old departmental structures; rather, new problems almost invariably cut across organizational lines. Unfortunately, recommendations to create new departments threaten the interests of a number of groups who usually can combine to defeat them.[34] Of the many recommendations for new federal departments and agencies in recent years, only the Department of Housing and Urban Affairs, the Transportation Department, and the Environmental Protection Agency have been created. The difficulty of taking anything away from established departments in order to create a new department better suited to handle new problems has led one writer to suggest that every government department or agency should be automatically disestablished after ten years unless there is positive action to continue it; such positive action would be permitted only after an impartial study group had reported the findings of a thorough study of it and the roles of each of its subunits.[35]

Although management literature would indicate that task forces and other project structure devices are the way to tackle new jobs, the common practice is to form an interagency committee or an intergovernmental coordinating council rather than to vest a temporary task force with real power.

SUMMARY AND CONCLUSIONS

A great array of types of organization structures, some new and some old, are used in business today. Also, many business managers take a flexible approach to established principles of organizing, utilizing them when they seem helpful but not hesitating to discard them when that seems advisable.

Continued computerization will no doubt bring further new types of structures and further modification of principles.

On the government side, there has been much less innovation. Although there is great need for many changes in government organization structures, the resistance to change is also great. Computerization is making progress in many branches of government, but these developments often do not carry through to changes in organization structure.

Academicians have developed and widely endorsed the contingency theory of organization; thus, what structure is appropriate in a given situation depends upon such factors as the nature of the task being performed, the characteristics of the leadership and of the work force, the objectives being sought, and various environmental factors. Increasingly, scholars and practitioners are able to describe the salient elements in a given situation and to prescribe the type of organization structure that probably would best serve that situation.

REVIEW QUESTIONS

1   Distinguish between:
    a   Functional structure
    b   Product structure
    c   Project structure
    d   Conglomerate structure
2   What conditions are necessary for effective use of flat organizational structures?
3   Explain why advanced stages of computerization may result in *either* recentralization or decentralization of authority.
4   Why is the project structure recommended for coping with change in capital-intensive businesses?

DISCUSSION QUESTIONS

1   With reference to the organization with which you are, have been, or plan to be associated, what are the main features of the structure? Do you feel this is an appropriate structure for the type of work being done (task)? For the type of leadership? For the types of persons employed?
2   In "collegial" working groups, the locus of authority to decide a question may depend more on the nature of the question than upon job title, job description, or staff/line distinctions. Comment on the short- and long-term organizational implications of this kind of authority distribution.

3 What forces that support change in organizational form do government and business share? What forces are unique to each sector?

4 New governmental agencies are created to deal with new problems. But too often there has been a reluctance or inability to disband the older, unnecessary agencies. What approach would you recommend to deal with this side-effect problem?

NOTES

[1] Peter Drucker, "New Templates for Today's Organizations," *Harvard Business Review,* January–February 1974, p. 49.

[2] The reorganization of Levi Strauss & Company, with annual sales of $328 million, was reported in "Levi's Tries on a Troika for Size," *Business Week,* Sept. 4, 1971. A functional structure was feasible until this size because it was essentially a one-product-line company.

[3] "The Brand Manager: No Longer King," *Business Week,* June 9, 1973, pp. 58–66.

[4] D. I. Cleland and W. R. King, *Systems Analysis and Project Management,* 2d ed. (McGraw-Hill Book Company, New York, 1975), pp. 15, 183–184; for illustrations of a number of different project structures, see chap. 11. For a different type of project structure chart and a discussion of the interpersonal relations problems, see "Teamwork through Conflict," *Business Week,* Mar. 20, 1971, pp. 44–49; also Clayton Reeser, "Some Potential Problems of the Project Form of Organization," *Journal of the Academy of Management,* December 1969, pp. 459–467.

[5] "Fluor Gambles On a Flock of New Orders," *Business Week,* Nov. 9, 1974, pp. 126–131. In this article the head of the firm attributes much of his firm's ability to handle jobs all over the world successfully to its project structure. Arthur H. Spiegel III, "How Outsiders Overhauled a Public Agency," *Harvard Business Review,* January–February 1974, pp. 116ff. Spiegel refers to project structure as the reformer's best tool.

[6] "Esmark Spawns a Thousand Profit Centers," *Business Week,* Aug. 3, 1974, pp. 48–52. The best-known unit of Esmark is Swift and Co., meat packers.

[7] James C. Worthy, "Organizational Structure and Employee Morale," *American Sociological Review,* April 1950, pp. 169–179. For a description of the Sears structure, see "How Giant Sears Grows and Grows," *Business Week,* Dec. 16, 1972, pp. 52–57. For another account of a flattening of structure see "Kaiser Aluminum Flattens Its Layers of Brass," *Business Week,* Feb. 24, 1973, pp. 81–84.

[8] T. Burns and G. M. Stalker, *The Management of Innovation* (The Tavistock Institute, London, 1961), p. 107; Richard M. Hill and J. D. Hlavacek, "The Venture Team: A New Concept in Marketing Organization," *Journal of Marketing,* July 1972, p. 46.

[9] A classic on the dysfunctional effects of traditional job descriptions, job structures, and supervisory practices, is Chris Argyris, *Personality and Organization* (Harper & Brothers, New York, 1957). Later Argyris works are *Integrating the Individual and the Organization* (John Wiley & Sons, Inc., New York, 1964) and *Applicability of Organizational Sociology* (Cambridge University Press, New York, 1972).

[10] Keith Davis, "Trends in Organizational Design," *Proceedings of the Thirty-third Annual Meeting* (Academy of Management, New York, 1973), p. 4. The same article appears in *Arizona Business,* November 1973, pp. 3–7. At this point in his article, Davis cites Don Hellriegel and John W. Slocum, Jr., "Organizational Design: A Contingency Approach," *Business Horizons,* April 1973, pp. 59–68. For a review of relevant literature and a very generalized model for designing a structure to fit a situation, see Y. K. Shetty and H. M. Carlisle, "A Contingency Model of Organizational Design," *California Management Review,* Fall 1972, pp. 38–45.

[11] Drucker, op. cit., p. 53.

[12] Ibid., pp. 47, 48.

[13] Joan Woodward, *Industrial Organization: Theory and Practice* (Oxford University Press, New York, 1965), pp. 51 and 69. A group of papers on the subsequent work of this research group, which has looked at the determinants of a number of facets of organizational behavior, is Joan Woodward (ed.), *Industrial Organization: Behavior and Control* (Oxford University Press, New York, 1970).

[14] Many volumes could be cited but one that summarizes it well is Jay R. Galbraith, "Environmental and Technological Determinants of Organizational Design," and other papers in *Studies in Organizational Design* (Richard D. Irwin, Inc., Homewood, Ill., 1970).

[15] Gerald C. Fisch, "Line/Staff Is Obsolete," *Harvard Business Review,* September–October 1961.

[16] David Oates, "Is the Pyramid Crumbling?" *International Management,* July 1971, pp. 10–13.

[17] By D. Ronald Daniel in the *Harvard Business Review,* November–December 1966, pp. 96–104.

[18] By E. W. Reilley in *Nation's Business,* July 1956.

[19] It is reported that fifty major American companies have opted for an office of the president or

some similar group structure at the top: "Can GM's New Top Team Cope with the 70's?" *Business Week,* Dec. 11, 1971, p. 70.

[20] A summary of many prognostications and researches on this subject is given in Charles W. Hofer, "Emerging EDP Patterns," *Harvard Business Review,* March–April 1970, pp. 16ff. For a summary of research findings, see Thomas L. Whisler, *Information Technology and Organizational Change* (Wadsworth Publishing Company, Inc., Belmont, Calif., 1970), especially p. 68.

[21] Herbert Simon, "The Proverbs of Administration," *Public Administration Review,* Winter 1946, pp. 53–67.

[22] Warren G. Bennis, *Changing Organizations: Essays on the Development and Evolution of Human Organizations* (McGraw-Hill Book Company, 1966), pp. 16–33.

[23] "Organizations for the Future," a symposium in *Public Administration Review,* July–August 1973. See "Introductory Note" and Herbert Kaufman's article, "The Direction of Organizational Evolution." The same general finding came out of a 1969 symposium focusing on current practice rather than projecting future structures: "Alienation, Decentralization and Participation," *Public Administration Review,* January–February 1969. See also F. C. Mosher, "The Public Service in a Temporary Society," *Public Administration Review,* January–February 1971, pp. 47ff.

[24] James E. Webb, *Space Age Management* (McGraw-Hill Book Company, New York, 1969).

[25] Leonard R. Sayles and Margaret K. Chandler, *Managing Large Systems* (Harper & Row, Publishers, Incorporated, New York, 1971). See pp. 166 and 191 for their closest approximations to an organization chart.

[26] Webb, op. cit., pp. 6 and 145.

[27] Amitai Etzioni, "The Third Sector and Domestic Missions," *Public Administration Review,* July–August 1973, pp. 314–322.

[28] For an account of how this issue has arisen repeatedly over many years in New York City, see Herbert Kaufman, "The New York City Health Centers," a case study, revised edition published by the Inter-University Case Program, 1959. For a discussion of this issue as experienced in Philadelphia, see Marianna Robinson, "Health Centers and Community Needs," in Frederic C. Mosher (ed.), *Governmental Reorganization: Cases and Commentary* (The Bobbs-Merrill Company, Inc., Indianapolis, 1967), pp. 61–103.

[29] Although the decentralized chart is *not* found in standard textbooks on police administration, it is implied in the writings of sociologists concerned with police-community relations, such as A. J. Reiss, Jr., and David Bordua, "Environment and Organization: A Perspective on Police," in David Bordua (ed.), *The Police: Six Sociological Essays* (John Wiley & Sons, Inc., New York, 1967), pp. 43–45.

[30] Roald F. Campbell, L. L. Cunningham, Roderick F. McPhee, and R. O. Nystrand, *The Organization and Control of American Schools,* 2d ed. (Charles E. Merrill, Inc., Englewood Cliffs, N.J., 1970), p. 16.

[31] Norman J. Ream, "The Computer and Its Impact on Public Organization," *Public Administration Review,* November–December 1968, pp. 494–503. This article is part of a symposium on computers in public administration published in this issue.

[32] The first case is reported in Chap. 9 of this book, and the second in Whisler, op. cit., p. 40.

[33] Ream, op. cit., p. 496.

[34] A fairly detailed account of how and why proposals for major reorganizations and creation of new federal departments have failed is given by Peri E. Arnold in "Reorganization and Politics: A Reflection on the Adequacy of Administrative Theory," *Public Administration Review,* May–June 1974, pp. 205–211.

[35] Peter Drucker, *The Effective Executive* (Harper & Row, Publishers, Incorporated, New York, 1967), p. 105.

RECOMMENDED READINGS

Costello, Timothy W.: "Change in Municipal Government: A View from the Inside," *Journal of Applied Behavioral Science,* March–April 1971, 131–145.

Goggin, William C.: "How the Multidimensional Structure Works at Dow Corning," *Harvard Business Review,* January–February 1974, pp. 54–65.

Perrow, Charles: "The Short and Glorious History of Organizational Theory," *Organizational Dynamics,* Summer 1973.

Symposium on Organizations for the Future, *Public Administration Review,* July–August 1973, pp. 299–335.

Chapter 7

Leading

DEFINITION OF MANAGERIAL LEADERSHIP

The managerial function here called "leading" is sometimes called "directing," "executing," "commanding," or even "communicating." Whatever the name, it concerns interpersonal influence, especially the pattern of a manager's influence upon his or her subordinates.

In most formally organized work groups, certain persons are given formal authority to supervise the work of others; that is, superior/subordinate relationships are established. At various levels, managers are referred to as "executive," "superintendent," "supervisor," "foreman," or simply "boss." The way in which any one of these managers influences subordinates—whether aggressively or passively, formally or informally, warmly or coldly, frequently or infrequently, stressing technical subjects or stressing personal matters, and so on—constitutes his or her style of leadership. When superiors are so uncommunicative that they have little influence over their subordinates, so-called informal leaders may take over the leaders' roles. In such a case, the leadership role is still part of the superior's job; but the superior has used a passive form of leadership and has thus, in effect, defaulted on that part of the job.

The point is that the function of leading is an inherent part of every managerial job in every kind of formal organization. It should be noted that this definition of "leaders" is quite different from the common usage, wherein it denotes the outstanding few. For example, the leading hitters in the American League are those with the highest batting averages, and a leading minister of religion is one of the most prominent, best-known ministers in the community. But in our definition, all managers (not just the outstanding few) are leaders—whatever the type and regardless of whether their work is effective or ineffective.

Managers exhibit their patterns of leadership in many different activities, including the way they plan, the extent to which they delegate authority, the manner in which they conduct performance reviews, the way in which they use control reports, their reactions to good performance versus poor performance, the extent to which they view themselves as coaches (or developers) of their subordinates, the way they react to emergencies, the extent of their influence with higher executive levels, their displays of loyalty or lack of loyalty to the organization, and in countless other ways. In short, the managerial process of leading pervades all the other managerial processes and is affected by such aspects of the work situation as the organization structure and the work activities being performed. Managerial leadership is the cumulative interpersonal influence that arises out of a manager's day-in and day-out working relationships with subordinates.

Now that managerial leadership has been defined, the question that naturally follows is: What kind of leadership is most effective? Unfortunately, the answer to that question is not simple, so it will be approached via the following topics:

What Are the Main Types of Managerial Leadership?
Which Type Is the Most Effective?
    The Case for Participative Management
    Motivation Theory Supporting Participative Management
    The Case against Participative Management as the Ideal Type
    A Second Look at Motivation Theory
    Conclusions: A Situational, or Contingency, Theory of Leadership
Can Effective Managerial Leaders Be Developed? How Good Are Executive
    Development and Organizational Development Programs?
Communication and Leadership
How Will Managerial Leadership Change under Systems Management?
Is Managerial Leadership Different in Government?
    Is Participation Really Coming?
    Government Situations Differ Too
    Organizational Development (OD) in Government?
    Conclusions on Managerial Leadership in Government

WHAT ARE THE MAIN TYPES OF MANAGERIAL LEADERSHIP?

There is some danger in setting up types of managerial leaders. It may oversimplify the subject. After all, leaders are human beings, and human actions are infinitely varied and sometimes quite subtle. Also, management calls for many different types of actions from a single leader; in consequence, a manager will sometimes be one type of leader, sometimes another type, and sometimes a leader who is difficult to classify. Despite this variety in kinds of actions taken by any one manager, most managers are basically one or another certain type of leader in the great bulk of their actions. Accordingly, it is enlightening to study types of leadership.

Although a long list of catchy types could be culled from the literature of administration, the following nine cover the subject:

Autocratic The "do it because I said so, I am the boss" type traditionally associated with the military and with business in the days when private ownership was dominant. One-way or "yes sir, ulcer" communications.

Benevolent autocratic Autocratic leadership toned down by the use of communications techniques that are less harsh, that show some consideration for the subordinate's integrity as an individual, and that are superficially two-way communications. Sometimes called the "let 'em have my way" type.

Bureaucratic The rules-centered, tradition-following, impersonal, noncreative type long associated with government management but also found in many large business organizations. Communications are plentiful and often two-way; however, they must pass through so many levels where responsibility is so diffused that the communications become meaningless.

Participative Though in political life democracy is associated with voting and majority rule, these features are *not* part of "democratic" managerial leadership. Rather, in management, "democratic" denotes genuine two-way communications, especially consultation by the superior with the subordinates on setting goals, suggesting new ideas, and deciding how to effectuate changes. Thus "consultative" or "participative" management would be more accurate than "democratic" management. This type can be broken down into two subtypes:

Individual-centered The manager who communicates effectively with individual subordinates and understands their personal problems and talents.

Group-centered The manager who understands not only the psychology of individual subordinates but also the sociology and dynamics of the work group, the team aspects.

Laissez faire The passive, "leave 'em alone" type who believes that most problems will simmer down and eventually go away if not aggravated by too prompt, too vigorous managerial action. Although sometimes no action is the best action, this type of manager takes no action most of the time.

Charismatic The administrator whose personal charm, cleverness, or technical brilliance dominates the situation, inspiring subordinates rather than creating the resentment sometimes generated by dominating (usually autocratic) leaders.

Technological The leader who makes most decisions on the basis of real or presumed superior ability in the technology involved. Communication chiefly concerns "how to do it" topics. This leader typically disdains all nontechnology matters as unimportant details to be handled by an administrative assistant.

Collegial The knowledge-oriented type usually associated with management of university faculties or research groups in government and industry. Subordinates are highly educated experts in their respective fields, so they are treated as colleagues rather than as subordinates. Lines of authority are deemphasized;

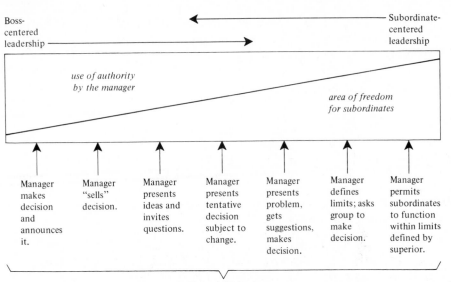

Range of Behavior

Figure 7-1 Continuum of style of leadership. (From Robert Tannenbaum, and Warren H. Schmidt, "How to Choose a Leadership Pattern," *Harvard Business Review,* March–April 1958, p. 96. This article was reprinted as an "HBR Classic" in the May–June 1973 issue, pp. 162–180.)

communications move freely along any lines that individuals prefer. (Sometimes described as "adhocracy.") Managers are seen as contributing coordination and necessary services to the whole rather than as bossing or supervising.

Political   The manager whose main strength is his or her influence in higher levels of the organization and/or in the surrounding community. The influence of such managers enables them to get things done for their subordinates and to represent their interests effectively. This feature of leadership can be found in combination with any of the other types except perhaps the laissez faire type.

A continuum, rather than discrete types, contains some of the same leadership elements, as illustrated in Figure 7–1.

Still other aspects of managerial leadership are reflected in the following definitions:

Leadership is the human factor which binds a group together and motivates it toward goals. . . . Leadership transforms potential into reality. It is the ultimate act which brings to success all of the potential that is in an organization and its people.

> Keith Davis, Human Relations in Business, *2d ed.,*
> *McGraw-Hill Book Company, New York, 1962, p. 103.*

Leadership in organizations involves the exercise of authority. It also involves making decisions for the organization.

> R. Dubin, Human Relations in Administration,
> *4th ed., Prentice-Hall, Inc., Englewood Cliffs, N.J. 1974.*

Leadership is the art of imposing one's will upon others in such a manner as to command their obedience, their respect, and their loyal cooperation.

G-I Manual, *Command & General Staff College, Fort Leavenworth, Kans., 1947.*

Leadership is "arrangement of the situation so that group results may be achieved."

Roger Bellows, Creative Leadership, *Prentice-Hall, Inc., Englewood Cliffs, N.J., 1959, p. 54.*

One ought to be both feared and loved, but as it is difficult for the two to go together, it is much safer to be feared than loved, if one of the two has to be wanting. Love is held by a chain of obligation which, men being selfish, is broken whenever it serves their purpose; but fear is maintained by a dread of punishment which never fails. I conclude, therefore, with regard to being feared and loved, that men love at their own free will, but fear at the will of the prince, and that a wise prince must rely on what is in his power and not on what is in the power of others, and he must only contrive to avoid incurring hatred, as has been explained.

Niccoló Machiavelli, The Prince *(about 1500)*
(The Prince and the Discourses, *Modern Library, Inc., New York, 1940, pp. 60–63).*

WHICH TYPE IS THE MOST EFFECTIVE?

The Case for Participative Management

Over the past two decades, most management literature and most management development programs have reflected a strong advocacy of the participative type of managerial leadership. Ever since the Hawthorne Experiments suggested that authoritarian order-giving might not be the most productive way to manage, many of the most influential writers on management have promoted participative management under various labels, each with a slightly different terminology and slightly different emphasis.

One of the best-known writers calls it "Theory Y," based on the assumption that people want to work, want to be creative, want to participate in making decisions that affect their working lives, and want to carry some responsibility for the results of their ideas. Theory Y is contrasted with older-style management, characterized as "Theory X," based on the assumption that people basically do not want to work, have to be monitored and disciplined in order to get work done, and do not want to be burdened with decision making or creativity or the responsibility that goes with them.[1]

Another leading writer calls his approach "System 4," in which managers are "supportive" of their subordinates—that is, they show interest in subordinates' ideas, personal problems, and problems at work.[2] The manager helps them in many ways, especially in developing their capabilities, and is the "linking pin" between the group and others in the organization, especially higher management. This manager helps subordinates by representing their interest to higher management. Under System 4, subordinates participate in the generation of new ideas and the setting of goals. This same writer admits that in some situations autocratic managers may achieve higher productivity; however, he contends that in the long run autocratic methods will drive the more creative, intelligent, and highly motivated workers out of the organization, with resulting lower productivity. Accordingly, he urges managers to measure the "intervening variables," those indicators (such as turnover, absenteeism, and poor morale) which reflect growing alienation on the part of the more competent employees. This advocacy of System 4 type leadership is based on a large body of research spanning many years and many types of business and nonbusiness organizations. The research sought to establish the differences between the characteristics of supervisors in high-producing departments and those of others in low-producing departments in the same firm. The data have shown better long-run productivity for System 4. Others closely associated with this research have reported dramatic productivity improvements in a firm after it was acquired by another firm in which System 4 had long been established.[3]

MBO and Participative Management A writer who has had extensive experience with MBO states that MBO has been applied without participation but that such top-down applications do not have the developmental and humanistic benefits of MBO which is tied to participative management.[4] Participative-style MBO entails two-way communications between superior and subordinate at every organizational level in setting objectives, identifying the achievement expected from each person and unit, and appraising actual results. MBO emphasizes discipline—as some other participative approaches do not—in the sense of expectations of excellence in performance. Thus, at one point, Drucker writes:

> For leadership is not magnetic personality—that can just as well be demagoguery. It is not "making friends and influencing people"—that is salesmanship. Leadership is the lifting of man's vision to higher sights, the raising of a man's performance to a higher standard, the building of a man's personality beyond its normal limitations. Nothing better prepares the ground for such leadership than a spirit of management that confirms in the day-to-day practices of the organization strict principles of conduct and responsibility, high standards of performance, and respect for the individual and his work.[5]

Many firms report improvements in return on investment and productivity after conversion to an MBO pattern of management; however, it is impossible to separate the effect of participative management from the effect of the other elements of MBO.

Two authors whose ideas have been widely used in executive development programs describe types of managers by use of the "managerial grid," a two-dimensional grid with "concern for people" on one axis and "concern for production" on the other.[6] Descriptive scales run from a low score of 1 to a high score of 9, so the ideal type is a "9,9" who has high concern both for people and for production (which is also the MBO ideal). Such a manager achieves high work accomplishment from committed subordinates who have a "common stake" in organization purpose. The superior/subordinate relationship is one of trust and respect.

Summary   The authorities whose ideas have been reviewed in the foregoing paragraphs and many other writers agree generally on recommending a style of managerial leadership that is humanistic, affords its employees security, is employee-supportive, and is strong on two-way communications. Also, they stress management development and the obligation of every manager to further the development of subordinates. And most of them advocate some degree of participation by subordinates in decision making, though there are differences among them as to how much participation, at what levels, and on what types of decision making. And, of course, there are success cases such as IBM, which reportedly has most of these features plus excellent work on job enlargement but not even a hint of "participatory democracy."[7] And there is the case of the Japanese-owned and managed firms in the United States that secure greater productivity than do American-managed firms in the United States making the same product in the same way. The difference has been attributed to a more humanistic attitude on the part of the Japanese managers, who show great interest in their subordinates as individuals and as workers.[8] Whether or not this amounts to participation in decision making is hard to say; while there is good two-way communications on any and all subjects at all levels, there is little explicit participation. In fact, the entire Japanese decision process is not very explicit.

Despite these difficulties in saying precisely what constitutes participative management and precisely what results it produces, there is still a strong trend in the direction of participative management. This trend is based not only on results achieved but also on strong support found in some theories of motivation, which will be examined in the next section.

Motivation Theory Supporting Participative Management

The widely accepted "hierarchy of needs" theory holds that workers who do not have the necessities of life are chiefly motivated by the need for food, clothing, shelter, and basic security but that workers who have such necessities are motivated by higher-type needs such as the need for belonging and the need for recognition of achievement. At the highest level is the need for "self-actualization," which is realized through such growth experiences as being responsible for one's own activities, being creative, and participating in decisions that shape the organization's goals and programs.[9]

Another widely heralded theory holds that workers have two kinds of needs that affect motivation in different ways.[10] The first group of needs is called environmental or hygiene factors; these comprise such matters as decent working conditions, adequate pay and security provisions, and reasonably pleasant and competent supervisors and higher-level managers. Workers take these factors for granted; though not positively motivated by their presence, they are negatively motivated by their absence. The second group of needs comprises factors similar to those in the highest levels in the hierarchy-of-needs theory, that is, achievement, challenging work, and the opportunity to grow professionally and psychologically and to take responsibility for one's own ideas. These are the positive motivating factors. Proponents of this theory recommend "job enlargement" to give workers and lower-level managers more chance to participate in determining how jobs shall be done as well as to make the jobs less boring.

Another writer on motivation has done a great deal of work measuring differences in different persons' needs for achievement, belonging, and recognition.[11] Some individuals have strong achievement drives, and such persons are most effective in situations in which they have some say in decision making and have some responsibility for results achieved. They are best suited for either high-achieving large firms or for small firms in which they can be the dominant personality.

Another influential behavioral scientist emphasizes the individual's need for psychological growth and maturation, or "self-actualization," in his or her working life; he sees the manager's job as making work meaningful for subordinates and at the same time accomplishing the organization's goals. He feels that a manager must understand the individual worker's needs, must be discerning in the selection and placement of workers in jobs, and must design jobs that achieve congruency of the individual's goals and the organization's goals.[12]

Clearly, there is a large area of agreement among these theories of motivation, and they all support the concept of participative leadership. Also, the 1960s were especially conducive to participative management; it was an era of high prosperity when lower-level needs and hygiene factors were generally being satisfied and when more people were acquiring more education than ever before in any nation.

The Case against Participative Leadership as the Ideal Type

Despite the trend toward participative leadership, many observers have serious reservations about it. However, because executives and consultants like to talk and write about their successes and not about their failures, there is much less documentation of the failures than of the successes of participative management. Nevertheless, there is a growing literature relating unsuccessful attempts to practice participative management and reporting research indicating that it does not always achieve high productivity.[13]

Perhaps the most frequent and best-documented error has been the attempt to teach participative management techniques in executive development programs both at universities and in companies. It has been found that often managers who, upon returning to their jobs, attempt to apply what they have been taught run into great difficulties.[14] Often they simply give up, returning to old patterns of working with subordinates; sometimes they become greatly frustrated and get into deep trouble with their superiors. In such situations, the established organizational climate, or character, is simply not prepared for the change in leadership methods; the resistance to change is strong, and there are good reasons why it is so.

Many other executives have learned this harsh lesson in another way. Sometimes, after reading a book or hearing a speech about the glories of participative management, executives have tried to convert overnight. They fail to realize that a powerful organizational climate, or character, has built up over many years of a different style of leadership, and mostly persons amenable to the old type of leadership have stayed with the organization. These are the very persons who are most frightened by a major change, especially one that demands that they show initiative and creativeness and assume some responsibility. On the other hand, most of the persons who would accept participative leadership and would grow with it have long since left the organization. For these reasons, then, sudden conversions to participative management are often quite unsuccessful. It may take years of careful effort to effect such a change without tearing an organization apart. The executives who do not realize this may decide that participative management does not work after all—that it is just a dream of crackpot professors—and go back to their previous way of working with their subordinates.

Good Idea, Wrong Person Sometimes the individual who attempts to use participation-type methods simply is the wrong personality for the technique. He or she has neither patience nor basic faith in the ability of subordinates; he or she may be psychologically so compelled to dominate that any attempt to solicit others' ideas will be insincere and will appear insincere. Such executives would probably be better accepted if they acted naturally rather than attempting to play a role which does not suit them.

Still other executives consciously take a manipulative, or "let 'em have my way" approach. This is a dangerous role, however, because it is a hard one to play well; if the subordinates realize that they are being manipulated, they may resent it greatly.[15]

Finally, some managers attempting the participative leadership style have used poor judgment about where and when to apply it. Some have sought participation on matters far beyond the subordinates' technical competence or on matters on which they have inadequate information. Others have sought participation on matters that are for all practical purposes already decided. If, for example, competitive conditions force a firm to install new methods or new equipment, it makes little sense to ask subordinates to discuss whether or not the firm should install such new methods or equipment. It might make sense, however, to discuss with them how the firm should go about effecting the change—the time schedule, who is given what assignments, and other topics on which the manager is truly free to use good ideas coming from the group.

The NLS, Inc., Story One of the most widely heralded successes of participative management was at Non-Linear Systems, Inc. (NLS), a 230-employee electronics company, which subsequently ran into difficulties and reverted to more traditional patterns of management.[16] During the 1960s, this company followed the guidance of a group of consulting behavioral scientists[17] by eliminating the assembly line, eliminating time cards, having work teams of six or seven workers free to organize themselves in whatever way they thought would be most effective, and having departments so autonomous that they kept their own financial records. Sensitivity training was used extensively to help workers and managers alike resolve their hangups so they could work together harmoniously. For a number of years these methods appeared to succeed—production jumped 30 percent, complaints on product quality dropped by 70 percent, and the company expanded and prospered.

But the aerospace slump of 1970 hit NLS's customers hard, and orders dropped off sharply; unfortunately, NLS was slow to react. Inventories mounted, and profits changed to losses. What was to blame for the slow reaction? Some observers feel that top management was so preoccupied with developing new theories of management that they failed to see the trouble coming in time; others feel that the essential controls were lacking; still others feel that the top managers were so friendly with their subordinate managers and workers that they could not bring themselves to take the harsh actions needed. Some observers blame the top executive; they say he was warned in time and urged to make the necessary cuts but simply refused to do so. Thus, while some feel that the participative methods were to blame, these latter observers disagree. Whatever the true explanation, the company has reverted to traditional budgetary controls with corporate management keeping close tabs on the department heads; also, assembly-line production techniques have been restored for some work. And after drastic cutbacks, the company has regained profitability.

Many scholars working on managerial leadership have been troubled by the fact that it has been difficult in research studies to say to what extent money rather than supervisory technique was the motivating factor; this problem arises because in most real-life situations higher productivity by workers is rewarded by higher pay. In order to cope with this problem, one research study of participative versus nonparticipative types of supervision has been conducted in a government agency where regulations forbade direct rewards for productivity. The study concludes that participative leadership has no discernible effect upon productivity.[18]

Research on Leadership and Productivity In a 1965 publication, a group of four social scientists, thoroughly experienced in industrial research, systematically reviewed all the then available evidence on the relationship between leadership methods at the first level of supervision and productivity.[19] They came to the following conclusions: (1) Many factors—technology, investment, materials, physical plant and layout, and the units and variety in which the product is marketed—as well as leadership methods influence productivity. (2) It is difficult to relate productivity changes to any one of these factors because in real-world situations it is virtually impossible to hold one factor constant while varying a single factor—here, supervisory methods. So there is little hard evidence upon which to base conclusions about the effect of supervision on productivity. (3) High morale, or worker happiness, does not always bring productivity. (4) In manufacturing (to say nothing of service and trade businesses), there are at least three different types of operations—unit, mass, and continuous flow (automated)—and it appears that different styles of supervisory leadership at the first level are required by each. The more a production process resembles unit (or custom) technology, the more skilled the workers are and the more appropriate is a type of supervision that allows some individual judgment and participation. The more it resembles mass production, the less skilled are the workers and the more the situation is dominated by the mechanics and speed of the line; here close supervision is more appropriate. Automated production involves few first-line workers, and they are usually highly trained, versatile, and self-reliant; a collegial-type relationship is thus more appropriate. This finding makes a direct tie with Joan Woodward's work, discussed in Chapter 6, which led to a contingency theory of organization structure.[20] (5) Even when the appropriate style is well applied to a particular situation, the amount of influence that supervision can have on productivity ranges from almost zero (where assembly-line speed dominates) to no more than 20 percent. Authors speculate, but cannot prove, that leadership styles may have greater productivity effects in higher management levels than in first-line supervision, that middle- and higher-level managers are the types of persons who desire a chance to participate and who have more ideas to contribute.

A later review of many relevant research studies came to a similar *situational* conclusion: Supportive, or people-centered, supervision makes for productivity under certain conditions—where decisions are not routine in nature, the information required for effective decision making cannot be standardized or centralized, decisions need not be made rapidly, and the subordinates feel a strong need for independence and see themselves as competent to contribute to decision making and are willing to do so.[21]

Later still, two scholars reviewed many research studies on this subject, including a number done by themselves and their associates. They stated flatly that "the empirical evidence generally has failed to support" McGregor's contention that Theory Y organizations and supervisors develop a work environment which maximizes human performance. While granting that there is some evidence supporting the principles of participative management as espoused by Likert, they find that "the benefits of this approach . . . are neither inevitable nor universal." They go on to state and support the contingency theory of leadership.[22]

Other writers have concluded that collegial-type leadership is most appropriate to research and intellectual-effort organizations.[23] Still another writer sees different types of leadership needed in crisis-oriented (such as the military, fire, and police departments), routine-oriented (typical bureaucracies), and knowledge-oriented (universities) organizations.[24]

A Second Look at Motivation Theory

If, as noted earlier, participative management appears to be firmly supported by leading motivation theorists, what can be said about these contingency approaches to leadership which contend that sometimes participative leadership is best but sometimes other types of leadership are best? Are the contingency approaches and motivation theory incompatible?

Perhaps the key question about the motivation of people at work is not the one usually asked: Why do people work? A more relevant question here is: Why do some free people work for low-paying or highly bureaucratic or highly autocratic organizations, especially in times of prosperity and labor shortages?

The very phrasing of the question in this way brings to mind the big, inescapable fact that many millions of persons elect to work for long spans of years in highly bureaucratic government offices, in relatively low-paying department stores, in banks, and in hundreds of businesses, utilities, universities, and social agencies that are neither high paying nor particularly participative in their management methods. What motivates these individuals to join and to stay with their particular organizations? Although inertia, convenience, or pension-plan provisions may explain some cases, certainly there are many other motivations. In some cases it is the challenge of technically demanding work or the pride of being associated with a leader who is technologically outstanding, while in others it is the nonchallenging nature of the work. Sometimes it is the opportunity for individual recognition and rapid advancement, and at other times it is the lack of challenge and the security of a highly bureaucratic situation. Sometimes it is the convenience of the work location or the pleasantness of the work, but in other instances it is the desire to do socially significant work, as in the case of social workers who will travel daily far from their homes to work hard in the most squalid sections of town. Some workers want to self-actualize, but to others the freedom to be creative is a burden.[25]

The conclusion is inescapable that there are all kinds of people, motivationally speaking. Some persons behave exactly according to the hierarchy-of-needs theory, but some do not. Some persons are motivated by the positive motivators, but others are indifferent to them. Still other persons are not particularly disposed in any one direction but are quite capable of adjusting, within limits, to any one or a few of the wide variety of motivating factors.[26]

Fortunately, there are also many different types of work situations to use the many different kinds of people.

Conclusions: A Situational, or Contingency, Theory of Leadership

1 *There is no one most effective type of managerial leadership.* Rather, the type that is most effective varies from situation to situation; it is *contingent* upon various factors in the situation. So, just as in connection with theory on organization structure, a *contingency theory* prevails today in managerial leadership.

2 *A number of factors should be considered in applying contingency theory to a given situation.* Both sides of the equation are difficult. On the leader side, defining types of managers requires categorizing human beings, which is not an easy task. On the other side, defining types of situations requires a level of diagnostic ability that is not common among managers in either business or government. The nature of the organization structure must be categorized; so also must the nature of the work processes. So, also, must the chief characteristics of the subordinates be evaluated; here one must take into account the history of the organization, especially what kind of leadership it has had in the past and how this has affected what kinds of subordinates have stayed and what kinds have left.

One writer who has devoted a great deal of effort to this problem is Fred E. Fiedler, whose "contingency model" provides fairly concrete guidance. He has developed a testing instrument that distinguishes those managers who are "task oriented" (more directive, structuring, goal oriented, efficiency oriented) from those who are "relations oriented" (more considerate, more concerned with human relations, more participative). He has defined eight types of situations based on combinations and degrees of the following three factors:

a *Leader-member relations,* whether the leader is accepted by the group (for whatever reasons) and whether or not the relationship is warm, friendly.

 b *Task structure,* whether the task requirements are spelled out so that the supervisor is in a strong position to give instructions, evaluate performance and exert control, and, conversely, where routine operations allow little room for creativity.
 c *Position power,* the degree to which the supervisor can hire, fire, instruct, etc.

At one extreme of Fiedler's eight types is the situation in which leader-member relations are good, task is quite structured, and the leader position has strong power. Thus, all factors are rated high. At the other extreme is the situation in which all factors are rated low: member relations are poor, the task is quite unstructured, and the leader position has weak power. The middle six types are situations in which the factors are neither all high nor all low but are mixed; in these more ambiguous situations there is room for consultation and creativity. Fiedler's finding is that the task-oriented leader is most effective in the two extreme situations and the relations-oriented leader is most effective in the middle-type situations.[27]

Fiedler's work appears most applicable at the lower managerial levels, where differences in the nature of tasks and workplace structure can best be defined and measured. His concepts and terminology require adaptation for use at higher managerial levels.

3 *Organizations have "characters," or "climates."* To say (as we just have), that what type of leadership is appropriate in a given situation is a function of a number of factors, is also to say that organizations develop characters, or climates, that vitally affect what results are achieved by a given managerial action. The understanding of these characters and their effects is a relatively new subject in management literature and one that will be considered in some detail later in this book.

4 *Parts of an organization may, and perhaps should, have different types of leaders.* In the chapter on organization structure, it was noted that some firms now structure the innovative parts of the company (usually the R&D and/or new-ventures sections) differently from the steady-state parts of the company (usually the established production or established selling sections). It follows that these different parts of a single organization probably need different types of managerial leadership too. Accordingly, it is incumbent upon higher-level managers to respect and work with managers with various leadership styles.

5 *Sound reasons underlie the trend toward more participative-consultative patterns of managerial leadership, yet it is often not effective.* The trend makes sense in view of the rising level of expectations of democratic treatment in all walks of life and in view of the increasing need to manage rapid change. Nevertheless, there still are many situations in which participative-consultative management is *not* the most effective style; further, there have been many misapplications of this style in situations in which it might have been appropriate.

6   *Participative-consultative leadership is potentially more potent in managerial levels than at the worker level.* Much research, writing, and discussion on participative leadership concentrates on its feasibility or infeasibility at the first-line supervisor level. Yet it is the managers, from vice president down through so-called middle management, who are most likely to have ideas for making important changes. It is these managers who are most likely to be utterly frustrated by a top executive who, often despite much talk to the contrary, really listens to no one. And in bureaucratically led organizations, it is the managers who are most likely to be frustrated by the operation of the "Peter Principle," whereby persons are promoted to their level of incompetence and remain there forever.

Note the repeated use of "most likely" in the foregoing paragraph. Certainly not all persons in middle and upper managerial ranks are well-suited to being managed in a participative style.

CAN EFFECTIVE MANAGERIAL LEADERS BE DEVELOPED? HOW GOOD ARE EXECUTIVE DEVELOPMENT AND ORGANIZATIONAL DEVELOPMENT PROGRAMS?

How effective have the great variety of executive development programs tried since World War II been? Have the university programs for mature executives, or the in-company programs, or the government-sponsored programs actually succeeded in making more effective managers of the participants?

The great difficulty of measuring the results achieved by these programs is readily apparent in view of the conclusion that we have just reached about the nature of managerial leadership. Thus, if there is indeed no one best type, training programs cannot be evaluated on how well they convey a certain type of leadership. If the effectiveness of leadership is contingent upon situational factors, then the programs can give only generalized techniques (such as the problem analysis technique that the universities using case method teach). The only meaningful measure of results, then, is a comparison of the person's effectiveness on the job before and after taking the training. But how can this be measured when there is no way of isolating what part of Mr. or Ms. X's performance is due to the fact that he or she attended the thirteen-week Advanced Management Program at Harvard or the two-year part-time Executive Program at UCLA? Or how can the change in a company's or a department's performance results be attributed to the fact that certain executives have been participating in an in-company management development program? How can one influence be isolated from all the other things happening in the economy, the industry, and the company at the same time? Obviously it cannot be done. Attempts have been made to measure results by gathering expert opinions about what changes have taken place in individual managers and companies as a result of on-campus programs,[28] by measuring the changes in the participants' thinking,[29] and by measuring the extent to which the conditions necessary for change are achieved by a given program.[30] Despite these rigorous efforts, however, the judgments are still far from objective, far from convincing. This is *not* to say that the programs have no value; it is to say that the value cannot be proved.

Many of the early management development programs for mature executives discussed the various types of leadership and provided supervised practice in communications, especially "the art of listening," to help a manager understand subordinates' needs and problems better. Communications of other types—group discussion leading, opinion polling, and writing—were also taught. Programs of this kind typically were heavily slanted in favor of participative-consultative leadership. But in time it was realized that this is not always the type of leadership needed; in fact, it was realized that sometimes the training did more harm than good because the trainee-manager got caught in a clash between what was taught in the classroom and how superiors actually worked and actually wanted the trainee to work. Strangely, despite the fact that these programs usually enjoyed the blessing of the chief executive of the organization, that individual's own methods were often in sharp disagreement with what was being taught.

Nonclassroom-Type Training   Another type of executive development program, variously called "multiple management," "junior boards," or "bottom-up management," avoids the classroom versus reality clash by not having classes. Instead, in these programs, selected manager-trainees are put on special project teams, or syndicates, assigned to recommend solutions to real, here-and-now, this-company problems. Since the assigned problems are beyond the scope of the trainees' regular jobs, such assignments widen a manager's experience and give him or her a chance to be seen and heard by top managers. It also gives the manager a chance to be criticized by the other trainees. Even more important is the fact that the organization encourages its junior executives to make recommendations that often imply criticism of the status quo. However, few organizations are ready for such criticism; classroom lectures or classroom discussions of published cases (about other organizations) are much less disturbing.

Another form of management development that gets away from the classroom situation and into real problems is so-called organizational development (OD), which was discussed in Chapter 6 as a means of identifying and working out organization structure problems. As a matter of fact, OD's greater use is in identifying, confronting, and working out interpersonal problems that are blockages to effective working together by superior and subordinate or by peers in an organization.

OD specialists, who often refer to themselves as "intervention agents," use a variety of methods to get a firm's managers to look critically at what is happening as they go about their usual managerial processes, that is, what is making for more effective managerial teamwork and what is blocking effective managerial teamwork. One method is to take an anonymous opinion poll on a variety of topics among the persons involved and let the analysis take off from there. Another method is to run through a managerial grid exercise, classifying the managers described in published materials and then shifting the discussion to the real in-company situation. Still another method is to have the participants describe the most effective and the least effective organizations they have ever worked in by checking off items on a list (such as the one illustrated in Figure 7–2) of examples of executive behavior. After discuss-

Organizational variable

e. Amount of responsibility felt by each member of organization for achieving organization's goals	Personnel at all levels feel real responsibility for organization's goals and behave in ways to implement them	Substantial proportion of personnel, especially at higher levels, feel responsibility and generally behave in ways to achieve the organization's goals	Managerial personnel usually feel responsibility; rank and file usually feel relatively little responsibility for achieving organization's goals	High levels of management feel responsibility; lower levels feel less; rank and file feel little and often welcome opportunity to behave in ways to defeat organization's goals	10
f. Attitudes toward other members of the organization	Favorable, cooperative attitudes throughout the organization with mutual trust and confidence	Cooperative, reasonably favorable attitudes toward others in organization; may be some competition between peers with resulting hostility and some condescension toward subordinates	Subservient attitudes toward superiors; competition for status resulting in hostility toward peers; condescension toward subordinates	Subservient attitudes toward superiors coupled with hostility; hostility toward peers and contempt for subordinates; distrust is widespread	11
g. Satisfaction derived	Relatively high satisfaction throughout the organization with regard to membership in the organization, supervision, and one's own achievements	Some dissatisfaction to moderately high satisfaction with regard to membership in the organization, supervision, and one's own achievements	Dissatisfaction to moderate satisfaction with regard to membership in the organization, supervision, and one's own achievements	Usually dissatisfaction with membership in the organization, with supervision, and with one's own achievements	12
3. Character of communication process					
a. Amount of interaction and communication aimed at achieving organization's objectives	Very little	Little	Quite a bit	Much with both individuals and groups	13
b. Direction of information flow	Downward	Mostly downward	Down and up	Down, up, and with peers	14
c. Downward communication					
(1) Where initiated	Initiated at all levels	Patterned on communication from top but with some initiative at lower levels	Primarily at top or patterned on communication from top	At top of organization or to implement top directive	15
(2) Extent to which superiors willingly share information with subordinates	Provide minimum of information	Gives subordinates only information superior feels they need	Gives information needed and answers most questions	Seeks to give subordinates all relevant information and all information they want	16

Figure 7-2 Sample page from profile of organizational characteristics. [From Rensis Likert, *The Human Organization* (McGraw-Hill Book Company, New York, 1967), pp. 200–201.]

ing what the manager-trainees have marked on these scales, the discussion can be turned to how their own practices agree with or deviate from what they have marked; or anonymous slips can be used to turn the discussion to real but undesignated persons in the organization. Sometimes sensitivity-group training is used to bring out the here-and-now problems. Sometimes the trainee-managers take on special assignments much in the manner of "multiple management" or "junior board" groups. One OD group is reported to have successfully handled the touchy problem of how to go about making a 15 percent reduction in work force.[31]

Whatever the particular starting device, the group in time takes on certain of the organization's real problems. As it works on a problem, one or two members are temporarily detached to serve as "process observers" to note what is happening, what actions build or impede effective teamwork, what actions build or destroy trust of one person or group by another, or what conditions encourage or discourage open communications. Sometimes it is possible to dispense with group meetings, special problems, and process observers altogether. It is then sufficient for the intervention agent to move about the company, hearing whatever organizational problems or ideas anyone cares to bring up, and to get the persons concerned to confront and solve the problems.[32]

Values of Nonclassroom Programs   The great strength of OD and the other types of problem-solving in-company programs is that they can concentrate on discovering and developing managerial practices that are effective in that particular situation. As Lawrence and Lorsch, whose research contributed so much to contingency theory, have predicted:

> . . . managements will rely increasingly on formally designated organizational development departments. These departments, staffed by trained specialists in the behavioral and administrative sciences, will be involved in planning new organizational forms for the effective utilization of human resources and in training managers to operate effectively in these settings.[33]

Another great advantage of these programs is that they can bring about change in the total situation instead of working on individuals detached from their real work situations. It is much easier for an individual to change when others know what the goal is and are sympathetic to those ideas. At the very least, these programs avoid the devastating inconsistency between what is taught in the classroom and what is actually practiced by the organization's managers.

These are the main reasons why the question "Can managerial leaders be developed?" is answered "Yes, and it is best done when the total situation is sympathetic to confrontation of its problems and receptive to change; also, when the program is more applied than academic." Clearly, some persons can never be made effective managerial leaders of any type; just as clearly, some persons are "naturals" (of one type or another) who need no training. But probably most managers and most managerial groups can benefit by periodically or regularly stepping back to reassess their tactics and internal relations.[34]

COMMUNICATION AND LEADERSHIP

The subject of communications has popped up at many points in this chapter; it is a key element in managerial leadership.

The aspect of communications that is usually stressed in management and organization development programs is interpersonal communications, or "The Fateful Process of Mr. A Talking to Mr. B."[35] It is called "fateful" because the failure of many individuals to understand one another fully lies at the root of much distrust, destructive rivalry, and frustration in managerial life. A and B fail to understand one another because one or both of them is (are) poor at the art of listening; also, one or both of them probably does (do) not know enough psychology to appreciate the great difficulties of one person accurately conveying feelings and thoughts to another person. In consequence of these difficulties, management training programs use role playing to teach problem solving and grievance drainage and sensitivity training to teach effective interpersonal communications. The impact of these techniques can be heightened by use of videotape playbacks that enable an individual to critique personal performance. These techniques are often supplemented by some fairly simple psychology concepts that are useful in understanding people's communications and reactions.

Another key aspect of communications in management is getting a message through the levels of management—another perilous process. What makes it so difficult is that each step in the hierarchical structure presents dangers of blockage, filtering, editing, and distortion. In fact, so strong is the tendency among managers to tell the boss only good news that sometimes what started out at a lower level as a complaint ends up at the top level so edited that it has become a compliment. And it has been proved many times over that people are simply incapable of passing a word accurately, by mouth, through a number of steps even when they have no incentive to distort or edit it. To combat these communications problems, some management training programs give training in grapevine (or rumor) analysis, in communicating around the channels as well as through them, in methods of conducting and using opinion polls, and in conducting group meetings. One large company has set up special communications channels and special communications experts to provide its employees with the opportunity to communicate effectively with upper-level executives.[36]

In government, the problem of getting a written report through the hierarchy is severe, not only because there are usually many levels but also because there is a premium on caution. At each level in the transmission, the government manager is tempted to demonstrate alertness by adding some precautions to the message; rarely does anyone take responsibility for eliminating anything. Thus are government "gobbledygook" communications created.

Still another difficult type of managerial communication is that involved in securing participation by subordinates in goal setting, planning, and performance review—the very heart of the managerial job. What complicates this type of communication is the fact that such participation sometimes involves (or at least implies) criticism of superiors' past decisions; unfortunately, few managers are able to handle criticism constructively. To overcome this, management development and OD programs use many methods to build a climate conducive to constructive criticism and suggestion giving.

In sum, managerial communications is a big and meaty subject, much too big to be covered thoroughly here. There is a sizable, fascinating literature on the subject, and almost every manager can profitably spend a great deal of effort studying it.[37]

HOW WILL MANAGERIAL LEADERSHIP CHANGE UNDER SYSTEMS MANAGEMENT?

This section is concerned *not* with the leadership problems involved in an organization's *transition to systems management,* formidable though those problems may be,[38] but with what changes will occur in the theory and practice of managerial leadership as the systems management concept comes into reasonably full use.

The contingency theory of leadership is entirely consistent with systems management theory. Thus systems management embodies the idea that everything is related to everything else, and contingency theory stresses that many factors interact to determine the type of leadership appropriate in a given situation. Further, systems management pays prime attention to environmental influences on the organization, and contingency theory includes environmental factors as among those to be considered in deciding what type of leadership will probably be most effective.

Despite this theoretical compatibility, however, there are many practical matters to be worked out before it will be clear just what managerial leadership will be like in the systems management era. Perhaps a useful way to review these matters and to indicate how speculative they are at present is to consider two alternative scenarios of what may have come to pass by 1985 or 1990.

Scenario 1

Computers will prove so powerful, via efficiency in operations and improvement in decision-making techniques, that data technology specialists (systems designers) will become dominant. They will design the information systems and the decision tools upon which top management depends; they will design the information systems, the project structures, and the procedures used by the operating sections of the organization.

Because systems design is a complex, highly technical field, only the few experts will be able to participate in systems design decisions. True, top executives will still make the major entrepreneurial decisions (about, for example, which fields to invest in and which to leave); however, these decisions will often be made with the aid of quantitative decision tools that the top executives use but do not fully understand.

At the middle levels, managers will have to take on faith the data, structures, and procedures given them. Few will be the opportunities for middle- and lower-level managers, lacking expertise in systems design, to participate in any significant decision making.

Operating units, typically project structures, will be fully integrated operations. Departmentalization as it is now known will have disappeared; work will move in an integrated flow rather than from department to department. Decision criteria will optimize (by focusing on the overall organizational objectives) rather than suboptimize (by focusing on departmental objectives, some of which may be in conflict with overall objectives). The results produced by lower-level managers along the line of work flow will not be identifiable or measurable. Accordingly, only the top managers for projects can be held accountable for results, and their responsibility will be diluted by the fact that they are operating a system designed by others. Thus, MBO, with its appraisal-by-results feature, will be workable, if at all, no lower than at the project-manager level.

Because complex information systems and automated operations are so expensive to design and build, there will be pressure to move ahead rapidly without fitting them to the people involved; rather the people—what few of them there will be—will be selected for compatibility with the automated technical system. Also, the great cost of changing such systems will bring resistance to change once a system has operated successfully. Paradoxically, although the coming era is seen as an era of rapid change, it will also be an era of inflexible, massive computerized systems.

In sum, technology specialists known as systems designers will dominate all but the very top level of management, and they will have considerable influence at that level, too. Managers at other levels will have little responsibility and little chance to participate in decision making. Established systems may show strong resistance to change. The form of leadership used will, perhaps, be called *technological bureaucracy*—impersonal, relatively rigid, based on expertise in information technology and automated equipment.

Scenario 2

Professional managers will have long since learned that a system (manufacturing, infor- mation, or other type of operation) can be designed by the finest engineers yet fail because it has neglected human factors. In fact, managers will have become so profes- sional that they will view an organization as a social system as well as an information system, a technical system, and an economic system. They will know that, for example, every feature designed into the technical system may affect the social system by affect- ing the type of workers needed, the type of leadership required by those workers, the type of training needed by those workers, or any of many other aspects of the social system. They will think in terms of human/machine systems rather than machine sys- tems; they will balance concern for human values with concern for production.

Top-level professional managers, now truly generalists, will, through OD proce- dures, diagnose each situation (the personalities of key executives, the demands of the technology, the types of workers required, etc.) to decide what instructions to give the systems designers. In some cases they will order a highly centralized decision-making system that offers little opportunity for participative patterns of management; in other cases they will order just the opposite or something in between.

The important point is that the higher-level executives will have sufficient under- standing of information technology and quantitative decision techniques to be able to direct the systems designers intelligently rather than be somewhat mystified by the complexities of systems analysis and systems design.

Middle- and lower-level managers will be freed of most of the detailed supervising of operations because operations will be automated; nonmanagerial technicians will maintain the operations. The managers will also be largely freed from data gathering and interpretation, because data will be gathered automatically and processed into just the form they need. They will be freed from having to pass data to superiors and subordinates, since each manager will receive the data that is needed. Thus, these managers will have time to plan improvements, time to be creative, time to coach their subordinates, time to work on improving organizational effectiveness.

Information technology will have advanced to the point where changes can be made readily in established systems. Thus, when managers at any level work out a desirable change, systems specialists can implement that change, at reasonable cost and without disrupting the total system. Also, as projects change from stage to stage, information systems can be readily adjusted.

Those systems that have been designed for delegation of substantial decision-making authority to lower levels and to encourage participative management will also provide organizational units (job structures and work flow) that make possible allocation of responsibility for the decisions made. Thus the appraisal-by-results features of MBO will be feasible at a number of managerial levels. In sum, managerial leadership will be *situationally effective,* the type of leadership being contingent upon the situational factors. There will be increasing use of participative styles, but other styles will be used too. Information technology specialists will serve managers rather than dominate them.

Significance of the Scenarios   If actual events follow Scenario 1, there will be a rebirth of the scientific management era, when technical rationality overpowered human considerations. If, however, actual events follow more along the lines of Scenario 2, the manager or administrator will be a generalist who integrates technical, informational, social, and economic systems into an effective organization.

IS MANAGERIAL LEADERSHIP DIFFERENT IN GOVERNMENT?

Only occasionally in this chapter have distinctions been drawn between leadership practices in private versus government organizations; rather, it has been assumed that the subject is essentially similar in the two fields. Perhaps that assumption should be probed a bit before this chapter on managerial leadership is concluded.

Some textbooks on public administration do indeed treat the subject much as it is treated in business literature; they cite the same writers, they note the same types of managerial leadership, they see the same trend toward more participative-consultative leadership, and they, too, conclude that a situational-contingency theory of leadership is most appropriate.[39] And there is, as noted in the chapter on organization structuring, a group of aggressive and impressive government-oriented writers proclaiming the theme "Democracy is inevitable." Their main argument is that traditional bureaucracy is too change-resistant, too slow-moving for today's pace of change.[40]

Some writers claim good results for participative methods in the U.S. Department of State,[41] and others claim successful adaptation of MBO to federal departments. However, there are, in total, few claims made that participative-consultative types of management are being practiced in public administration. The problem is not in the communications aspects of participative management; typically there is much communication. The problem is in being able to use innovative suggestions and in being able to delegate meaningful responsibility down the line. Perhaps a realistic evaluation of the extent to which newer forms of leadership are used in government is given by the author of a 400-page book describing the contributions to management of the federal government's managers. It gives only one-third of a page to the subject of managerial leadership, mentioning that the Department of Defense has made constructive criticisms of the leadership practices of some defense contracting firms.[42]

Is Participation Really Coming?

Among the numerous writers who are *not* sanguine about the prospects of participative leadership in public administration, one points out that the founders of public administration were reformers bent on rectifying the disorganization, haphazardness, amateurism, and dishonesty which characterized the governmental administration of their times. The antidote lay in an emphasis on centralization, hierarchy, and discipline as means to the central administrative value of efficiency. This has led to a tradition of strict accountability of public administrators for performance according to prescribed processes and regulations—a tradition not conducive to democratic-participative methods. Accordingly, he concludes:

> . . . there is little to be found in orthodox public-administration theory or doctrine explicitly supportive of behavioral-science concepts of participative or democratic processes in internal organizational control and governance. Nor do participative concepts appear to have made substantial impact in practice, whether with or without supporting doctrine. Participative administration in the context of internal systems of organizational government can hardly be judged to be an emergent reality in the public sector.[43]

And another writer states the same conclusion in stronger terms:

> As for the mainstream of public administration, the conclusion is inescapable that we will *not* find a panacea in participative belief. We cannot drown our failures in moonshine, albeit labeled behavioral science.[44]

Other writers point out various reasons why the bureaucratic pattern perpetuates itself. Thus bureaucracies tend to attract and hold persons who are not seeking challenge and to repel those who are; also, reward is more likely to come from loyalty and service than from trying innovative ideas that run some risk of failure. Civil service regulations make it difficult to reward innovation and creativity. One textbook concludes that the task of leadership is to minimize bureaucracy; the need for entrepreneurial leadership in government is recognized, but so also are the practical limitations on such leadership.[45]

Government Situations Differ Too

This diversity of views as to what is happening and will happen in public administration leadership follows naturally from the fact that public administration is a vast field covering many kinds of enterprises, many kinds of managers, and many kinds of subordinates. There can be little doubt that the NASA managerial leadership was different from that of the typical established agency; although a collegial type leadership with tight planning and control worked in NASA, that is no justification for supposing that it would work in a metropolitan department maintaining streets and sewers or in a federal patent agency. But it appears to have worked in TVA (Tennessee Valley Authority), and it might work in a crusading type of public research agency such as the organization administering the cancer program.[46]

Public administration literature is just beginning to cope with the diversity of situations and styles of leadership. One contribution is an article that identifies four types of leaders: the innovator, the developer, the maintainer, and the figurehead.[47] The emphasis here is partly on the organization's stage of development and partly on the character of its mission. Surely it is important that in the selection of high-level public executives, some consideration be given to these factors; in other words, work on a contingency approach is needed. This classification also points up that in some public organizations, especially those newly undertaking great social change, external participation (that is, community involvement) may be as important or even more important than the kind of participation usually discussed in connection with managerial leadership (that is, internal participation by members of the staff of the organization). One study finds that federal program managers spend perhaps 60 percent of their time "applying the so-called command skills of direction, staffing, controlling, planning, and evaluating." They spend a good deal of the rest of their time trying to persuade those over whom they have no control to their viewpoints.[48] Or in the words of another writer:

> A public executive works in a milieu where he must sell every day: his superiors on needs, the legislature for the tools, his peers in other agencies on jurisdiction, his subordinates on productivity.[49]

Because of this "selling" function, part of the "endless lateral brokerage" required of government officials, some writers see managerial leadership primarily in terms of policy-deciding and support-building activities essential to the implementation of broad legislative mandates.[50] Perhaps one person cannot be expected to do both the external and internal communications and the securing of participation.

Organizational Development (OD) in Government?

As to OD and other problem-solving types of management development, again there is much interest in the literature but there are relatively few reports of actual programs. A symposium on OD in the *Public Administration Review* does report a number of programs in state and federal units.[51] In another article, a pair of authors enthusiastically endorses OD as a technique useful in public administration; however, only one actual application is cited, and that one concerned a foreign government which, in fact, tried only the first phase of an OD program and decided to go no further with it![52] Another writer laments that government agencies have *not* followed the trend toward the use of the OD approach in management development. He comments: "It is ironic that the drift in government is toward adoption of training and development systems which industry is leaving. Industry is moving away from individual development and moving into organizational development."[53]

It is especially difficult to carry out a real-problem type of management development program in a government organization. The reason is that constructive criticism from within government operations is dangerous because it can easily be picked up by press or politicians and made to appear to be a scandal or gross incompetence.

Conclusions on Managerial Leadership in Government

Sweeping generalizations about all government administrators being incurable bureaucrats are invalid; so also are claims that participative leadership is making strong gains and will inevitably be predominant in public administration. Although there are undoubtedly many inveterate bureaucrats and some others who sooner or later succumb to the numbing pressures of the more bureaucratic situations, there are others in nontypical situations who are successfully using collegial, participative, or technological patterns of leadership.[54]

It may well be, as found by one researcher, that the typical government managers, in comparison to their business counterparts, have less favorable attitudes and less commitment to their organizations.[55] Undoubtedly, as he suggests, efforts should be made to give more government managers a chance to make identifiable contributions and to receive recognition for them. For example, a number of the older, established agencies (such as the logistics sections of the various armed services and the Internal Revenue Service) have made outstanding managerial use of computers. But little is known about the managers who are responsible for these achievements or about their leadership methods.

REVIEW QUESTIONS

1 List the major types of leadership outlined in the text and identify the predominant characteristic of each.
2 In what type of situation might each of these leadership types be most appropriate or most effective?
3 What are the basic elements in the definition of leadership adopted in the chapter?
4 Why is it more difficult to carry out a "real-problem type of management development program" in a government organization than in a business organization?

DISCUSSION QUESTIONS

1 With reference to the organization with which you are, have been, or hope to be associated, what style of leadership was practiced by your immediate superior? By the chief executive? On what specific actions do you base these judgments? In each case, are these appropriate styles in the particular situation?
2 What are the advantages of conceptualizing a manager's leadership style along a continuum?
3 Do the arguments supporting participative leadership outweigh those against? How can a manager reconcile those differences in the light of conflicting research evidence?
4 Construct your own scenario about management leadership under systems management conditions, using whatever parts of this textbook's two scenarios that seem convincing to you plus whatever additional ideas you have.

NOTES

[1] Douglas McGregor, *The Human Side of Enterprise* (McGraw-Hill Book Company, New York, 1960), pp. 33–35, 45–49, and 88–89.
[2] R. Likert, *The Human Organization* (McGraw-Hill Book Company, New York, 1967), pp. 4–10.
[3] Ibid., chap. 3; also Alfred J. Marrow, David G. Bowers, and Stanley E. Seashore, *Management by Participation* (Harper & Row Publishers, Incorporated, New York, 1967).
[4] George Odiorne, "The Politics of Implementing MBO," *Business Horizons,* June 1974, pp. 14–15.
[5] Peter F. Drucker, *The Practice of Management* (Harper & Row, Publishers, Incorporated, New York, 1954), pp. 159–160.

⁶ Robert R. Blake and Jane S. Mouton, *The Managerial Grid* (Gulf Publishing Co., Houston, Tex.,1964).

⁷ Peter Drucker, *Management: Tasks, Responsibilities, Practices* (Harper & Row, Publishers, Incorporated, New York, 1974), pp. 260–265.

⁸ Richard T. Johnson and Wm. G. Ouchi, "Made in America (under Japanese Management)," *Harvard Business Review,* September–October 1974, pp. 61–69.

⁹ A. H. Maslow, *Motivation and Personality* (Harper & Row, Publishers, Incorporated, New York, 1954).

¹⁰ F. Herzberg, *Work and the Nature of Man* (The World Publishing Company, Cleveland, 1966). For a criticism of Herzberg's research methods and a questioning of the validity of the dual types of motivation rather than a uniscalar approach, see O. Behling, G. Labovitz, and R. Kosmo, "The Herzberg Controversy: A Critical Appraisal," *Academy of Management Journal,* March 1968, pp. 99–108.

¹¹ David C. McClellan, *The Achieving Society* (D. Van Nostrand Company, Princeton, N.J., 1961).

¹² Chris Argyris, *Integrating the Individual and the Organization* (John Wiley & Sons, Inc., New York, 1964) and *Management and Organizational Development* (McGraw-Hill Book Company, New York, 1971).

¹³ For two articles that relate a number of such experiences, see R. C. Albrook, "Participative Management: Time for a Second Look," *Fortune,* May 1967, pp. 166ff: and James A. Lee, "Behavioral Theory vs. Reality," *Harvard Business Review,* March–April 1971, pp. 20ff.

¹⁴ E. A. Fleishman, Edwin F. Harris, and Harold E. Burtt, *Leadership and Supervision in Industry: An Evaluation of a Supervisory Training Program,* Monograph no. 13 (Bureau of Business Research, Ohio State University, Columbus, 1955), p. 94.

¹⁵ William M. Fox, "When Human Relations May Succeed but the Company Fail," *California Management Review,* Spring 1966.

¹⁶ "Where Being Nice to Workers Didn't Work," *Business Week,* Jan. 20, 1973, pp. 98–100.

¹⁷ One glowing account of the experiments at this company was given by Abraham Maslow in *Eupsychian Management* (The Dorsey Press and Richard D. Irwin, Inc., Homewood, Ill., 1965).

¹⁸ Reed M. Powell and John L. Schlacter, "Participative Management: A Panacea?" *Journal of the Academy of Management,* June 1971, pp. 165–173.

¹⁹ R. Dubin, George Homans, Floyd Mann, and Delbert Miller, *Leadership and Productivity* (Chandler Publishing Company, San Francisco, 1965).

²⁰ Ibid., pp. 11–16.

²¹ Alan C. Filley and Robert J. House, *Managerial Process and Organizational Behavior* (Scott, Foresman and Company, Glenview, Ill., 1969), pp. 404–405.

²² Fred E. Fiedler and Martin M. Chemers, *Leadership and Effective Management* (Scott, Foresman and Company, Glenview, Ill., 1974), pp. 51 and 78–91.

²³ Keith Davis, *Human Behavior at Work,* 4th ed. (McGraw-Hill Book Company, New York, 1972), chaps. 20–25; also Warren O. Hagstrom, "Traditional and Modern Forms of Scientific Teamwork," *Administrative Sciences Quarterly,* December 1964, pp. 241–263. For a full chapter entitled "Scientists and Professionals in Organizations," which cites the two foregoing studies and many other sources, see F. Kast and J. Rosenzweig, *Organization and Management: A Systems Approach,* 2d ed. (McGraw-Hill Book Company, 1974), chap. 17.

²⁴ Waino Suojanen, "Management Theory: Functional and Evolutionary," *Journal of the Academy of Management,* March 1963, pp. 14–16, and in the same journal, "Comments," September 1964, p. 229.

²⁵ George Strauss, "The Personality versus Organization Theory," in David R. Hampton, Charles E. Summer, and Ross A. Webber (eds.), *Organizational Behavior and the Practice of Management* (Scott, Foresman and Company, Glenview, Ill., 1968), pp. 265–268. See also Robert N. McMurry, "The Case for Benevolent Autocracy," *Harvard Business Review,* January–February 1958, pp. 82–90.

²⁶ Psychologist Conrad Graves is reported as estimating that possibly less than half the population are not and never will be the type of workers envisioned in McGregor's Theory Y. Graves identifies seven personality types but warns that they are only fairly distinct and that some persons are motivationally flexible: The "autistic," which requires close care and nuturing; the "animistic," which must be dealt with by sheer force or enticement; the "ordered," that responds best to a moralistic judgment; the "materialistic," which calls for pragmatic, hard bargaining; the "sociocentric," which is motivated by a need for belonging; the "cognitive," whose need is for information; and the "apprehending," whose need is for understanding. Only the latter three types are well suited to participative techniques. See "Participative Management: Time for a Second Look," op. cit., pp. 196–197. See also Edward E. Lawler III, "The Individualized Organization: Problems and Promise," *California Management Review,* Winter 1974, pp. 31–39.

[27] Fiedler and Chemers, op. cit., especially chap. 5. Also F. E. Fiedler, "Engineer the Job to Fit the Manager," *Harvard Business Review,* September–October 1965, pp. 115–122, and *A Theory of Leadership Effectiveness* (McGraw-Hill Company, New York, 1967), p. 34. Similar analyses are presented by John J. Morse and Jay W. Lorsch in "Beyond Theory Y," *Harvard Business Review,* May–June 1970, pp. 61–68.

[28] Kenneth R. Andrews, *The Effectiveness of University Management Development Programs* (Bureau of Research, Graduate School of Business, Harvard University, 1966).

[29] Fleishman, Harris, and Burtt, op. cit.

[30] Robert J. House, *Management Development: Design, Evaluation, and Implementation* (University of Michigan Press, Ann Arbor, Mich., 1967), p. 13.

[31] "Teamwork through Conflict," *Business Week,* Mar. 20, 1971, pp. 44–48.

[32] For general reading on OD, see the following: Harold M. F. Rush, *Organizational Development: A Reconnaisance* (The Conference Board, Inc., New York, 1973); a seven-article symposium, "Organizational Development: An Overview," *Journal of Contemporary Business,* Summer 1972; M. G. Evans, "Failures in OD Program," *Business Horizons,* April 1974, pp. 23–28; and Wendell French and Cecil Bell, *Organization Development* (Prentice-Hall, Inc., Englewood Cliffs, N.J., 1973).

[33] Paul R. Lawrence and Jay W. Lorsch, *Organization and Environment* (Richard D. Irwin, Inc., Homewood, Ill., 1969), p. 238.

[34] George Strauss, "Organizational Development: Credits and Debits," *Organizational Dynamics,* Winter 1973, p. 19. While critical of and skeptical about many OD practices, Strauss comes to substantially the conclusion stated in this sentence.

[35] This title is borrowed from a classic article by Wendell Johnson, "The Fateful Process of Mr. A Talking to Mr. B," *Harvard Business Review,* January–February 1953.

[36] Bruce Harriman, "Up and Down the Communications Ladder," *Harvard Business Review,* September–October, 1974, pp. 143–151.

[37] For full textbooks on communications, see Lee O. Thayer, *Administrative Communication* (Richard D. Irwin, Inc., Homewood, Ill., 1961); and Ralph G. Nichols and Leonard A. Stevens, *Are You Listening?* (McGraw-Hill Book Company, New York, 1957). See also K. Davis, op. cit., p. 359; and Carl Rogers and F. J. Roethlisberger, "Barriers and Gateways to Communication," *Harvard Business Review,* July–August 1952, pp. 46–52.

[38] Lawrence K. Williams, "The Human Side of a Systems Change," *Systems and Procedures Journal,* July–August 1964; G. W. Dickson and John K. Simmons, "The Behavioral Side of MIS," *Business Horizons,* August 1970, pp. 59–71; E. F. Huse, "The Impact of Computerized Programs on Managers & Organizations," in C. A. Myers (ed.), *The Impact of Computers on Management* (The M.I.T. Press, Cambridge, Mass., 1967); and Robert J. Mockler, "The Systems Approach to Business Organization and Decision Making," *California Management Review,* Winter 1968, pp. 53–57.

[39] Felix A. Nigro, *Modern Public Administration,* 2d ed. (Harper & Row, Publishers, Incorporated, New York, 1970), chap. 11; also John M. Pfiffner and Robert Presthus, *Public Administration* (The Ronald Press Company, New York, 1967), pp. 90–91.

[40] Philip E. Slater and Warren G. Bennis, "Democracy Is Inevitable," *Harvard Business Review,* March–April 1964, pp. 51–59; also David S. Brown, "The High Cost of Hierarchy," *Civil Service Journal,* January–March 1967, pp. 17–22.

[41] Alfred J. Marrow, "Managerial Revolution in the State Department," *Personnel,* November–December 1966, p. 10.

[42] David S. Brown, *Federal Contributions to Management: Effects on the Public and Private Sectors* (Frederick A. Praeger, Inc., New York, 1971), p. 367.

[43] Marvin Meade, " 'Participative Administration'—Emerging Reality or Wishful Thinking?" in Dwight Waldo (ed.), *Public Administration in a Time of Turbulence* (Chandler Publishing Co., San Francisco, 1971), pp. 175–177. Meade takes the material before the quotation from Dwight Waldo, "Development of the Theory of Democratic Administration," *American Political Science Review,* March 1952, pp. 85–87.

[44] Herbert G. Wilcox, "Hierarchy, Human Nature and the Participative Panacea," *Public Administration Review,* January–February 1969, p. 62. This article is part of a symposium entitled "Alienation, Decentralization and Participation."

[45] Marshall E. Dimock and Gladys O. Dimock, *Public Administration,* 4th ed. (Holt, Rinehart and Winston, Inc., New York, 1969), p. 296.

[46] One study of this agency reveals strong desire by the workers in TVA for a participative style of leadership: Arthur A. Thompson, "Participation in Decision-Making: The TVA Experience," *Public Personnel Review,* April 1967, pp. 82–88.

[47] Sandra P. Schoenberg, "A Typology of Leadership Style in Public Organizations," in L. A. Rowe

and W. B. Boise (eds.), *Organizational and Managerial Innovation* (Goodyear Publishing Co., Inc., Pacific Palisader, Calif., 1973).

⁴⁸ J. J. Corson and R. S. Paul, *Men Near the Top: Filling Key Posts in the Federal Service* (John Hopkins Press, Baltimore, 1966), p. 43.

⁴⁹ Barry Passet, *Leadership Development for Public Service* (Gulf Publishing Company, Houston, Tex., 1971), p. 6.

⁵⁰ See, for example, the selection of articles in chaps. 4 and 5 of Louis C. Gawthrop (ed.), *The Administrative Process and Democratic Theory* (Houghton Mifflin Company, Boston, 1970).

⁵¹ In the March–April 1974 issue.

⁵² Samuel A. Culbert and Jerome Reisel, "Organization Development: An Applied Philosophy for Managers of Public Enterprise," *Public Administration Review,* March–April 1971, pp. 159–169.

⁵³ Passet, op. cit., p. 89.

⁵⁴ Illustrations of the types of personalities and the motivation patterns found among federal government executives are given in Norman H. Martin, "Three Personality Profiles" and other sections of *The American Federal Executive* edited by W. L. Warner, P. P. Van Riper, N. H. Martin, and O. F. Collins (Yale University Press, New Haven, Conn., 1963). Studies of higher-level federal administrators have failed to show any significant differences between them and their counterparts in private business: David Stanley, *The Higher Civil Service* (The Brookings Institution, Washington, 1964); Dean E. Mann, *The Assistant Secretaries: Problems and Processes of Appointment* (The Brookings Institution, Washington, 1965).

⁵⁵ Bruce Buchanan II, "Government Managers, Business Executives and Organizational Commitment," *Public Administration Review,* July–August 1974, pp. 339–347.

RECOMMENDED READINGS

Berlew, David E.: "Leadership and Organizational Excitement," *California Management Review,* Winter 1974, pp. 21–30.

Fiedler, Fred E.: "How Do You Make Leaders More Effective? New Answers to an Old Puzzle," *Organizational Dynamics,* Autumn 1972, pp. 2–18.

Stogdill, Ralph M.: *Handbook of Leadership: A Survey of Theory and Research* (The Free Press, New York, 1974).

Zaleznik, Abraham: "Power and Politics in Organizational Life," *Harvard Business Review,* May–June 1970, pp. 47–60.

Chapter 8

Staffing

WHAT IS STAFFING?

Traditionally the managerial process of staffing has covered those activities involved in procuring employees (recruitment, testing, interviewing, investigating, and evaluating), training and developing employees (skills training, supervisory and executive development), compensating employees (job description and evaluation, incentive plans, etc.), appraising performance and promoting, controlling some conditions of work (safety and health hazards), and communicating with employees (newsletters and publications, opinion polls, and other forms of communications). In short, staffing in the past has comprised those activities associated with the personnel department and, in unionized situations, the department that negotiates with unions and administers collective bargaining contracts (whether it be called labor relations or industrial relations or is simply part of the personnel department).

In actual business practice, staffing was for a long time typically rather separated from the other managerial processes. The personnel management specialists provided certain services to the rest of the company, but they did so without working closely with the line managers, without having much impact on how line managers perform their jobs, and without being regarded as a part of top management. Many chief executives, focusing hard on the manufacturing and selling activities, were prone to leave personnel management to college-trained specialists—"clean hands" types who do not get involved in the nitty-gritty of the shop floor or applying the hard sell to customers. In the federal government, this separation was for many years quite complete; personnel management was concentrated in the Civil Service Commission. The separation of personnel management from the rest of management has prevailed in the academic world too. In fact, in most schools the staffing function has been taught in personnel management courses with little or no attention given to it in courses in general management (administration).

Some observers came to the conclusion that this separation of personnel management from the rest of management kept the human relations specialists from making full use of those skills and insights that they possess. These observers concluded that since the human resource represents the greatest cost element in many types of businesses and in virtually all government operations, the knowledge possessed by personnel specialists should be applied in every phase of management in order to attain a work force and a management team that are as effective as they can become.

In recent years, the separateness of personnel management has been somewhat reduced in both business and government; the specialist in personnel relations has been brought much more into the core managerial activities. In business, this has sometimes been done by formally making the personnel manager (or industrial relations director) a member of top management, sometimes by having a management training program that truly permeates all managerial activities, and sometimes by using the concept of "manpower" management. The latter approach emphasizes thorough planning of the personnel side of every corporate plan in order to achieve the full development and most effective placement of each individual, the best use of the human resources.

In the federal government, integration has been sought by decentralizing personnel management activities to operating departments and agencies (but still keeping an important staff role for the Civil Service Commission).

In both business and government, there has been a bit of movement toward systems management, more particularly some use of quantitative methods on personnel problems and some computerization of personnel records systems. Integration of personnel management into the rest of management constitutes a move to holistic decision making.

OBJECTIVES AND OUTLINE OF THIS CHAPTER

The structure of this chapter parallels this history of moving from separation to integration. First it discusses the traditional personnel management activities. These are described in just enough detail to indicate the nature of each activity and how it can contribute to the overall managerial processes. Detailed presentation of techniques is left to courses in personnel management, wage and salary administration, and collective bargaining.

The chapter then moves on to the newer approaches in which personnel management is more integrated with the other managerial activities, with particular attention to personnel aspects of the current productivity problem.

Staffing activities are, of course, essential to all forms of enterprise—government, charitable, and religious as well as business. Although there are some differences between staffing in a business versus a nonprofit, nongovernment setting, they are handled together in the first part of this chapter. Inasmuch as civil service procedures make government personnel management quite different, that subject is covered separately. Thus this chapter is presented under the following headings:

Traditional Staffing Activities and Their Importance to General Management
    Employment
    Training and Development
    Performance Appraisal
    Communications
    Wage and Salary Administration
    Other Staffing Activities
Modern Staffing Concepts and the Productivity Problem
    "Manpower" Management
    The Productivity Problem
    Responses to the Productivity Problem
Collective Bargaining's Impact upon Staffing
Special Problems of Staffing in Government
    Chronology of Main Developments in Federal Personnel Management
    Problems and Trends in Federal Personnel Management
    How Effective Is Federal Personnel Management?
    Staffing in State and Local Government
    Collective Bargaining in the Public Sector
Systems Management and the Staffing Process
    Quantitative Methods
    Human Resource Accounting
Summary on the Staffing Process

TRADITIONAL STAFFING ACTIVITIES AND THEIR IMPORTANCE TO GENERAL MANAGEMENT

Employment

An expertly designed and aggressively run employment program is far different from the perfunctory efforts made by most organizations. A professional program is rooted in two kinds of research studies. The first study inquires into the costs of a mistake in hiring, that is, the hiring of a person who does not stay or who does not perform satisfactorily. When these costs are carefully compiled by a business firm for a number of different positions, the results usually surprise executives because they are far higher than had been supposed. In many cases, once the true costs of employment mistakes are known, it is realized that elaborate efforts to reduce such mistakes are economically justified. The firm is then ready to go all out in improving the employment process.

The second type of study seeks to discover the factors that make for stability or instability and success or failure in a particular company. Once these factors have been determined, the knowledge can be used to focus recruitment efforts on the most fruitful sources of applicants and to screen out (via diagnostic application forms and the use of tests) the most unlikely candidates. Such early elimination of the poor bets makes it possible to spend more time and do a better job on the better prospects in the latter part of the selection process. The entire process includes:

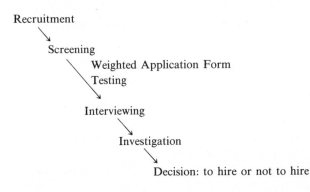

Recruitment

    Screening

        Weighted Application Form

        Testing

       Interviewing

         Investigation

           Decision: to hire or not to hire

A great deal of know-how has been accumulated at each step in this integrated process. The recruitment step involves having a clear definition of what kinds of persons are needed, of the particular sources most likely to yield significant numbers of these types of persons, and of the advertising and communications channels and messages most likely to reach them. The construction of a weighted application form requires ability to do correlation analyses that identify the factors (perhaps age, educational level, type of previous experience, location of residence, etc.) that distinguish between successful and unsuccessful employees. These factors are then applied in a rough screening process that eliminates some of the less likely candidates while losing very few, if any, of the likely candidates. [Under federal law it is now illegal to ask ages of applicants between forty and sixty-five years of age; in some states it is illegal to inquire about the age of any applicant. As a matter of fact, there are now many legal restrictions (federal law plus the rulings of the Equal Employment Opportunity Commission and state laws) on what questions may be asked a job applicant. And violations of these restrictions have already led to legal actions and heavy judgments against some firms. Restrictions apply not only to such discrimination-related matters as race, religion, and sex but also to physical data, criminal record, and type of military discharge held.] The testing step requires expert knowledge of the many kinds of tests (proficiency, aptitude, interest, intelligence, maturity-personality, etc.) and their proper use (validation for particular situations and knowing how much reliance to place on a particular score). There is a vast difference between the expertise needed to use tests for some objective proficiency measurement (such as typing speed) versus using them for screening as to intelligence level (where there are many different types of tests and screening should be on fairly wide tolerances) versus using them in understanding an applicant's psychological makeup (where there are many different types of tests that require highly expert administration and interpretation, and where the test findings are only one bit of input that supplements the insights gained in the interviewing and investigation phases of the selection process).

Interviewing is the step at which the greatest mistakes are made. Partly because most individuals believe that they possess some innate ability to evaluate other persons and partly because they simply do not realize how fallible ad hoc methods really are, many interviewers have never learned sound interviewing methods. Such methods are based on an understanding of how to go about determining what an applicant *can do* (i.e., innate talents plus acquired capabilities and experience) and what an applicant *will do* (i.e., prediction of actual performance in view of basic habit patterns, personality, and maturity-immaturity). A systematic approach to these subjects requires an organized method of reviewing the applicant's personal, social, and work history; it involves, also, knowledge of how to put together the information received in order to bring out the applicant's basic behavior patterns. Further, a professional interviewer knows how to avoid the common errors (such as talking too much or revealing one's values). He or she is also aware of the need for getting a full and accurate record of the applicant's history so that that information can be used effectively in the investigation process.

Investigation Is Important   The investigation step can be the most penetrating step in the entire selection process if it involves direct contact with the applicant's former supervisors. A great deal can be learned about an applicant via three or four telephone conversations with former supervisors; by contrast, written inquiries and letters of recommendations from references are virtually worthless.[1] But to get the most out of such telephone conversations, employment specialists must know exactly what they are seeking to confirm, how to use the data gathered in the other steps in order to make the investigation productive, how best to approach the contact, and how to use the information gained from the contact in order to strengthen the final evaluation of what the applicant *can do* and *will do* if hired.

In sum, employment selection is a process consisting of a number of integrated steps, and there are a substantial number of proved techniques that can be used at each of these steps; unfortunately, many people drift into this type of work without ever learning the techniques or even without realizing that the techniques exist.

At the rank-and-file worker level, a soundly conceived and executed selection program can contribute greatly to building a work force of properly qualified and productive persons; also, such a program can go far toward solving an expensive turnover problem in times of tight labor markets. In the managerial levels, a sound selection program can do much to shape the character of an organization by acquiring the types of persons who will fit the existing character or will help to bring about a planned change in that character.

In the selection of managers, the personnel specialist plays a limited role; it is the line executives who make the yes/no selection decisions. This is true both in the selection of managers from outside the organization and in the promotion of supervisors-managers from within the organization. In the promotion situation, there is increasing use in business and government of "assessment centers" at which candidates are evaluated by selection specialists who observe them in various trial situations.[2] But, again, it is the line manager who must make the final decision on promotion. Thus it is important that line managers understand enough about the selection process to appreciate the help of the professional selection specialists and to cooperate with them.

Training and Development

Another staffing activity, training, has a big role to play alongside selection in producing a productive work force and in shaping the character of managerial leadership.

At the worker level, the training specialists conduct not only induction programs but also many types of skills training that help upgrade unskilled labor into semiskilled and semiskilled labor into skilled. Although the bulk of this training is done on the job, more formal classroom training is also used extensively.

At the lowest managerial ranks, the training department can help with the difficult transition experienced by many persons upon taking their first step into supervisory-managerial life. The newly appointed assistant section head or supervisor often needs training in training, or in how to instruct workers in order to upgrade their skills. Often he or she needs instruction in record-keeping, work scheduling, material control, and similar supervisory duties. And the most important need at this stage of development often is for human relations-communications training to better understand and deal with workers' needs and grievances. Such training involves role playing, case analysis, and practice sessions in conference leading.

If managerial training for middle and higher levels, which has been discussed in the chapter on leadership, is done by members of the personnel department, this is another reason for the top personnel management executive to be a member of top management. This executive should be in a position to let the high-ranking executives know when there is a gap, or even a contradiction, between their practices and what is being taught in the management training program.

Another type of effort that requires a strong training input is the introduction of new management methods—methods exemplified by the introduction of MBO. Introduction of MBO is a big change, because it requires formal planning from managers who have never before planned, new two-way communications about those plans, and new types of written reports. Merely announcing the new requirements often gets only incomplete and poor-quality compliance; a great deal of instruction, hand-holding, and persuasion is sometimes needed to achieve change in basic managerial practice. In the case history presented earlier (of a state government having difficulty instituting PPBS), a problem was that that government simply did not have a training capability that could provide the needed instruction, hand-holding, and persuasion. That particular state government lacked enough professional trainers; also, the trainers that were assembled lacked the knowledge of management methods and the close working relationship with top executives that were needed to do the job.

In sum, training can contribute in numerous ways to the building of a productive work force, to the development of managers, and to the nurturing of a constructive organizational climate; however, these things can be achieved only if the efforts of training specialists are closely integrated with the actual workings of line management.

Performance Appraisal

A process in which line managers need a great deal of help and training from personnel specialists is the appraisal of performance of subordinates. This is probably done poorly, or even defaulted, more often than any other managerial duty. Poor appraisals can yield counterproductive results; but effective appraisals can contribute importantly to the subordinate's development and to the firm's promotion and placement programs.

Appraisals can misfire because they involve criticism, and criticism can undermine a person's self-esteem, which must be strong if he or she is to try new methods of doing things and take on new challenges. Criticism can also cause anxieties that interfere with good performance; it can lead to exaggerated overreactions and can cause alienation.[3] One research study found situations in which the better-performing employees were being discouraged (because they were given short interviews in which most of the time was spent on criticism) and weaker employees were showing no improvement (because in their longer interviews the criticisms were so guarded and so balanced with praise that they did not realize that change was needed).[4]

Other formidable problems involved in performance appraisal center about objectivity, that is, the danger of the appraiser being unduly influenced by recent events, by positive or negative "halo" effects (predispositions of which the appraiser is unaware), or by the psychological phenomenon of "projection" (by which the superior tends to apply personal value judgments to people and situations for which they may be inappropriate). In addition, there are problems arising from the lack of clear criteria about what results are expected from the subordinates (usually because the superiors themselves are not sure about how their own performance is being judged).

When the performance appraisal is linked to wage and salary administration, there is often a temptation to make ratings favorable in order to justify pay increases that may be advisable for other reasons. Another baffling problem is that of equity— should a person who achieves 80 percent of a challenging goal be denied a pay raise while a person who achieves 100 percent of an easy goal *is* given an increase? For these reasons, some experts in this field believe that there should be no tie between performance appraisal and compensation; rather, the emphasis should be kept on development of the individual.

Because many supervisor-managers are aware of these various problems—some only vaguely and instinctively, some quite explicitly—they either neglect to do appraisals or do them in the most passive, noncontroversial way possible. They often will "go down the middle" on the rating forms, avoiding the need for a serious discussion with the subordinate. This tendency is especially pronounced in government administration, because the appraiser often must defend an unusually high or low rating before a review board. Officers in the Armed Forces are given periodic "fitness report" ratings by their commanding officers, and the file of these ratings is all-important at those career junctures when promotion boards decide who goes on to the high ranks and who drops out. As the process has evolved, commanding officers are reluctant to rate critically because such a rating can stop an individual's lifelong career; in consequence, overrating is rampant. A commentary by a retired naval officer gives the following translation table for understanding the ratings:[5]

Outstanding	a stellar officer
Exceptional	not quite stellar
Superior	a bit dull
Excellent	mediocre
Acceptable	unacceptable
Marginal	criminality suspected
Unsatisfactory	criminality proven

When the present author was a naval officer, he was reviewed periodically by his commanding officer on a form containing a place for the ratee's signature below the statement "I have had an opportunity to discuss this rating with my commanding officer and I understand the reasons underlying this rating of my performance." The procedure was made a farce by the captain, who required his officers to sign the form in blank and never discussed their ratings with them.

Many different types of rating forms and procedures have been developed in the hope of making performance appraisal meaningful, constructive, and objective. These include graphic rating scales in which traits are evaluated; rank-order listings on various traits plus overall performance; the assessing of the ratee's performance in critical incidents; and the forced choice (from among many) of statements that best describe the ratee. Also, various design features, such as reversing the scale direction randomly or slipping in an occasional placebo, have been built into the forms to keep the rater from filling out the form without thinking. Also used have been ratings by peers (sometimes so-called buddy ratings) and self-ratings to be used for comparison with the superior's rating and discussion of the differences.

Although no one form or procedure has solved all the problems of performance appraisal, some do yield good results when (1) the overall organizational climate is conducive to personal development; (2) the line supervisors-managers are trained to know enough about performance appraisal to do a sound job of it; and (3) higher-level managers insist that the job be done and that the ratings actually be used in deciding promotions.[6]

One of the main aims of MBO is to strengthen performance appraisal by (1) bringing the subordinate in on the determination of performance criteria; (2) making those criteria measurable, preferably objectively measurable (rather than using nonmeasurable traits such as "industrious" or "gets along well with others"); and (3) setting the standards *before* the start of the period to be reviewed. This participative working out of things in advance brings the superior and subordinate into communication about the problems to be solved and possible ways of solving them. This, in turn, makes it possible for the review of performance to be on a constructive, helping basis rather than on a criticizing basis. While the MBO format does not always work out so ideally, it is nevertheless probably the most satisfactory approach to performance appraisal.[7]

Communications

Because communications up and down the line often prove inadequate and unreliable (as indicated in the discussion in Chapter 7 of the communications training given in executive development programs), the personnel department typically has responsibility for many supplementary forms of communications. These include the company newspaper, newsletters, in-plant broadcasts, suggestion systems, and anonymous polls of employee opinion. The polls can provide clues as to which communications are succeeding and which are not, what needs to be communicated, and which supervisors are in need of what types of training. Much of such information can be secured only through anonymous channels. Exit interviews with departing employees can, if done with tact, yield valuable feedback on these same subjects.

Wage and Salary Administration

Still another area in which line managers need help from personnel specialists is wage and salary administration.[8] Sound design of a job classification-evaluation program requires considerable knowledge of the different types of plans available and the suitability of a particular type of plan to a particular organization's work. As important as the original design of a wage and salary plan is its continuing administration—the reclassifying and reevaluating of jobs as they gradually change over time. Another continuing task is the taking of community wage surveys and making of the pay readjustments needed to remain competitive in the labor market.

The design and administration of incentive pay systems is another field in which line management needs the help of experts, as is also the design and administration of so-called fringe-benefit programs. Many incentive pay systems have been counterproductive because they have been administered in ways that engender human fears of being exploited and being treated unfairly. Somewhat similarly, many expensive fringe benefits have bought little or nothing for the employer because the communications aspects have been poorly handled.

High rates of inflation have made wage and salary administration particularly difficult. Many firms through the years have maintained the policy of giving merit increases rather than general increases, but inflation makes it necessary to give everyone something. Firms that try to maintain merit increases in addition to general increases find themselves giving double-digit wage increases. Also, inflation distorts profit figures through profits on inventory; such profits increase the pressure for wage increases or automatically increase the distributions under profit-sharing plans. Furthermore, inflation has hurt the equity securities market, crippling the investment earnings of many retirement plans. Keeping employees satisfied and still maintaining control over total compensation costs under such conditions requires considerable know-how in wage and salary administration.

Other Staffing Activities

This chapter could go on and on describing other staffing activities that can, if done correctly, contribute to productivity and economical operation. One is the safety program, with its humanistic and economic (via the costly workmen's compensation rate) aspects. Another is the in-plant health program. Both of these can be part of a larger program to make the company a physically safe, healthful and pleasant place to work. Tying in with this are the other employee services, especially employee eating facilities and parking, both of which are often fraught with status differentiations that create alienation not only between worker and manager but also between certain levels of managers.

A novel way to assure workers fair treatment and a greater voice in their own destinies is to borrow from government the ombudsman concept. The Xerox Corporation reports favorable results from the establishment of such a position to hear and do something about the complaints and ideas of workers.[9]

MODERN STAFFING CONCEPTS AND THE PRODUCTIVITY PROBLEM

"Manpower" Management

As personnel management became better integrated with the main body of management activity, the concept of "manpower" management became popular. This approach involves far more personnel planning than was done previously; the personnel specialist participates in the organization's basic planning. This specialist's role is to ensure that the skills required by growth as well as by increasing computerization and automation will be available when needed. In developing these skills, the manpower management specialist takes a comprehensive approach that seeks to realize each individual's potential (including the potential of women and minority group members). The specialist builds and maintains inventories of skills, creates new career paths, and develops versatile training programs that help individuals progress along the career paths that appeal to them most. In short, manpower management is more long range, more comprehensive, and more humanistic than was the earlier approach to personnel management.

The manpower management program faces particularly formidable problems when a traditional work force must be shifted over to newly computerized and automated processes. In such situations, which are now occurring frequently, new kinds of jobs (e.g., systems monitors, systems maintainers) fit together into new kinds of structures built around computerized information flows. The manpower management specialist must use selection know-how (1) to identify those workers who are capable of learning new and more sophisticated skills and (2) to help them acquire those skills. Also, the problem of those workers who cannot absorb the new and more sophisticated skills must be handled in ways that minimize upset, insecurity, and resistance.

The Productivity Problem

In recent years the United States has experienced a serious productivity problem. In some years it has been a slowdown in the rate of productivity improvement; in one period of almost two years there has been an absolute drop in productivity. For the first time in this century, the United States is being outproduced by other nations, and certain major United States industries (e.g., autos and steel) are losing not only foreign markets but also part of the domestic market.[10] Part of the problem lies in the widespread alienation of labor. This has come to be called the "Lordstown syndrome," after a General Motors plant in Lordstown, Ohio. Designed as the last word in assembly-line efficiency, the Lordstown plant has become instead the focal point of the absenteeism, high turnover, poor quality, grievances, local strikes, and low productivity that were plaguing GM and many other companies before the sharp 1974–75 recession that brought widespread unemployment to the auto industry.[11]

How can this happen in the 1970s—when American industry is supposed to have learned so much over the past four decades about motivation and leadership, about humanizing jobs through job enlargement, about manpower management, and about grievance handling under mature union-management relationships? Does this mean that much of what behavioral scientists think they have learned is wrong? Or that it is being applied ineffectively? Or that it is not being used?

It is possible that the answer lies along these lines: What has been learned about motivation, communications, and leadership methods is mostly valid; it is being used, but not as much or as effectively as it might be. In addition, conditions have changed, and behavioral scientists and managers have not yet learned to apply their ideas to the new conditions.

Although it is exceedingly difficult to establish causal relationships between broad-scale changes taking place in our society and economy, it does indeed appear that a number of changes have been taking place that have seriously eroded human motivation and performance. According to extensive studies conducted between 1971 and 1973 by the National Commission on Productivity into the causes and cures of the productivity problem, it is the following types of forces that have produced the problem:[12]

1 *People's expectations of how they should be treated.* This is the oldest and best-established of the basic trends. For over two decades it has been recognized that much of the population is better educated than ever before. Also, prosperity and its high living standards have interacted with the educational factor to give people—in both worker and managerial ranks—new expectations of having some voice in deciding how they should do their work and in determining the conditions surrounding the work. Recognition of these rising expectations has long since led to widespread use of MBO and other participative management approaches that foster two-way communications at all levels. Now further movements in this direction appear to be needed.

2 *Alienation from the established values.* Many individuals—again, in both worker and managerial ranks—are now less motivated by material goals and more concerned with the quality of working life. At the worker level this has led to the Lordstown syndrome of worker revolt (wildcat strikes, excessive absenteeism, sabotage of product) against highly engineered production lines. At the lower- and middle-management levels, it has led to the entirely new phenomenon of managerial dropouts.

Apparently this alienation is not a universal fact of life. One study of another General Motors plant (that is, one other than Lordstown) found that 95 percent of the workers are satisfied with their jobs and that 71 percent of them find no part of their jobs to be tiring or upsetting.[13]

Despite this finding—which may reflect an older work force and stabilized community—and others like it, there does appear to be widespread worker alienation. An ambitious interviewing project, involving talks with workers from many kinds of organizations in many parts of the United States, found widespread dissatisfaction over the meaninglessness of jobs.[14]

3 *Makeup of the work force.* In many sectors, minority groups comprise a large and steadily increasing proportion of the labor force. They have social and cultural values and attitudes that are not well understood by their predominantly Caucasian middle-class supervisors. This lack of understanding produces frustration and resentments, and these, in turn, produce much the same alienation, revolt, and sabotage noted earlier.

Responses to the Productivity Problem

Part of the solution lies in the elimination of boring jobs through capital investment in more automation via computers, numerically controlled machine tools, and word processing equipment. But not all the problem situations are amenable to solution via automation; part of the solution lies in new ways of utilizing the human resource, ways more compatible with the new conditions.

In part, GM's response has been to redouble its personnel management–human relations efforts. It has added a vice president with a staff of 144 persons, including 5 psychologists, to do organizational development (OD) work throughout the corporation's thirty-four divisions worldwide. The OD program is seeking to generate worker participation in such matters as how to rearrange the plant work area when a new model changeover occurs. Even though one job-enlargement experiment in a truck assembly line has failed, clearly GM intends to use the job-enlargement idea in many situations. Another thrust at GM is to increase the number of blacks and other minority group members in supervision and management; the college graduate recruitment program is bringing in far more blacks and women, and admission to the GM Institute's management program is changing along the same lines. It is hoped that management trainees from minority group ranks will in time be able to make more effective application of behavioral sciences ideas to present-day work forces.[15]

Job enlargement, one of the elements of the GM program, has become a fairly widely and successfully used technique for increasing worker satisfaction and productivity since its introduction over a decade ago.[16] An approach much like GM's—that is, using job enlargement along with OD and other programs—has been strongly advocated by the head of Westinghouse Electric Corporation.[17] And a bold program of job enlargement and participative team planning, called "People and Asset Effectiveness," is being used by in-house behavioral scientists at Texas Instruments. The TI efforts grow out of long emphasis on the human factor at that corporation, which appears to have achieved extraordinary productivity.[18] And the Bell Telephone Companies have used job enlargement, as it is sometimes called, in connection with both white-collar and blue-collar jobs.[19] Frederick Herzberg, the originator of the concept, feels that straightaway job enrichment—which sometimes amounts simply to restoring jobs to the way they were before industrial engineers "rationalized" them—is more effective in achieving individual growth and competence than is the use of job enrichment in conjunction with participative management or group incentives.[20]

Another approach to greater job satisfaction and increased productivity involves fundamental change in the design of jobs. Sometimes called "work structuring," it encompasses the job enrichment idea but goes beyond that, even to the design of the plant plus considerable participation in decision making by groups of workers. Variations of this approach are included in the innovative ideas reported in the thirty-four case studies—most of them claiming strongly favorable results—reported in the National Productivity Commission's study *Work in America*.[21] One case concerns a new plant of a pet food company, a subsidiary of one of the giant food companies.[22] The new plant, which replaced one that had experienced considerable costly employee discontent, featured autonomous work groups, integrated support functions (that is, the work group did its own specialty work, such as maintenance, quality control, etc.), challenging job assignments, job mobility and rewards for learning new jobs, facilitative leadership, absence of many of the usual status symbols of position, managerial information for operators, and self-government (with respect to plant rules) for the plant community. Although standard industrial engineering studies estimated that 110 employees would be required to operate the plant, it produces at capacity with 70 employees. In addition, the new plant's fixed overhead rate was 33 percent lower than in the old plant, there was a dramatic drop in quality rejects, and there was a modest improvement in absenteeism. While new equipment was no doubt responsible for some of these results, the author of the report estimates that half the improvements derived from the innovative human organization.

Two Swedish Experiments   Another case of work structuring is that of a new Volvo automobile plant in Sweden. One feature is the elimination of the steadily moving assembly line for battery-powered carriers that move individually, enabling teams of workers to set their own pace as long as they meet a preset production goal. A second innovation is the division of workers into teams of about fifteen people, each team having responsibility for one production phase such as installing the electrical system, or interior upholstery, or underbody fittings. The teams can organize their own work into a mini–assembly line with each doing a different job in sequence on a number of cars, or each worker or group can do the complete installation on one car. They can rotate jobs in order to avoid boredom and to distribute equally the good and bad jobs. The plant's odd design, combining four 6-sided shapes on one level and three 6-sided shapes on a second level, gives each team its own exterior section with ample sunlight and view of the landscaped grounds. Teams have their own entrances as well as locker and coffeebreak rooms, and they are encouraged to make collective decisions and suggestions about their own production practices and working conditions.

Production in the new Volvo plant has met both quantity and quality quotas,[23] and the company is confident that in time it will recover more than the greater construction cost (about 10 percent over the conventional plant) through reduced absenteeism and lower personnel turnover. A 5 percent increase in productivity has been achieved in a similar experiment (without the benefit of new construction) in a Swedish plant manufacturing rock-drilling machines. Here too, the managers are confident that improvement in turnover, which had been an expensive problem for the firm, will in time produce greater economies.[24]

Conclusions on Cases   Some observers are quite skeptical about the cases and the general conclusions drawn in *Work in America,* while others are highly enthusiastic. Thus an economist critiquing the report argues that there is not widespread alienation in the blue-collar work force in America, and he cites numerous surveys to support his view. He feels that the 1971–72 productivity problems were a function of maladjustments in the economy that will disappear when business conditions improve. He feels that the pay envelope, rather than job design, governs workers' satisfaction.[25] An opposite view is expressed by a Harvard Business School professor who is so impressed by the cases reported in *Work in America* that he predicts that in time, "probably in most" plants, work teams will perform without supervision and many decisions will be based on employee consensus.[26]

The present author, while not as enthusiastic as the Harvard Business School professor just quoted, does feel that these cases point to a real possibility for improving productivity by designing the technosocial system as a whole. In other words, the personnel management specialist should be in on job design; it should not be left wholly to the industrial engineer. In many situations this will mean much more freedom for teams of workers to organize their own assignments and methods.

Clearly, today's work environment is different in many ways and in many places from what it was in the decades when the traditional staffing techniques—selection, training, appraisal, incentive compensation, etc.—were developed. Although these techniques are still useful, the new conditions bring new problems that demand new answers. To supply these new answers, the personnel specialist must be integrated into the total management effort, including job design, to help make the total organizational system work—which, incidentally, is a step toward systems management.

A decade after the pioneering work in the British coal mining industry by the Tavistock Institute in Great Britain,[27] this lesson is being applied by a few firms in the United States, Sweden, and India. To some extent it is a more mature, broader, and deeper application of the ideas gathered in the Hawthorne Experiments over four decades ago.

Flexi-Time and the Four-Day Week   Still other approaches to changing jobs to increase productivity are so-called flexi-time and the four-day week. Flexi-time is an arrangement that allows workers a couple of hours of latitude in starting and stopping work each day without reducing the total time worked per week. Some plans require a given employee to work the same hours every day in the week; other plans permit variations from day to day. Started in Europe, the idea has been well received and, it is estimated, is used by about 5,000 firms who find that it helps reduce their turnover rate in very tight labor markets.[28] Apparently employees enjoy the freedom of adjusting their commuting hours to escape peak traffic or adjusting to other family members' schedules. It is estimated that in the United States the number of firms with flexi-time grew from less than a dozen in mid-1973 to more than 100 in mid-1974. Results to date are promising, although benefits seem to be more on reduced turnover than increased productivity. Also, some firms' work routines are such that they simply cannot use the idea.[29]

The four-day week, virtually nonexistent in 1969 in the United States, reportedly was in effect in from 700 to 1,000 organizations by mid-1974; about 60 percent were on forty-hour weeks and the remainder were on shorter weeks.[30] It is not yet clear whether the idea is an effective antidote to worker boredom and alienation. Results to date have been mixed, and there are indications that fatigue may be a serious drawback.

COLLECTIVE BARGAINING'S IMPACT UPON STAFFING

In unionized situations, the character of staffing activities is affected by the terms of the collective bargaining contract. Invariably, all aspects of wage administration are covered by the contract. Also, the employment process is dominated by the union in those industries in which union hiring halls and the closed shop are established. Often training at the worker level is supplied by the union, particularly in craft situations. Sometimes the union participates in training at the lower supervisory levels. Almost always the union has its own communications program running side by side with the management's communications. Performance appraisal systems at the worker level are generally discouraged by unions in favor of a procedure whereby managers must give written notice of unsatisfactory performance to the worker and the union shop steward.

With respect to some of the newer practices involving work teams, setting of the work pace and work assignments by workers themselves, and job enlargement schemes—in short, the methods that are being used to combat the productivity crisis—unions have a mixed reaction. Some unions resist such methods, seeing them as schemes whereby managers hope to come between worker and union. Other unions feel that they serve their members best by being in the forefront of such new methods; they engage in "productivity bargaining," whereby unions help encourage productivity improvements if the workers are assured of a share in the gain. (This is not too different from the twenty-five-year-old Scanlan plan, whereby unions participated in productivity improvement programs if guaranteed a share via keeping the labor percentage cost fixed.) And at least one prominent union leader is said to regard the concern over worker disaffection with assembly lines as nothing more than "elitist nonsense"; he sees worker unrest and poor productivity as arising when workers are dissatisfied with their paychecks, vacations, and retirement plans.[31]

In sum, unions can, and often do, profoundly affect some staffing activities. The way a particular union influences staffing activities is a function of its strength, its philosophy, and the institutionalized practices of its industry.

Obviously union-management relations, collective bargaining, and contract administration are big subjects that cannot be covered, even sketchily, in this book. In many universities they fill three or four semester-long courses, and in some they constitute a major field.

SPECIAL PROBLEMS OF STAFFING IN GOVERNMENT

Chronology of Main Developments in Federal Personnel Management

The following listing sets forth the main steps in the development of the present system of personnel management in the federal government:[32]

1883 *U.S. Civil Service Commission (CSC)* established by the Pendleton Act to develop a merit system in employment to replace the spoils–political patronage system.

1912 *Job security* established by the Lloyd-LaFollette Act, prohibiting removal of employees from office except on the basis of written charges accompanied by an opportunity to reply (the "open back door" system). This was replaced in 1962, after many years of debate, by a system under which the CSC can reverse the line manager's decision to dismiss an employee (the "closed back door" system).

1923 *Rational pay structures* were established by the Classification Act, calling for the sorting and ranking of positions in a hierarchical sequence according to the comparative difficulty and responsibility of the job. Positions were divided into two major categories, white collar and blue collar. The act applied only to white-collar positions in the District of Columbia identified as professional and scientific; subprofessional; clerical, administrative, and fiscal; and custodial (later changed to crafts, protective, and custodial). The blue-collar positions were identified as the apprenticeable work in a recognized trade or craft.

1938 *A positive, decentralized personnel management program* was begun by presidential order, establishing personnel management sections in each major federal department and agency. Previously all personnel management activities had been centralized in the CSC and were focused on preventing abuses; now the decentralized, expanded, and professionally staffed offices focused on positive improvements such as new recruitment procedures to attract better applicants, new selection procedures to improve the quality of those selected, and new procedures to protect the rights of employees.

1940 *Extension of civil service coverage* by presidential action, spreading coverage to 200,000 more persons, one of a series of such orders by different presidents, bringing the coverage to 85 percent of all federal government employees. A 1969 order placed 70,000 postal workers under merit procedures, virtually completing the process.

1944 *Veterans' Preference Act* provided preferential treatment of veterans in hiring and retention; granted them a right to a hearing in appeals to the CSC of an adverse action.

1949 *"Supergrades" created* by adding grades 16–18 to the top of the classified service. By early 1972, the top pay of a classified grade had reached $36,000. Also, the Classification Act of 1949 and amendments to it have established various groupings of federal employees and designed appropriate methods of setting pay scales for each, thus removing the need for legislative action for each pay adjustment. The three white-collar categories were integrated within a single general schedule (GS) consisting of eighteen grade levels of work difficulty and responsibility. The blue-collar positions were excluded from coverage. A new, separate pay system was established which allowed each agency to maintain and control its own wage- (blue-collar) and pay-grade system to meet its individual needs.

1958   *Government Employees Training Act* established general authority for the training of federal employees to increase the economy and efficiency of the government. Prior to this legislation, any federal agency lacking special authorization from Congress for training of its employees was limited, by rulings of the Comptroller General of the United States, to training which was of brief duration and special or limited in nature. In 1963, a live-in institute for middle-rank managers (Executive Seminar Center) was established at Kings Point, New York, followed in later years by the establishment of other such institutes at Berkeley, California, and Oak Ridge, Tennessee. In 1967, a report by the Presidential Task Force on Career Advancement, finding that all the businesses reputed to be the ten best-managed firms had continuing management development programs, made many suggestions for executive training. In carrying out these suggestions, the CSC has established regional training centers throughout the country and the Federal Executive Institute for in-residence training for top-level executives (discussed in Chapter 3).

1959   *Merit promotion* regulations, formulated by the CSC and strengthened in 1969, greatly reduced the influence of seniority in promotion considerations.

1962   *Federal Salary Reform Act* established the principle of pay comparability between general schedule employees and those in private enterprise; the government moved toward implementation of this principle through several acts in the 1960s, finally achieving full pay comparability in July 1969. *The Federal Executive Salary Act of 1964* governs the pay of top executives (Cabinet members, undersecretaries, bureau heads, and chairpersons and members of boards and commissions) above the highest classified grade, GS-18.

1962   *Collective bargaining rights* of federal employees were formalized by executive order establishing a program of employee-management cooperation. Following this, organizing activity expanded so rapidly that in 1966 the CSC found it necessary to establish an Office of Labor-Management Relations, which has moved steadily toward mature, sophisticated patterns of union-management relations and government.

1962   *Appeal rights,* the same as veterans have, were granted to nonveterans in the competitive service by executive order; agencies were required to establish an appeal system.

1965   *A single Coordinated Wage System for Federal Employees (CFWS)* in the trades and labor occupations, completely exempt from the Classification Act, was established by a presidential directive.

1967   *The Executive Assignment System (EAS)* was made fully operational. In addition to establishing a new appointment system for "supergrades," the EAS provided for cooperative personnel planning between the CSC and the various agencies, a computerized inventory of executives in grades GS-15 and above, and the continuing development of executives. These features have assured a very broad search for qualified candidates before filling career executive positions in the supergrade category and have fostered the movement of executives between agencies.

1969   *Executive interchange between government and industry* established under President's Commission on Personnel Interchange.

1969   *Discrimination on basis of sex, race, color, religion, or national origin* prohibited in federal employment by Executive Order 11478. It directs heads of executive departments and agencies to establish and maintain affirmative programs of equal employment opportunity for all civilian employees and applicants for employment. The CSC administers this order, reviews all complaints of discrimination by federal employees, and issues regulations and instructions as necessary.

1970   *Equal employment opportunity programs* strengthened governmentwide.

1970   *The Intergovernmental Personnel Act (IPA)* provides for grants to states and localities to upgrade public service there to achieve improved personnel systems at the grass roots to handle the work to be delegated under the "new federalism" concept. The IPA also provides for technical assistance to state and local governments in recruitment, examining, and other personnel management areas; cooperative recruiting and examining among federal, state, and local governments; and temporary interchange of employees between federal, state, and local governments and institutions of higher education.

1970   *Labor-management relations program* was strengthened with the issuance of a new Executive order creating third-party machinery to resolve disputes and administer the program governmentwide. For overall program administration, a Federal Labor Relations Council was established, consisting of the Chairman of the CSC (as chairman of the council), the Director of the Office of Management and Budget, and the Secretary of Labor.

1970   *New Federal Information Centers, expansion of federal executive boards, and establishment of "listening posts" in large cities* all aimed at helping the CSC (in cooperation with the General Services Administration) become more "responsive."

1970   *Federal Pay Comparability Act* continues the principle, established by the 1962 Federal Salary Reform Act, of fixing federal pay at rates comparable with private enterprise pay rates for the same levels of work. In addition, the 1970 statute, while transferring primary responsibility for general schedule salary adjustments from Congress to the President, gives employee unions a role in the pay-setting process and establishes an impartial three-member Advisory Committee to advise the President on federal pay. Pay rates are now adjusted annually by the President to keep them at levels comparable with private enterprise pay rates.

1971–73   *Productivity measurement and improvement program,* a joint effort of the CSC, General Accounting Office, and the Office of Management and Budget, representing a far stronger effort than had ever previously been made on these problems. Resulted in establishment of a permanent productivity measurement system covering more than 60 percent of the federal civilian work force and creation of a CSC program to apply the latest knowledge from the behavioral and management sciences to improved personnel management (Clearinghouse on Productivity and Organizational Effectiveness).

1972   *The Equal Employment Opportunity Act of 1972 (EEO)* requires that all personnel actions affecting employees or applicants for employment shall be made free from any discrimination based on race, creed, color, religion, sex, or national origin. The CSC has authority for enforcing the Act and may order whatever remedies are appropriate, including reinstatement or hiring of employees with or without back pay. Each federal department and agency is required by the Commission to submit an annual EEO action plan for review and approval at the national and regional levels. Also, an employee or applicant for employment who has alleged discrimination based on sex, race, color, religion, or national origin may, if he or she is dissatisfied with the final action taken by an agency or by the Commission's Appeals Review Board, file a civil action in an appropriate federal district court.

1972 *Computerized, nationwide personnel data* (Central Personnel Data File and Federal Automated Career System) on federal civilian employees in a system to facilitate promotion and development across agency lines and to provide an information resource for federal personnel program.

1972 *New Centralized Federal Wage System,* containing most of the provisions of the CFWS, enacted into law (Public Law 92–392.) The responsibility for managing and operating the centralized system was placed in the CSC. Pay was to be based on the prevailing area wage locales established in the continental limits.

1974 *CSC designated sole agency to hear employee appeals,* by Executive order. Agency appeals systems abolished. The Federal Employee Appeals Authority, independent of all other Commission functions, was provided. Open hearings provided upon request.

1975 *The National Productivity Center* established to coordinate and extend previous productivity efforts.

Problems and Trends in Federal Personnel Management

The dominant feature of federal personnel management has been the role of the civil service, and it has been quite controversial. Starting out as a reform movement to replace the political spoils system with merit employment, the federal civil service in time came under strong attack as a musty, paper-shuffling, incompetence-protecting, bureaucratic bottleneck. One critic went so far as to charge that the CSC was the single biggest obstacle to the successful waging of World War II.[33] Although other writers have not gone that far, they have made many serious criticisms: (1) Merit principles were administratively distorted into overprotection of the incompetent. (2) Emphasis on credentials and test scores, with the tests often being not relevant to the job to be done, outweighed considerations of performance, so that good performance was usually not rewarded. (3) Centralization of many decisions in the Commission reduced the power of line supervisors to discipline and reward their subordinates. Thus the federal government, like private business, has suffered from separation of personnel management from line management. (4) The Commission was trying to serve too many different purposes—fairness in employment, worker security, training, merit, veterans' preference, union rules, equal opportunity, etc. Put another way, the merit principle has been given two conflicting meanings—one being the reward for being *deserving* and the other the reward for being *excellent*.[34] (5) The job descriptions used have been so narrow and the organization structures so rigid that line supervisors cannot make effective use of their employees.[35]

From the chronology presented at the start of this section, it is clear that many actions have been taken (1) to solve the problems brought up by these critics, especially by decentralizing personnel management functions so that line managers have an opportunity to be effective and, (2) to match in the federal government the pay scales, quality standards, and managerial techniques used by the best-managed businesses.

One way in which the government has paralleled business is in the increasing emphasis on "manpower" management. As one writer puts it: "Public personnel administration as traditionally conceived has now been invaded from an intellectual quarter called 'manpower.' "[36] He goes on to explain that in the public sector this entails emphasis on career mobility, personnel forecasting and planning, personnel development, professionalism, and collective bargaining.

Still another parallel to the business field lies in the productivity programs mounted by the federal government in the last few years. Since service industries show less productivity improvement than do manufacturing industries, and since the government is such a huge purveyor of services, the government aspects of the problem have been of top importance. Among the personnel management actions suggested for increasing productivity of government workers are these:

Use of incentive pay systems in certain amenable operations; now, most feed-back about their work that government workers receive is critical, negatively motivating.

Granting of more discretion to line managers in making budget cutbacks; currently they operate under rules that require a "rif" (reduction in force) to hit productive and unproductive workers alike.

Granting of more discretion to managers in hiring and in awarding promotions and pay increases; the present emphasis is too much on credentials and test scores.

Better feedback on managerial performance and enforcement of performance standards; now there is too much protection of the nonperforming manager.

Use of job enlargement and self-direction techniques similar to those being used effectively in a few private industries.[37]

How Effective Is Federal Personnel Management?

What have been the results of all these efforts to cope with criticisms and to match business pay and the best business personnel management programs?

Despite the many reforms made by the CSC, it is still blasted in terms almost as harsh as those heard three or four decades ago. Thus the summary of a 1972 symposium entitled "Productivity in the Public Sector"—featuring experts from government (federal, state, and local), foundations, business, and academic institutions—contains the assertion:

Waste, mismanagement, bureaucratic empire building, and slipping services feed on each other. . . . Archaic civil service rules cripple efficiency, and some of the tactics of public employee unions puff up budgets with no particular increase in output! . . . Government managers, no less than their brethren in private enterprise, are afflicted with many workers who see themselves engaged in dehumanizing chores and no longer care about performance.[38]

One textbook writer summarizes as follows:

In practice, merit systems—meaning the programs of civil service agencies—have often been unimaginative, inflexible and unresponsive to the real needs of the employees. Outmoded policies and procedures actually harmful to the employees have been perpetuated in the name of "merit." The staunchest defenders of civil service do not deny that "merit systems" have often failed to live up to their promise.[39]

Yet the same writer feels that, with all its faults, the government's program of promotion by merit is better than the "typical business firm's" practice of promoting "conformists, yes-men and other kinds of favorites."[40] (Certainly many persons knowledgeable about big business practice would object violently to this judgment, but others would accept it as valid for perhaps a third of the country's large firms.)

To the present author the greatest government failures have been in the weakness of promotion practices which clog the channels of promotion and in discharge practices which tolerate poor performance. It is reported that about 26,000 classified employees per year are fired for cause.[41] Although this indicates that some discipline is being applied despite all the protective rules and procedures, the figure represents a bit less than 1 percent of the 2,800,000 employees covered by civil service regulations. Compared with the annual voluntary quit rate of from 12 to 20 percent (mostly younger and newer employees, presumably including some with high potential), the discharge rate seems hardly adequate to build a strong work force. The government may be losing a substantial part of its best employees because it gets rid of only a relatively few of its worst.

It is the managers in the civil service structure who have drawn the criticism of reformer Ralph Nader's organization. A major Nader report alleges that managers are protected from criticism and from discharge for nonperformance. Claiming that federal managers have become masters at ducking or passing responsibility, the report cites many cases of employees being ostracized and forced out of government for revealing instances of waste and mismanagement. The capable and conscientious government workers get into trouble, according to this report, while the incompetent and noncaring move along well in the system. The report urges establishment of an accountability and review board through which citizens and employees could seek redress of agency policies they believe are being carried out improperly or not at all.[42]

A symposium entitled "The Merit Principle Today" comes to no overall conclusion about civil service, but the editor does draw from the various papers a number of recommendations for improvements, including these: (1) Make political endorsements for merit-systems jobs punishable crimes and police the processes accordingly. (2) Use selection methods that are clearly relevant to the job and the career, because using irrelevant qualification requirements or tests in the name of objective competition is harmful nonsense. (3) Quit the "rule of one, rule of three" nonsense; let the appointing officer choose the candidate he or she wants for the job from a "well-qualified" list. (4) In promotions, refuse to accept seniority as the only criterion for supervisory jobs or highly specialized positions. (5) When staffs are cut—and more of that should be done—put employees in quality categories and cut the lowest first. However, structure the categories so that there is no decline in performance on equal employment opportunity goals. A detailed suggestion is also made for a major research project that would, if carried out well, yield a reliable answer to the question: How good is the public service?[43]

At the other extreme, a civil service official claims that in the federal work force "people are so dedicated about what they are doing (that) they get their rewards from the job."[44] A government union official describes them "As a whole, the hardest working, most loyal group we have in this country today."[45] A more modest claim was stated by the head of the CSC when he summarized his first two years in office:[46]

> I think our image is better, but we'll always draw criticism. It's ingrained in Americans to continually reexamine their governmental institutions. . . . I'm particularly pleased at the progress we've made in moving basic reforms along. And I'm proud of the way our staff has taken up the challenge to make the agency more responsive—to leave no doubt that we are what we should be—the servant of the people.

An academic study concludes that tenure is worth the cost of merit systems that have little to do with merit in order to avoid the corrupting extremes of political patronage that once prevailed.[47]

Have "Supergrades" Performed Well?   What about the "supergrades," those highly qualified and highly paid career persons at the top of the civil service who exercise considerable influence on the political appointees of Cabinet or commission-head rank? Do these criticisms apply to them, too, or are they able to escape the frustrations that plague lower-level managers? Have these supergrades been able to instill some aggressiveness and innovation into the picture?

Again, the evidence is conflicting. Most reports on business-government executive interchange programs claim that the participating business managers acquire a substantial respect for their government counterparts. There is one account of an antipollution expert, loaned by his company to help a government agency temporarily, who decided to stay with the government. He contended that the really important work in his field is being done by the government.[48] In contrast, an aerospace scientist-manager, lured to the government by the opportunity to head a sophisticated project, quit in disgust, saying: "I find less challenge in government than I found in industry. This is because of the bureaucracy; it's a big, huge organization and the inertia is very high. . . . A lot of people get into situations where there is no challenge. They have a lot to offer. They are pressured to stay and they do stay, but their personality changes. If I compromise once, twice, three times because I have a family to feed, then I just survive and I don't care."[49]

Above the supergrades of the civil service are the five levels in the executive structure (level I includes Cabinet secretaries at $60,000 per year, level II includes major agency heads at $42,500 per year, and so on through level V, which includes minor agency heads at $36,000 per year—all as of 1974). For the past decade at least, the executive structure has suffered a turnover rate that would mean ruin to an industrial firm. With almost half these executives serving less than two years, they barely have time to learn their jobs and establish sound working relationships with their superiors, much less accomplish anything.[50] It has been suggested that this turnover be cured by filling assistant secretary positions and possibly others in the executive structure with civil service personnel. While this emulation of the British system would reduce turnover, it would also strengthen what have been called "the unholy alliances"—long-standing underground alliances between a veteran congressional committee member, a high-level bureaucrat, and a special-interest lobbyist concerned with the same subject matter.

One reason for high turnover in the executive structure is that pay is adjusted only every four years (extended to five by Nixon), so incumbents suffer approximately a 25 percent pay cut in five years because of inflation. (Because the top GS grade is prohibited by law from receiving higher pay than level V in the executive structure, pay in the supergrades has been so compressed that all were for years receiving the same base pay.)[51]

Data and Conclusions   Amid all these conflicting views about the efficiency or inefficiency of the various grades of the civil service and the appointive executive service, some productivity figures have been developed. These are the first fairly comprehensive productivity data ever developed for federal agencies. The figures indicate that, for the four-year period 1967–71, productivity in the federal service improved at an annual rate of about 1.8 percent.[52] This is about the same rate of annual improvement achieved by private business during the same four years; however, for private business that rate represents a serious decline that has helped cause the United States to lose out competitively in many international markets. The 1.8 percent rate is a composite of government sectors, some of which showed a much larger increase (particularly those operations that are chiefly data processing, where improvement is associated with increasing computerization and word-processing equipment), and the more traditional government operations that showed virtually no productivity improvement.

In summary, we cannot give a clear-cut answer to the question: How effective is federal personnel management today? First, productivity measurements present a mixed picture. Second, it is difficult to know just what has caused the substantial increases in productivity that have occurred. As the National Commission on Productivity has concluded, the major factor in increasing federal agency productivity has been, and probably will continue to be, capital investment in computerization and automation. The other programs may be making a contribution to productivity; however, these activities should be buttressed with more measurement of output (not activity) by the agencies as a whole, by major sections of agencies, and by individual managers. Also, there is great need for recognition of strong performance and much more pressure to get rid of those who do not perform. A drastic reform would be to provide that an annual performance rating in the lowest 2 percent—by agency at each level having at least fifty persons—is cause for automatic dismissal.

Staffing in State and Local Government

Within the last decade, ten states have enacted comprehensive merit systems, bringing the total to thirty-three; in addition, a merit system functions in all state agencies administering federally aided programs for welfare, health, civil defense, and employment security. Only about one-tenth of the nation's counties have merit systems, but most of the large cities do. However, in some jurisdictions the merit system is far less rigorous than is the federal system, particularly in that it allows much more influence to seniority in promotion.[53] In some areas local groups, with an ethnic or other type of base, can manipulate the merit system rules and legally appoint and promote favorites.

With respect to training and management development, state and local governments are also following the federal lead, but to a lesser degree. The movement toward more such activities at the state and local levels has been furthered by federal subsidization of programs and by the practice of local branches of federal agencies inviting other governments to participate in their programs.

Some observers feel that the real productivity problem is at the state and local levels because (1) that is where the great numbers of personnel are, the figure being in the neighborhood of 11 million against almost 3 million in federal employment, and (2) much less has been done toward measuring and/or improving productivity.[54] Further, it is projected that employment by state and local governments for purposes other than education will almost double (that is, go from 4.3 million to 7.9 million) between 1970 and 1990.[55] Employment in local government is growing faster than in either state or federal; it is probably growing faster than in any major industry.[56]

The productivity measurement problem is, of course, difficult. For example, one city has established a bonus program for police based on reduction in reported crime. In order to keep police from simply refusing to report some crimes, historical ratios between citizen-reported and police-reported crime have been written into the agreement.[57] For another example, one city reports substantial savings via a bonus plan for garbage collectors in which workers were given 50 percent of the savings, most of which was savings in overtime work. To make this plan work, it was necessary to develop an effective inspection system to ensure that the work was actually getting done and done not too sloppily. Despite such difficulties, New York City in its major productivity drive during 1972–73 established 300 productivity targets for 16 city agencies, ranging from street potholes filled per day through water meters read (industrial engineering studies indicated that the standard should be 100, but the actual was 39), to restaurant sanitation inspections completed, to court cases processed, to infant mortality reduction, to welfare cases processed (social workers were observed playing chess and reading novels at their desks).

In some cases unions have cooperated fully; "productivity contracting" has devised numerous formulas for sharing of cost savings. In other cases, however, unions have vigorously opposed productivity programs of any type for fear that they would result in work speedup and job loss. In one case, unions actually secured legislation prohibiting implementation of any of the productivity recommendations made by a firm of management consultants.

Although incentive systems have been the favorite device for eliciting greater productivity from local government workers, there have been some fruitful operations research studies that have produced more economical personnel deployment programs and work scheduling. In New York City, a traditional-type industrial engineering study reduced the number of sanitation department vehicles out of service at any particular time from over 35 percent to around 16 percent. Still another approach is the use of sophisticated technical consultants. In one case, a Rand Corporation scientist retained by a city invented a chemical additive that greatly increased the effectiveness of water pumped onto fires; this "slippery water" in turn made it possible to use lighter hoses and to reduce the number of fire-fighting personnel required to run a fire engine.

One fascinating aspect of productivity programs at the local level is that many of the good ideas developed can be replicated in dozens or even hundreds of other localities with astronomical potential savings to the national economy. It has been estimated that a 1 percent productivity improvement by all local government employees could cut expenditures by almost $50 billion by 1985[58] or that a 3 percent improvement in municipalities having over 50,000 population could immediately mean a saving of $1 million per day.[59]

About 800 local governments, according to the National Commission on Productivity, have formal programs to improve productivity. Undoubtedly the City Managers Association's TAP (Technology Application Program) will secure fairly widespread adoption of some of the better productivity ideas. The need is great, the improvement opportunities are everywhere, and the know-how is available; the motivation and managerial control problems are what remain to be solved in most situations.

Collective Bargaining in the Public Sector

The decade of the 1960s was a period in which employees in the public sector on a widespread basis were granted, and began to exercise, rights of organization and bargaining. In the early 1960s the time was propitious for the organization of public employees who found themselves in the same position as industrial workers in the 1930s—numerous, needed, and neglected. Sensing this, President Kennedy in January 1962 signed an Executive order making it federal policy to grant recognition to unions of government employees. By 1964, about 60 percent of the employees of the Post Office Department, 33 percent of the blue-collar workers in other federal departments, and 14 percent of the white-collar workers were unionized.[60] Unionization has progressed steadily since then, as is evidenced by the membership figures of the American Federation of Government Employees: 76,000 in 1964 and 530,000 in 1972, making it the largest union in the federal service. By 1972, 85 percent of the postal service workers and 31 percent of all other federal employees were covered by collective bargaining agreements.[61] The percentage of federal employees in units with recognized bargaining agents was 58.

Although New York City and the state of Wisconsin had granted recognition to public unions before President Kennedy issued his historic order for the federal government, unionization at both the state and local levels followed developments at the federal level. By 1969, twenty states had passed some form of legislation dealing with public employees.[62] By the end of 1973, thirty states had granted collective bargaining rights to public employees; of those, twelve authorized broad-scope collective bargaining for both state and local government employees, an additional ten states offered limited collective bargaining to some government workers, and eight others offered bargaining rights just to teachers.

The most controversial issue in public collective bargaining is this: Which, if any, public employees should have the right to strike? Or, put another way, should employees in the vital services (police, fire, sanitation, etc.) be permitted to strike? Although strikes are illegal in the federal service and for employees of all but a very few states—in 1970, Hawaii became the first state to grant the right to strike to all employees in all categories—strikes of government workers occurred with increasing frequency once unionization was established. In the first year of the 1960s, there were only 26 strikes at all jurisdictional levels; in the last year of the decade, there were 411 of them—372 by local government employees, 37 by state employees, and 2 by federal employees.[63] Although labor leaders have been jailed and the Armed Forces have been called upon to operate transportation facilities, there appears to be no effective deterrent to public emergency strikes.[64]

The second most controversial issue in public collective bargaining is: What items are bargainable? This issue is being thrashed out on many different items in many different jurisdictions; the outcome of this process could add further inflexibilities and restrictions on the amount of discretion managers have in promoting and otherwise rewarding the most competent and aggressive employees. Union action could not only limit managerial discretion but also undermine the merit principles.[65] There are many other areas, such as workloads, use of labor-saving devices, and discipline, where unions could have either a helpful or harmful effect on work-force effectiveness. Some observers feel that so far the unions have had a salutary effect in limiting the arbitrariness of officials and in giving workers some voice in the huge bureaucratic process.[66] However, there is a serious question of how to settle disputes. How far can arbitrators go in spending monies from the public treasury? In connection with productivity improvement programs, as has been noted, some public employee unions have been quite cooperative while others have been completely resistant.

Perhaps the most basic question to be asked is: What will happen to the public interest? Will public collective bargaining diminish the role of legislatures while building up the roles of executives and union officials? Especially when the executive and the union officials are close political allies, how will runaway spending and financial disaster be avoided?

Unfortunately, the subject of public collective bargaining is too big to be covered in this book; in-depth consideration of these fascinating issues must be left to other courses and other textbooks.

SYSTEMS MANAGEMENT AND THE STAFFING PROCESS

Much of what has been happening in personnel management in both business and government over the past decade constitutes a movement toward systems management. The integration of personnel management with the rest of management has brought holistic decision making to staffing; the personnel specialists' work on job design, personnel management, and organizational development does much more to make total organizations effective than did their earlier isolated efforts in selection or training.

Another way in which the staffing function has been moving toward systems management is in the use of computers. On the government side, where an organization such as the Air Force has more employees than any single business firm, there has been substantial progress in computerizing personnel records systems. These systems enable personnel specialists to make decisions, for example, on utilization of an individual's skills or on personnel development programs on the basis of up-to-date and thoroughly processed data on all Air Force personnel.

All the personnel specialist's skills are vitally needed as an organization moves more deeply into computerization and automation. In most cases there will be fewer but more sophisticated jobs. The person who formerly occupied a station on an assembly line or who maintained a certain type of machine will probably have to learn how to monitor and maintain a number of different kinds of equipment on the automated production line and/or the computerized information system. This ties in with the idea of training people to do a number of jobs, a form of job enlargement. Also, it presents the selection and training specialists with a tremendous task of determining which workers can absorb such sophisticated training and which must be placed in more traditional types of operations. But, above all, it provides an opportunity for designing jobs anew.

Training will also be required at middle and higher managerial levels, where it will be necessary to get managers to make systems decisions rather than departmental decisions.[67]

Also, after a fairly advanced stage of systems management has been reached, it will be necessary to build a new type of employment relationship. Project management structures will probably be used extensively to handle the rapid changes of products and processes. Projects will come and go. Workers will have less permanent relationships with a given supervisor, department, or even type of operating activity. Psychologically, they will have to be prepared for this temporariness, this recurring need for retraining and regrouping. Probably it will be necessary to build loyalty to the overall organization by keeping the worker informed of the firm's planning and of his or her role in those plans. There will be stress on the ability to form a project team and bring it to effective operation. Performance appraisal may be more by group than by individual. Promotional paths may involve fewer but bigger jumps.

Quantitative Methods

Another hallmark of systems management is the use of quantitative methods. As personnel specialists become more deeply involved in the design of work systems and with all the activities of line managers, it is inevitable that they become involved with quantitative methods of decision making and quantitative measurements of the effectiveness of their techniques.

A recent article explains a cost-effectiveness technique applied to personnel programs by the Xerox Corporation.[68] This technique instills considerable discipline into deciding which and how many personnel management programs to fund by subjecting them to a careful analysis worked out around the following questions:

> *Determining the state-of-the art requirements.* Are the necessary skills available?
> *Determining the ease of implementation.* Will line management accept and execute the program?
> *Determining the net economic benefits.* Will the program be cost-effective?
> *Determining the economic risks.* Can the company afford not to act?

Use of the first two factors makes it possible to attach a probability factor to a straight cost versus benefit comparison.

Pointing out that in most businesses the personnel element constitutes between 40 and 70 percent of total costs, while personnel staff costs usually range between 1 and 2 percent of payroll, the proponent of this technique argues that companies would have stronger personnel programs if they built lists of possible projects arrayed in priority order according to their cost-effectiveness.

A technique potentially useful in manpower planning is Markov chain analysis, a way of analyzing sequential decisions. Recent articles have explored application of it to evaluating alternative personnel policies (e.g., promotion from within for certain openings, establishing particular qualifications and certain job progression paths, etc.), especially their effects on the supply of qualified workers and on the advancement achieved by current employees.[69] Also, simulation models can project the effect of particular policies under various possible expansion and contraction conditions.

Human Resource Accounting

Another attempt to bring quantitative methods to the staffing process is what is called "human resource accounting." Still in its infancy, this idea seeks to apply to an organization's human assets the same investment analysis—attention to the condition of the asset and reporting of the investments made as well as their depreciation—that is applied to physical assets.[70]

In order to measure the payback on an investment in human resources (such as a supervisory training program, for example), it is necessary somehow to measure the ultimate effect of that program on productivity and/or sales. Sometimes these ultimate effects do not occur for a long time; also, sometimes it is virtually impossible to say how much of an increase in productivity is due to new equipment and how much to improved supervision. Sometimes it is possible to get an earlier indication of the effect of a training program or some other personnel management program by measuring "intervening variables" such as turnover, absenteeism, grievance rate, or morale. Such measures are often reliable indicators of real costs or savings that will sooner or later be reflected in the P&L statement and balance sheet.

One technique being used experimentally is to capitalize the cost of a training program (that is, instead of treating it as a current expense, add it to an asset account such as "net investment in human resources") and depreciate that asset over time and/or when the trained employee leaves the organization.[71] If fully incorporated into an organization's public reports, this practice would increase earnings at the time that the asset was written up and decrease earnings when it was written down; such effects might be sharp in times of heavy layoffs or heavy hiring and training. However, such accounting for human assets could be confined to internal reports; it would certainly focus attention on the magnitude of an organization's human assets, on ways of determining the tangible effects of personnel management programs, and on the desirability or undesirability of investing in human assets versus investing in other kinds of assets.[72] Again, personnel decisions would become much more integrated into an organization's total management strategy.

SUMMARY ON THE STAFFING PROCESS

The managerial process of staffing comprises a number of specialist activities that over the years have been quite highly developed, involving a considerable body of technique. These techniques have been only lightly considered in this chapter, leaving most of their discussion for other courses and other textbooks.

The personnel management techniques, if properly integrated into the total managerial process, can contribute significantly to the performance of business or government organizations. Moves to achieve such integration have, in many situations, been successful over the past decade. One problem spurring such integration has been the productivity crisis of recent years. In the attempt to develop organizations that meet the needs of today's workers, personnel specialists have become deeply involved in job design, personnel management, and organizational development in addition to their more traditional activities of employment, training, wage and salary administration, and other service activities.

The integration of personnel management activities into the bigger management picture constitutes one step toward systems management. So does the computerization of personnel records. Both are moves toward holistic decision making. But many challenges remain for personnel specialists to use their techniques in shifting work forces from traditional-type operations to computerized, automated operations. Achieving organizational effectiveness in the new types of operations will require not only technological change but also a great deal of wise adaptation to today's economic and sociological environment.

REVIEW QUESTIONS

1 List and briefly explain the activities traditionally included in the staffing function.
2 What information is involved in determining (*a*) what an employment candidate *can* do, and (*b*) what the candidate *will* do?
3 In what ways can an MBO program strengthen the performance appraisal process?
4 Why does the significant productivity problem within government occur at the state and local levels?
5 Describe the ways in which changes occurring in the staffing function constitute movement toward "systems management."

DISCUSSION QUESTIONS

1 With reference to the organization with which you are, have been, or hope to be associated, what factors should be investigated in a study designed to determine the costs of a mistake in hiring at a middle-management level?
2 Develop pro and con arguments as to whether government employees providing vital services should be permitted to strike.
3 The federal civil service has been praised and criticized. From what you know about the civil service:
   a Does it do more harm than good for the employee, for the agency, and for the general public?
   b Are unions making the civil service superfluous?
   c How do good managers work within the civil service system?

NOTES

[1] This statement has been disputed by students who are government employment specialists. They contend that letters of inquiry from government agencies do elicit useful information, especially from other government agencies.

[2] "Where They Make Believe They're the Boss," *Business Week,* Aug. 28, 1971, pp. 34–35, reports that the Internal Revenue Service is using this technique, which was pioneered by the American Telephone and Telegraph Company. For a recent report that thoroughly covers the literature and research on this subject, see Ann Howard, "Assessment of Assessment Centers," *Journal of the Academy of Management,* March 1974, pp. 115–134.

[3] James Conant, "The Performance Appraisal: A Critique and an Alternative," *Business Horizons,* June 1973, p. 78.

[4] H. H. Meyer, E. Kay, and J. R. P. French, Jr., "Split Roles in Performance Appraisal," *Harvard Business Review,* January–February 1965, pp. 123–129.

[5] Walter "R." Thomas, *From a Small Naval Observatory* (Naval Institute Press, Annapolis, Md., 1972), p. 28.

[6] The latter point is disputed by Alan L. Patz in "Performance Appraisal: Useful but Still Resisted," *Harvard Business Review,* May–June 1975, p. 79. He feels that promotions should be based on potential to handle the new job more than performance on the past job.

[7] This judgment is shared by Conant, op. cit., p. 78; however, Patz, in the article cited in the immediately preceding footnote, feels that performance appraisal should be kept separate from MBO. He reasons that MBO focuses on the future, on goals, while performance appraisal focuses on past performance. He sees performance appraisal as purely a counseling, development device.

[8] This subject often constitutes a full-semester course in itself. For one leading textbook, see David Belcher, *Compensation Administration* (Prentice-Hall, Inc., Englewood Cliffs, N.J., 1974)

[9] "How the Xerox Ombudsman Helps Xerox," *Business Week,* May 12, 1973, pp. 188–189.

[10] National Productivity Commission, *First Annual Report* (U.S. Government Printing Office, 1972), p. viii. See also the section by Herbert Stein in National Productivity Commission, *The Meaning and Measurement of Productivity,* September 1971. Also C. Jackson Grayson, "An Expanded Concept of Productivity and Its Implications for Economic Policy Makers," *Sloan Management Review,* Spring 1974, especially p. 87.

[11] "GM Zeroes In on Employee Discontent," *Business Week,* May 12, 1973, p. 148.

[12] National Commission on Productivity, *Second Annual Report* (U.S. Government Printing Office, March 1973), especially the Introduction by Peter Peterson.

[13] I. Siassi, Guido Crocetti, and Herzl R. Spiro, "Loneliness and Dissatisfaction in a Blue-Collar Population," *Archives of General Psychiatry,* February 1974, pp. 261ff.

[14] Louis (Studs) Terkel, *Working* (Pantheon Books, a division of Random House, Inc., New York, 1974).

[15] "GE Zeroes In on Employee Discontent," op. cit., p. 144.

[16] W. E. Reif, D. N. Ferrazzi, and R. J. Evans, Jr., "Job Enrichment: Who Uses It and Why," *Business Horizons,* February 1974, pp. 73–78. This article reports the findings of a mail questionnaire to large firms on usage of job enrichment.

[17] Donald C. Burnham, *Productivity Improvement* (Carnegie Press, Carnegie Institute of Technology, Pittsburgh, 1973).

[18] "How Texas Instruments Turns Its People On," *Business Week,* Sept. 29, 1973, pp. 86–90; Charles L. Hughes, *Goal Setting: Key to Industrial and Organizational Effectiveness* (American Management Association, New York, 1965).

[19] Robert Ford, *Motivation through the Work Itself* (American Management Association, New York, 1969).

[20] Frederick Herzberg, "The Wise Old Turk," *Harvard Business Review,* September–October 1974, pp. 70–80. The basic Herzberg works are *Work and the Nature of Man* (Thomas Y. Crowell Company, New York, 1966) and (with coauthors) *The Motivation to Work* (John Wiley & Sons, Inc., New York, 1959).

[21] *Work in America,* a report of a special task force to the Secretary of Health, Education, and Welfare, prepared for Committee on Labor and Public Welfare of the U.S. Senate (U.S. Government Printing Office, February 1973). The thirty cases are summarized in the appendix. See also Judson Gooding, *The Job Revolution* (Walker Publishing Company, Inc., New York, 1972).

[22] This case is reported by Richard Walton both in *Work in America* (pp. 77–80) and in "How to Counter Alienation in the Plant," *Harvard Business Review,* November–December 1972, pp. 74–79.

[23] Statement by Perh Gyllenhammar, president of A. B. Volvo, in a speech reported in *HBS Bulletin,* January–February 1975, pp. 33–34.

[24] L. E. Bjork, "An Experiment in Work Satisfaction," *Scientific American,* March 1975, pp. 17–23.

[25] Harold Wool, "What's Wrong with Work in America?—A Review Essay," *Monthly Labor Review,* March 1975, pp. 38–44.

[26] Walton, "How to Counter Alienation in the Plant," op. cit. pp. 70 and 77. Walton examines the question of why these success stories have not been widely imitated in "Explaining Why Success Didn't Take," *Organizational Dynamics,* Winter 1975, pp. 3–21.

[27] Eric Trist, G. W. Higgins, H. Murray, and A. B. Pollock, *Organizational Choice* (Tavistock Publications, London, 1963).

[28] "Europe Likes Flexi-Time Work," *Business Week,* Oct. 7, 1972, pp. 80–81; and A. O. Elbing, H. Gadon, and J. R. M. Gordon, "Flexible Working Hours: It's About Time," *Harvard Business Review,* January–February 1974, pp. 18ff.

[29] J. C. Swart, "What Time Shall I Go to Work Today?" *Business Horizons,* October 1974, pp. 19–26.

[30] M. J. Gannon, "Four Days, Forty Hours: A Case Study," *California Management Review,* Winter 1974, pp. 74–80.

[31] Leonard Woodcock, president of the United Automobile Workers, as quoted in "Blue Collar Blues?" *Newsweek,* Apr. 29, 1974, p. 90.

[32] This chronology is borrowed from Marshall E. Dimock and Gladys O. Dimock, *Public Administration,* 4th ed. (Holt, Rinehart and Winston, Inc., New York, 1969), p. 184; however, a few deletions and many updating entries have been made. Help from both the Washington and the Honolulu offices of the U.S. Civil Service Commission is gratefully acknowledged.

[33] John Fisher, "Let's Get Back to the Spoils System," in Dwight Waldo (ed.), *Ideas and Issues in Public Administration* (McGraw-Hill Book Company, New York, 1953).

[34] Enid F. Beaumont, "A Pivotal Point for the Merit Concept," *Public Administration Review,* September–October 1974.

[35] Robert T. Golembiewski, "Civil Service and Managing Work," *American Political Science Review,* December 1962, pp. 961–974; also reprinted in Robert T. Golembiewski (ed.), *Public Administration: Readings in Institutions, Processes, Behavior* (Rand McNally & Company, Chicago, 1966), pp. 175–189.

[36] E. B. McGregor, Jr., "Problems of Public Personnel Administration and Manpower: Bridging the Gap," *Public Administration Review,* November–December 1972, p. 889.

[37] *Measuring and Enhancing Productivity in the Federal Sector,* a study prepared for the Joint Economic Committee of the U.S. Congress by the CSC, the General Accounting Office, and the Office of Management and Budget (U.S. Government Printing Office, 1972), pp. 20ff. For an article based on this report, see Elmer B. Staats, "Measuring and Enhancing Federal Productivity," *Sloan Management Review,* Fall 1973, pp. 1–9.

[38] Sig Gissler, "Productivity in the Public Sector: A Summary of a Wingspread Symposium," *Public Administration Review,* November–December 1972, p. 841. This article is part of a fourteen-article symposium in this issue entitled "Productivity in Government."

[39] Felix A. Nigro, *Modern Public Administration,* 2d ed. (Harper & Row Publishers, Incorporated, New York, 1970), p. 296.

[40] Ibid., p. 304.

[41] Harry F. Rosenthal, in an Associated Press release in the *Honolulu Star-Bulletin,* Jan. 25, 1972, p. C-16.

[42] Robert Vaughn, *The Spoiled System* (Public Interest Research Group, Washington, D.C., 1972).

[43] David T. Stanley, "Merit: The Now and Future Thing," *Public Administration Review,* September–October 1974, pp. 451–452.

[44] Raymond Jacobsen, Director of the Bureau of Policies and Standards in the Civil Service Commission, quoted in the Associated Press story cited in footnote 41.

[45] Ibid., quoting John Griner, president of the American Federation of Government Employees.

[46] Robert Hampton quoted in Samuel Stafford, "Civil Service Commission's Hampton Aims at Achieving Agency 'Responsiveness,' " *Government Executive,* February 1971, p. 30.

[47] Charles Perrow, *Complex Organizations* (Scott, Foresman and Company, Glenview, Ill., 1972), p. 11.

[48] "Middle Managers Swap Jobs," *Business Week,* Oct. 16, 1971, p. 68.

[49] Associated Press story, op.cit.

[50] Arch Patton, "Government's Revolving Door," *Business Week,* Sept. 22, 1973, pp. 12–13.

[51] Arch Patton, "Government's Pay Disincentive," *Business Week,* Jan. 19, 1974, pp. 12–13.

[52] *Measuring and Enhancing Productivity in the Federal Sector,* op. cit., p. 18.

[53] Nigro, op.cit., pp. 256–257 and 302–303.

[54] Richard S. Rosenbloom, "The *Real* Productivity Crisis Is in Government," *Harvard Business Review,* September–October 1973, pp. 156ff.

[55] *The U.S. Economy in 1990,* prepared by the National Industrial Conference Board for the White House Conference on the "Industrial World Ahead: A Look at Business in 1990," 1972.

[56] Harry P. Hatry, and Donald M. Fisk, *Improving Productivity and Productivity Measurements in Local Governments,* a report prepared for the National Commission on Productivity (The Urban Institute, Washington, D.C., 1971), pp. 4–5.

[57] "Boosting Urban Efficiency," *Business Week,* Jan. 5, 1974, pp. 37–39.

[58] Ibid., p. 37.

[59] Rosenbloom, op.cit., p. 158.

[60] Ira Sharkansky, *Public Administration: Policy Making in Government Agencies,* 2d ed. (Markham Publishing Co., Chicago, 1972), p. 136; this account relies upon Frederick C. Mosher, *Democracy and the Public Service* (Oxford University Press, Fair Lawn, N.J., 1968), chap. 6.

[61] Richard J. Murphy, "The Difference of a Decade," *Public Administration Review,* March–April 1972, pp. 108 and 111. This article is one of five in a symposium in this issue entitled "Collective Bargaining in the Public Sector: A Reappraisal."

[62] Gus Tyler, "Why They Organize," another of the articles in the symposium mentioned in the immediately previous footnote, p. 101.

[63] U.S. Department of Labor, Bureau of Labor Statistics, *Work Stoppages in Government, 1958–68* (U.S. Government Printing Office, 1970), p. 2.

[64] John S. Greenebaum, "A Partial Solution to Strikes by Essential Workers," *State Government Administration,* July–August 1971.

[65] Frank P. Zeidler, "An Overview of Labor-Management Relations in the Public Service," *Public Personnel Review,* January 1972.

[66] Felix A. Nigro, "The Implications for Public Administration," *Public Administration Review,* March–April 1972. This is the concluding article in the symposium mentioned in earlier footnotes.

[67] L. H. Mantell, "The Systems Approach and Good Management," *Business Horizons,* October 1972, pp. 43–51.

[68] Logan M. Cheek, "Cost Effectiveness Comes to the Personnel Function," *Harvard Business Review,* May–June 1973, pp. 96–105.

[69] P. C. Nystrom, "A Job Vacancy Model for Organizational Manpower Management," *Academy of Management Proceedings,* annual meeting, 1972; and T. A. Mahoney and G. T. Milkovich, "Internal Labor Markets: An Empirical Investigation," *Academy of Management Proceedings,* annual meeting, 1972.

[70] "A New Twist to 'People Accounting,' " *Business Week,* Oct. 21, 1967, pp. 67–68; R. L. Brummet, W. C. Pyle, and E. G. Flamholtz, "Human Resource Accounting in Industry," *Personnel Administration,* July–August 1969; R. B. Frantzret et al., "The Valuation of Human Resources," *Business Horizons,* June 1974, pp. 73–80; and a set of three articles in *California Management Review,* Summer 1974.

[71] Although it might be fairly simple accounting to attach the cost of a training program to the individual employees who attended the training session and to depreciate the cost over the careers of

those employees, it is much more difficult to handle an organizational development program, for example, because the sessions are less formal and there is less definition of who is participating and how much.

[72] Thomas W. McRae, "Human Resource Accounting as a Management Tool," *The Journal of Accounting,* August 1974, pp. 32–38.

RECOMMENDED READINGS

Foulkes, F. K.: "The Expanding Role of the Personnel Function," *Harvard Business Review,* March–April 1975, pp. 71–84.

Gibson, Charles H.: "Volvo Increases Productivity through Job Enrichment," *California Management Review,* Summer 1973, pp. 64–66.

Mills, Ted: "Human Resources—Why the New Concern?" *Harvard Business Review,* March–April 1975, pp. 120–134.

Sorensen, James E., and Thomas L. Sorensen: "The Conflict of Professionals in Bureaucratic Organizations," *Administrative Science Quarterly,* March 1974, pp. 98–106.

Chapter 9

Managerial Decision Making and Information Systems

The dramatic improvements in managerial decision making over the past two decades have been rooted in many aspects of management. In addition to the obvious contributions of new quantitative decision techniques and improved information via computerization, there have been significant contributions to decision making from new planning and control techniques, new organizational structures and leadership methods, and new behavioral sciences insights into the decision processes. The ways in which all these developments have affected decision making, plus the role of computerized information systems in decision making, are brought out under the following headings:

Managerial Decision Making
    Decision Making and Planning/Controlling Techniques
    Decision Making and Organizational Structure
    Decision Making, Leadership, and Communications
    Behavioral Sciences Insights into Decision Making
    Decision Making and Quantitative Methods
    What Does an Administrator Need to Know about Quantitative
        Techniques?
Information Needs and Information Technology
    Introduction
    Historical Perspective on the Role of Information in Decision Making
    Current Status of Management Information Systems (MIS)
    What Does a Manager Need to Know about MISs?
The Future: Systems Management, Decision Making, and Information Systems

MANAGERIAL DECISION MAKING

Decision Making and Planning/Controlling Techniques

The great advances made since World War II in both the theory and practice of planning/controlling have done much to raise the quality of managerial decision making. After all, it is in the processes of planning/controlling that most managerial decision making is done.

Perhaps the greatest strengthening of decision making has come from the greater attention to objectives which has been a big feature of MBO, project management, and virtually every management curriculum or executive training program. The emphasis on objectives and on strategy helps (1) to keep decision making consistently focused rather than going off in many directions, which often produces bad decisions, and (2) to ensure that the specific decision techniques are harnessed to serving purposes and programs that are well thought out. Since many of the developers of decision techniques are not managers, they tend to emphasize technique over purpose. Guided by a strong structure of objectives and strategy, they are better able to see the really fruitful applications of their techniques.

It is not claimed that all business firms are doing a textbook job of thinking out their objectives and planning/controlling for them; however, it does appear that large numbers of companies have made substantial progress in these respects. That such progress has been less certain in the field of public administration is clear from the general failure of PPBS, the public administration counterpart of MBO. As noted in the chapter on planning, some decision theorists in public administration, known as incrementalists, reason that the public decision process is too pluralistic, too compromising, and too pragmatic for long-range objectives, rational analysis, and systematic planning. They feel that incremental budgeting is more realistic. A leading writer of this school, who has popularized the "muddling through" concept, writes:

> Except roughly and vaguely, I know of no way to describe—or even to understand— what my relative evaluations are for, say, freedom and security, speed and accuracy in governmental decisions, or low taxes and better schools than to describe my preferences between specific policy choices that might be made between the alternatives in each of the pairs.[1]

The incrementalists feel that day-to-day approaches to small pieces of major problems may achieve significant aggregative results but that comprehensive, integrated, rational programs eventually fall of their own weight. Another group of decision theorists, with roots in behavioral sciences empirical research, favor the "existentialist" approach, a "now generation" philosophy.[2]

It is, then, not surprising that less progress has been made on formulating and using objectives and that therefore less improvement has been made in decision making.

Increased professionalism in planning and controlling has also meant greater as well as more effective use of decision techniques. This applies to the older techniques which were often neglected in business, such as breakeven charts, return-on-investment analyses, capital investment payback calculations, and ratio analyses. It applies, also, to older decision techniques which had hardly entered the management field, such as the use of matrixes and field-force analyses. The former is a simple method for systematically analyzing a number of alternative actions on a number of criteria (which may be weighted to add precision to the process). Field-force analysis, also a simple method, involves the systematic listing of all the forces favorable to a certain course of action and all those against; then the planner can work out a program that strengthens the favorable and avoids or weakens the unfavorable forces. And obviously, more professionalism in planning has meant far more use of the newer quantitative decision techniques such as PERT and PERT/ Cost (which have been described in the planning chapter) and others (which will be described later in this chapter).

Decision Making and Organizational Structure

Some large organizations have sought to sharpen decision making via three different organizational devices. One is decentralization of decision-making authority to profit centers, an approach that moves decision making closer to the actual activity and provides incentive for people down the line to be creative. The second device is the project or product structure, that is, matrix or crosshatched structures which seek to preserve the best features of two ways of structuring, by function and by project. Utilizing PERT and other computerized data reporting methods, a project manager may pull together all information pertinent to a given project; this manager is, thereby, able to make better decisions about that project than can the manager whose attention is spread over many different projects. The third device is the flat organization structure which seeks improved decision making by placing it closer to the scene of action (decentralization) and by shortening lines of communications.

Decision Making, Leadership, and Communications

The quality of decision making has no doubt been enhanced in some situations by participative patterns of leadership that use more people's ideas and that encourage creativity. Participative leadership is consistent with the trend toward greater delegation of authority in decentralized decision structures, getting some part of decision making into the hands of persons closer to operations.

Some organizations have increased participation in decision making by using brainstorming, a technique for establishing a climate that encourages creative thinking.

The increasing size of firms has also encouraged the so-called multiple executive (or office of the president) and committee decision making. Both are formats for bringing more talent into decision making.

Behavioral Sciences Insights into Decision Making

In addition to their input on participative management, behavioral scientists have made other contributions to decision making. Herbert Simon, basing his early work on Barnard's descriptions of the realities of the decision-making process, has been a leading figure in bringing realism to decision theory. His concept of the "administrative man" has effectively replaced the unrealistic and not too helpful "economic man" of earlier decision theory.[3] Simon contended that decision makers typically reason from a simplified model of the real situation; also, their individual psychological makeups result in a subjective rationality rather than an objective one. He pointed out, further, that the search for alternative courses of action is rarely complete; instead, decision makers accept satisfactory alternatives rather than insisting on optimum solutions. He also described the role of the searcher's expectations or aspirations, born of previous successes and failures, in determining what is satisfactory.

Simon's associates at the Carnegie-Mellon Institute have conducted many studies of actual decision processes, elaborating and modifying his insights. One set of experiments developed models of the decision-making processes in specific real business situations, and the models then successfully predicted subsequent real decisions.[4] Simon has sought to learn more about human decision making by attempting to duplicate human decision processes on computers, including the processes of intelligence activity (finding occasions for making a decision), design activity (finding possible courses of action), and choice activity (choosing among alternative courses of action).[5] Others are studying the risk attitudes of decision makers and means for measuring an individual's risk aversion.[6]

Decision Making and Quantitative Methods

One legacy of World War II to management was a new group of quantitative tools for analyzing problems. Mathematically trained analysts developed models and used statistical search techniques that enabled British and American military commanders to make better decisions about the assignment of scarce submarines to convoy duties, the use of planes in air strikes and air defense, the maintaining of inventories of scarce aircraft parts at bases all over the world, and other problems.[7] A few years after the war, when computers became available to handle the lengthy computations involved, operations research (OR) specialists proceeded to develop various techniques that have been applied to many different kinds of managerial decisions.

Linear Programming[8] One computer-facilitated technique that has found considerable and increasing use over the last fifteen years or so is linear programming. It is a method for stating a problem in a series of mathematical equations and then finding the optimum solution to the equations by a systematic trial-and-error procedure.

Linear programming can be used in short-range planning, such as scheduling the jobs to go on each machine in a machine shop for a week's operation (or scheduling a month's production in an assembly plant). Here the problem is to secure maximum profit from a number of machines, each with a number of different capabilities, processing a number of different products, each of which returns a different profit and each of which might be machined by any one of a number of different combinations of machines. The machine-shop problem might be complicated by various constraints such as current sales rates of each product, inventory space available, inventory policies, and contingency factors (such as a policy of not loading three particular machines too heavily at the same time because they are subject to frequent breakdown and are the only machines that can perform certain vital operations).

Linear programming can also be used on somewhat longer-range planning, such as how to improve a large firm's distribution system (number and location of warehouses, modes of transport and costs of each mode, locations of customers, quality of customer service under each plan, and many other considerations and constraints).

One thing that these two problems and many other real managerial problems have in common is a large number of variables or factors to consider; in fact, these problems typically have far more variables than the unaided human mind can process systematically. However, each of the conditions may be stated in an equation, and the complete set of equations can be solved rapidly by a computer.

For example, the fact that a certain machine can be run no more than 300 hours per month and that a unit of product 1 requires 5 hours on it, a unit of product 2 requires 3 hours on it, and a unit of product 3 requires 1 hour on it may be expressed as:

$$5X_1 + 3X_2 + X_3 \leq 300$$ which is the math way of saying that the total production must be some mixture of the three products that can be accomplished in no more than 300 hours

Or a need to limit production of product 2 to no fewer than 100 units and no more than 400 units may be expressed as:

$X_2 \geq 100$ which says that production of product 2 shall be greater than or equal to 100

$X_2 \leq 400$ which says that production of product 2 shall be less than or equal to 400

Another feature that these problems have in common is that the desired solution (sometimes called the objective function) may be stated in specific, definite terms, such as to make the greatest profit or to produce a certain quantity at the least cost. These problems are said to be *deterministic*. This, too, may be put into an equation. For example, if the profit for each unit of product 1 is $10; for product 2, $7; and for product 3, $6; the objective may be stated as follows:

Maximize $z = 10X_1 + 7X_2 + 6X_3$ which is the math way of saying that the solution sought is the maximization of profits

Another feature that these problems have in common is that the relationships are linear or reasonably so. Thus the profit on each unit of product 1 remains $10 and does not increase or decrease as the volume of product 1 changes within the limits used. (If the relationships are not linear, a more complex form of programming must be used.)

A problem with a large number of variables and constraints would involve larger equations and a dozen or dozens of them. The mathematical process for solving such a set of equations is tedious, involving repetitious procedures for systematically withdrawing one variable, then another, then another, until the optimal solution is identified. But a computer working with standardized software (that is, computer programming that enables the machine to carry out the procedure) that is now readily available can quickly define the optimum machine-shop schedule, distribution system, or product mix that will give maximum profit or whatever solution the problem is designed to produce.

This exposition of linear programming has obviously dealt with only the most simple, straightforward applications. Specialists may do much more with the technique. For example, they can give the manager more than just the answer to the stated problem; they can often use the same analysis to demonstrate to the manager that even better results are obtainable by using more of the same or different types of the resource (equipment, fertilizer, etc.). Thus, it is said that every linear program has a shadow, or dual, program which provides additional information and insights into the problem. Also, the specialist can use related mathematical procedures to reveal the consequences of slight changes in the variables; this type of sensitivity analysis lets the manager know what the critical and noncritical ranges for any factor in a problem are. Such analyses may alert the manager to the feasibility of ideas that have never before been tried in the operation or to dangers of ideas that might be contemplated. Again, the analyst may simplify complex problems by use of a technique known as decomposition, which breaks the problem into simpler problems and then reassembles it into a solvable problem.

Probability Techniques[9]   In many planning problems, the quantitative relationships cannot be stated precisely; rather, they must be "guesstimated." In contrast to the deterministic problems discussed earlier, these are *nondeterministic* problems. For example, a manager is required to decide what production facilities to acquire for a new product line about to be put on the market. The safest course of action would be to subcontract the production to some established organization; this would require a minimum quantity guarantee, which would involve far less risk than there would be in building a special production facility for the new product. But if the product achieves a big sales volume, the subcontractor may not be able to handle it; also, the manager will then wish, for many reasons, that a special facility had been built immediately. But if the manager starts out by building a large factory and the product then does not sell well, there will be a big loss. Perhaps the best answer is the middle course—a small factory. The middle course would produce medium-happy results if the sales are high, happy results if the sales are medium, and medium-unhappy results if the sales are weak.

A group of quantitative techniques called probability (or uncertainty, or nondeterminate, or stochastic) methods can help managers with this problem and a host of others that are somewhat similar. Probability techniques perform calculations on the basis of a mixture of hard (factual) data and soft (estimated) data. For example, in the problem just discussed, the hard data are the facts about the investment required by each course of action and the operating profit or loss that would be sustained at each level of sales under each course of action, or strategy; the soft data are estimates of the sales volume—the probability that the product will achieve only a low volume of sales, the probability that the product will achieve a moderate volume of sales, and the probability that it will achieve a high volume of sales. Although these estimates may be based on experience with similar products in times past, they are still only estimates—therefore, soft data. Accordingly, these decision techniques cannot supply foolproof answers, but they can help managers by giving them many keen insights into the pros and cons of alternative strategies.

In the matrix in Figure 9–1a, the alternative strategies (i.e., to subcontract, build a small factory, or build a large factory) are on the vertical axis and the possible sales volumes (called "states of nature" by decision theorists, who seem to have a penchant for vague terms) are on the horizontal axis. The numbers in the boxes are the payoffs, or the net results (profit or loss in millions of dollars) for each strategy under each possible volume.

In Figure 9–1a it is assumed that the probabilities of A, B, or C occurring are equal; therefore, the value of each course of action is the average of the three results.

Under probability analysis, however, an estimate is used for the probability of A, B, or C occurring; the same payoff figures used in the first matrix are modified in the matrix in Figure 9–1b by that probability (which is shown in the top box in each vertical column). Much different payoff figures and a much different relation among the expected values result; alternative 2 emerges as the best choice. If the estimates of probability used in the second matrix are at all realistic, this procedure gives the manager a much more accurate picture of the gamble involved than does the first matrix.

Figure 9-1a Matrix without Probabilities

	States of nature			
Alternative decisions ↓	A (small sales)	B (medium sales)	C (large sales)	Expected value (average of A, B, C)
1 (subcontract)	0.0	+ 2	+ 4	+ 2
2 (build small plant)	− 4	+ 4	+ 8	+ 2.66
3 (build large plant)	− 10	0.0	+ 20	+ 3.33

Figure 9-1*b* **Matrix with Probabilities**

Alternative decisions ↓	States of nature			
	A (small sales) (0.30)	*B* (medium sales) (0.50)	*C* (Large sales) (0.20)	Expected value (sum of *A, B, C*)
1 (subcontract)	0.0	+ 1.0	+ .8	+ 1.8
2 (build small plant)	− 1.2	+ 2.0	+ 1.6	+ 2.4
3 (build large plant)	− 3.0	0.0	+ 4.0	+ 1.0

Decision Criteria The user of probability techniques must be clear as to the basis for the manager's decision. Thus, a payoff matrix for another problem might indicate that:

Strategy *x* yields the greatest potential profit under certain conditions (states of nature), but also, under other conditions, the greatest loss.

Strategy *y* yields only a modest profit at best but does not expose the company to loss under any conditions.

Strategy *z* yields a fairly substantial profit under the most probable conditions and a slight profit or loss under other conditions.

Which course of action does the manager choose? A number of decision criteria (maximum, average, minimum-maximum, least regrets, etc.) have been precisely stated and implemented mathematically. By using these criteria, the decision maker not only becomes much clearer about exactly which criterion is being used but also can use neatly packaged mathematical procedures and computer programming for solving the problem according to that criterion.[10] These criteria are *alternatives* to using the maximum-expected-value approach illustrated above.

Other Probability Techniques The foregoing matrixes are quite simple, having only three strategies, three states of nature, and one variable (the sales volume achieved). Many variations of this basic technique, much more sophisticated mathematically, have been developed to handle different types of problems. Thus the decision tree[11] and Markov chains[12] techniques are designed for problems that involve a sequence of decisions—that is, dynamic problem analysis. In the example of choosing between subcontracting, building a modest plant, or building a large plant, a decision-tree analysis can consider what conditions and results might be faced at later points in time under each present alternative. Sometimes an alternative that looks best under two-year analysis does not look so good if evaluated over three

2-year periods; thus, a decision tree can combine short-run and long-run analyses.

The *Monte Carlo* and *queueing* techniques are used for problems involving random occurrence of events and waiting lines, as in deciding how many toll gates to have on a bridge, how many checkout counters to have in a grocery store, how many tool cribs to have in a large manufacturing plant, or how to schedule staff in a hospital outpatient clinic.[13] And *Bayesian analysis* is a method used to apply statistical techniques to expert opinions in problems such as that facing a product manager who must decide between using box or bag packaging.[14] In this type of problem, a number of factors can be quantified objectively (e.g., the costs of the packages, the costs of the different packaging processes, freight charges associated with each type of packaging, etc.), but a number of other factors must be estimated and assigned a probability (e.g., the consumer acceptance of the different packages, the damage-prevention value of each type of package, the retailer's reaction in terms of shelf space allotted, etc.). Bayesian analysis builds equations that combine the objective and subjective data, and these equations are designed to approximate the net effect of using each type of packaging. By varying the subjective data, the manager can get an idea of which factors are the critical or sensitive elements in the problem. The manager might, then, concentrate the market research on learning more about what the actual magnitudes of the critical factors might be. In this box versus bag case, even the most pessimistic estimates on the box showed it to be superior to the bag.

Although these probability techniques are not widely employed, their use is growing steadily. For example, the Wells Fargo Bank in California gives much of the credit for its highly successful "Gold Account" to research and analysis done by its in-house group of management scientists.[15]

That these techniques do not always supply correct answers is illustrated by the failure of Corfam, the new shoe material which was launched after much "venture analysis" by a highly sophisticated marketing group at Du Pont.[16] In this case, apparently, the subjective judgments built into the equations were far off on the market strength of other emerging shoe materials, particularly plastics. More important than this celebrated failure, however, is the fact that in the same period the same group at Du Pont launched twenty-four new products, most of which have been successful.[17] The loss flowing from a failure can be turned off; the profits flowing from a success can keep flowing for years and years.

Among the new techniques for new applications that continue to appear is one for the complex but programmable problems of selecting securities for an investment portfolio with defined objectives and policies.[18]

Inventory Methods   Perhaps the most thoroughly developed and widely used quantitative decision techniques are those applied to inventory control. Such data as rates of past usage of an item, quantity-price discounts, shipping time, and costs of "stock outages" may be fed into models (formulas) which can determine when and how much to reorder. Such decision outputs can be used as advisory to human decision makers or can be automated even to the extent of typing out reorder letters to the supplier company.

Cost-Benefit (or Cost-Effectiveness) Analysis   In an earlier discussion of the use of newer decision techniques in the Department of Defense, it was mentioned that this technique was applied to major decisions on selection of weapons systems. Also, there have been attempts to use it in selecting from among alternative approaches to major socioeconomic problems such as medical care for the needy, pollution, and slum clearance.[19]

Cost-benefit analysis can be a rather simple technique, literally comparing cost with benefit where both can be easily calculated; but where both cost and benefit are difficult to define (that is, when they involve complex calculations or subjective elements), the technique can be quite complex.

Simulation Models[20]   The quantitative technique having perhaps the greatest potential in both business and government management may well be the use of simulation models. Their potential is so great because they can be applied to major decisions. Thus the chapter on planning has discussed reports on the use of simulation models in projecting the long-run impact on a corporation of a contemplated acquisition, in undertaking development of new product lines, in evaluating possible changes in financial structure, and in invading new marketing territories. However, it has also been noted that some companies have been unable to solve the complexities of a model of a total organization and that some of the most publicized simulation models have not fulfilled the promises made for them.

Although simulations will not provide definitive answers to ill-structured problems, they can, when they *are* effective, give many insights that will sharpen an executive's analysis and open up new ideas. News accounts tell of one chief executive, with a computer console beside his desk, who regularly uses simulation;[21] one writer contends that many more top executives will, in the not-too-distant future, operate in this way.[22] This prognostication is based on the belief that breakthrough conditions now exist. Many younger executives reaching the top have been trained to understand these techniques, adequate libraries of relatively inexpensive standard programs are now available, and the advantages accruing to the users of this technique will be so great that competitors will have to jump on the bandwagon.

What Does an Administrator Need to Know about Quantitative Techniques?

Over the past two decades during which these newer quantitative techniques have been available, organizations that might use them have been faced with a dilemma: Persons who understand the techniques usually do not understand the managerial problems; conversely, persons who understand the managerial problems usually do not understand the techniques. Or put another way, managerial types, who are suited to handling ill-defined and sometimes emotion-laden problems, are by nature disinclined to use mathematics; conversely mathematicians, who are precise persons seeking precise answers, do not understand management problems in their real-life complexity. Or, put still another way, managers alone will miss many fruitful applications of quantitative methods; mathematicians alone will produce useless answers to unrealistic problems.

In order to solve this dilemma, it is not necessary to make managers into mathematicians or to make mathematicians into managers.[23] (Although this is being done with good results by the increasing numbers of persons who take an engineering undergraduate degree and an administration graduate degree.) But managers can be given enough understanding of these techniques—of when they are useful and when they are not useful, of when the output should be relied upon as a definitive answer and when it should be regarded as just added insight into the problem—to enable them to work effectively with specialists in quantitative decision techniques. The separate and joint responsibilities of the two parties, manager and specialist, may be outlined as follows:

1 Identifying the problem, including a definition of the objectives sought in solving the problem. (The manager's responsibility.)
2 Devising alternative ways of attacking the problem; selecting the way best suited to the data available. (A joint responsibility of manager and specialist.)
3 Stating the problem in mathematical form, securing or devising a computer program to process it, and translating the output into nonmathematical terms. (The responsibility of the specialist.)
4 Deciding how to use the output, that is, how much reliance should be placed upon the output. (The manager's responsibility.)

Middle- and higher-level line managers can learn the essence of what they need to know about quantitative methods (in order to work in the way just outlined) in a short training program—of perhaps four to eight hours—based on the "thought process" (or "decision logic") chart displayed in Figure 9–2.[24] One big problem in such a training program is the special terminology involved, terminology that appears to be essential to mathematicians but which scares off nonmathematicians. But in today's vernacular, it is "not all that difficult." For example, in Figure 9–2, the first step after identifying the problem is to decide whether or not it can be expressed in quantitative terms. When it cannot be directly expressed in quantitative terms, the diagram leads to the strange words "utility function." A "utility function" is simply a device, or procedure, for putting nonquantitative factors into quantitative terms such as units of satisfaction, "utils," or points. Thus, a certain change in employee morale may be measured by a point rating scale (and if desired, those points may be arbitrarily assigned dollars-and-cents value). So cross out the box containing the confusing term "utility function" and write in "Can it be translated into reasonably accurate quantitative terms?"

Once that hurdle is jumped, the nonmathematician reader of this chart encounters a terribly frightening use of symbols, $y = f(x)$, which means simply that one thing (y) changes as some other thing (x) changes. The f denotes the relationship between changes in the two things—perhaps y increases two units every time x increases one unit, or perhaps y increases three units every time x decreases one unit.

Having conquered the fear caused by the $y = f(x)$ symbol, the reader is then confronted by the strange term "stochastically," but that whole box can easily be changed to read: "Is the relationship definitive, or does it involve probabilities?" (If definitive, move to right; if probabilities, move down.) Still another strange term

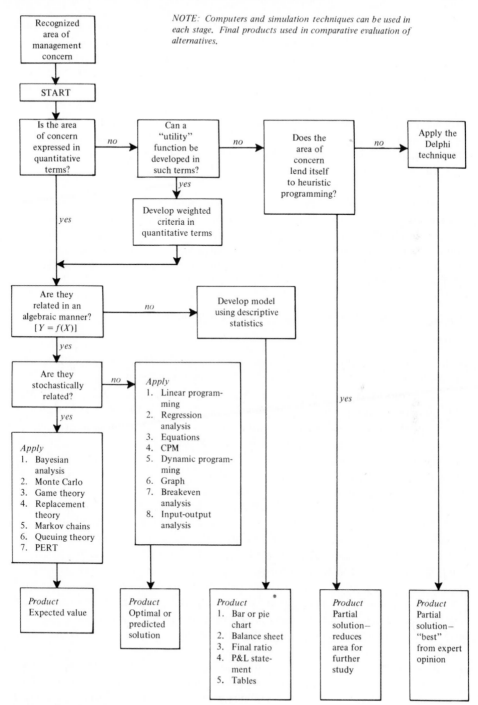

Figure 9–2 Quantitative methods logic chart.

is "heuristic," which simply means that judgment is used to simplify or estimate complex parts of the problem if this can be done without changing the basic nature of the problem. The rest of the strange terms in this diagram are names of particular techniques, some of which have been discussed in this chapter and all of which could be adequately explained in a short training program.

It would appear, then, that if managers do not panic at the first sight of strange jargon and symbols, they can, in a short training program, learn the basic logic of quantitative methods. They will then be over the fear of the unknown and well on their way to understanding the range of techniques available—what they can and cannot do. So prepared, such managers can work effectively with technical specialists in quantitative methods.

Is it necessary that managers acquire the capability of working effectively with specialists in quantitative decision techniques? In the great majority of cases the answer is clearly yes. Even though some of the techniques are little used today and some of the more sophisticated techniques have yielded disappointing results, the trend is clear: these techniques will be used more often and more effectively, especially in larger businesses and at higher staff levels in government.[25]

INFORMATION NEEDS AND INFORMATION TECHNOLOGY
Introduction

One of the great truths of management lies in the simple statement that "Decisions are only as good as the information on which they are based."

Everyone recognizes that this statement applies to highly factual operating decisions (for example, how many units to manufacture next week) or to decisions based on quantitative decision techniques (for example, how many warehouses to have and where to locate them on the basis of linear programming). But some managers do not realize that this statement also applies to the less structured, more judgmental decisions that managers make; rather, such managers have the romantic idea that big decisions are made by strokes of genius or sharp intuition unburdened by a body of information. In fact, such is rarely the case. A high-ranking executive making a sweeping strategy decision (for example, how fast the firm should grow) needs to base that decision on solid information about market and demographic trends, competitors' strengths and weaknesses, the executive's own firm's strengths and weaknesses, probable technology developments over the next few years, and other information. Even a lower-ranking executive making an almost casual decision about how to handle an employee's informal complaint needs to have a sound factual background about current operating pressures, morale conditions in that employee's group, the characteristics of the employee's immediate supervisor, and the provisions of the collective bargaining contract.

Because managers make many different kinds of decisions, they need many different kinds of information—market information, product information, inventory information, cost information, financial information, historical information, current information, projective information, precise information, approximate information, crude information, workforce information, economic conditions information, and many other kinds.

Two points about these introductory remarks should be noted:

1 The term "information" rather than "data" has been used. Data become information when they are put into useful form. Although some managers can use data effectively, most managers do much better with data that have been put into a form useful for them. Hence, this section will deal with information.

2 The popular phrase "management information system" (MIS) has not been used because it needs to be introduced carefully; it is currently being used with various meanings. At one extreme, it denotes the total flow of all kinds of information to all kinds of managers in an organization. Admittedly, such an MIS is not very systematic in its construction or its application. At the other extreme, it denotes only such highly organized and systematically handled information as is quantitative and computerized and as flows from a single, integrated data base. Sometimes the phrase is used, as it will be used in this chapter, to denote a condition between these two extremes—a collection of quantitative, computerized, but not necessarily integrated information flows (such as marketing information plus production information plus financial information and possibly others).

This section will, then, look at the information needs of managerial decision makers and how these needs have been met in the past, how they are being met now, and how they probably will be met in the future.

Historical Perspective on the Role of Information in Decision Making

A basic element of scientific management, or Taylorism, one of the first great revolutions that laid the foundation for modern management, was the collection and analysis of facts—facts about such mundane activities as the size of shovels used in loading coal, the speeds at which metals were cut, the way assembly jobs were laid out, and many other production activities. From such data, Taylor and others produced information that enabled them to devise the "one best method" of doing certain jobs, thereby greatly enhancing production. Taylor's insistence on having factual bases for decisions is still followed today by industrial engineers; although in some instances extreme rationalization of work methods has been found to be somewhat counterproductive, industrial engineering plays a vital role in production management.

Another great change leading to modern managerial practice was the development of planning and controlling capabilities, with General Motors and Du Pont leading the way in the 1920s. One famous manager of that era attributes GM's rise to preeminence in the automobile industry, and its position as possibly the best-managed of all American corporations, mainly to its "passion for facts."[26] Thus GM simply gathered more information than its competitors had about who was buying what type of car and why. This enabled the corporation to sharpen its planning and control and thereby to outcompete its rivals. As others learned to gather information, GM stayed ahead by gathering more and different types of information.

As managers during the 1940s and 1950s learned more and more about how to plan and later about how to plan strategy, they realized greater and greater needs for external information (such as market-trend books, sets of economic indicators, etc.). As they learned more and more about how to control, they learned to put internally generated information into useful form (such as the Du Pont return-on-investment form or chart-room displays).

These growing demands for information in forms other than the traditional accounting-financial reports placed great strain on the accountants-controllers who were the information technologists of that day. They had difficulty working with these new kinds of information; also, they had difficulty keeping different kinds of information current and coordinated. For example, the author recalls encountering, about twenty years ago, a situation in a defense manufacturing company in which each of five different sections (customer relations, industrial engineering, purchasing, cost accounting, and billing) was working with a different bill of materials for the same product. The customer had kept requesting changes in the product as each new shipment was received, and the firm's information system simply was not fast enough or accurate enough to put these changes through to all departments quickly. During this period, the ability of managers to use information ran ahead of the ability of information specialists and their equipment to supply that information.

But a third great revolution affecting managerial practice—computerization—has made it possible to supply more information than most managers can use. Progress in both equipment and software has been so great that one writer concludes: "The computing power is available; the major challenge is management's ability to harness the power."[27] Computing power is available not only via big computers but also in smaller packages via the minicomputers that came into widespread use in the mid-1970s; these machines make many new kinds of installations possible, make it possible for medium-sized companies to have their own computers, and make possible the computerization of certain activities in decentralized units of large organizations.[28]

As new generations of ever more powerful computers became available,[29] many new possibilities in managerial planning and control emerged. These can perhaps best be grasped by considering the stages of progress in the nonscientific use of computers in business and government:

First Stage The first computers were put to work on clerical jobs (payroll, customer billing, accounts receivable, etc.), substituting machine power for human clericals but not changing procedures. This type of usage continues to expand, having extended in many instances to almost every clerical activity within a large business or government agency.[30]

Second Stage Some decisions of the operating and middle-management type were automated or semiautomated. Examples are an airline reservation system, an inventory control system that not only determines reorder points and amounts but also initiates reorders, a production scheduling system, or an internal revenue application that automatically sorts out those tax returns that are to be considered for special audit. Although some large organizations have initiated many such systems over the last decade, most computer-using companies are only now moving into such applications.

Third Stage   Computers used in higher-level managerial decision making. Applications include the use of simulation models in projecting possible results of various growth strategies or various financing moves or the use of quantitative decision techniques in evaluating risk versus gain potentials in alternative methods of launching a new product or choosing between two potential new products. A few leading organizations have been making such applications over the past five to seven years, but they are still only a small percentage of all computer users.

Although the first stage may be described as electronic data processing, the second and third stages get into management information systems.

Clearly, the twenty years since computers first appeared on the management scene have been hectic ones; new developments have cascaded in, one on top of another, too rapidly to be thoroughly understood and carefully assimilated even by the specialists in the field. It is not surprising then, that the average practicing manager is considerably confused. In order to help reduce this confusion, the next section will seek to summarize some things that have been learned about the application of computerized information flows to managerial decision making and about the design and management of information systems.

The Current Status of Management Information Systems

Impact of Computerization at Different Managerial Levels   Considerable confusion can result when writers discuss "the impact of computers on management," because different readers may be thinking of different levels of management. Hence writers should talk of "the *impacts* of computers on management," because impacts have been quite different at different levels. A leading writer on this subject summarizes the differential impacts as follows:

> There is no question that computers and MIS have had and will have progressively more impact on management. Existing systems have influenced lower levels of management, particularly operating management. The effect on middle management has been slight, while the impact on top management has been almost non-existent.[31]

Explaining why the impact on top managers has been slight, the same writer points out that top managers are primarily concerned with planning, while middle and operating-level managers are primarily concerned with control. Computers are more adept at control than at planning. Moreover, the planning that top managers do is partly based on external data and concerns problems that are loosely structured—both of these are conditions which limit the usefulness of computers.[32] The planning that the lower levels do (for example, production scheduling) is much more tightly structured and has much better developed computer programs (software) available.

The differential impact between middle managers and operating-level managers can be seen by considering the control activities of each level. Budgeting is a main use of computers in many companies. A middle manager in production focuses on results against quarterly and annual budgets in a number of different production activities; an operating-level manager focuses on daily and weekly budgets in a single production activity. Although computerization can strengthen the control reports at both levels, the impact is much greater at the operating level, particularly if the system is on-line and real-time. For another example, the manager of inventory control is usually a middle-level manager who watches control reports on the performance of various subordinate managers and on overall inventory levels, production slowdowns due to material shortages, and the like—areas in which computers can be of some help. However, the lower-level managers in this area (perhaps called buyer supervisors) control inventory levels of specific items. This is an activity which computers can perform automatically, leaving the manager to handle only the exceptional cases. Thus, in these areas, the computer has had a profound effect upon the jobs and numbers of operating-level managers. It has had some, but less, effect upon the jobs of middle-level managers.

Drawing such distinctions between the impacts of computerization at different managerial levels can help clear up still other confusions in the literature on management information systems. For example, the debate between those who feel that real-time, on-line information systems are practical and those who believe they are not appears to be rooted in the fact that the pro writers are looking at lower-level management while the con writers are looking at top-level management.[33]

Increasing Effectiveness of MISs   Another subject on which a reader of management literature can become considerably confused concerns whether such systems are generally useful or useless. Some writers have contended that managers have been glutted with so much information that they cannot use any of it and also that they often get managerially useless information.[34] According to this view, this wastefulness occurs because managers do not understand computers and computer specialists do not understand management; the two groups simply have not learned to work together to produce useful subsystems and systems. However, other writers who have surveyed managers' attitudes toward computerized information systems report that in general managers know what they want, know how to get what they want, and know how to make effective use of what they get. The explanation of these differences in findings appears to lie in the fact that the latter writers made their surveys some five to six years later than did the writers who came up with such unfavorable views of MISs. The more recent writers reason as follows:

> . . . if these middle managers were once at the mercy of the technical systems designers, they now have or are gaining the confidence, knowledge, and organizational power to reduce the flow of irrelevant information.[35]

The attitude of managers toward MISs is also relative to the organizational level of the manager being surveyed; it has been found that higher-level managers find the information outputs less useful than do the middle- and lower-level managers.[36]

In summary, when considering such questions as the impact of computerization on management or the usefulness of MISs, it is necessary not only to differentiate between managerial levels but also to be sure that one is dealing with current views of this rapidly developing field.

Higher-Level Managers and the MIS   Although the previous two sections of this chapter have indicated slight involvement of high-level executives with computerized information systems, this condition is changing and can be expected to change at an increasing pace. In fact, as mentioned earlier in this chapter, a few top executives have already learned to use simulation models to project possible outcomes of alternative new-product programs, alternative financial structures, or contemplated acquisitions.[37]

Early in 1974, the U.S. Air Force completed implementation of the advanced data system that enables top-level commanders at USAF Headquarters in Washington, D.C., or at the Military Personnel Center in San Antonio, Texas, to make decisions (such as the assembly of an emergency task force of certain specialized skills to assist in some diplomatic negotiations) on the basis of personnel data that are no more than a few days old. A decade or so ago when the phased development of this new information system was started, it took three months for new personnel information about who had acquired what skills or experience and where the individual was located to be transmitted through various levels and to be processed into a form useful at the top.[38]

A number of things are happening which will accelerate the pace of top management involvement in, and satisfaction with, computerized information systems. First, persons who have been exposed to computers early in their lives, usually in college or graduate school, are now mature enough to move into high positions; such persons encourage rather than resist such developments. Second, "direct-access" (or "user-oriented") languages are being developed which enable a person with only brief training to interact directly with the computer. Third, better and better software is available off the shelf for such applications as economic forecasting, sales forecasting, simulating part or all of an organization's operation, projecting balance sheets and P&L statements, or using quantitative decision techniques (such as multiple correlation-regression analysis or those for solving waiting-line problems discussed in the first half of this chapter). Fourth, useful data banks on the external (to the firm) information needed in high-level planning are becoming easily accessible. Fifth, and probably most important, occasionally a top manager using computerized decision techniques scores a competitive success, and that spurs many others to "get with it."

Although all these developments will increase the usage of computerized information systems by top-level executives, one authority predicts that most of that usage will continue to be with the assistance of computer specialists rather than directly by the executives.[39]

Integrated MIS—Realistic, Practical?   Perhaps the biggest debate of all in the literature on information systems is: Is the idea of an integrated MIS technically possible and/or managerially practical?[40] Here again, writers on opposite sides of the subject appear to be talking about different things but using identical terminology. At this point in time the answer to the question appears to be: If by "integrated" is meant a single, totally integrated system including all the organization's needs for quantitative information, the answer is "No, it's neither technically feasible nor managerially practical." However, if by "integrated" is meant an integrated smaller piece of the total package, then the answer is "Yes, it is technically feasible and managerially practical."

In a totally integrated system, a piece of information (such as order number, customer's name and address, or description of item ordered, etc.) is entered only once; thereafter, all or any part of that information can be recalled instantly by any section within the company that has a legitimate use for it. If the entries are made on line (that is, automatically as production items tumble out of the machines that manufacture them) and if they are processed in real time (that is, put through the system immediately), then the information that each user gets is not only up to date but also identical to the information that any other user gets. No longer would different parts of a given company be working with different bills of material on one product; no longer would a customer's name have to be manually retyped again and again (on order acknowledgements, shop orders, shipping labels, bills of lading, invoices, etc.). From a single data bank, each manager in the entire organization would have flowing to him or her the information needed to plan and control a particular activity, and only that information would be received.

At its extreme, the concept of total integration can tie in with a great deal of marketing decision making and manufacturing processing. Thus, as noted in an earlier chapter, some lumber companies have systems that automatically weigh and measure a log, comparing these data with stored data about the wood requirements of various products to decide what products might be made from it. If to this system is added a flow of information about market prices and inventory levels of all products, then an elaborate model could automatically decide what products should be made from that log, direct the plant equipment to so route and process the log, and even store the resulting products in the right places in the warehouse and send them to the loading dock when ready to be shipped. If all this were further integrated with computerized cost accounting and order filling, the information would flow through into the cost reports and final P&L statement and balance sheet.

A beautiful concept but neither realistic nor practical now.

Although some lumber companies have developed parts of such a system, none has put it all together in a single system.[41] Such total integration requires near perfection in accounting design, systems design, computer programming, and the design of automated production facilities. The original cost would be staggering in dollars and in time, and the system might well be too inflexible to accommodate frequent changes in product design or marketing practices. And, as has been noted, top management simply does not need up-to-the-minute details or even daily P&Ls; in fact, such information may be so lacking in perspective that it would be more harmful than helpful to top executives. What is needed for top-level planning is a great deal of externally generated information—much more than just current market prices—which at present is not available in computer-accessible form.

Retailers, Airlines, Buses A type of operation that appears to lend itself to a high degree of automation is retailing. Some electronic cash registers enable the clerk to punch in data, others can read merchandise tickets, and still others read (with a wand) codes printed on merchandise labels or packages. In any case, the data are fed to a computer and processed (in real time or later in batches) to set up sales records, merchandising analyses, inventory records and perhaps automated reordering, and the revenue and cost-of-goods-sold parts of the P&L report. In some applications, one section of the ticket remains with the merchandise in order that all the entries can be reversed in case the merchandise is returned by the customer. A late 1972 report pointed out that ninety or so large retailing organizations had by then gone to such systems, most fairly recently;[42] obviously many more organizations have gone to such systems in the years since 1972. Indications are that the systems will pay for themselves through labor saving within from 1½ to 3 years while speeding up customer service and reducing inventories. The saving is calculated at about 1 percent of sales; this may sound small, but it amounts to doubling the rate of the profit on sales of grocery retail chains.

These retail systems are not total systems in that they do not tie in with physical operations (except the checkout and inventory operation), personnel records, or long-range planning; however, they do integrate a wide and important swath of a retail operation.

Airlines, by the nature of their operations, have almost been forced to become leaders in extending operations information systems into use in management decision making.[43] The computerized on-line reservation systems, which store the customer's name and other information when the reservation is made, also furnish information for sales planning and forecasting, for route planning, and for food catering. The flight operations systems that feed the operations control centers, discussed in the chapter on control, also furnish information for maintenance and safety decisions; they may soon be tied in on some airlines with crew assignment decisions. Although the two major systems have some interconnections, they will not be tied in with revenue accounting until automatic ticketing and machine-readable tickets are in use.

Metropolitan bus operation and management is another field in which considerable integration has taken place. The Kansas City Area Transit Authority has a revenue collection system that not only curtails thefts but also provides operating data on its buses. Integrated circuits in the buses keep track of fare box revenues, passenger numbers, routes, and mileage. At the depot, a vacuum unit sucks coins from the fare box while the data go to a minicomputer; also, as servicing is done, gas consumption and other information is also fed into the computer. The system provides basic data for revenue accounting, analysis of which buses consume how much gas, maintenance scheduling, and marketing analyses.[44]

A Manufacturing-Selling Firm Looking at a manufacturing-selling firm, one writer shows the interrelationships among fifteen different subsystems (strategic

planning, marketing, financial accounting, order processing, requirements generation, purchasing, materials control, production scheduling, production control, inventory control, engineering and research, sales outlets, maintenance, quality control, and transportation) as in Figure 9–3. The subsystems, which are interrelated,
unfortunately flow into one another in a complex pattern. Full integration of such
a pattern is not feasible because of the difficulties mentioned earlier. The author who
developed this diagram feels that each of these subsystems should be developed
separately, using a common data base insofar as is possible but realizing that one
all-encompassing data base may not be possible in many cases. Other authors recognize three types of managerial decisions—operational control, management control,
and strategic planning— that call for three separate and quite different data bases:

> . . . the "totally-integrated-management-information systems" ideas so popular in the
> literature are a poor design concept. More particularly, the "integrated" or "company-
> wide" data base is a misleading notion, and even if it could be achieved would be
> exorbitantly expensive.
>
> Information differences among the three decision areas also imply related differ-
> ences in hardware and software requirements. On the one hand, strategic planning
> decisions require access to a data base which is used infrequently and may involve an
> interface with a variety of complex models. Operational control decisions, on the other
> hand, may require a larger data base with continuous updating and frequent access to
> current information.[45]

These authors go on to point out that the three types of decisions also call for
different types of managerial and analyst skills and different forms of organizational
structures around which to build the information system.

In summary, the point seems clear that in most large organizations a totally
integrated system is at this time not feasible; however, neither is it practical to
develop each subsystem entirely independently. Rather, the recommended procedure is to have centralized, expert data-base management that will so design subsystems that some can be easily integrated and there will finally be perhaps three or
more separate systems, each with its own data base.

What Does a Manager Need to Know about MISs?

Obviously, the answer to this question varies considerably with the manager's position in the organizational hierarchy. A manager at the lowest level who does not
expect to rise any higher needs to know little more than how to put data into it and
how to use the information that comes out of it. Such managers probably will have
little to say about what their information needs are or how one subsystem relates
to another. They will probably see electronic data processing systems chiefly as
means of mechanizing clerical tasks, a process that can be handled by data technologists. The more interesting case, of course, is that of the higher-level manager who
sees the computerized information system as a means of automating certain programmable decisions and/or of acquiring better information which leads to better
human decision making. What does such a manager need to know about information

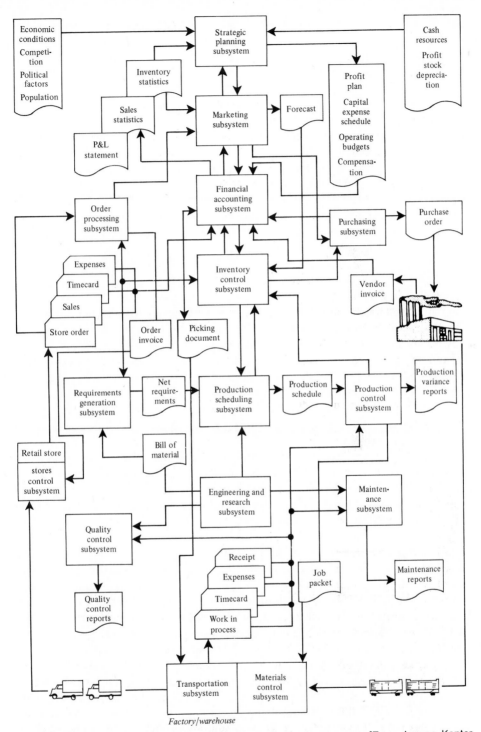

Figure 9–3 Information system model for a manufacturing company. [From Jerome Kanter, *Management Oriented Management Information Systems* (Prentice-Hall, Inc., Englewood Cliffs, N.J., 1972), p. 65. Reproduced with permission of Prentice-Hall, Inc.]

systems and information technology? The following five points can be made in answer to this question.

1 *It is the user's system, not the specialist's.* Probably the biggest lesson that has emerged from the first two decades of computerized information systems is that it is the manager who must decide *what* the system is to do; the computer specialist decides only *how* the system is to do it. It is the organization's objectives and plans (i.e., its strategy) that determine all the activities involved in executing the organization's strategic plans. Decisions about what information is needed are the manager's to make; they are in no way within the competence or responsibility of the computer specialist. Or, in the words of one authority, "marrying a computer to a business operation begins with management and a thorough study of business operations, not with the computer."[46]

2 *A larger plan should underlie work on a specific subsystem.* Another big lesson that has emerged over the past few years is that it is a mistake to proceed first with one limited subsystem, then another, and then another without providing for common data-base management and for some integration of data bases eventually. Often it is discovered too late that some subsystems could have and should have been integrated, and correction of the mistake involves costly recoding and redesign. Clearly, it is desirable to do as much "system specification" as possible, (that is, deciding how much of what kinds of data the system is to take in and what kinds of output will be required) before designing any specific subsystems. Again, these are chiefly managerial-type decisions—decisions about *what* the system is to provide—although the computer specialist should participate in order to keep the decisions feasible from the technology and cost standpoints. Only after the systems specification decisions have been made can the computer specialist make sound systems design decisions—the *how* it is to be accomplished questions (e.g., which computers, what kinds of memories, and what kinds of output and other peripheral devices to use).

3 *Managers must make the cost-benefit calculation, comparing the specialists' estimates of the costs with their own estimates of the benefits.* Only the manager can know whether real-time data are worth the cost in a particular situation or can understand the problem of excess or unneeded information.[47] On the cost side, there are three categories: (1) hardware-software costs, running about 35 percent of the total; (2) system design and programmer costs, running about 40 percent of the total; and (3) operating costs, including the salaries and supplies involved in storing, accessing, and maintaining data, which run about 25 percent of costs.[48] On the benefits side, there are the possible reductions in clerical costs and the less tangible benefits. The latter benefits are usually the more important, including such considerations as better and faster information for decision making, ability to use decision techniques not feasible without computers, and improvement of customer service. Unfortunately, the calculation of these less tangible benefits is often largely guesswork. The *valuation of information* is a vague and difficult subject for many managers. It is reasonable and logical to assume that better information will lead to better decisions; in fact, it has long since been demonstrated in considerable detail, as set forth in Figure 9–4, how a well-developed information system can give a marketing manager, for example, excellent information on which to base plans.[49] As enlightening as this display is, it does not tell a manager how much of what kind of information will lead to how much better decisions. Only rather abstract techniques for information valuation are available;[50] one hopes that more precise measurements will be developed as more and more successful applications are made of new information systems and new decision techniques. If that is done, then managers will be able to make relatively tangible cost-benefit calculations on proposed management information systems.

4 *Computerization involves classic "change management" problems.* Much has been learned the hard way about the human problems attendant upon moving into each succeeding stage of computerization. Highly perceptive leadership is required to avoid resistances and conflicts that result in waste, confusion, and even sabotage.

In the first phase, when clerical tasks are being mechanized, a big human problem is that of insecurity on the part of workers and first-level managers. Either job insecurity (will the machine replace me?) and/or ability insecurity (will I be able to understand the new methods?) can lead to resistance or sabotage.[51] So insecure were the personnel in one government agency observed by the author that the operation was "double tracked" (that is, the manual system was maintained alongside the computerized system) for six years before employees were ready to acknowledge that the new system would work! The antidote to insecurities of this sort is, obviously, communications, training, and participation. The personnel must be given reassurances about which and how many jobs will be abolished and when. And they must be carefully trained in the new procedures and given plentiful opportunities to voice their problems and fears.

In later phases, when the information system is being extended to high-level planning and control, there are big problems in manager-specialist relationships. If the technology specialists dominate these phases, there is a real danger that they will flood managers with too much not-very-useful information and decision techniques. But line managers will not be able to maintain control (over MIS budgets and over issues such as real time versus batching) unless they are given adequate training and consistent top-level support. Steering committees should be so constructed and run as to achieve manager-specialist coordination and sound consideration of each functional department's interests.[52] High-level managers have the responsibility not only for supporting line subordinates but also for seeing that consistently poor performers on either side—line managers moved into MIS work or computer specialists—are removed.

5 *Responsibilities may be stated by specific steps.* The general points made in the foregoing sections may be specifically stated if the process of developing an information system is broken down into the following steps:

Reports Formerly Used for Planning

Reports Used after the Management Information Study

DEFECTS | **ENVIRONMENT** | **COMPETITION** | **INTERNAL**

DEFECTS

No information on the total market for gasoline and other automotive products—its size, its location, its rate of growth, etc.

No information on competitors—what they are doing, where, and how well

Marketing profit-and-loss concept encouraged faulty planning because of arbitrary transfer prices

No information that discloses the company's marketing strengths and weaknesses by class of trade, e.g., company-owned stations, independent dealers, distributors, etc.

Marketing expense information misleading because of allocations of headquarters' overhead

Inadequate data on size "mix" of stations, e.g., number and percentage of stations selling different volumes of gasoline

Inadequate data on the sales performance of newly built or acquired stations

- Division and district expenses
- Sales volume by product for divisions and districts
- Marketing department profit and loss
- Capital budgets by division for five years

ENVIRONMENT

Ten-year industry sales by product, by marketing division, and where possible, by trading area

Ten-year car registration records by state and trading area (where possible)

Ten-year population records by trading area

Ten-year record of new road-mile construction by state and trading area (where possible)

Five-year projection of 100 fastest growing trading areas in country—by percentage and absolute numbers

Five-year projection of car registration by state and trading area (where possible)

Report on federal road-building program

Five-year report (and five-year projection) on composition of country's automobile population by size, weight, horsepower, etc., for each division

Purpose: to provide an overall picture of the market, its composition, its size, its location, significant trends affecting any of these factors, etc.

COMPETITION

Ten-year share-of-market reports by product, by division, and where possible, by trading area

Special price reports intended to show (a) competitor's price strategy and (b) areas of the country classified by the nature of price conditions—stable, volatile, strong, weak, etc.

Five-year record of new station construction by competition, by division and trading area

Five-year summary of new refinery, terminal, and bulk plant construction by competition

Analysis of 100 largest and 100 fastest growing markets (trading areas) showing leading competitors in terms of volume, market share, laid-down costs, facilities, construction or acquisition activity, etc.

Special reports on key market developments, e.g., rebrander activity, additional quantities of gasoline, multiple octane pumps, etc.

Purpose: to identify who competitors are, how well they've been doing, and the likely direction of their future efforts

INTERNAL

Five-year sales and realizations by product, by division, by class of trade

Division and district expenses per gallon (without allocations of headquarters' expenses)

Marketing "net back" statements by product, by division, by district, and by bulk plant (realizations less expenses)

Laid-down costs by product, by terminal and bulk plant

Frequency distribution studies of gasoline sales by size of retail stations, by division and district

Share of company's total sales by product for each state

Five-year report of number of stations by type (owned, leased, etc.) by division and district

Five-year report of capital budgets by division and district (amounts authorized and spent)

Purpose: to assess the company strengths and weaknesses, thus permitting a correlation between the company's capabilities and the opportunities of the marketplace

Figure 9–4 Marketing planning information under old and new information systems.

    a Setting *organizational goals and objectives.*

    b Setting *strategy* for achieving the objectives and goals; that is, determining the main activities to be carried out, their scale and scope and other features that will help the organization succeed. These, in turn, indicate the *kinds of decisions* that will have to be made in the operation of the organization.

    c Setting the overall *system specifications;* that is, determining the kinds of information needed to make those decisions and carry out those activities—the kinds and approximate amounts of data to be inputted, the types of processing needed, and the forms in which the information is to be outputted. Plans for data bank(s) and for the amount of integration of subsystems to be sought. Setting of priorities among potential applications. Making overall cost-benefit calculations.

    d *Designing the system* involves selection of a computer and other hardware such as file storage media, input devices, printing facilities, computer and printing, capacities, methods of accessing and processing.

    e *Subsystem specification,* the specification process (described earlier) repeated at the subsystem level, identifying in detail the information that the subsystem needs in order to function and the sources of that information.

    f *Subsystem design* includes data coding and detailing the steps in acquiring, processing, and outputting data, ensuring that they blend together to meet the subsystem specification.

    g *Programming* includes writing computer instructions and forming them into a program that the machine can execute.

    h *Operation,* including the training of operators, operating per se, and maintenance.[53]

This is obviously an idealized process in that it assumes starting with a clear slate (no given objectives-goals or hardware) and in that it calls for considerable planning of the overall system before work on a particular subsystem is begun. Despite this unrealness, this listing can provide a vehicle for the following consideration of what a manager needs to know about information systems.

Although it would be desirable for both managers and information specialists to be thoroughly knowledgeable on all steps in the process, it is unrealistic to expect that many persons will be so completely trained. A more realistic but still ambitious hope is that each side would understand enough about the other's area to appreciate the skills and problems involved.

The manager bears full responsibility for steps *a* and *b.* Also, the manager is heavily involved in steps *c* and *e,* where he or she must work closely with the information specialist in gaining a synthesis between what managers desire and what the information specialist can deliver; the system must be consistent with the accounting system, the state of the programming art, and the machine capability. It is particularly important that the manager have a strong voice in the setting of priorities among possible applications because it is here that the readiness-resistance of the operating personnel must be considered.

The information specialist bears the chief responsibility for steps *d, f,* and *g.* Although it is desirable that the manager have some knowledge of at least one machine language, it is not necessary that he or she be able to do professional programming or be able to work on such technical questions as how to convert data and programs from one computer system to another, setting up audit and checking routines, deciding when to use simultaneous or multiprogramming, or designing testing programs.

The last step, operation, is again a joint responsibility, with the information specialist supplying the technical content of training and the manager handling the human aspects. The operation per se is supervised by managers, while maintenance is supervised by specialists.

THE FUTURE: SYSTEMS MANAGEMENT, DECISION MAKING, AND INFORMATION SYSTEMS

Decision making is best understood as flowing from the whole management system, and that is why this chapter first traced the many advances made in managerial decision making via better planning and control, via leadership techniques that bring more persons' talents into problem solving, via behavioral studies of the psychology and sociology of decision making, and via new types of organization structures. Only after this were quantitative decision techniques and computerized MISs discussed as factors making for improved decision making.

It is probably valid to say that both quantitative methods and management information systems are today in their infancies despite all the advances noted. Certainly there have not been as many applications of quantitative technique as would be indicated by the proliferating literature, and there have no doubt been more unsuccessful applications than have been reported.[54] Little has been learned about flow-type (holistic) decision making. And we can only guess at what a true systems management organization structure would look like. Presumably it would be designed primarily around decision making, far more so than are today's structures.[55] Design of a systems management structure would probably proceed along the following sequence, starting from the top:

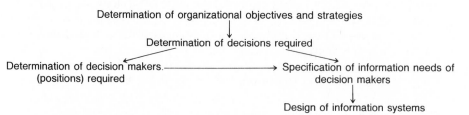

Government organizations would appear to present special difficulties in moving toward such rationally designed information systems and decision processes; there is always the danger of becoming bogged down in pluralistic politics and bureaucracy. Yet it is only in a government organization, NASA, that this type of structure has been approached in actual practice. But business firms rarely have the opportunity to build a new structure from a clear slate; rather, structures and data flows are changed bit by bit, so they usually represent compromises with the ideal. And this is the situation that many business organizations are in today—groping toward new kinds of decision-making positions, new types of information flows, and new kinds of organization structures. This is why it is difficult at this stage to say what a complete systems management structure and information system would look like.

Because computerization can only increase, younger managers and prospective managers are well advised to learn about the new decision techniques and information systems. This chapter has provided only the briefest introduction to these subjects; it indicates what needs to be learned but does not present the material that needs to be learned.

In the systems management era which lies ahead, the managerial job will be seen as the solution of problems whose key variables are people, economics, technology, and information. That last one, information, is the new requirement—the new basic element of virtually all managerial jobs. Of course, managers have always used information; however, only recently has enough been learned about information to make it a basic field of study for managers.

REVIEW QUESTIONS

1   Distinguish between "data" and "information."
2   Discuss the reasons why top-level managers will have increasing involvement with computerized information systems.
3   Describe the organizational devices used to improve decision making in business firms.
4   What are the critical differences between inputs of the manager/user and the computer specialist in the design of a computerized information system?

DISCUSSION QUESTIONS

1   With reference to the organization with which you are, have been, or plan to be associated, which old quantitative methods are used in decision making? Which newer ones? Why does this pattern prevail? Would the training program suggested in this chapter be effective in this organization? On what considerations do you base your answer?
2   How can business firms avoid the disadvantages of bit-by-bit changes toward new kinds of rationally designed information systems and decision processes while maintaining the advantages associated with experience gained during the firm's existence?
3   Briefly outline how costs and benefits could be determined and compared in evaluating a proposed computer information system for a city fire department.

NOTES

[1] C. Lindblom, "The Science of Muddling Through," *Public Administration Review,* Spring 1959, pp. 83–84. See also the primer for incrementalism by C. Lindholm and R. Dahl, *Politics, Economics and Welfare* (Harper & Row, Publishers, Incorporated, New York, 1953).

[2] A. Richter, "The Existentialist Executive," *Public Administration Review,* July–August 1970.

[3] Herbert A. Simon, *Administrative Behavior* 2d ed. (The Free Press of Glencoe, a division of the Macmillan Company, New York, 1957).

[4] R. M. Cyert and J. G. March, *A Behavioral Theory of the Firm* (Prentice-Hall, Inc., Englewood Cliffs, N.J., 1963).

[5] H. A. Simon, *The New Science of Management Decision* (Harper & Brothers, New York, 1960).

[6] Ralph O. Swalm, "Utility Theory—Insights into Risk-Taking," *Harvard Business Review,* November–December 1966, pp. 123–136. John S. Hammond III, "Better Decisions with Preference Theory," *Harvard Business Review,* November–December 1967, pp. 123–141.

[7] Florence N. Trefethen, "A History of Operations Research," in Joseph F. McCloskey and Florence N. Trefethen (eds.), *Operations Research for Management* (The Johns Hopkins Press, Baltimore, 1954), pp. 3–35.

[8] Almost any textbook on quantitative methods of decision making includes a substantial treatment of linear programming. This account has relied on Van Court Hare, Jr., *Systems Analysis: A Diagnostic Approach* (Harcourt, Brace & World, Inc., New York, 1967), pp. 164–166; and Frederick S. Hillier and Gerald J. Lieberman, *Introduction to Operations Research* (Holden-Day, Inc., Publisher, San Francisco, 1967), pp. 127–167.

[9] For more detailed descriptions of some techniques of this type, see Martin K. Starr, *Management: A Modern Approach* (Harcourt Brace Jovanovich, Inc., New York, 1971), chaps. 5 and 6; C. W. Emory and P. Niland, *Making Management Decisions* (Houghton Mifflin Company, Boston, 1968), chaps. 11 and 12; and Harvey Wagner, *Principles of Operations Research with Application to Managerial Decisions,* 2d ed. (Prentice-Hall, Inc., Englewood Cliffs, N.J., 1975), chaps. 16 and 17.

[10] Almost any text on quantitative methods of decision making covers this subject; however, for a thoughtful discussion of decision criteria and their uses, see David W. Miller and Martin K. Starr, *The Structure of Human Decisions* (Prentice-Hall, Inc., Englewood Cliffs, N.J., 1967), chap. 5. Marketing applications are presented in Philip Kotler, "The Use of Mathematical Models in Marketing," *Journal of Marketing,* October 1963.

[11] For explanations of this technique, see Edward A. McCreary, "How to Grow a Decision Tree," *Think,* March–April 1967, pp. 13–18; and Hammond, op. cit.

[12] For a discussion of this technique and an example of its application, see Philip Kotler, *Marketing Management: Analysis, Planning, and Control* (Prentice-Hall, Inc., Englewood Cliffs, N.J., 1967), p. 510.

[13] For an explanation of this technique, see Abe Shuchman, "Queue Tips for Managers," in Abe Shuchman (ed.), *Scientific Decision Making in Business* (Holt, Rinehart and Winston, Inc., New York, 1963), p. 300.

[14] For an explanation of this technique and another application of it, see Paul Green, "Bayesian Decision Theory in Pricing Strategy," *Journal of Marketing,* January 1963, pp. 5–15; also Starr, op. cit., pp. 225–233.

[15] "What Wells Fargo Wants in California," *Business Week,* June 2, 1973, p. 49.

[16] "Poromeric Heel Dragging," *Chemical Week,* July 26, 1969, pp. 43–44. See also the following articles from *Business Week:* "DuPont's 'Answer Machine,' " Dec. 20, 1969, pp. 68–70; "Picking Customers Out of the Mob," June 5, 1971, p. 71; and "Corfam Walks Again," July 10, 1971, p. 26.

[17] "A Management Leapfrog at DuPont," *Business Week,* Dec. 15, 1973, p. 48.

[18] Emory and Niland, op. cit. This volume gives a summary of techniques. For a nontechnical, journalistic treatment, see R. C. Weisselberg and Joseph G. Crowley, *The Executive Strategist* (McGraw-Hill Book Company, New York, 1969); also see David B. Hertz, *New Power for Management* (McGraw-Hill Book Company, New York, 1971).

[19] A. W. Marshall, *Cost/Benefit Analysis in Health* (The Rand Corporation, Santa Monica, Calif., 1965), p. 3274; R. A. Crystal and Agnes Breustu, "Cost Benefit Analysis and Cost Effectiveness Analysis in the Health Field," *Inquiry,* The Blue Cross Association, December 1966; Olaf Helmer, *The Application of Cost-Effectiveness to Non-Military Government Problems* (The Rand Corporation, Santa Monica, Calif., 1966), p. 3449; John Haldi, "Issues of Analysis in Cost-Effectiveness Studies for Civilian Agencies of the Federal Government," in D. I. Cleland and W. R. King (eds.), *Systems, Organizations Analysis, Management: A Book of Readings* (McGraw-Hill Book Company, New York, 1969), pp. 272–278.

[20] All the textbooks on managerial decision making cited in this chapter have sections on this subject; also, Ernest C. Miller, "Simulations," in *Advanced Techniques for Strategic Planning,* Research Study no. 104 (American Management Association, New York, 1971).

[21] "Running the Show with a Keyboard," *Business Week,* July 13, 1968, p. 778. See also "Adjusting the Mix at Pillsbury," *Business Week,* Sept. 30, 1967, pp. 167–172.

[22] Robert F. Vandell, "Management Evolution in the Quantitative World," *Harvard Business Review,* January–February 1970, pp. 83–92.

[23] For an article that supports this statement after making a rather probing study of the differing cognitive styles of managers and management scientists, see James L. McKenney and Peter G. W. Keen, "How Managers' Minds Work," *Harvard Business Review,* May–June 1974, pp. 79–90.

[24] Developed by Jerry E. Allen.

[25] David B. Hertz, "Has Management Science Reached a Dead End?" *The McKinsey Quarterly,* Winter 1972, pp. 44–53, reprinted in Ernest Dale, *Readings in Management: Landmarks and New Frontiers,* 3d ed. (McGraw-Hill Book Company, New York, 1975); R. D. Eck, "Treading Softly with Management Science," *Arizona Business,* January 1975, pp. 3–7; C. West Churchman, "Management

Education," *Organizational Dynamics,* Summer 1972, pp. 12–20; and C. Jackson Grayson, "Management Science and Business Practice," *Harvard Business Review,* July–August 1973, pp. 41–48.

[26] Alfred Sloan, *My Years with General Motors* (Doubleday & Company, Inc., Garden City, New York, 1964), p. xxiii.

[27] Jerome Kanter, *Management-oriented Management Information Systems* (Prentice-Hall, Inc., Englewood Cliffs, N.J. 1972), p. 135.

[28] For a highly informative article on the various ways in which minicomputers may be used and the advantages and disadvantages of each way, see G. J. Burnett and R. L. Nolan, "At Last, Major Roles for Minicomputers," *Harvard Business Review,* May–June 1975, pp. 148–156.

[29] Van Court Hare defines four generations of computers, as follows: (1) The vacuum tube computers of the 1950s. (2) The machines of the early 1960s whose electronic components were made of individual transistors mounted on circuit boards and assembled in a fairly modular form. (3) The computer of the late 1960s and early 1970s featuring integrated circuits, very small devices in which a number of transistors are put together by a photo-arts-type process and etched on a small chip of silicon. Integrated circuits, which are used in a very large number of the machines on the market today, drastically reduced the price of computers and especially the price of a unit of computing. This development also made possible minicomputers. (4) This technology, involving large-scale integrated circuitry, will bring a new drastic reduction in cost of a unit of computing. This generation was in small-scale production in 1972 and is advancing rapidly. See Van Court Hare, Jr., "Fourth Generation Technology: Hardware and Software," *Management Information Systems for the 1970s* (Center for Business and Economic Research, Kent State University, Kent, Ohio, 1972), pp. 7–9.

Frederick Withington writes of five generations of computers. He lumps the third and fourth in the above listing into one generation; then he adds two more: (4) in the period 1974–82, featuring very large file stores and satellite computers; and (5) in the period after 1982, featuring magnetic bubble and/or laser holographic technology and "distributed systems." See "Five Generations of Computers," *Harvard Business Review,* July–August 1974, p. 101.

[30] C. F. Gibson and R. L. Nolan, "Managing the Four Stages of EDP Growth," *Harvard Business Review,* January–February 1974, p. 77. Gibson and Nolan divide this first stage into two, the second one being the proliferation of applications into such areas as cash flow, general ledger, budgeting, order processing, sales, and forecasting.

[31] Kanter, op. cit., p. 203.

[32] Ibid., pp. 8–9 and 180–185.

[33] A set of articles on this issue is contained in P. Schoderbek (ed.), *Management Systems,* 2d ed. (John Wiley & Sons, Inc., New York, 1971). Included are D. G. Malcolm, "Exploring the Military Analogy—Real-Time Management Control," *Management Control Systems* (John Wiley & Sons, New York, 1960); J. Dearden, "Myth of Real-Time Management Information," *Harvard Business Review,* May–June 1966; and R. V. Head, "Real-Time Management Information? Let's Not Be Silly," *Datamation,* August 1966.

[34] Russell L. Ackoff, "Management Misinformation Systems," *Management Science,* December 1967, pp. B147–156x; and Arlene Hersman, "A Mess in MIS," *Dun's Review,* January 1968, pp. 26ff.

[35] Carl R. Adams and Roger G. Schroeder, "Managers and MIS: 'They Get What They Want,' " *Business Horizons,* December 1973, pp. 63–68.

[36] Robert L. Johnson and Irwin H. Derman, "How Intelligent Is Your MIS?" *Business Horizons,* February 1970, pp. 55–62.

[37] T. Hanold, "An Executive View of MIS," *Datamation,* November 1972.

[38] *Air Force Times,* Apr. 24, 1974, and *Advanced Personnel Data System Manual* (The Military Personnel Center, San Antonio, Tex., 1971), chap. 2.

[39] Kanter, op. cit., pp. 183–184, 191–192, and 210.

[40] A set of articles taking various sides of this controversy is in Peter Schoderbek, op. cit., containing the Johnson-Derman article cited earlier; R. L. Martino, "The Development and Installation of a Total Management System," *Data Processing for Management,* April 1963; A. T. Spaulding, Jr., "Is a Total System Practical?" *Systems and Procedures Journal,* January–February 1964; and W. M. A. Brooker, "The Total Systems Myth," *Systems and Procedures Journal,* July–August 1965. See also John Dearden, "MIS Is a Mirage," *Harvard Business Review,* January–February 1972, pp. 90–98.

[41] The abandonment of a number of highly publicized models, including a sawmill model, has been reported by Hayes and Nolan, op. cit., pp. 105 and 107.

[42] "The Retailers Go Electronic," *Business Week,* Aug. 29, 1972, pp. 38–39.

[43] "Where Airlines Must Pioneer," *Business Week,* March 1970, pp. 86–94.

[44] "Using Automation to Save the Bus Lines," *Business Week,* Oct. 6, 1973, p. 117.

[45] The three types of decisions were identified by R. Anthony, *Planning and Control Systems: A Framework for Analysis* (Harvard Graduate School of Business Administration, Boston, 1965). The quotation used here is from an article that elaborates upon Anthony's categories: G. A. Gorry and M. S. S. Morton, "A Framework for Management Information Systems," *Sloan Management Review,* Fall 1971, pp. 78 and 80.

[46] Kanter, op. cit., p. 71.

[47] Guidance on these and numerous other practical considerations are given by Felix Kaufman in "On Understanding the Computer," *The Conference Board RECORD,* October 1974.

[48] Estimates from Kanter, op. cit., p. 80. Clearly, in a system that runs for years without changes in hardware or programs, the third category of costs will run a higher percentage. However, it is a rare system that is that stable.

[49] From a now classic article by D. Ronald Daniel, "Management Information Crisis," *Harvard Business Review,* September–October 1961, p. 118. Reproduced with special permission from the publisher.

[50] See, for example R. R. Andrus, "Approaches to Information Evaluation," *MSU Business Topics,* Summer 1971, pp. 40–47; H. J. Watson, "A New Approach to Valuing Information," *Managerial Planning,* November–December 1973, pp. 18–21; and Charles A. Gallagher, "Perceptions of the Value of a Management Information System," *Academy of Management Journal,* March 1974, pp. 46–55. These three articles give three very different reviews of the literature.

[51] Gibson and Nolan, op. cit., p. 80. Also Chris Argyris, "Management Information Systems: The Challenge to Rationality and Emotionality," *Management Sciences,* February 1971, pp. B275–B292.

[52] See suggestion in Kanter, op. cit., pp. 90–92. See also "A Transplanted Dean Makes an S&L Swing," *Business Week,* June 22, 1974, pp. 66–68. In setting up a group to establish the company's first MIS, the president picked as chairman the man most critical of the idea, with the result that, "Now we're second to no company in this field. We can massage our loan portfolios for the best yields. I can punch buttons and in two or three seconds tell you what we have in inventory. I can get hourly exact deposits and withdrawals in every single branch. I can tell in any bracket the makeup of employees—minorities, females, age—and the bracket in which each was hired."

[53] This material is adapted from Kanter, op. cit., pp. 18–20 and 210–213. Because of liberal adaptations, the present author bears full responsibility.

[54] Some indication of the extent of this phenomenon, with respect to production management techniques, is given in Robert D. Smith and Daniel Robey, "Research and Applications in Operations Management: Discussion of a Paradox," *Academy of Management Journal,* December 1973, pp. 647–657.

[55] For ideas about designing a structure from the decision standpoint, see R. J. Mockler, "The Systems Approach to Business Organization and Decision-Making," *California Management Review,* Winter 1968, pp. 53–58.

RECOMMENDED READINGS

Argyris, Chris: "Management Information Systems: The Challenge to Rationality and Emotionality," *Management Science,* February 1971, pp. B275–B292.

Hammond, John S. III: "Do's and Don'ts of Computer Models for Planning," *Harvard Business Review,* March–April 1974, pp. 110–123.

Hayes, Robert H., and Richard L. Nolan: "What Kind of Corporate Modeling Functions Best?" *Harvard Business Review,* May–June 1974, pp. 102–112.

Hurtado, Corydon D.: "Establishing a Government MIS," *Journal of Systems Management,* June 1971, pp. 40–43.

Kaufman, Felix: "On Understanding the Computer," *The Conference Board RECORD,* October 1974, pp. 52–53.

Part Three

Integration and Summary

The final section of this book integrates and summarizes the subject of management in business and public organizations in three ways:

1   Chapter 10 summarizes management *theory*. Four main ways of theorizing about management—that is, four ways of organizing what is known about management—are reviewed. After considering the advantages, uses, and limitations of each approach, a fifth integrating approach is formulated (in two diagrams—one in business terminology and one in public terminology). This constitutes this book's final statement of the theory, or the basic nature, of management.

2   Chapter 11 summarizes management *practice*. This is done in two ways: *(a)* An examination of the current status of actual managerial practice is made, asking such questions as: How professional are today's managers in business and government? How well are they meeting the challenges facing them? What is the current state of development of managerial practice? This examination leads to identification of some of the main opportunities and frustrations that young managers face today and in the years immediately ahead. *(b)* A discussion of how to evaluate the quality of the management of a particular organization is undertaken. In order to evaluate the quality of some particular managerial group, the evaluator must clearly understand what the truly key elements in the practice of management are.

3 Chapter 12 helps readers to integrate their thinking about management, particularly concerning their own careers in management, by discussing the *philosophy* of management. This is done by stating one manager's philosophy—his attitude toward some of the main issues, problems, and opportunities in management—as a stimulus to readers to think out their own philosophies.

All three of these chapters range back over many of the topics discussed in the first nine chapters, pulling the material together first in one way, then another, and then still another. Some readers, because of their backgrounds and particular interests, will find the Chapter 10 summary and integration most helpful; others will find Chapter 11 the most helpful; and still others will feel that Chapter 12 is the most meaningful.

The Appendix presents "Building a Career in Management," still another way to summarize and apply the material presented in this book.

Summary on Management Theory

PURPOSE OF THIS CHAPTER

This chapter will review four theories of management. Then it will present an integrative summary of management theory. First, however, it will answer these questions: What is the use of theory? Why is it important to have such a summary of management theory? Accordingly, the chapter will be presented under four major headings:

The Uses of Management Theory
Four Ways to Summarize Management
    Theory 1—Integration of Specialists
    Theory 2—The Fundamental Processes of Management
    Theory 3—The Skills of an Administrator
    Theory 4—A Basic Systems Approach
An Integrative Summary—The Full Systems Management Theory
Summary and Conclusions

THE USES OF MANAGEMENT THEORY

Throughout this book it has been made clear that managers work in an endless variety of situations: organizations varying in size from gigantic to minute; in age from centuries-old to brand new; in product from established routine products (or services) to exciting new products (or services); in structure from traditional bureaucracy to modern horizontal forms; in technology from the simplest handicraft to research in space exploration; in social importance from none to a great impact upon our lives; in freedom of action from the classic free market enterprise to regulated utilities to government agencies; and in organizational health from buoyant to sick.

Can centuries of experience and all this variety be summarized in a brief, neat theory? Obviously, formulating such a summary is a difficult task; inevitably, any brief statement must leave out the detail and even some significant ideas. However, a good theory can provide a quick, clear overall grasp of the subject, a nondetailed road map that enables a person to understand the basic nature of management. This is why it has been said that nothing is as practical as a good theory.

In other words, a person equipped with a sound theory has an organized foundation, a basic understanding of management from which to proceed to study particular situations. By adding the details of a particular situation, a person may determine how well a particular management group is performing or evaluate the usefulness of particular techniques, programs, or strategies in that situation.

FOUR WAYS TO SUMMARIZE MANAGEMENT

Of the many possible ways of summarizing management, the following four are among the most useful. These include both older and newer approaches, and that is where management theory stands today—in transition from older approaches that have become somewhat outmoded to newer approaches.

Theory 1—Integration of Specialists

Management is the process of achieving an organization's goals through the efforts of other people by integration (by generalists) of the capabilities of specialists in engineering design, production, marketing, accounting, finance, industrial and personnel relations, transportation, and purchasing (sometimes R&D and/or overseas operations are added to this list). As applied to government, the listing would include some of the same departments—accounting, finance, industrial and personnel relations, purchasing—and others unique to the organization's particular kind of activity. (For example, for the Federal Aviation Administration, flight operations standards and aviation medicine might be included; for a police department, patrol, investigation, and detention facilities might be listed.)

This is an old approach, one that used to be prominent in the literature of business administration and general public administration but is no longer used in these fields. It is, however, still found in the literature of some governmental fields such as police administration or welfare administration. It should be noted that the current curriculums of most schools of business have as their core requirements courses in these "specialist" fields. Also, many firms and government agencies are still organized along these lines; departments with these specialist titles dominate or are at least prominent in their structures.

The current value of this theory lies in the reminder that capabilities in some or all of these specialist fields are still essential to an organization's success. Although this book has not dealt with production management, it should be recognized that it is today highly important. Securing improved productivity involves technological knowledge of processes, equipment, and materials. It also requires skill in making big, risky capital investment decisions to achieve advanced degrees of mechanization or full automation.

Again, although this book has ignored the field of marketing, this field is today of great importance in management. With shorter and shorter product life, skill in evaluating product proposals and securing market acceptance for new products is vital.

And so it goes with all the other specialist fields; each represents an important aspect of getting the overall job done. Even if the advent of systems management removes some of the old familiar specialist departments from prominence in the organization charts, replacing them with new units (such as project management teams, or process maintenance departments, or information-flow specialists), managers will still have to know a great deal about how to design, make, sell, and distribute the product or service. And there will still be a purchasing function, a labor relations function, and a finance function to be performed.

Although top-level managers need not be highly skilled in each of these specialist fields, they will still have to know enough about them to be able to determine whether or not their specialists are competent. And they will have to know enough about them to be able to formulate overall strategies that are realistic in light of the organization's design, production, marketing, and finance capabilities. Middle-level managers will still need to be expert in one or more of these specialist fields, even though the field may be somewhat reshaped in content and in working relationships under systems management.

Theory 2—The Fundamental Processes of Management

Management is the process of defining and achieving an organization's goals through the efforts of others by performing the processes of planning, controlling, organizing, staffing, and leading. This approach was illustrated earlier in this book with the accompanying diagram.

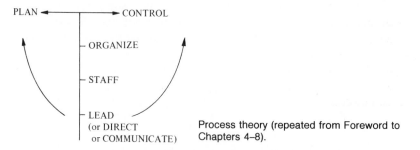

Process theory (repeated from Foreword to Chapters 4–8).

This theory focuses on the processes performed by all managers regardless of their level, field of specialty, or type of organization (public or private). Once predominant, this approach is today regarded by some writers as outdated because (1) having been formulated long ago, it has not been successfully geared to computer-age structures and techniques, and (2) it is associated with an era that was mechanistic and efficiency-oriented, neglecting purpose and values.

Despite these criticisms, the main part of this book has been built on a process outline; however, each process chapter has contained updating material on how the process is changing under the impact of increasing computerization, increasing use of quantitative methods, new behavioral sciences insights, and today's great concern for purpose and values.

The process theory is still relevant; even in the most modern systems management format, managers must plan, control, organize, staff, and provide leadership. The processes may, indeed, be reshaped under systems management. Planning may be more environment-oriented. Control may be more automated. Organizing may feature more horizontal and flexible structures. Staffing may emphasize different qualities in selection and different goals in training. And leaders may be communicating different messages by different means. But all the basic managerial processes will still be required, and it will still be essential that managers learn them. Although some of the techniques that have developed around each of the processes will become obsolete, along with some of the associated principles, many of them will still be indispensable.

Theory 3—The Skills of an Administrator

Management is the process of defining and achieving an organization's objectives by applying three kinds of skills: technical, human, and conceptual.[1] The focus is on broad kinds of skills rather than, as in the first two approaches, on specialist capabilities or on basic processes. This theory indicates, as in Figure 10-1, how the nature of the managerial job changes as one moves from lower to middle to high organization levels. Used in this way, it may be called a "levels theory of management," which stresses the differences in the nature of the managerial job at different levels.

This theory emphasizes the human aspects of management at all levels. However, at the lower level it stresses that individuals have some specific task to perform. Whatever that task—whether manufacturing a product, providing insurance underwriting, or operating a state's welfare department—there are technical know-how factors that a manager should understand. He or she should know not only designing, manufacturing, or marketing in general but also how to design, manufacture, or market a particular product line (or how to render a particular service). It is at

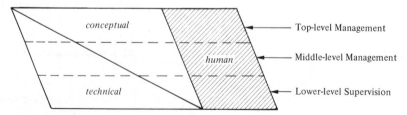

conceptual — Top-level Management

human — Middle-level Management

technical — Lower-level Supervision

Figure 10-1 The skills of a manager.

this level that managers devote much time to maintaining their operations. They must work out problems with managers of departments upstream and downstream from their own departments; also, they must work out day-to-day problems with the purchasing department, the employment office, and other "staff" groups that do certain jobs for their departments. To do such maintaining, or coordination, the manager must know the ins and outs, the technical aspects, of the industry and of the specialist field involved.

Figure 10-1 indicates that a manager's early training should be primarily a combination of technical and behavioral sciences (or human relations) training —usually called "supervisory training." While a manager is still at the lower levels, planning is routine and of minor importance. But as a person moves into and through middle-management levels, he or she should get more training in planning. And the top manager must be able to think conceptually, which includes far more than routine planning.[2] Conceptual thinking focuses upon the choice of an organization's objectives: what role it chooses to play, what environmental opportunities it chooses to seize, what contributions it chooses to make. In short, it is concerned with purpose. It is broad-gauged strategy formulation and sophisticated decision making involving an appreciation of the changing environment and how external factors affect the organization's mission.

This theory's main contribution lies in its treatment of conceptual thinking, and this goes far to satisfy those who criticize business and government managers as persons narrowly concerned with efficiency rather than broadly concerned with purpose.

This technical-human-conceptual framework may be used to gain insights into other management problems too. For example, it can be used to diagnose the type of high-level leadership needed by a given organization at various stages of its growth or under differing competitive conditions. Sometimes the overriding need is for stress on technical excellence—quality of product or service and/or cost of production and/or ability to develop worthy new products. Sometimes the greatest need is in the area of human skills—as, for example, when there is dissension and high turnover in an organization. But most often the greatest need in high levels is for the conceptual skills.

Theory 4—A Basic Systems Approach

Management is the process of determining an organization's objectives and then accomplishing those objectives by integrating four main subsystems—the human, technical, informational, and economic-financial. This theory can be illustrated with a diagram that was used in Chapter 2 and is repeated on the next page.

An advantage of the four subsystems diagram is that it shows the range and depth of a manager's responsibility—a responsibility that (especially at the higher levels) stretches over four major subsystems. Like Theory 3 (skills of an administrator), this theory insists that the manager must understand both human relations and technical processes, bringing the two together effectively. In addition, this theory contains two emphases that the other three theories neglect. One is the key role of the relatively new field of information flow. The other is the idea that an organization

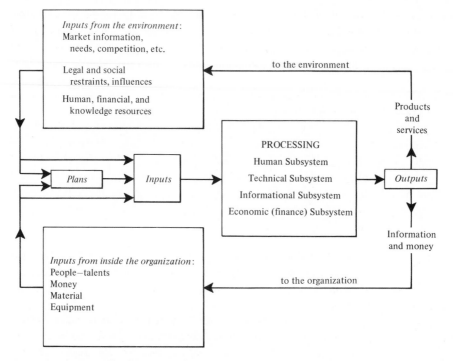

Figure 2-1 (repeated)   An organizational system.

must be kept economically and financially sound. This latter consideration involves constant attention to such questions as: Are we providing a product (or service) that the market still needs? Are we doing it at a cost that the market will accept? Are we doing it profitably enough that we will continue to attract, through equity investments and loans, the money needed to fuel the operation? In public enterprises, these questions would be: Are we effectively fulfilling some legislated task or some social need? Are we doing it within budgetary limits?

By placing four subsystems on an equal footing, this theory points up the inadequacy of approaches that make any one of the subsystems the most important, such as put forth in books entitled *A Behavioral Approach to Management, Management: A Sociological Approach,* or *Management Science.* An effective general manager realizes that weakness in any one of these main subsystems can plunge the organization into deep trouble.

AN INTEGRATIVE SUMMARY—THE FULL SYSTEMS MANAGEMENT THEORY

The four theories that have just been reviewed are in no way contradictory one to another; rather, they are mutually compatible, with considerable overlap between them. Each theory stresses certain aspects of management and neglects other aspects. Logically, then, an integration of these four theories should present a relatively complete theory of management, and that is what the full systems management theory does—depicted in Figure 10-2*a* in business terminology and in Figure 10-2*b* in public/government terminology and as defined in the following (repeated from Chapter 2):

> *Systems Management:* Management (the process of working with and through other persons to define and achieve the objectives of a formal organization) that is characterized by the following practices: (1) views the organization both as a system with its own subsystems and as a subsystem of larger environmental systems; (2) takes a holistic approach, using techniques of analysis that emphasize the interrelationships among the component parts of the organization; (3) uses flexible, changing organization structures, served by computerized information flows, to keep structure adjusted to changing tasks; (4) designs information flow and uses quantitative techniques to strengthen decision making; and (5) views the organization as a social structure and as a series of human/machine relationships.

These diagrams are relatively complex, but this should be seen as a desirable feature inasmuch as management is a complex subject. A simple diagram cannot cover the subject; witness the fact that each of the four theories reviewed earlier did neglect some important aspect of management.

Clearly, the full systems management diagrams are based on Theory 4—basic systems management. They simply incorporate Theories 1 (integration of specialists) and 2 (the managerial processes) via two boxes in the lower left-hand part of the diagram. And they incorporate, also, two-thirds of Theory 3 (skills of an administrator) via the human and technical subsystems in the "processing" box; the conceptual part of Theory 3 is captured by placing "formulation of objectives" prominently at the head of the process and linking it both to the environment and to the organization's values and its planning process. Conceptual thinking chiefly concerns what role the organization (with its values, strengths, and weaknesses) should play (i.e., what its objectives should be) in view of the changing environment (with its opportunities, threats, and needs). Consistent with Theory 4, systems theory, this approach regards the organization as a part of the larger environmental system, helping to keep the manager aware of the changing environment and the need for responding to some of those changes.

Some other aspects of these diagrams should be noted. One is that "research and development management" has been added to the list of traditional specialist capabilities and has in fact been placed at the head of the list. This has been done because it is a unique specialist capability that is increasingly important in these times of rapidly changing technology. Linked to the awareness of environmental factors discussed earlier, a strong R&D capability helps keep an organization effectively tomorrow-minded. Also, the word "decision" has been inserted into the information subsystem in order to make explicit the strong interest of systems management in decision making and in using the newer tools for decision making when appropriate.

The government version of this diagram, Figure 10-2*b,* contains changed wording throughout; however, there are two main distinctions from the business version.

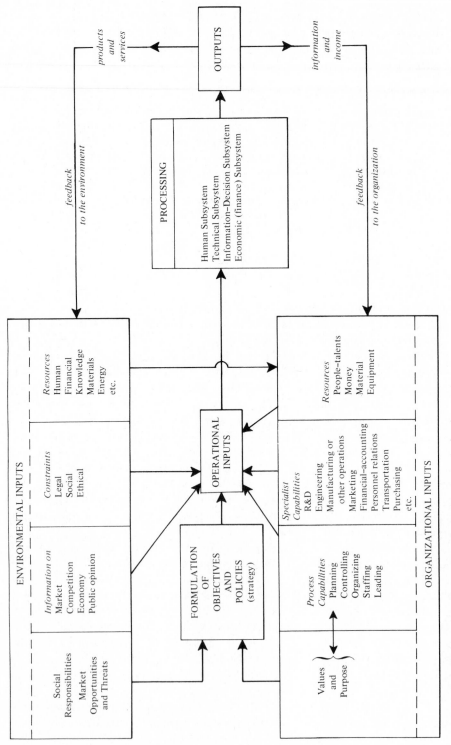

Figure 10-2a Full systems management (in business terminology).

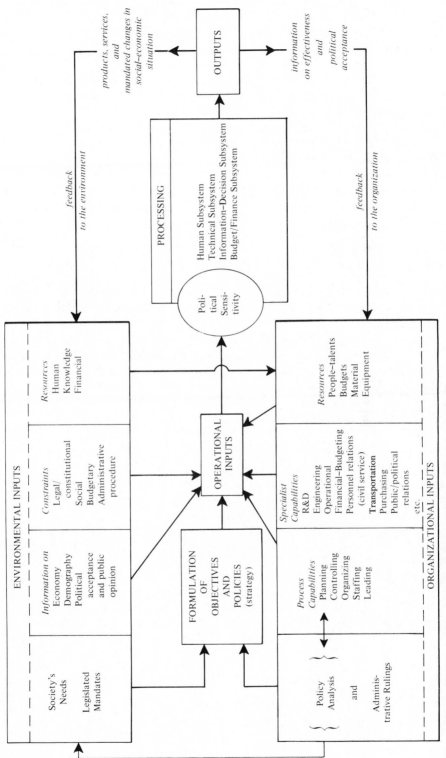

Figure 10-2b Full systems management (in public/government terminology).

One is in the box in the upper left-hand corner where "legislated mandates" is entered to note that government agencies typically receive a good part of their objectives in the form of legislated mandates; these are, of course, often supplemented and even modified from within the agency by the process of administrative rulings. Another distinction from business is in the insertion before the "processing" box of a filter labeled "political sensitivity" to signify that government organizations are never fully neutral politically. In legislating new programs, there is always political compromise rather than pure rational analysis. In determining administrative rulings, there is always an awareness of whether or not the rulings will be politically acceptable. In working with employees and in serving the public, there is always negotiation and persuasion rather than pure economic rationality. In short, public administrators, even though protected by civil service, must be somewhat responsive to political pressures; or, as has been said of even the aloof Supreme Court justices, they "watch the election returns."

SUMMARY AND CONCLUSIONS

The full systems management theory is, then, integrative; it indicates the full complexity of management. Part of that complexity arises from the fact that management theory and practice are in transition. Those organizations that are well into systems management will be reminded by this theory that the managerial processes and some of the specialist capabilities are still important even though the operation is highly automated and traditional departments have been moved off or far down in the organization chart. Those organizations that are moving slowly, if at all, toward systems management will be reminded that they still must work with the human, the technical, the informational, and the economic-financial aspects.

Perhaps the prime use of management theory is to give students a quick, clear grasp of the overall shape and nature of the subject. The full systems management approach has been designed to do just that without favoring or neglecting any significant aspect. Another use of management theory is that made by managers who need checklists to help them determine whether they are neglecting any major part of their complex jobs. Still another way that management theory can be useful is to help young managers think about their career plans. What do diagrams such as those shown in Figures 10-2a and b suggest to a person planning a career in management? That question is discussed in the Appendix ("Building a Career in Management").

REVIEW QUESTIONS

1 What is the reasoning behind the statement "There's nothing as useful as a good theory"?
2 What is the main contribution to the better understanding of management made by each of the following theories: the integration of specialists, the fundamental processes of management, the skills of an administrator?
3 What does the basic systems approach to management offer that the other three theories discussed in this chapter do not offer?

4 In what ways is the full systems management theory, as expressed in Figure 10-2*a*, different from the basic systems approach as expressed in Figure 2-1 (repeated in this chapter)?

5 What is the significance of the insertion of "political sensitivity" in front of the "processing" box in the public administration version of the full systems management diagram, Figure 10-2*b*?

DISCUSSION QUESTIONS

1 If, indeed, "there is nothing as useful as a good theory," why are students usually bored with or unreceptive to theory? Why do they so often say, "Ugh, another damned theory course!"?

2 With reference to Figure 10-1, in what ways does or does not Theory 3 (the skills of an administrator) accurately reflect the main competencies required of managers at the different levels in the particular organization with which you are associated or with which you plan to be associated?

3 It was stated in the Preface that one of the main ideas underlying this book is that it is complete, balanced. Does this balanced treatment, as expressed in the full systems management diagram (Figure 10-2*a*, or Figure 10-2*b* for those interested in public administration), leave you with a fulfilled (satisfied) feeling or with a feeling of frustration? What questions do these diagrams raise in your mind?

4 In what ways is the full systems diagram (either Figure 10-2*a* or Figure 10-2*b*) useful to you in thinking about your career plans? How does it help you realize what further courses you should take, plan the kind of work experiences you should seek, define the kind of position you want to work toward as an objective, or decide whether you want to be a manager or some sort of specialist? Give specifics underlying your answers.

5 What changes would have to be made in the full systems management diagram (Figure 10-2*a* or Figure 10-2*b*) to make it more relevant to the particular kind of organization in which you work, have worked, or may work in the future?

6 Which management theory appears to be predominant in the literature in your particular field? Is the theory used explicitly, is it implied in the literature, or does there appear to be no theory?

NOTES

[1] This approach was formulated by Robert Katz, "Skills of an Effective Administrator," *Harvard Business Review,* January–February 1955. It has been reprinted as "An HBR Classic" in the September–October 1974 issue.

[2] This diagram could be criticized for understating the importance of technical capability in top-level positions in certain kinds of organizations. The small triangle in the upper left-hand corner, representing no more than 20 percent of the total, probably understates the technological capability requirement for high-level executives in smaller organizations featuring sophisticated technology.

RECOMMENDED READINGS

"General Systems Theory," the theme of nine articles in *Academy of Management Journal,* December 1972.

Kahn, Herman, and Bruce B. Biggs: *Things to Come: Thinking about the 70's and 80's* (The Macmillan Company, New York, 1972).

Kozmetsky, George: "Reflections of a 21st Century Manager," *Bell Telephone Magazine,*

March–April 1969. Reprinted in Robert M. Fulmer and Theodore T. Herbert, *Exploring the New Management* (The Macmillan Company, New York, 1974).

Luthans, Fred: "Contingency Theory of Management: A Path Out of the Jungle," *Business Horizons,* June 1973.

Perloff, Harvey S. (ed.): *The Future of the U.S. Government: Toward the Year 2000* (George Braziller, Inc., New York, 1971).

Schoderbek, Peter, Asterios G. Kefalas, and Charles G. Schoderbek: "The Systems Approach to Management," in *Management Systems: Conceptual Considerations* (Business Publications, Inc., Austin, Tex., 1975), chap. 9.

Scott, William G.: "Organization Theory: An Overview and an Appraisal," *Academy of Management Journal,* April 1961.

Chapter 11

The Current Status of
Managerial Practice

NATURE OF THIS CHAPTER

Whereas the previous chapter focused on management theory, this one will focus on managerial practice. It will do so by exploring two questions, first with respect to business and then with respect to government and public organizations. (1) On the general level, the question is: What is the quality of managerial practice? Do today's managers have command over a solid body of knowledge that they are able to apply effectively? (2) On the specific level, the question is: How can one evaluate the quality of managerial practice in a specific organization? What main criteria should an evaluator use in deciding whether a given organization is well or poorly managed?

This will be presented under the following headings:

In order to judge how well or poorly today's managers are performing, it is advisable to look chiefly at large organizations. In business it is the large ones that can be expected to be the most professional, setting the pace for others to follow; in government, most organizations are large. Also, large firms determine to a significant extent what foods we can buy and how much we pay for them; they determine what kinds of jobs most of us work at and the conditions under which we work. Further, they importantly influence the nation's strengths and weaknesses in international trade and the quality and amount of the equipment that supports the Armed Forces.

Large public organizations determine the quality of education our children receive, the type of medical care we get from hospitals and what we pay for it, the strength of the police protection we receive, and the quality of many other vital services.

How well or how poorly are managers of the large business and government organizations performing vis-à-vis these great responsibilities? How well are they performing vis-à-vis their narrower responsibilities of running effective, healthy, and profitable organizations?

BUSINESS: WHAT IS THE QUALITY OF MANAGERIAL PRACTICE?

Any answer to this question, from excellent to poor, can be documented if the writer is selective in choosing the evidence.

The Case for an Answer of Excellent

On the "excellent" side there is the long history of our country's high standard of living based on outstanding productivity of goods and services (although productivity was slipping during the first half of the 1970s).

Also, every observer of American business can name a large number of companies which have turned in fine performances consistently for many years. Such names as IBM, Sears-Roebuck, Procter and Gamble, Coca-Cola, Eastman Kodak, and General Motors stand not only for profitable operation but also for worthy products and exemplary working conditions and employee benefit programs. Such relative newcomers as Xerox and Hewlett-Packard indicate that it is still possible for a well-managed organization with new products to become a large company. These companies give some assurance that there is such a thing as professional managers effectively applying a sound body of management knowledge; such sustained success cannot be entirely due to luck or mysterious genius at work. Buttressing this assurance is the fact that American management methods are being applied (selectively and with modifications, of course) in many parts of the world. Within the last decade, graduate schools of business administration modeled after United States schools have been started in Great Britain, a number of European countries, India, and the Philippines.

The Case for an Answer of Poor

There is, however, also considerable evidence to support an answer of "poor." One need only read daily newspapers over the past few years to recognize valid, severe criticism of large business and government on the ecology, quality of life, and consumerist fronts. The automobile industry has failed to disprove charges of producing unsafe cars, the cereal industry has failed to disprove charges that it urges young children to demand products that contain little or no food value, and many industries—including steel, the most basic of all—stand convicted of killing some of our finest rivers and lakes with polluting discharges. Further, the public accounting profession is under great pressure to reform its practices and the "generally accepted accounting principles," so that certified statements will not so often conceal, rather than reveal, corporate troubles.

A growing antibusiness mood, even among Republicans and the affluent, was documented in a study by the Opinion Research Corporation. Between 1965 and mid-1972 (thus before the main impact of the Nixon/Watergate scandals), the share of the United States public expressing low approval of business climbed from 47 percent to 60 percent.[1] Similar declines were reported in the public's confidence in leaders in education, medicine, and the executive branch of the government; much of this criticism concerns managers' failures to adopt and achieve socially significant objectives for their organizations. As one article points out, chief executives must learn to cope with a new set of challenges:

> The men who have been groomed to succeed the retiring chieftains will not only be
> operating in a different economic climate, they will be grappling with issues that were

once peripheral: pollution control, minority-hiring practices, consumerism, and women's liberation. Moreover, they will be challenged increasingly to demonstrate that
continuing economic growth is indeed desirable. Keeping pace with technology will
exacerbate the pressures. In brief, the priorities have drastically changed from the time
their predecessors were elevated to the top job.[2]

To this list could be added the problems of disorganization and depletion of capital
markets, of extraordinarily high prices for oil and other forms of energy, of a
slow-growth economy, of inflation, and of chronic mismanagement of the economy
by both the President and the Congress. Clearly, the managerial job, at least in the
upper ranks, is getting harder and harder.

Another serious charge against big business managers, noted in an earlier
chapter, concerns their performance in the area of productivity and international
competition:

> The root of the problem, however, is not so much a question of scientific or technical
> knowledge as a question of management. In the Sixties, U.S. companies were outproduc-
> ing and outselling their European competitors. . . . And U.S. management was making
> more efficient use of the corporation's resources. The great U.S. strength was the ability
> to adapt such scientific principles into commercial products and put them into mass
> production at a price people wanted to pay. . . . U.S. companies have become less
> innovative, less willing to gamble on new products, and less adept at translating a
> scientific development into a commercial product.
>
> While the rest of the world has been managing its technology better, the U.S. has
> been managing worse. One reason is that many U.S. companies have banked on acquisi-
> tions of other corporations for their growth rather than building internal growth from
> new products.
>
> More money for research and development is not the sole answer. In the Fifties,
> many U.S. companies went on an R&D binge, building research laboratories, hiring
> large staffs, in the blind belief that money spent on research inevitably would return
> as greater sales. It didn't, and a lot of those companies became disenchanted.
>
> Money is only one of the ingredients required to put U.S. technology back in the
> race. The government's program must zero in on specific goals and assure that each
> project is well managed. Otherwise, much of the proposed R&D subsidy will be wasted.[3]

On the same subject, the then Secretary of the Treasury told a group of business
leaders, "The rest of the world is at work while we're worrying. . . . They're
out-working us, they're out-thinking us, and they're out-planning us, day after
day."[4]

Behind these charges lies the fact that the official productivity index declined
for a record seven consecutive quarters ending in the first quarter of 1975; instead
of the usual level of about 3.5 percent per year advance, the negative figures reached
as high as 5.9 percent during one quarter.[5]

Even when the focus is shifted to specific firms' operations, there is still evidence
of widespread managerial weakness. The last few years have witnessed a series of
spectacular corporate collapses. A decade ago the Convair Division of General
Dynamics Corporation set an all-time corporate record by losing $450 million on

its venture into commercial jet aircraft; more recently the corporation was hobbled by another huge misadventure, this time in shipbuilding.[6] The new record was set by the Lockheed Aircraft Corporation's loss of over $600 million and subsequent rescue from bankruptcy by a huge loan guarantee from Congress.[7] That these gigantic losses are not confined to the defense contractor is demonstrated by RCA, Inc., which suffered a loss estimated at between $250 million and $490 million upon abandoning its computer business.[8] In 1972, the Great Atlantic & Pacific Tea Co. (A&P) ran into deep red ink after ten years of declining earnings and erosion of its once preeminent position in the grocery business. By fiscal 1975, its annual loss had reached $157 million.[9] Probably all these debacles will be topped by the Penn Central Railroad fiasco if an overall dollar figure is eventually attached to that long story of mismanagement and deception.

In the 1970–71 recession, a dozen or so large conglomerates (including Litton Industries, whose extraordinary success seemed to be "rewriting the book" on management) took spectacular falls. During that same period, three of the country's largest brokerage firms merged with healthier firms as the only way to avoid bankruptcy. In the same period, the business press carried accounts of the collapse of a large publishing empire (Cowles Communications, Inc.),[10] deep losses and complete organizational disarray in the second largest maker of heavy trucks (White Motor Corporation),[11] the drastic decline of a giant textile firm (J. P. Stevens & Co.),[12] a $100 million write-off by the American Standard Inc.,[13] a story of gross mismanagement and great deficits at Pan American World Airways,[14] and a sharp earnings decline and a top-level shakeup at (horrors!) the largest management consulting firm, Booz, Allen, & Hamilton, Inc.[15]

A few years later, Pan American was on the verge of collapse and another giant retailer, the W. T. Grant Co., recorded a series of loss years topped by a loss of $177 million in 1974 and bankruptcy in 1975.[16] Also, the head of the Federal Maritime Commission taunted a meeting of shipping industry executives as follows: "How many of you, knowing what you do about your own industry, would invest in 10 shares of stock of any American flag steamship line?"[17] To all this may be added the frequent and well-publicized breakdowns in telephone service and electric power in New York City and the surrounding area and the financial difficulties of New York's power company.

What Can Be Learned from the Cases of Companies in Trouble?

Two of the companies (A&P in the first half of its decade of travail and J. P. Stevens & Co.) appear to provide classic examples of old, entrenched managers failing to adapt their product line and/or marketing methods to changes in the environment. At one point, A&P's two elderly top executives (each over seventy-five years old) retired and were succeeded by two long-time A&P men, each over sixty-five!

The Cowles Communications story appears to be another classic type, the "one-man show" that could not keep up with the increasing size or the pace of change. The early Pan Am difficulties appear to have been due to sheer incompetence in top management; the firm's later troubles centered on unfortunate investment decisions on new aircraft. A number of other cases (White Motors and most of the conglomerates) appear to have suffered from ill-conceived acquisition programs that multiplied management problems faster than management capability could be increased. As a matter of fact, there have been dozens of companies in trouble for this same reason since acquisition fever ran high in the 1960s. The W. T. Grant Co., too, expanded too fast (but not by acquisition), losing managerial control over its merchandising and credit operations.

Two companies (General Dynamics, RCA) made unfortunate decisions on major new product-line ventures; perhaps they should be classified as "faulty strategy formulation." But what is not clear are the answers to questions such as these: What factors underlie these poor decisions? How can leading companies, enjoying the benefits of all types of technological and analytical expertise, make such huge blunders?

What management lessons can be drawn from this history of big-name companies in trouble? For one thing, they appear to reaffirm some long-established, obvious principles such as those against elderly, ingrown management and against one-person rule. But beyond this, the causes of trouble are so varied that they seem to yield only the lesson that management is a many-sided process in which there are various ways of going wrong; or put another way, many things must be done well to have continuing solid results.

Are There Patterns of Successful and Unsuccessful Management?

What can be learned by shifting the search from specific practices to broad patterns of management? The answer appears to be: Not much, because (1) available reports are usually more journalistic than scientific, quite unstandardized and unsystematic, and (2) what solid evidence there is is mixed.

Take, for example, the pattern of management used by so many successful "diversified majors," as described in Chapter 3. This pattern features decentralization into profit centers but centralization of policy coordination, long-range planning, and financial controls. These features usually are supported by highly competent corporate staff specialists as advisers/coordinators and by strong management information systems; also, the chief executive typically is an organization builder rather than one who chooses to rule alone. The problem is that although this pattern is one that has had much success, it also has been used by some of the deeply troubled companies. For example, an account of the National Cash Register Company's sharp decline points out that it occurred during the regime of a Harvard Business School graduate who used "all the modern methods" including decentralized profit centers.[18] And other accounts tell of highly successful companies that are quite centralized (Marriott Hotels, Inc., motels and tourism)[19] and of others in which the top executive is, indeed, a solitary ruler (Northwest Industries, which somehow combines the dominating top executive with some degree of decentralization).[20]

What about the popular MBO approach—does it have a record of success? Before we attempt to answer this question, it should be noted that MBO is quite similar to the just discussed pattern of decentralized profit centers with some centralized controls. In fact, at the higher levels it is impossible to distinguish one from the other. However, MBO does attempt to push participation in setting objectives down the line to lower levels of management. Another problem is that there are no comprehensive data on how many firms are using MBO or how many firms have attempted to use it. Nor are there comprehensive success-failure data on MBO. Most writers, especially those who are selling consulting services, write much about their successes and little about their failures. Probably a valid indication of the extent of usage is the statement of one person in a position to know: "So many firms have adopted it that it would almost seem that a company cannot claim to be modern if it does not profess to practice Management by Objectives."[21]

A review of the few systematic reports that have been made on MBO applications indicates that here, too, results have been mixed.[22] The more successful applications cite such benefits as the following: Goals were clarified; the level of goals was increased over time; the degree of goal achievement, as well as overall productivity, was improved; an increasing number of measurable goals were established in areas other than production; there was an improvement in overall attitude among participants and an increase in the level of participation by managers; and more objective performance reviews led to the identification and removal of obstacles to better performance. Among the problems encountered, which in many cases led to abandonment of MBO, were these: Too-difficult goals led to a reaction by managers that they were being subjected to an unfair "speedup"; some executives pursued certain goals so single mindedly that undesirable side effects (such as neglect of maintenance or, as in the case of the electrical equipment companies, illegal collusion in pricing) resulted; linking performance reviews to wage and salary adjustments caused distortion of the reviews; and clashes developed between the overall goals and the goals of particular work groups or individuals (some of whom undoubtedly did not want their performance measured). Most companies found it difficult to carry the two-way discussions of what each unit's objectives ought to be farther than one or two levels down without taking excessive time in discussions and/or creating excessive paperwork. It is probably accurate to say that the benefits of MBO have been manifested mostly in its effect upon managers one or two levels immediately below the chief *operating* executive (not the chief executive).

What about systems management—what results have been achieved by this approach? On the business side, it appears that few, if any, firms have applied the full concept; so there are no results to report. It is clear, however, that many firms are making progress with such elements of the full concept as project management and computer-based management information systems that are aiding management decision making.

In sum, there are, indeed, patterns of management that have achieved many successes. The patterns of decentralization with centralized policy control and MBO, which are very similar, are two that are generally successful. New, generally successful patterns consistent with systems management theory no doubt will develop in the years ahead. Yet these patterns are not failproof; they can be misapplied and they cannot prevent all errors. And less generally favored patterns can be successful too if properly applied in selected situations.

If, then, it is not possible to say that a given pattern of management is good or bad per se, how can one evaluate the quality of the management of a given organization? That is the subject of the next section; that is the next approach to understanding the status of managerial practice.

BUSINESS: HOW TO EVALUATE AN ORGANIZATION'S MANAGEMENT

The methods of evaluating management that appeared in the literature during the 1950s and early 1960s had little validity; in fact, they have been shown to yield evaluations that were often proved wrong by subsequent events.[23] These methods were mechanistic, featuring lists of specific managerial practices and awarding so many points if such and such a degree of that practice were present. Unfortunately, management is not that simple.

The evaluation methods in the literature since the mid-1960s have, indeed, been more sophisticated. These newer methods have typically featured an analysis of the external situation (competition, market trends, technology trends, etc.) facing the organization and an analysis of internal factors (strengths, weaknesses, and quality of strategy) to see if they are adequate for success vis-à-vis the external situation.[24] A method of this newer type will be presented here; it is organized around two basic questions:

1 *Results achieved:* What results have been achieved by the organization over the past few years? Who is responsible for these results?
2 *Future capability:* Does the organization have the capability of remaining or becoming effective for the next five to ten years?

Results Achieved

This part of the evaluation is based on the ancient adage "The proof of the pudding is in the eating." Or, in management terms, "Judge an organization by the results it achieves." Financial analysis techniques for judging results are highly developed and widely used. There are many different measures of profitability (return-on-investment, net profit/sales, share of market, etc.), and for most industries there are published norms and ranges on some of these measures. In fact, most industries have available, also, more detailed data such as cost-structure figures, departmental productivity figures, and a number of balance-sheet ratios. It is not difficult to compare a firm's data for recent years with data from similar firms.

Three complications do arise, however. One concerns the time lag between managerial actions and results. Sometimes a poorly managed firm may continue to show good financial results for a few years because it enjoys a particularly strong product line or a uniquely strong marketing position or exceptionally efficient equipment; conversely, a well-managed firm may not show good results for a few years because it is correcting mistakes made by earlier managers. Accordingly, an evaluator must be sure that the results being examined are those achieved by current managers rather than by their predecessors.

Another complication concerns the need for multiple objectives. Companies can get into deep trouble via single-minded pursuit of profits. Today a company must plan and control to multiple objectives that define the market need to be fulfilled, the market position to be held and the means by which it is to be held, the financial stature to be achieved, and the social, ethical, and employee-relations responsibilities to be fulfilled.

The third complication, closely related to the second, is that a firm may be making short-run profits at the expense of long-run investment. That is why there is a second part to this evaluation method, a part focusing on the future.

Future Capability

This part requires at least four types of analyses: (1) What has been the basis of the firm's past success? Will these factors continue to be sufficient, or are environmental changes taking place so that new kinds of strengths will be required in the next few years? (2) Does the organization have the capability to develop new products as environmental changes require them? (3) Is the character (or climate) of the organization, especially as affected by its organizational development and management development activities, such that its health will be maintained or even improved, or is the character such that the organization will deteriorate over time? (4) Is the financial structure adequate to withstand substantial developmental investments and temporary setbacks?

The Basis of Past and Future Success   Each line of business has its "success imperatives"—things that it must do well in order to succeed. If these things are done well, sometimes the business will succeed even if its performance of other functions is not particularly strong. But these success imperatives can change over time.

In the early days of aerosol packaging, for example, a certain firm succeeded chiefly because it was highly competent in conceiving and developing new applications of the aerosol technique and because it produced quality products. Thus the firm helped customers shift many types of products into aerosol packaging and did it without severe headaches from spotty quality or long delays. However, over the years, most products that could make the shift to aerosol form had done so; also, many more firms had learned to do aerosol can filling, including product manufacturers who had their own "captive" aerosol canning facilities. In this way the basis of competition shifted to economical mass production—this was a new success imperative. Also, this capability needed to be marketed inasmuch as customers were no longer coming to the packager, but the company had not developed either mass production capability or a marketing competence.

Again, a medium-sized electronics firm's early success for almost a decade was based chiefly on its ability to manufacture two new electronic components when very few other firms knew how to make them. Since the new products were small parts that made big differences in aircraft guidance systems, price was not an important consideration; neither was marketing capability. But as many firms learned to make these items, price competition set in. The firm then had to choose between abandoning these products in favor of other new products or developing the manufacturing and marketing capability to compete with the established products under the changed competitive conditions. Unfortunately, this firm did not have the financial strength or the managerial depth to go both ways at once, and it suffered financially for two years while it refused to face up to this choice.

In order to know when the success imperatives are changing and a new strategy is needed, a firm needs to have (1) some means of systematically measuring environmental change, (2) some means of objectively evaluating the strengths and weaknesses of its departments and functions vis-à-vis the emerging conditions, and (3) the type of leadership that can think in terms of strategy.[25]

Capability for Developing New Products and Services Obviously, it is not enough to recognize the need for a new product-line strategy; the organization must be capable of creating the new products (or services) and of manufacturing and/or marketing them. The research phase requires not only technological ability in product conception and design but also the managerial capability to conceive, plan, and control a research program. Research management is a special kind of management that understands what technological skills are needed for a given program, what type of leadership gets the results from technologists, and what the control indicators are that signal whether a research project is headed for success or for a blind alley. The research phase is then followed by the development and marketing phases, which are described in this way by one drug industry executive: "Once you discover something, you need a tough, structured sequence of events in development to launch it commercially."[26]

Such R&D capabilities—technological and managerial—are not acquired overnight; hence the evaluator looks for evidence that these skills have been carefully developed and proved effective. Also essential is the reserve financial strength needed to carry these inevitably expensive programs, as is the earning power needed to attract new equity or loans to support growth and change.

Organizational Character (or Climate) Over the years every organization develops a character that has a potent influence, for better or worse, on the organization's future capability. For example, one organization's character may be such that the firm attracts and holds talented managers, stimulates the professional growth of its managers, and steadily increases in ability to cope with internal and external changes. A second organization may have a character that discourages talented subordinate managers and causes them to leave the company; also, the organization may be steadily becoming less flexible, less able to realize that change is needed, and less able to cope with that need. In short, the dynamic of the first organization is such that it will remain a healthy, effective organization; the dynamic of the second is such that, even though it may currently be successful, it will not long remain a healthy, effective organization.

A climate is built up through years of a certain type of leadership, a certain level of performance, a certain discipline or lack of discipline, and possibly many other factors such as the nature of the product being made (Is it technically challenging? Is its quality something that builds pride?) or social factors in the community. But usually the main factor in setting the climate of a company is the leadership action (not words!) of the top executive. Thus, sometimes a hard-driving, autocratic chief executive can achieve good short-run results from an organization; however, such leadership usually is not conducive to attracting, holding, and developing talented subordinate managers, so the organization's capability may in time deteriorate.[27] Or a leader who is too long in power may become less and less likely to make major changes in the firm's success pattern; in time an unproductive bureaucracy grows up under such a leader—a bureaucracy dedicated to the status quo.

Sometimes an organization's character changes under the strains of growth and/or as time takes its inevitable toll on a leader. For example, at an earlier date a certain chief executive enjoyed an open, effective relationship with the heads of the two operating divisions and with the other key executives of his firm. However, over the years the firm acquired subsidiaries that not only were located on different continents (instead of being in one state, as previously) but were also in a dozen different types of businesses (instead of two, as previously). In addition, the leader's health began to slip. Without his realizing it, his pattern of communications with his division heads became much less open and much less effective.

Some companies make positive efforts to mold the organization character, regularly increasing the capacity of its executives to work together effectively, to keep communications open, to retain the flexibility required to cope with change. As has been noted in Chapters 7 and 8, some firms have structured their executive development programs to achieve these ends; others work at it via an "organizational development" format involving ongoing, conscious confrontation with actual or potential barriers to communications and cooperation.

Another type of dynamic that sometimes prevails is that once formed, an organization's character tends to be self-reinforcing. Therefore, an organization attracts and holds the type of people who fit its character and repels those who do not fit that character. Because it becomes ingrained, the organization's character is not changed easily.

An evaluator seeking to determine a firm's tomorrow-mindedness should first determine what the organizational character and dynamic is; then, a good estimate can probably be made of whether or not that character and dynamic are appropriate to the challenges facing the firm and what the effects will be on the firm's future capabilities.[28]

Financial Capability   With equity markets tight and interest rates on borrowings high (conditions which apparently will prevail long range in the United States), managers must be especially astute in building financial strength if their firms are to make the improvement investments needed to keep competitive—to say nothing of expansion investments. Has the firm followed a modest dividend policy? That is, has it plowed back its earnings into investments in its future? Has the firm maintained a modest debt/equity ratio so that it will be able to borrow when necessary?

GOVERNMENT/PUBLIC: WHAT IS THE QUALITY OF MANAGERIAL PRACTICE?

Although there are some rays of hope in government management and in the hospital and school management fields, accounts of excellently managed government/public organizations are still rare, while accounts of poor management are plentiful.

Successes

In recent years the shining example of successful management, noted in Chapter 3, has been that of the NASA moon exploration organization, which precisely integrated the efforts of many large and small business and government agencies. The NASA format—a flat structure of project units; collegial leadership; a strong, computerized management information system; and strict control to plans via chartroom sessions—is seen by some observers as the prototype of a new and better way of managing public enterprises. Yet there is little evidence that this approach has succeeded anywhere other than under the exceptional circumstances of the moonshot program.

In earlier years, the favorite example of successful management was the Tennessee Valley Authority, a huge, federally owned and operated electric power, irrigation, flood-control, and fertilizer project. Here the key to success appears to have been clearly set priorities and vigorous quality control; perhaps a better way to say it is that a strong personality began with well-defined goals and insisted upon excellent performance in working toward those goals.

The same clear definition of what is expected and strong controls to achieve it seem to be the basis of another of the long-time success stories in the government sphere, the Marine Corps.

Surely among such public institutions as universities and hospitals, some not government owned, there are some that are well managed; however, there have not been systematic studies of what distinguishes a well-managed hospital from a poorly managed one.

On the local government level there is an occasional account of excellent management, as in the case of Toronto, Canada, where thirteen suburban jurisdictions and the city were in 1953 merged into a single metropolitan district with five boroughs. The Toronto metropolitan administration and the Metro Council are given joint credit for achieving balanced growth and enhanced livability.[29] The area's crime rate, housing conditions, and transportation compare favorably with other Canadian and United States areas of comparable population density.

In addition to these cases of overall successful management in the government/public sphere, there are many instances of more specific improvements being made. Thus it has been noted earlier in this book that at least two large federal agencies have made highly effective use of computerized information systems. Even in the accounts of the general failure of PPBS, it has been noted that some jurisdictions have used that concept quite effectively, achieving much-needed reforms in budgeting, and other jurisdictions are working on less elaborate systems for accomplishing the objectives at which PPBS aimed. Furthermore, in the wake of the massive

McNamara–Defense Department revolution in management methods, it appears that there will be, at least, a permanent legacy of better cost-effectiveness studies and more thorough analysis of alternative approaches to accomplishing defined missions.[30] All these developments provide some basis for hoping that the systems management approach will in time prove useful at federal, state, and local levels of government.

Among other specific improvements noted in earlier chapters have been the following: (1) the work on productivity done in some cities and by the government section of the National Productivity Commission; (2) the sustained efforts of the Office of Management and Budget to improve federal budgeting; and (3) the launching of many intragovernment and government-university executive development programs.

Still another encouraging development has been the assault by a large task force of business management specialists on one of the most notoriously ineffective and inefficient agencies, the New York City Welfare Department. Taking care to work with (rather than against) established agency management and the civil service, the task force was able in two years to reduce the agency's error rate by 50 percent, increase staff productivity by 16 percent, trim the caseload by 109,000 people, and generate a $200 million savings in welfare payments. All this was accomplished by using such techniques as project management, enforcement of accountability, step-by-step (instead of all-at-once) implementation of changes, elimination of inept managers (despite civil service) and issuance of photographic identification cards to welfare recipients.[31]

In Minnesota, a somewhat similar program that also showed substantial results took place at the state level. Here a group of business executives on six-months loan to the state instituted MBO, better cash management and investment, improved revenue and cost data, new departments that focused certain responsibilities, a cost-control program, and incentive pay (under which part of a manager's compensation was tied to achievement against objectives). It appears that savings will approach $40 million per year on an investment of less than $1 million.[32]

Failures

Far outweighing these few evidences of effective management in the government/public sphere, however, are many charges of poor management. Two highly qualified observers, as noted in earlier chapters, have charged that (1) virtually all government administration structures—national, state, and local—have lost command of themselves and their future and (2) state governments are "mostly feeble" and local governments "archaic."

In a more specific criticism, an experienced writer on public administration contends that administrative shortcomings caused the failure of President Johnson's Great Society programs. He describes the situation this way:

> The Great Society piled new programs alongside old in a tangle of separate grant categories, program requirements, administrative channels, and delivery mechanisms. Many departments found it difficult to ascertain what they were purchasing or accom-

plishing with the funds they distributed. Program coordination in Washington and in the field was inadequate. It was difficult to coordinate related activities when they were managed by separate organizations.[33]

Although warned in 1967—by his Task Force on Government Organization—of impending failures, Johnson used only weak coordinating devices such as interagency coordinating committees rather than the stronger program management structure which was recommended to him.

Sweeping charges of failure—partly political and partly administrative—of federal agencies to achieve social reform objectives have been made by a number of younger academics. Representative of these is the following:

> Public administration has shared in this rhetoric of promise: promises to end racism, poverty, hunger, and social injustice; promises to redistribute wealth and the burden of taxation; to provide employment or adequate, dignity-preserving welfare for those unemployed; to dampen inflation and spread material prosperity, public goods, and personal liberties to ever-growing numbers of Americans. Moreover, public administration has made some promises of its own. Not only would it serve as one of the instruments for fulfilling political promises and benevolent social purposes, but it would do this with economy, efficiency, good management, attention to the public interest, careful consideration of the social and human consequences of its actions; and perhaps above all, it would act as a means of social betterment and not as a mode of governance.
>
> The record contains persuasive evidence that these promises have not been kept at all well. . . . Even with all the advances duly noted and all the appropriate caveats entered and exceptions made, the record is dismal. In the richest society in the world, one-fifth of its members remain in poverty while the vast preponderance of national public expenditures goes into myriad military and security activities. This poverty and the general maldistribution of public and private wealth of the nation is linked with the scourge of racism, which continues to stain our social, political, economic, and legal fabric. Access to justice, to education, to employment, to health and to power remains unequal. The environment in which we live, work and play is becoming despoiled, dehumanized and intolerably commercialized. On the other hand, antisegregation laws, the repeated peace and poverty offensives, urban- and human-renewal programs, "bootstrap" projects of bewildering variety, and creative federalisms of one kind or another, all appear to lead to few tangible improvements and little moderating of demands.[34]

Although the foregoing quotation is extreme, it nevertheless is true that one great federal program after another has become an administrative morass. Thus medicare and medicaid have run out of control in some states;[35] welfare is virtually everywhere a jungle of mismanagement; and the subsidized low-cost housing program has been described as "bankrupt."[36] To these problems in the socially relevant fields can be added the well-known administrative weakness of one of the oldest and most routine of all government operations, the post office. After showing some initial progress, it appears to be doing about as poorly in its new quasipublic corporate form as it did as a federal department.[37] A Congressman who is also an advanced student of management writes: "I submit to you that our nation is in serious difficulty today because we have badly mismanaged the public business. . . . We are using horse-and-buggy techniques in the space age. And we are producing horse-and-buggy results."[38]

Noting that the budget has virtually run out of control, the Congressman points out that the Appropriations Committee has no mechanism for evaluating the trade-offs between one functional area and another, nor does it have the capability to perform sensitivity analyses on spending proposals. Further, members of Congress do not have available any electronic device that could display such pertinent information as budget data or current economic statistics. (It should be noted, however, that in 1974 Congress enacted a reform measure designed to impose some spending discipline upon itself. The bill established a Budget Committee in each house of Congress and established a procedure requiring Congress to set overall budget limits. Also, it provided a formidable congressional budget staff to help these committees do their job.)

Perhaps the most serious management error noted by the Congressman is the practice of appointing leadership strictly by seniority (a problem on which some progress was made in 1975 when a number of elderly chairmen were deposed). A minor but fascinating management weakness is the lack in Congress of a simple electronic device for roll calls (each of which takes thirty-five minutes). He notes that one day a series of six roll-call votes and three quorum calls consumed over six hours. (At what cost per hour of maintaining Congress?)

Another study finds that on both the federal and state levels, one systems analysis (not systems management) effort after another, with the exception of the NASA program, has failed. Citing reports on waste management, water resources utilization, education, and many other subjects, this study concludes: "Review of 10 years' literature and experience with systems analytic techniques in the public sector discloses iteration and reiteration of platitudes and promises, but little improvement in either the state-of-the-art of systems analysis or of government."[39]

Summary

This brief review of managerial practices in government/public organizations suggests a mixed picture: Although there are some well-managed organizations and many efforts are being made to improve managerial practice, the indication is that bureaucracy is far from dead. Both Parkinson's Law and the Peter Principle appear to be still operative in many situations.[40] Although big efforts are being made to bring the budgeting process under control and to improve the quality of planning (main features of PPBS), it is a fact that PPBS has in most jurisdictions been discontinued. While big improvements are made in one New York City agency, the rest of that government continues to slide into chaos and bankruptcy.

Perhaps the point to be remembered here is that, as noted in Chapter 7, there are all kinds of people in this world. Of all the managers in government/public organizations, some want better management, some definitely do not want it, and some just do not know much about it.

Further insights into the quality of management in the government/public sphere may be gained by considering the problem of how to evaluate the management of those organizations. That is the subject of the next section.

GOVERNMENT/PUBLIC: HOW TO EVALUATE AN
ORGANIZATION'S MANAGEMENT

One reason why the evaluation of management in the government/public sphere is difficult is that often the two prime factors used in the business sector are not applicable; thus there is usually no summary concept as tangible and useful as return-on-investment, and organizational tomorrow-mindedness is a concept far from the thinking of most government managers. Another big reason why evaluation is difficult is that even when productivity-efficiency measurements are possible—which is not often in government—they are not vital considerations. This is *not* to say that productivity and efficiency are unimportant in government/public organizations; they are important, but they are not as crucial as considerations of the quality of objectives and effectiveness (which is different from efficiency) in accomplishing those objectives.

Evaluating Efficiency and Productivity

As has been noted in earlier chapters, considerable progress in measuring productivity has been made in recent years; and in late 1975 the National Center for Productivity and the Quality of Working Life was created by Congress. It has also been noted that city agencies performing refuse collection, as well as police, fire, and other departments, have developed data on cost per client and data on cure rate (e.g., persons enabled to become self-supporting, or reduction of incidence of a particular disease). Such data can have tremendous value because they can be used as standards of comparison by many other jurisdictions.

The way that political factors can prevail over efficiency considerations in public administration is brought out in the comments of a successful businessperson who became mayor of a large American city. After pointing out that he was elected on a platform of bringing "business methods to government," he states:

> . . . I realize that the "business" answer is not always the answer to the question of "good government." The good business executive by that very fact may well be a poor government executive.
>
> Government is a business. The largest in our country. But government is more than a business. Government presides over a way of life. And if the government executive applies only the priorities and goals of business to the American government and to the American people, he will inevitably destroy the purpose of the American government.
>
> Business methods can be applied by the government executive to the common housekeeping functions of government: computerizing records, regularizing contracts, systematizing inventories, bidding purchases, cultivating public relations, professionalizing budgets, etc.
>
> But as mayor . . . I came to realize that these methods would not adequately solve the major urban problems of discrimination, poverty, riots, and social tension.[41]

The ex-mayor then goes on to illustrate his point with examples of instances in which the efficient solution to a problem was unacceptable because it would have aggravated racial problems, or would have deprived certain neighborhoods of amenities, or would have in some other way generated more political opposition than it was worth. (Thus the reason for inserting "political sensitivity" into the public version of the full systems management diagram in Chapter 10 is illustrated.) He concludes: "The business of government is government, not business."

Evaluating Objectives and Effectiveness in Achieving Them

The primacy of purposes/objectives is expressed by a leading management authority in his list of "principles of effectiveness in service institutions":

  1 They need to define "what is our business and what should it be. . . ."
  2 They need to derive *clear objectives and goals* from their definition of function and mission.
  3 They then have to think through *priorities* of concentration which enable them to select targets, to set standards of accomplishment and performance, that is, to define the minimum acceptable results; to set deadlines; to go to work on results; and to make someone accountable for results.
  4 They need to define *measurements of performance*—the customer satisfaction measurements . . . or the literacy figures. . . .
  5 They need to use these measurements to *feed back* on their efforts, that is, to build self-control from results into their system.
  6 Finally, they need an organized audit of *objectives and results,* so as to identify those objectives that no longer serve a purpose or have proven unattainable.[42]

The suggestion in the last point about an "organized audit" is being carried out in some states that have established legislative auditors to do evaluations of the quality of management of their agencies. Such auditors, if given independence and security via long-term appointments by the legislature rather than by the executive, can do evaluations that give high visibility to instances of strong management as well as to instances of weak management.

A Legislative Auditor's Approach

The evaluation manual used by one legislative auditor emphasizes objectives, effectiveness, and measures of efficiency. Thus this legislative auditor's manual provides for program audits, operation audits, and financial audits. The program audits assess the quality of the agencies' planning-programming-budgeting processes by which the executive formulates recommendations to the legislature as to what government ought to do, what results it ought to seek, what program it ought to pursue, and how limited resources are to be allocated.[43] The subjective nature of the evaluation is clear in the following criteria applied to program planning:

  1 *Identification of needs to be met by government* may be said to be adequate to the extent to which the needs

- describe situations or conditions of people or their environment.
- describe the difference between what does exist and what should exist.
- are those to which governmental attention should be given, either alone or in conjunction with individuals or private interests.
- express values which are in harmony with the overall value system of our society. . . .

2 *The development of objectives to be sought* may be said to be adequate to
the extent to which each statement of objective:

- describes the state of condition or result that is being sought.
- states the "real" objective.
- states the end-result being sought in quantitative form or in such manner
that it is possible to identify and develop criteria to measure the degree of success
or failure in achieving it.
- contributes to the attainment of overall goals.
- is consistent with other governmental objectives and the objectives formulated at higher levels of the program structure.
- is attainable.
- is reasonable, logical and understandable.
- is expressed in a manner which will permit consideration of alternatives for
its accomplishment.
- is meaningful to the people responsible for its attainment.
- serves to guide, direct, and control human effort.
- motivates people toward its accomplishment.
- is a reflection of current conditions.

3 *The identification or establishment of measurements* with which to judge
effectiveness or progress in relation to the stated objectives may be said to be
adequate to the extent to which the criteria identified or established:

- are appropriate and enable measurement of progress toward the objective.
- consider all major effects relative to the objective.
- are related to and consistent with higher-level criteria.
- describe the quantitative bases for measurement, or if any criterion is not
itself measurable in quantitative terms, specify the quantitative measures that are
satisfactory proxies for such criterion.

This manual proceeds to examine in like manner the costing and cost-benefit
analysis, programming and time phasing, budgeting, structuring, and other aspects
of program planning and control. Despite the subjective nature of these criteria, this
particular legislative auditor has issued a number of hard-hitting reports.

Program Evaluation

Another technique for evaluating the management of government organizations is
actually a group of techniques that have collectively come to be called "program
evaluation."[44] One form this has taken is that of a controlled experiment, with
"control" and "experimental" groups sometimes provided for in the legislation
establishing the program or sometimes set up after the fact. In either case, controlled
experiments with human beings are exceedingly difficult, especially when politicians
all insist that their constituents not be in the group that does not receive whatever
benefits the program is dispensing. A second form that it can take is that of a
cost-effectiveness study; however, as has been amply demonstrated in the PPBS
experience, both the cost and the effectiveness sides of cost-effectiveness studies can

be difficult and controversial. A third form of program evaluation is the policy analysis approach, which assesses the appropriateness of objectives much in the manner of the legislative auditor's material described earlier.

Although there is obviously great need for evaluation of the many programs that the United States government undertakes so that lessons may be learned about what makes for effective programming and effective program implementation, most observers are not too optimistic that either politicians or administrators will encourage systematic, strongly analytical evaluations on a continuing basis.[45]

Summary on Evaluation of Government/Public Management

The material that has just been reviewed demonstrates that the ex-mayor's remarks about using business methods only in connection with "housekeeping" matters should be amended. Good business methods include formulating objectives and planning and controlling to them; these are vital in government too. To recap, the evaluation of management in a government/public agency focuses on:

1   The quality of the objectives and purposes
2   The measurement of effectiveness in achieving those goals
3   The measurement of efficiency in carrying out operations

Another point should be added; although it might be seen as part of the first point, it should be made a separate item because of the reluctance of government agencies to discontinue activities and because of the tendency of hospitals and universities to try to do everything:

4   The periodic, systematic pruning of no-longer-needed programs and the elimination of services better rendered by some other organization

Evaluative criteria in the first two steps are often subjective. Despite the general failure of PPBS, some progress is being made toward devising objective criteria and applying them systematically via such devices as a legislative auditor or program evaluation. Another device is the "operational readiness" exercise, as used in the Armed Forces by the Inspector General, which tests without warning the current operational capabilities of a unit. If these exercises are oriented to future types of emergencies (rather than to the last war), they can be truly valuable evaluations. Another device is the independent, high-level special commission in the tradition of the Brownlow, Hoover, and other studies of government. This idea could be used often at every level of government and by other public organizations; however, it would be necessary somehow to generate enough sustained public support that the findings—unlike those of these famous groups—would actually be used.

This section has not discussed the concepts of organizational character and success imperatives which were dealt with in the section on evaluation of a business organization. Although they are completely relevant to the evaluation of government/public organizations, they, as concepts, are harder to apply in this area than in business.[46]

CONCLUSIONS

One purpose of this chapter has been to sharpen the reader's ability to identify effective or ineffective management and to know why it is effective or ineffective. In business there is now available a fairly solid body of knowledge about how to evaluate management, but progress on this subject has been slower in government, partly because it is a much more difficult task there.

Another purpose has been to impress on the reader, especially the younger reader, that there is unlimited opportunity for the improvement of managerial practice. In order to provide this emphasis, the chapter has accentuated the negative, emphasizing the examples of poor management more than the examples of good management. These opportunities for improvement exist in the great majority of private businesses and government/public organizations. In some fields where vast numbers of people are employed—such as police, education, library work, social work, and public health—the move toward professional management is in its infancy.

Some of these challenges are heavy in social significance, others are heavy in private reward for those persons who can perform, and some offer both.

At the operating level, there are opportunities for improvement in productivity, especially as operations are automated and as better management comes to the service industries. At all levels there is opportunity for making subordinates' working lives more satisfying. At the higher levels there is a great deal to be learned about how to keep organizations healthy and effective despite the strains of growth and change. And at the highest level there is need for managers who can think in terms of purpose as well as process and in situational, or contingency, terms. These needs are becoming greater as environmental and economic conditions become more difficult, more demanding.

Graduate schools of business administration have been criticized for teaching the solving of problems (that is, teaching people how to be process specialists) rather than the finding of problems (that is, showing people how to conceptualize what the organization *might* be doing and *should* be doing, how to shape and reshape the strategy—or total package of missions—in order to keep the organization adjusted to environmental change).[47] It is hoped that this chapter's emphasis on how to evaluate the management of the total organizational system, especially how it is defining its objectives in relation to the changing environment, provides some answer to that criticism.

REVIEW QUESTIONS

Business

1 What evidence is there to support the argument that generally the level of managerial practice in business is excellent?
2 What evidence is there to support the argument that generally the level of managerial practice in business is poor?
3 Which patterns of business managerial practice are felt to be generally successful? Why are these patterns often not successful?

4 What are the main criteria used in evaluating the quality of managerial practice in a particular firm?

Government/Public

5 What evidence is there to support the argument that bureaucracy is dying or, put another way, that many specific improvements are being made and are tending toward an overall improvement in the quality of managerial practice in government/public organizations?
6 What evidence is there to support the argument that bureaucracy is *not* dying or, put another way, that it is only in extraordinary circumstances (e.g., the moon-shot program) that good managerial results have been achieved in government/public organization?
7 What are the main criteria to be used in evaluating the quality of managerial practice in a particular government/public organization?

DISCUSSION QUESTIONS

Both Business and Government/Public

The following questions are to be answered with reference to the particular organization in which you are working, have worked, or plan to work.

1 What is the character (or climate) of the organization? What are the main factors molding this character?
2 What are the success imperatives of this type of enterprise?
3 What is the quality of current managerial practice in this firm? Is it the same at all levels, or does it vary by level?
4 Has the organization in recent years been the subject of a systematic, written evaluation? If yes, by whom (i.e., insider or outsider, consultant, auditor, etc.) was it done? What criteria were used? How do they compare with the criteria used in this chapter? What were the findings? Do you agree with them? If no evaluation has been done in the last five years, what, do you feel, is the reason?

Business

5 How do you explain the fact that despite all that is known about management today, so many large, well-known companies get into such deep trouble, make such huge mistakes?
6 Have you had any experience with MBO? In what form did it come to you? What effect did it have at your level? What good and bad results did it have overall in the organization? Has it been modified or abandoned? Do the results agree or disagree with what has been said in this chapter?

Government/Public

7 With reference to your particular organization, is bureaucracy dying?
8 What measures of productivity are used in your organization? What motivating effect do they have? What learning value? How did the method of measuring originate—from efforts of managers inside the organization, from specialists from higher jurisdictions, from associations or commissions?

NOTES

[1] Reported in "America's Growing Antibusiness Mood," *Business Week,* June 17, 1972, pp. 100–104. A 1975 poll of college students revealed that only 20 percent believed that the moral and ethical

standards of business executives are high; see a Gallup Poll report released by the Field Newspaper Syndicate, May 9, 1975.

[2] "Old Bosses Bequeath New Problems," *Business Week,* Jan. 1, 1972, p. 50.

[3] "Why U.S. Technology Lags," an editorial, *Business Week,* Jan. 15, 1972, p. 80.

[4] "Tough Talk from Connally," a column by James Reston, syndicated by the New York Times Service in January 1972.

[5] *Monthly Labor Review,* April 1975, tables 32, 33, and 34, pp. 124–125.

[6] "The Major Dilemma at General Dynamics," *Business Week,* June 3, 1972, pp. 74–76.

[7] "Why the Public Has Lost Faith in Business," *Business Week,* June 17, 1972, p. 116.

[8] "The $250-Million Disaster That Hit RCA," *Business Week,* Sept. 25, 1971, pp. 34–36. The $490 million figure is used by Katherine Davis Fishman in "Programmed for Disaster," *The Atlantic,* May 1973, pp. 33–42.

[9] "A&P's Ploy: Cutting Prices to Turn a Profit," *Business Week,* May 20, 1972, pp. 76–79; "A&P Expects to Post 'Very High' Deficit for Its First Quarter," *Wall Street Journal,* June 21, 1972, p. 6; and "Can Jonathan Scott Save A&P?" *Business Week,* May 19, 1975, p. 128.

[10] "What Finally Crippled the Cowles Empire," *Business Week,* Sept. 25, 1971. See also an exposé-type book by Don Gussman, who sold his business to Cowles: *Divorce Corporate Style* (Ballantine Books, Inc., New York, 1972).

[11] " 'Bunkie' Knudsen Redesigns White Motors," *Business Week,* Oct. 30, 1971, pp. 44–48; and "Semon Knudsen Has His Share of Problems Running White Motors," *Wall Street Journal,* Apr. 5, 1973, pp. 1ff.

[12] "The Flaw in the Fabric at J. P. Stevens," *Business Week,* Nov. 13, 1971, p. 64.

[13] "The Fear That Set a Write-off Record," *Business Week,* Jan. 15, 1972, p. 25.

[14] "Pan Am Fights to Revive Its Credibility," *Business Week,* Feb. 3, 1973, pp. 54–55.

[15] "Booz, Allen Tries to Cure Its Own Ills," *Business Week,* Jan. 20, 1973.

[16] "How W. T. Grant Lost $175 Million Last Year," *Business Week,* Feb. 24, 1975, pp. 74–76; "Deeper in the Red," *Business Week,* Oct. 13, 1975, p. 46; and "Kassuba's Painful Precedent," *Business Week,* Dec. 1, 1975, p. 66.

[17] Helen D. Bentley, as reported in a United Press International story by Marguerite Davis, published in the *Honolulu Star-Bulletin,* June 13, 1971, p. A-19.

[18] "The Rebuilding at National Cash Register," *Business Week,* May 26, 1973, pp. 82–86.

[19] "Marriott Tries Its Tricks on New Ventures," *Business Week,* June 17, 1972, pp. 61–64.

[20] "One-Man Rule Works for Northwest Industries," *Business Week,* May 26, 1972, pp. 60–61.

[21] Walter Wikstrom, "Management by Objectives or Appraisal by Results," *The Conference Board RECORD,* July 1966, p. 27. Mr. Wikstrom is associated with the Conference Board's Division of Personnel Management.

[22] Stephen J. Carroll, Jr., and Henry L. Tosi, Jr., *Management by Objectives: Applications and Research* (The Macmillan Company, New York, 1973), especially chap. 7. Also John J. Villareal, "Management by Objectives Revisited," *Advanced Management Journal,* April 1974.

[23] In writing an earlier book, the present author researched methods of evaluating management. It was found that few practicing executives have systematic approaches to this subject; rather, their methods were impressionistic and sketchy. Consultants usually have fairly well developed techniques for doing this, but they guard them as trade secrets. For more on this subject, including detailed separate methods for evaluating management in small and large firms, see the present author's *Business Policy in Growing Firms* (Chandler Division of International Textbook Co., Scranton, Pa., 1967).

[24] W. F. Glueck, "Appraising the Company's Status," in *Business Policy: Strategy Formation and Management Action* (McGraw-Hill Book Company, New York, 1972), chap. 3. Also David E. Hussey, "The Corporate Appraisal: Assessing Company Strengths and Weaknesses," in Max D. Richards and W. A. Neilander (eds.), *Readings in Management* (South-Western Publishing Company, Incorporated, Cincinnati, 1974).

[25] Perhaps using the diagram in Fig. 10-2a as a framework.

[26] Gerald D. Laubach, president of Pfizer, Inc., and formerly the firm's R&D director, as quoted in *Business Week,* June 16, 1973, p. 68.

[27] It is for this reason that Rensis Likert has stressed keeping tabs on the "intervening variables"— those indicators (such as turnover, absenteeism, or others) that occur before the overall profit performance begins to tell that an organization is deteriorating.

[28] This highly useful concept is just now becoming well developed in management literature. For a set of papers on various aspects of this subject, see R. Tagiuri and George Litwin, *Organizational Climate: Exploration of a Concept* (Bureau of Business Research, Harvard Graduate School of Business Administration, Boston, 1968). For an article describing four organizational characters and the ability

of each to deal with internal and external conflicts, see Roger Harrison, "Understanding Your Organization's Character," *Harvard Business Review,* May–June 1972, pp. 119–128. For an approach to organizational climate based on communications, flexibility, creativity, and genuine commitment to goals, see the chapter entitled "Organizational Effectiveness" in Edgar Schein's *Organizational Psychology,* 2d ed. (Prentice-Hall, Inc., Englewood Cliffs, N.J., 1965). For some examples of how organizational character can radically affect the results that different firms achieve with identical training programs or job evaluation plans, see R. B. Buchele, "Company Character and the Effectiveness of Personnel Management Techniques," *Personnel,* January 1955.

[29] "Toronto Learns to Live with Bigness," *Business Week,* Aug. 19, 1972, pp. 64–65.

[30] Allen Schick, "A Death in the Bureaucracy: The Demise of Federal PPB," *Public Administration Review,* March–April 1973, pp. 147–148. See also A. C. Enthoven and K. Wayne Smith, *How Much Is Enough?* (Harper & Row, Publishers, Incorporated, New York, 1971).

[31] Arthur H. Spiegel III, "How Outsiders Overhauled a Public Agency," *Harvard Business Review,* January–February 1975, pp. 116ff.

[32] D. J. Dayton, "Loaned Executives Shake Up a State's Government," *Harvard Business Review,* November–December 1974, pp. 14ff.

[33] Schick, op. cit., p. 150.

[34] A more complete statement of the material by Peter Savage cited in Chap. 4, footnote 31.

[35] "California Reels under Impact of Medicaid Scandals," *National Observer,* June 23, 1969, pp. 1ff. Also, see statements by Rashi Fein in "The $60 Billion Crisis over Medical Care," *Business Week,* Jan. 17, 1970, pp. 51–54.

[36] "The Bankruptcy of Subsidized Housing," *Business Week,* May 27, 1972, pp. 42–48.

[37] "The Postal Service Tries the Hard Sell," *Business Week,* Oct. 21, 1972, pp. 38–42.

[38] Donald W. Riegle, Jr., "Business and Government at the Crossroads," *Northwestern Management Reporter,* Spring 1972, pp. 6–10.

[39] Ida Hoos, "Systems Techniques for Managing Society: A Critique," *Public Administration Review,* March–April 1973, p. 157.

[40] Parkinson's Law holds, not entirely facetiously, that there is no relation between the number of persons employed and the work to be done; in fact, work expands to occupy however many persons are available. The Peter Principle contends that employees (including managers) in a bureaucracy tend to rise to the level of their incompetence: unfortunately, removal of incompetents is rare.

[41] A. J. Cervantes, former mayor of St. Louis, Mo., in "Memoirs of a Businessman-Mayor," *Business Week,* Dec. 8, 1973, pp. 19 and 20.

[42] Peter Drucker, *Management: Tasks, Responsibilities, Practices* (Harper & Row, Publishers, Incorporated, New York, 1974), pp. 158–159. Under "service institutions" Drucker includes government agencies, public utilities, and certain nonprofit organizations.

[43] *Manual of Guides of the Office of the Legislative Auditor* (The Auditor of the State of Hawaii, 1972 revision), p. A-6. For a description of management audits done by the federal government's General Accounting Office, see W. L. Campfield, "Auditing Management Performance," *Financial Executive,* January 1971, pp. 24–34.

[44] The classification of types given here follows O. F. Poland, "Program Evaluation and Administrative Theory," *Public Administration Review,* July–August 1974, pp. 333–338. This is the concluding article in a five-article symposium, edited by Poland, on program evaluation.

[45] Ibid. See also James W. Davis, Jr., "Evaluating Government Programs," in *An Introduction to Public Administration* (The Free Press, New York, 1974).

[46] For one attempt to define organizational character in a government setting, see Larry Greiner, "The Simple Complexity of Organizational Climate in a Government Organization," in Tagiuri and Litwin, *Organizational Climate: Exploration of a Concept* (Bureau of Business Research, Harvard Graduate School of Business Administration, Boston, 1968).

[47] J. Stirling Livingston, "The Myth of the Well Educated Executive," *Harvard Business Review,* January–February 1971.

RECOMMENDED READINGS

Buchele, R. B. : *Business Policy in Growing Firms* (Chandler Division of International Textbook Company, Scranton, Pa., 1967). Contains detailed evaluative outlines, one for small firms, one for large firms. The large-firm evaluation repeats material in the author's

"How to Evaluate a Firm," *California Management Review,* Fall 1962, which has been reprinted in a number of books of readings in management.

Drucker, Peter F.: *Management: Tasks, Responsibilities, Practices* (Harper & Row, Publishers, Incorporated, New York, 1973). Chaps. 11–14, on service institutions, cover government, public nongovernment, and public utility organizations.

Glueck, W. F.: "Appraising the Company's Status," in *Business Policy: Strategy Formation and Management Action* (McGraw-Hill Book Company, New York, 1972).

Greiner, L., D. Leitch, and L. Barnes: "The Simple Complexity of Organizational Climate in a Government Organization," in R. Tagiuri and G. Litwin, *Organizational Climate: Exploration of a Concept* (Bureau of Business Research, Harvard Graduate School of Business Administration, Boston, 1968).

Charles Perrow, *Organizational Analysis: A Sociological View* (Wadsworth Publishing Company, Inc., Belmont, Calif., 1970).

Chapter 12

A Philosophy of Management . . . and Some Implications for Managerial Practice

WHY A PHILOSOPHY?

This chapter presents one person's philosophy of management. It is offered as a stimulus to thinking, *not* as a recommendation or even as a representation of the majority view. It is hoped that each reader will formulate a personal philosophy, altering this one as much as is necessary to bring it into line with his or her own thinking.

Just as different situations call for different types of leadership, so do they call for different management philosophies. There is need for managers who agree with most or all of the planks in this philosophy and for managers who feel that some of these planks are simply not viable in their organizations, or that some of the planks are too idealistic, or that some of them are (horrors!) academic.

Of the many possible reasons why it is important that managers formulate their own philosophies, three are most cogent:

1   A manager who has thought out what kind of manager he or she wants to be will probably be more effective than a manager who has no philosophy. The reason for this is the same as in the case of organizations that have become more effective after developing their basic objectives and policies—going through such a process helps channel efforts toward important matters.

2   A manager who can keep in clear perspective the broader purposes of management—broader, that is, than merely surviving or beating competition—generates a personal sense of worthwhileness and humaneness that, in turn, is transmitted to subordinates.

3   The younger generation—not only the extremists but also many young men and women who will be needed in government and industry during the next decade —are far more value-conscious than were their predecessors. They want to know the boss's and the organization's value systems; the manager who does not have satisfying answers to their questions may lose many of these future managers.

One hopes that the revelations in 1973–74 of dishonesty and poor ethics on the part of the President of the United States, the Vice President, some Cabinet officers, and some of their supporters in the business world will produce a sustained reaction toward higher ethical standards. It is in the hope that such an improvement will take place among government and business managers (and the belief that if it does not occur, our country is in deep trouble) that this chapter is presented. It is outlined as follows:

A Philosophy of Management
    On the Nature of the Managerial Job
    On the Human Responsibilities of Managers
    On the Social Responsibilities of Managers
    On Personal Aspects of Managerial Effectiveness
Conclusion

A PHILOSOPHY OF MANAGEMENT

On the Nature of the Managerial Job

Plank 1   *The managerial job can offer great intellectual and professional challenge.* Management is complex, many faceted, ever changing. As has been brought out in the theory diagrams in Chapter 10, management involves not only decision making but also getting work done through human beings and groups of human beings. The decision-making component sometimes requires ability in information gathering and analysis, in consultation and negotiation, in using sophisticated quantitative techniques, and in taking risks. The component that calls for getting work done through others requires the ability to communicate plus considerable understanding of psychological and sociological factors. Management at the higher levels also involves study of many aspects of the changing political and market environment and conceptual thinking about what those changes mean—threats and opportunities—to the organization and its people. Management involves short-run planning and design of controls on current results and long-range planning and the design of very different controls on long-run results. Sometimes management involves substantial knowledge of technologies required in product design or in the design of manufacturing processes; sometimes it involves deep knowledge of trade practices in a particular industry or profession. Sooner or later almost every administrative job requires an understanding of tool subjects (such as accounting, statistics, or information technology) and some of the specialty fields (such as finance, manufacturing, marketing, industrial relations, transportation, business law, design engineering, and plant engineering) and how the specialty fields affect one another. Further, management involves capability in the basic managerial processes of organizing and staffing as well as the planning, controlling, and leading mentioned previously. On top of all this, government managers must understand the political process.

Thus the truly professional manager needs some competence in the academic fields of psychology, sociology, economics, mathematics, semantics, and political science as well as in the managerial processes and techniques.

The integration of all these kinds of knowledge and the effective application of them to a given situation is no small task; furthermore, all these managerial practices and strategies must be frequently reevaluated and adjusted to the organization's new stage of growth, a changing competitive picture (or a government agency's changing mission), or rapidly changing technologies.

What is the significance of this complexity? Why is it placed at the very start of this statement of philosophy?

Recognition of the complexity of management can help managers in two big ways: First, it helps them see the intellectual challenge of the managerial job. Managers who appreciate this challenge will continue to grow professionally and will find their work exciting and enjoyable. Second, it helps managers realize that no one ever completely masters the managerial job; put another way, even the best managers need help.[1] Acceptance of this viewpoint will encourage a manager to overcome what is probably the greatest single weakness of today's business and government executives—the inability to be truly open to suggestion when such help carries with it some criticism.

Plank 2   *There is no "one right way" to manage and no one organizational character to be achieved.* Although Plank 1 stresses the intellectual challenge that can be found in management, it is *not* intended that every manager should approach a job and a career in that spirit. Rather, the point is that the intellectual challenge *can* be there if an individual chooses—as this writer does—to approach the managerial job in that spirit.

Similarly, it is *not* contended that all organizations should attempt to mold a character built on the highest talents, the greatest creativity, the truly excellent performance. An all-out MBO approach, vigorously measuring an individual's actual achievement against preset objectives, is not always feasible. After all, there are many kinds of persons in this world; those who prize security over challenge would be miserable under a pattern of management focusing on excellence of performance and individual accountability; those who are dependent personalities prefer receiving strong direction to being asked to participate in decision making and creative planning.

Fortunately, there are many routine jobs to be done, hence persons looking for security and some regimentation can be happy and effective if they are in the right type of organization. In fact, there are some basic, repetitive jobs to be done even in some organizations whose overall character is exciting and dynamic.

Also calling for a contingency rather than a "one right way" approach to management is the fact that organizations are dynamic; significant changes often develop from within as well as from the outside environment. Thus the growth process itself can change an organization's character and its problems, and managers must change their ways of managing in order to cope with these internally generated changes. One author describes five growth phases, each with a relatively calm period (evolution) that ends with a management crisis (revolution). He demonstrates how early entrepreneurial creativity can bring size that the creative entrepreneur cannot manage, how decentralization can in time lead to loss of control, how too much control and coordination can lead to red tape—unless managers take action to deal with these unwanted developments.[2]

In sum, professional managers realize that management can be far more than applying principles in a "one right way" cookbook approach; they recognize that, in its highest form, management requires conceptual thinking—the ability to diagnose and prescribe for a situation and to manage organizational dynamics. Fortunately, modern management literature contains concepts (such as organizational character, key crises, stages of growth, strategy formulation, and contingency theory) that help managers to do such conceptual thinking.

Plank 3 *There is need for encouragement of risk-taking change agents.* Trends toward managers using the soft voice, negotiating rather than issuing orders, and engaging in patient "lateral brokerage" among the many technical experts involved in today's complex programs have been noted at various points in this book. So, also, has the increasing use of participative-consultative methods of leadership in business decision making and in the planning of public programs where community involvement is desired. These trends toward less direct action constitute a healthy development, a logical response to today's level of general education and to increases in the complexity of the jobs to be done.

Yet there is a danger too. The danger is that decisiveness and innovation will be downgraded in importance, that concern for the process leading to a decision will lead to neglect of the quality of the decision. At the very time when the pace of change (in products, processes, markets, and social needs) is tremendous, the pace of organizational decision making is slowing down. At the very time when there is a premium on new products, new services, and new technologies, there is less and less praise of decisiveness—yet decisiveness is essential to innovation and risk taking.

In public administration, the problem is compounded by the fact that individuals often have more to lose than to gain by decisiveness. Thus a public administrator who forcefully pushes through an ultimately unsuccessful program is freely criticized by columnists, editorial writers, politicians, and "irate citizens." However, if a public administrator's bold action is successful, there is rarely any public acknowledgement or generous reward. Can we solve such staggering problems as mass transportation, urban renewal, organized crime, and pollution under a system that castigates failure, tolerates inaction, and does not reward achievement? Clearly, we need a strong system of rewards and recognition for public administrators who solve problems creatively. There is need, too, for "buck stoppers"; sometimes even a poor decision is better than none at all. Perhaps our public officials should experiment with unique positions (e.g., a state "housing czar" with authority to suspend rules and procedures that restrict production of housing) structured to get action on certain vital problems. Conversely, there is need of some technique for identifying and eliminating those public "servants" who chronically emphasize what cannot be done, who know all the restrictive rules and none of the means of getting around them.

Some private businesses provide more recognition and much more reward for initiative, but too many of them base promotions on steadiness, conformity, dependability. These latter firms are guilty of the charge hurled by a prominent radical: "Industry pretends to admire tigerhood but actually rewards tabbiness."[3] As has been noted earlier, few firms have executive development programs that encourage younger managers to dig into real problems and recommend important changes; apparently either egotism or insecurity still causes many high-level executives to regard proposals for change as threats or criticism. Yet one recent writer contends that now change itself should be the central object of managerial attention, charging that:

> Up to now, with rare exceptions, the administration of change has been handled as a supplement to the administration of established ongoing activities. . . . Most companies, including many with reputations for being well managed, are organized primarily to administer yesterday's ideas. Investments and operations are measured by efficient performance, with relatively short-term targets for achievement, and a primary focus on taut administration of existing resources and markets. This was an appropriate corporate design concept when the rate of changes within and outside the company was slow.[4]

The point of this plank is *not* that we should revert to the rugged individualism of the legendary risk taker of olden days. No, this individual was a poor organization builder and, often, a poor decision maker. Again, the point is *not* that change for change's sake is good. Certainly there is such a thing as too much change, too hasty flitting from one fad to another; certainly there are many organizations (a quality restaurant, for example) in which stability is a key virtue. In many organizations the need is for a balance between stable, efficient operations and enough change to remain vital and competitive. In fact, some companies have established separate structures so that they can foster a "change agent" climate in the new-products part of the organization without upsetting the stability of other departments.

The point of this plank is that in some organizations (at least, in parts of them) there is increasing need for combining participative methods with strong delegations of decision-making authority, enforcement of accountability for results, recognition of achievement, and tolerance of error. It is the potential for emphasizing change and its achievement that makes the MBO-PPBS approach so attractive.

The need is to train managers to be change agents rather than smooth presiders over the status quo. Such training focuses first on recognizing a need for change, and it includes such subjects as assessing the environment, studying product life-cycle curves, and understanding organizational dynamics (as discussed under Plank 2). The training then should cover communications and participation—letting the persons involved at least know what is going to happen and why or at best allowing them to participate in the decision making. This phase includes two-way communications to relieve anxieties and to evaluate implementation progress. The next step in change management is the organizing for it, and here project structuring is often appropriate. Then comes the planning and control (or implementation) phase where much that has been learned about R&D management is applicable; here PERT and other control techniques are often needed. The final area in which change agents need training is in the leadership styles that are particularly effective in working in a change setting.[5]

On the Human Responsibilities of Managers

Plank 4 *A manager can greatly affect the quality of life of subordinates.* Although progress has been made toward more use of consultative leadership, there are still frustrated and discouraged managers at various levels of many business and government organizations. A $65,000-per-year vice president confided to the author: "I wish I had the guts to give up this salary and all the fringes; not being allowed to do this job the way I know it should be done is killing me. I mean it literally—it's killing me!" A senior vice president of a large firm put it this way: "The boss is having a wonderful time, but the rest of us are developing the biggest crop of ulcers you ever saw, except for Joe_____ ; he's just drifting toward retirement in two years, doing nothing, letting nothing bother him."

Despite the increasing use of the MBO technique, it is still common to encounter remarks like the following, received when the division heads of a large firm were asked to record, anonymously, their key problems: "I really don't know what the boss expects of me; he keeps me utterly in the dark. I got a swell bonus last year, but I'll be darned if I know why!" *Dun's Review* reports: "Bluntly, middle managers are expressing much the same dissatisfaction with the status quo and the same agitation for change as the younger generation."[6]

Executives who feel that this statement does not apply to their subordinates should, as a matter of insurance, arrange for an evaluation of their subordinates' feelings by an outsider who can afford to be objective. We are notoriously inaccurate in evaluating the attitudes of our own subordinates.[7] This writer's experience is that for every manager who finds work fulfilling, there are three or four who are quite frustrated; for every one who can claim to be performing to capacity and growing professionally, there are many who feel that they are being prevented from doing so. For every manager who truly respects his or her boss, there are a number who do not.

The manager who can reverse such situations can make a tremendous social contribution. The problem of disheartened managers, whose talents are being wasted and whose viscera are being corroded, is important in itself and because it creates problems for their subordinate supervisors and workers down the line as well as for their families. Thus, a strong multiplier effect, for good or for bad, flows from the patterns of leadership used by higher-level managers.

Critics of "the establishment" see business managers as moneygrubbers or the stooges of moneygrubbers. Also, many people on our campuses glibly write off the business school as a place that teaches only "how to make money." Yet the fact is that only a small part of the business school's efforts focuses on moneymaking (although that is a necessary function in our society). A far larger effort is directed to teaching (1) communications skills that enable a manager to solicit and use the ideas of subordinates, (2) the "linking-pin" role whereby a manager represents subordinates in higher management councils, (3) a form of performance-review interviewing that will recognize subordinates' achievements and their developmental needs, (4) the coaching-training role of managers that fulfills those developmental needs, and (5) job design and other aspects of industrial psychology and sociology that contribute to making workers' lives less frustrating, more satisfying.

In short, there has long been emphasis—in the schools and in practice—on those managerial activities that contribute toward a better quality of life at work for managers at various hierarchical levels as well as for workers. It is a huge social responsibility, and there is still a long way to go.

Plank 5   *Of all an organization's resources, the human resources are the most unique and have the greatest potential for improvement.* Even in those organizations that attract the less aggressive and ambitious workers, performance will be enhanced if each employee feels that superiors are concerned with his or her needs and problems. Accordingly, top managers really believe, as well as say, that people are the organization's greatest asset; indeed they are, at least potentially. Employees should know the objectives and plans of their own units and how they fit into the whole. And working conditions and equipment should be such that they help workers build self-respect. The job itself should have enough content that the worker can maintain self-respect.

In situations where workers have ambitions and growth potential, far more must be done. Workers must have a chance to develop not only their skills but also their creativity. Here is where participation in the design of jobs and working conditions is vital.

And it must always be remembered that these ideas apply fully to persons in the managerial ranks too.

It is a hopeful sign that, as noted in Chapter 8, some firms are attempting "human resource accounting" to focus on the huge investment that every firm has in its human resources and the professional and psychosocial development of those resources.

Plank 6   *There is no inherent conflict between participative management and excellence of performance; in fact, they can reinforce one another.* Some managers still suffer a nagging fear that somehow "democratic" ("consultative" and "participative" are better terms) leadership leads to softness, lack of discipline, and sacrifice of productivity in favor of a shallow sort of happiness. Some persons vaguely link participative leadership with such bogeys as "progressive education" or "permissive parenthood," thus keeping the nagging fears alive, although they have in many situations been proved groundless, as noted in Chapter 7.

One strength of the MBO approach, effectively applied in an appropriate situation, is that it neatly meshes consultative supervision with a strong focus on results, that is, with a demand for high standards of performance. The consultation process features give-and-take discussion between superior and subordinate about what the person's (or the unit's) objectives for a given period should be and how the results can be defined (or measured). Such consultation puts the focus strongly on the results to be expected. Then further consultation, in the form of a performance review, compares what actually was achieved with the results expected. Under such procedures it is much more possible to recognize and reward true achievement and to discipline nonachievement than it is when the objectives are vague and/or their measurement is not defined and/or the subordinate has had no chance to understand them fully.

Plank 7   *To "know thyself" is a basic obligation of all managers because it is a prerequisite to understanding subordinates and to keeping pace with change.* A great part of any managerial job involves getting work done through other people. The variables in the problem are the manager, the other person(s), the work, and the surrounding situation. Of these four variables, the manager completely controls only one—the first; however, this often is the variable that is hardest to judge objectively because the manager gets the least objective information on this subject.

As a person rises in an organization, more and more people—both inside and outside the organization—have more and more to gain or lose from his or her favor or disfavor. Sometimes consciously and sometimes unconsciously, people slant the information that they pass on to this individual. In contrast to elected officials, who are subjected to the criticism of their political opponents and of the press, corporation executives are shielded from criticism.[8] These executives are insulated from important reactions and events by staffs and levels of organization structure, each person having his or her own interest in editing and filtering information going toward the top. This difficulty of communicating frankly (including the art of listening) with subordinates is heightened by the fact that every manager must judge subordinates in ways that affect their rewards, promotions, and development. Thus, subordinates have vested interests in flattering a manager (just as all students have a motive to flatter their teachers) or at least to avoid making criticisms. Increasingly unable to communicate effectively with subordinates, the manager understands them—their strengths and weaknesses, their problems and aspirations—less and less. In the end there is danger of failing not only to "know thyself" but also to "know thy subordinates." The two dangers are interlocked.

Especially after some successful years on the job, an executive is not only flattered by many persons but is praised in the press and in industry circles for those techniques and strategies that brought success. In this way the very fact of success tends to shut this person off from recognition of market changes or other changes that require new techniques—that is, that require changes in the success formula with which he or she is identified.

Just as external competitive conditions change bit by bit, so does each person grow a bit older and change a bit every day. In time, both kinds of small changes can accumulate into big changes. But it is extremely difficult to detect these subtle changes, especially at the top. It is for these reasons that some observers claim that "organizations die from the top down." It is tragic when a potentially strong organization is limited by the strengths and weaknesses of one person, and it is especially tragic when that one person has developed a somewhat unrealistic self-image.

If this criticism of some executives seems too harsh, consider the following actual case history. Some years ago a graduate class devoted a full semester to intensive study of one large, diversified company. At various stages high-ranking managers from the company appeared before the class; all stated the same view of the firm's prospects, namely that earnings per share would be doubled over the next five years. As the semester progressed, the students became increasingly incredulous because they simply did not see the strength of product line, the managerial competence, the staff organization, or the financial leverage required for such performance. When, toward the end of the semester, the president of the company appeared before the class, the students' questions were quite challenging. However, he put them down rather gruffly, repeating the prediction: "We'll double in five!" Almost unanimously the students, in their term papers, disagreed with him. However, when these papers were sent to the company, the president's aides decided not to show them to him. Now the five-year period in dispute is over. The company not only failed to "double in five" but actually regressed a bit in earnings per share. Incredibly, the young, inexperienced students had a more realistic grasp of the firm's prospects than did the man who was being paid $150,000 per year to understand the firm's strengths and weaknesses!

Professional management watchers (such as professors, consultants, writers) see situations such as this one so often that they urge high-level executives to make sure that they get reasonably accurate communications. This means obtaining anonymous views via opinion polls from subordinates as to their (the bosses') effects upon subordinates and as to the strengths and weaknesses of the organization. It is recommended, also, that these communications be supplemented periodically by the views of outsiders who can afford to be objective.[9] Such outsiders can, on a confidential basis, tap the internal company grapevine and the external (customers, suppliers, etc.) grapevine as well.

Management experts increasingly recommend the "ten-year rule" under which the tenure of key persons (heads of organizations or of major subunits of organizations) is limited to ten years. The present author strongly endorses this rule, feeling that (1) most of what a person is going to accomplish will be accomplished well within the ten years; (2) for reasons discussed in connection with this plank, chances are that after ten years the person's contribution will be less and less positive and possibly even negative; and (3) if the person moves, he or she probably will enjoy a new burst of creativity and will be quite effective.

On the government side, one need only mention the case of J. Edgar Hoover at the Federal Bureau of Investigation to prove the need for such a rule.

On the Social Responsibilities of Managers

Plank 8 *The social responsibilities of managers are varied and compelling, and they are currently changing fundamentally.* The first social responsibility of a business is to make a profit by fulfilling some legitimate market need. This comes first because (1) without profit the business will not survive to serve any other social responsibilities and (2) if it is profiting by some means other than serving a legitimate market need, either it is ethically questionable (from a consumerist viewpoint) or its future is precarious because it may not receive continuing support in the market-place. Government agencies have a similar responsibility, but the enforcement mechanism is not so strong and relentless as is the marketplace.

The second social responsibility is to treat employees fairly, selecting and rewarding them strictly on merit. This is vital because discrimination, especially by race, is a cancer on the body of society. Government agencies have the same responsibility, and here the enforcement (civil service) is strong, perhaps too strong (as noted in Chapter 8) from an effectiveness-efficiency standpoint.

The third area of responsibility covers such subjects as supporting charitable and civic causes. Although the validity of this responsibility has long been debated, a preponderant majority of managers now accept it.[10]

The revolution that is taking place is the recognition of a new area of social responsibility—the responsibility for helping solve some of the major socioeconomic problems such as urban renewal, mass transportation, adequate medical care for all, housing, clean water, clean air, and others. Thus this new responsibility impinges upon the most basic managerial decisions—decisions as to the kind of work the organization does and the intrinsic value of the activities to which it devotes its resources.[11]

This new emphasis carries both opportunities and threats. One opportunity is to learn to do these great jobs profitably; there are many jobs to be done. Another is to win the loyalty of a greater number of the young, who feel that these socioeconomic problems must be solved. The threat is that if business cannot solve these problems, government organizations will have to do so, taking an ever-larger role in our economic life.

For a long time a part of the American genius for production has been spent on tail fins, striped toothpaste, and ever-fancier cosmetics because that is what consumers seemed to want. But now it is clear that a substantial part of the body politic is concerned with deeper values. Industry and government combined have the technical and managerial know-how to solve some of these big socioeconomic problems. But to achieve this will take far better management than has been exhibited by those defense contractors who have produced only at the cost of astronomical overruns on bid prices.

Peter Drucker makes similar points about the opportunities and threats that lie behind these major socioeconomic problems:

> . . . it is an ethical demand on business to convert into profitable business the satisfaction of social needs and wants. . . . Social awareness is organizational self-interest. The needs of society, if left unfilled, turn into social diseases. No institution, whether business or hospital, university or government agency, is likely to thrive in a diseased society.[12]

Drucker points out that one hundred years ago there were community wants that have been satisfied by what are now the modern electrical industry, the telephone industry, and urban transit systems.

A large, diversified company (TRW, Inc.) has expressed the same idea in this way:

> An immense opportunity lies in an area TRW labels "civil systems." The company is using its systems analysis and management expertise to tackle a wide variety of civilian problems like environmental pollution, water management, police communications, urban mass transportation systems, traffic control, medical systems, land use, and community planning and development. As a case in point, TRW is currently helping to plan the development of an entire 3,000-acre urban community in Ontario, Canada. . . . Being flexible and responsive to change is going to be extremely important if one can believe the ecologists, economists, and population experts when they say the seventies will be the most critical decade in history. The problems of maintaining a decent quality of life can now be predicted with almost complete certainty.
>
> In an environment that will marry the profit motive to . . . society's needs, there are immense opportunities for those with the technological skills necessary to pursue these interests. TRW is such a company, and it looks to a cycle of challenge and response that should lead to the highest level of productivity and growth in its history.[13]

Finally, *Business Week* has commented editorially as follows:

> If U.S. cities eventually are saved from the decay and collapse that threaten them, it may well turn out that private enterprise rather than government has the answer . . . across the country an increasing number of large corporations and land developers are pushing big-scale, master-planned projects that promise to remake the ravaged faces of downtown areas. . . .
>
> There is nothing charitable about these enterprises. Their backers simply are betting that, with proper planning, downtown development can be made to pay its own way. And as urban sprawl covers more and more territory, making land on the fringes more and more remote, basic economics promises to give the private efforts a boost. . . .
>
> With a little good sense in city government and some careful work by the planners, it just might be that the profit motive could save the city as society's major marketplace for goods, services, and ideas.[14]

The reference to "a little good sense in city government" points up the social responsibility of government officials to work effectively with business managers and vice versa. And in peacetime, there is a social responsibility on military managers, too, to use their great resources for the benefit of socially valuable projects.

Plank 9 *If social goals are to be achieved, managerial controls must focus upon them.* Acknowledging the social responsibilities enumerated in Plank 8 is only a first step. In order actually to achieve them, managers must learn to include these in their statements of objectives and to generate control reports on them. In other words, managers must learn to control to multiple objectives—the socially oriented goals in addition to the traditional financial, production, and sales goals.

There are many financial, production, sales, and product-line controls, but how many firms actively measure progress against their social objectives? How many firms have well-developed control reports for doing this? How many firms regularly measure what the body politic thinks of the projects the firm is undertaking and how it uses its resources? How many government agencies do this regularly?

One technique for making such measurements is the "social audit," which a few firms are attempting to implement. As developed by one firm, the audit takes the form of a balance sheet. The asset side contains entries such as "staff trained for social projects," "equipment and buildings equipped for work on social projects," and "completed research on social problems;" the liabilities side is headed "social commitments, obligations, and equity" and contains such items as "contract commitments to certain projects," "costs of pollution," and "costs of government services consumed" (net of tax payment).[15] Social audits can be helpful in comparing the cost-effectiveness ratios of alternative corporate social programs; such comparison studies improve the decision making involved in setting the corporate social or *pro bono* budget.

Plank 10   *Management is required universally, and the quality of management is a factor in rivalry between ideologies.* One hopes that rivalry between large nations is shifting from military conflict to a competition to demonstrate which ideology or national system can produce a better quality of life for its people. In such competition, the multiple goals of productivity, effectiveness, satisfying working lives, and the solution of major socioeconomic problems are sought by every nation. Thus management is required universally, and the quality of its managerial performance helps or hurts the international appeal of a nation's political-economic system.

In the past the United States' productivity and high standard of living, as well as our willingness to give economic help to other nations, have helped us to win friends; conversely, recurring massive agricultural failures in the Soviet Union and China have hindered the propagation of those nations' ideologies. Also, in industry the Soviets appear to have had great difficulty in designing managerial incentives and controls that do not result in unfortunate distortions in production. Neither of our two great rivals has had much surplus to give to other nations.

Unfortunately, however, the United States is no longer the productivity leader of the world, and the dollar is no longer the currency on which all others are based. We have been hurt not only by mismanagement of the economy by elected officials but also by managers who tolerate superfluous and unproductive government workers. Also harmful are business managers who use high-pressure advertising to sell worthless cereals or to sell 11 cents' worth of after-shave lotion for $1.29. And we are not helped by those who produce damage-prone automobiles, or sell certain United States–made drugs for two or three times as much at home as they cost abroad, or who bribe government officials and make illegal political contributions. That some of these managers loudly extol the private enterprise system and denounce other systems is distressing; they could serve the system better by more effective performance and higher managerial ethics.

A useful ethical criterion, especially for public executives but also for business-people, is to ask: If this action is held up to public scrutiny, will I still feel that it is what I should have done and how I should have done it?[16]

On Personal Aspects of Managerial Effectiveness

Plank 11 *Management is not for everyone; some highly intelligent people would be far more effective in nonmanagerial positions.* President Harry Truman used to say of a career in politics: "If you can't stand the heat, get out of the kitchen!" The saying has relevance to management (administration) as a career if the "heat" is interpreted to mean the inevitable frustrations of the managerial job.

Although there is value in studying management in highly rational terms (define objectives, set plans, design control reports, etc.), it must be recognized that these definitions do not present a realistic picture of day-to-day managerial life. Rarely is the actual process so smooth, logical, or straight-line. No matter how systematic a manager tries to be, there are times when management appears to be "just one damned thing after another." After all, managers work through other people—and people are nonstandardized and subject to emotional states; each is equipped with a set of communication filters (i.e., a unique personal history) that may cause him or her to receive much different messages than the manager intends to convey. Also, managers regularly must make decisions on incomplete data and faulty forecasts. Finally, managers must control to multiple goals, which are sometimes conflicting. And when managers in desperation turn to textbooks for help, they are frustratingly advised to use a "situational" or "contingency" approach, to adapt the often conflicting principles to infinitely varying situations.

Thus managers who have been educated in economic analysis, quantitative methods, and logical planning find that the skills they most need on the job are those of negotiation, persuasion, compromise, and decision making without benefit of scientific technique.

Especially in huge business or government organizations, the weight of accumulated irrationalities often threatens to break a manager's spirit, causing him or her to lose momentum, to shift into neutral, to coast. Yet this is exactly what must be resisted, because it is the beginning of "contagious frustration" that spreads to subordinates. A manager who can overcome the frustrations and keep working toward meaningful goals can keep subordinates alive and effective. Some leaders can maintain an island of meaningfulness even though the next higher manager has quit trying; they instill in their subordinates some goal, or what Ohmann calls a "sense of special significance" strong enough to resist the spreading contagion.[17]

Some persons simply are not cut out for these irrationalities, discontinuities, ambiguities, and compromises. Such persons would be happier and more effective pursuing such specialties as engineering, science, or writing; still others would be happier and more effective in staff jobs where they could specialize in analyzing problems or in dealing with a limited range of problems rather than handling the full range of processes and problems confronting a manager.

Certainly management is not for everyone. Unfortunately, many persons who should not be in management are forced into it because that is the only way they can continue to progress in rank, pay, and status. Organizations should provide special pay grades and titles that enable gifted specialists to continue progressing without being forced into management.

Plank 12 *A manager has an obligation to try to achieve vigorous physical and mental health.* A manager who becomes physically stodgy is likely to become a victim of the contagious frustration that has just been discussed; conversely, a vigorous, healthy manager is more likely to maintain a sense of mission that helps make the working lives of subordinates more meaningful. Also, a healthy manager is better able to take the time and more likely to have the sincere empathy required to communicate well with subordinates so that they will enjoy their lives better.

The word "vigorous" is used here to denote something more than merely having an annual physical examination. The minimum requirement includes a systematic exercise program, a reasonable diet, workdays of sensible length, and a relaxing recreational, artistic, or intellectual off-job interest. Mental health is helped, also, by the kind of "know thyself" communication discussed earlier in this chapter.[18]

Plank 13 *Time is a precious managerial resource.* "Irrevocable," "irreplaceable," "highly perishable," "precious"—these adjectives describe time as a managerial resource, and they indicate why managers should periodically do some hard thinking about time utilization.

Such hard thinking involves three types of analyses: Is the manager actually in control of his or her own time? Does the manager's actual time usage match the existing objectives? Might certain timesaving procedures be helpful?

First, in determining whether managers are actually in control of their own time, they must look at the patterns of their relations with superiors and subordinates.[19] Many bosses, often unwittingly, do not allow their subordinate managers to control their (the subordinates') own time; rather, they keep subordinates on call, ready to jump immediately into any assignment that the boss may give them. While this is quite convenient for the boss, it keeps the subordinates from organizing their own time usage toward the accomplishment of their own objectives; it keeps the subordinates from being accountable managers. Some managers, when presented with evidence that they are using their subordinate managers in this way, will change their way of working.

In looking at their relationships with their own subordinates, managers must ask themselves whether they are supervising them so closely that they (the superiors) inevitably get involved in the details of the subordinates' work. Some managers are seduced, through subtle flattery, into taking on tasks that subordinates could handle. One way to check on this is to ask oneself at the end of every conference with a subordinate or group of subordinates: Did the meeting result in a list of things for me to do, or in a list of things for my subordinates to do? Managers who ask this question often find that, in fact, their subordinates are "delegating" jobs upward to them. It helps, also, to insist that subordinates recommend solutions rather than just raise problems in memos and in meetings.

Second, in order to find out whether or not his or her time utilization matches objectives and priorities, a manager should first find out exactly how this time is actually being used; that is, the manager should periodically keep a time log. Then the record of actual time use should be compared with a statement of ideal use of time. Is the time actually being used to work on objectives (in priority order or strategic sequences) or might it be that telephone calls, drop-in visitors, conference schedules, unnecessary trips, or the demands of superiors or subordinates actually set the priorities?

After making this comparison, a manager should have two signs posted in his or her office. One sign, tying in with what has been said earlier about managers being change agents, reads, "The managerial job is to bring about change, improvements; it is not to preside over the status quo." Under this motto there should be a recap of the main objectives of the current six-month or one-year period. In fact, some executives post the current objectives where all visitors may see them, the idea being that such public commitment increases the manager's private commitment.

The other sign reads, "The big gains are made by doing the right things, not by doing things rightly." The "right things" are those things necessary to achieve change; the other things are established procedures that the manager may be handling expertly or precisely even though they are no longer essential or though it is now possible for nonmanagers to handle them. Or, in Drucker's terms, is the manager spending time on products that are in the decline phase of their life cycles instead of on products that are today's and tomorrow's winners? Everyday pressures on a manager always favor yesterday. They always favor what has happened over the future, the crisis over the opportunity, the immediate over the relevant.[20]

The third step is to apply timesaving techniques and devices, such as ways of scheduling telephone time to minimize interruptions, ways of quickly answering correspondence, techniques for using a secretary efficiently, and many other ideas that are readily available in management literature. [21]

This plea for more effective use of time should *not* be seen as a plea for high-pressure scheduling or hyperactivity; that would conflict with the plank on health and the one on the quality of the lives of one's subordinates. On the contrary, a relaxed pace (considerable "brooding time") is required to determine what changes need to be made and what actions are required to achieve "the right things to do."

CONCLUSION

It is fitting that this book be brought to a close with a discussion of management philosophy. A main theme throughout has been that management is undergoing profound change, and in time of change it is especially important that managers be clear in their own minds about what they want to accomplish and why. Armed with a strong philosophy, managers are better able to sort out the many new ideas and challenges cascading upon them and to concentrate on those that will help them formulate and achieve worthy objectives.

REVIEW QUESTIONS

1 Why is it important that managers (and potential managers) think through their own philosophies of management?
2 In what ways can recognition of the complexity of management influence a person's actual managerial practices?

3 How can the concept of corporate character be put to practical use in a given situation?

4 Why is it especially important at the current stage of development of management to encourage risk taking and the viewing of managers as "change agents?"

5 What are the four main topics of the philosophy planks under the heading "On the Human Responsibilities of Managers"?

6 What does the author feel is the big, fundamental change taking place in the area of the social responsibilities of managers?

7 What are the sources of frustration in the managerial job that lead to the idea that managers should have high "frustration tolerance"?

DISCUSSION QUESTIONS

1 Describe at least two changes (additions, subtractions, or modifications) that you would make in the philosophy stated in this chapter in order to bring it more into line with your own philosophy. Explain the reasoning that underlies each of your changes.

2 What are some of the philosophy differences that contribute to the "generation gap" as it affects managerial practice? What can persons on each side do to help bridge the gap?

3 Some writers contend that managers' main social responsibility is to run a profitable business and also that devotion of time and money to other social responsibilities constitutes a diversion from the main social responsibility. Discuss pro and con.

4 What problems do you see as limiting the widespread use of "human resources accounting?" Of "social audit"?

5 How can the long-running debate between human relations proponents (derided as "do-gooders" or "happiness happy" by their critics) and those who stress performance-productivity (derided as "Neanderthal" or "shortsighted" types by their critics) be resolved?

NOTES

[1] Peter Drucker feels that "few executives attain one-tenth of the effectiveness their abilities, their knowledge, and their industry deserve." *The Age of Discontinuity* (Harper & Row, Publishers, Incorporated, New York, 1969), p. 200.

[2] Larry E. Greiner, "Evolution and Revolution as Organizations Grow," *Harvard Business Review,* July–August 1972, pp. 37–46. Also, as in footnote 8 in Chap. 4, the present author has identified seven "key crises" in the growth of new small firms.

[3] Remark by Tom Hayden at a seminar sponsored by the General Electric Company to explore antiestablishment views.

[4] Melvin Anshen, "The Management of Ideas," *Harvard Business Review,* July–August 1969, p. 102. See also Howard W. Johnson, "Education for Management and Technology in the 1970's," *Science,* May 10, 1968, pp. 620–627.

[5] For a listing of principles of change management, see Charles A. Dailey, *Entrepreneurial Management* (McGraw-Hill Book Company, New York, 1971), last half of chap. 2. Dailey's seventeen principles include: "Innovation is accepted faster in small packages," "Most inventions are made by outsiders," "The outside expert must be introduced by the hometown 'good ol' boy,' " and "The chances of change by written directive are near zero."

[6] George J. Berkwitt, "The Revolt of the Middle Managers," *Dun's Review,* September 1969, p. 39.

[7] Ralph G. Nichols, "Listening, What Price Inefficiency?" *Office Executive,* April 1959. William H. Read, "Communication in Organizations: Some Problems and Misconceptions," *Personnel Administration,* March–April 1963, pp. 4–10.

[8] Ralph Nader's "raiders" and other self-appointed critics of corporate managers are now creating such criticism in the form of protests at annual meetings, stockholders' lawsuits, and proposals for legislation on the makeup of boards of directors. For an account of how government officials work under the glare of publicity, see Frederick V. Malek, "Mr. Executive Goes to Washington," *Harvard Business Review,* September–October 1972, p. 64.

⁹ With their need for maintaining volume of billings to carry overhead, most management consulting firms can ill afford to be critical or even objective if they might thereby lose an account. Thus a contract arrangement for a number of years is best for assuring objectivity from the consultant.

¹⁰ For an excellent set of papers on various aspects of this subject, see "Social Responsibility of Business," *Journal of Contemporary Business,* Winter 1973. Also *Bibliography: Corporate Responsibility* (Bank of America, San Francisco, May 1974).

¹¹ George A. Steiner, "The Second Managerial Revolution," *The Conference Board RECORD,* July 1973.

¹² Drucker, op. cit., pp. 205–206.

¹³ Excerpted from an undated pamphlet titled *TRW: A Focus on Growth* (TRW, Inc., Cleveland).

¹⁴ Editorial section, Feb. 17, 1973. See also the Spring 1974 issue of *Journal of Contemporary Business,* which has as its theme "Corporate Responsibility and the Problems of the City."

¹⁵ R. A. Bauer and Dan H. Fenn, Jr., *The Corporate Social Audit* (Russell Sage Foundation, New York, 1972). "The First Attempts at a Corporate 'Social Audit,' " *Business Week,* Sept. 23, 1972, reports on the book; so also does an article by Bauer and Fenn, "What Is a Corporate Social Audit?" *Harvard Business Review,* January–February 1973. For a depth analysis of the accounting problems involved in social audits, see Neil Churchill, "Toward a Theory of Social Accounting," *Sloan Management Review,* Spring 1974, pp. 1–17.

¹⁶ Harlan Cleveland, *The Future Executive.* (Harper & Row, Publishers, Incorporated, New York, 1972), Chap. 8.

¹⁷ O. A. Ohmann, " 'Skyhooks' with Special Implications for Monday through Friday," *Harvard Business Review,* May–June 1955, pp. 9–10.

¹⁸ For more on mental health, see "The Executive under Pressure," a *Business Week* supplement, May 25, 1974, pp. 119–130, including recommended readings from among the plethora of self-help psychology books. Among those recommended are Thomas A. Harris, *I'm OK—You're OK* (Harper & Row, Publishers, Incorporated, New York, 1969), and Eric Fromm's, *The Art of Loving* (Harper & Row, Publishers, Incorporated, New York, 1959).

¹⁹ William Oncken and Donald L. Wass, "Management Time: Who's Got the Monkey?" *Harvard Business Review,* November–December 1974, pp. 75–80.

²⁰ Peter Drucker, *Managing for Results* (Harper & Row, Publishers, Incorporated, New York, 1964), chap. 4; and *The Effective Executive* (Harper & Row, Publishers, Incorporated New York, 1966), p. 111.

²¹ Some basic ideas plus some gimmicks are contained in Drucker's *The Effective Executive,* chaps. 1 and 2; F. D. Barrett, "The Management of Time," *The Business Quarterly,* a publication of the School of Business Administration, University of Western Ontario, London, Ontario, Canada, Spring 1960; and Leo B. Moore, "Managerial Time," *Industrial Management Review,* Spring 1968. Also, a description of an electronic device used in analyzing an executive's work day is given in "Are Executives Efficient?" *Business Week,* December 1973, pp. 52–55. A list of timesaving tricks and a discussion of ideas featured by some consultants is given in "Teaching Managers to Do More in Less Time," *Business Week,* Mar. 3, 1975, pp. 68–69.

RECOMMENDED READINGS

Anshen, Melvin: "The Management of Ideas," *Harvard Business Review,* July–August 1969.

Cassell, Frank: "The Politics of Public-Private Management," *MSU Business Topics,* September 1972.

Leys, Wayne A. R.: *Ethics for Policy Decisions* (Greenwood Press, Westport, Conn., 1968).

Lodge, George C.: "Business and the Changing Society," *Harvard Business Review,* March–April 1974.

"Social Responsibility of Business" (issue theme), *Journal of Contemporary Business,* Winter 1973.

Steiner, George A.: "The Second Managerial Revolution," *The Conference Board RECORD,* July 1973.

Stover, Carl F.: "Changing Patterns in the Philosophy of Management," *Public Administration Review,* Winter 1968.

"Symposium on Social Equity and Public Administration," *Public Administration Review,* January–February 1974.

Appendix

Building a Career in Management

Note: *This appendix is designed for young managers with enough work experience to have some idea of what their career objectives are and in what field they will pursue those objectives. Undergraduates or others whose preoccupation is with finding a first job and who are vague on their career objectives should benefit from an exercise such as that set forth by J. D. Weinrauch in "Term Project: A Simulated Life Cycle,"* Collegiate News and Views, *Fall 1974, pp. 15ff.*

Building a career in management is essentially a planning/controlling task that uses four concepts developed earlier in this textbook:

   1 *Know thyself*—which calls for the assessment of your own strengths, weaknesses, and interests so that your objectives will be realistic.
   2 *Organizational character*—which recognizes that organizations differ vastly in the amount of development they offer and in the kind of performance they value and reward.
   3 *Complexity of management*—which reminds a manager that it is possible, though not always essential, to take a "lifelong learning" approach to a career in management.
   4 *Scenario planning*—a technique for bringing together the three foregoing concepts and many specific ideas into a workable career plan that provides for periodic measurement, evaluation, and replanning.

This appendix will first discuss the use of each of these concepts in career building. Then it will get into the specifics of separate scenario career plans for persons planning to go into (1) small businesses, possibly as owners, (2) large firms, or (3) government organizations.

THE BASIC CONCEPTS OF CAREER BUILDING

Know Thyself

Today a person in management may pursue any of a variety of goals—the traditional goals of position and wealth or goals having to do with the development of people, the improvement of communities, the solution of socioeconomic problems, or many other kinds of activities. All these are attainable through *some* businesses. In addition, there are many nonprofit, nongovernmental organizations working directly on educational, medical, scientific, and cultural pursuits of great challenge. And, increasingly, there are government enterprises doing vital work in these same fields; in fact, on large projects, a government group often provides the coordinating management for project teams from business and nonbusiness organizations.

The common denominator of these different kinds of enterprises is that they all require managers at many levels. Perhaps a young person seeking a job and having a hard time of it may not realize that such a wide choice lies open. Nevertheless, the choice is there, although finding it may take time, considerable intelligent search activity, some trial and error, and even some temporary compromises.

Faced with so much choice and such a formidable search task, young managers need to define their objectives—that is, what they want to get out of their management careers in the long run. Having objectives well defined is essential to the process of determining what it will take to reach those objectives. And the process of thinking through "what it will take" brings young managers face to face with the big "know thyself" questions: What are your true interests—the things that motivate you? Do you have the talents required to pursue such interests, especially the talents required to achieve the needed formal education? Do you have the ambition required to succeed at each step of the experience you must acquire? Are career plans consistent with your values on family life and intellectual or cultural activities?

Without realistic answers to these questions, a manager's objectives and plans may prove to be mere wishful thinking; even worse, they might prove greatly frustrating by leading the manager down inappropriate paths. But securing realistic answers to these questions requires a great deal of inquiry not only at the start of one's career but also at every major step in that career.[1] The inquiry must tap the wisdom of persons who know the manager's strengths and weaknesses—associates, bosses, psychologist-counselors, knowledgeable friends, and spouse—and of persons who are actually achieving the same kinds of objectives. The latter are especially valuable sources and (even when they have no organizational tie with the inquirer) are usually willing to help because they are flattered that someone else admires their values and that someone else sees them as successful.

As in all managerial planning and control, in career building it is necessary to measure progress against objectives regularly. And sometimes a mature under-standing of oneself will lead to the conclusion that objectives should be changed—to be less ambitious, more ambitious, or different in character.

Organizational Character

How can a person determine from outside whether an organization will be sympathetic to his or her interests, will appreciate the values he or she holds important, will reward the kinds of achievements he or she will attain, will offer the kinds of work experience and the rate of advancement that he or she has envisioned in objectives and plans? The first year or two are critical in setting one's attitude toward a managerial career—in either "being turned on" or "being turned off."[2]

It is a big, difficult assignment. To start with, most published materials on this subject are naïve and unrealistic. Further, many high-ranking executives in large firms are unrealistic about their organizations (for reasons recounted in Chapter 12); many lower-ranking spokespersons—public relations specialists and recruiters—are paid to be promoters, not objective analysts. And, most discouraging of all, many managers simply have not learned to think analytically about organizational character—how it is formed, what shapes it takes, and how much impact it has on careers.

The most effective procedure is to make many inquiries of people from within and outside the organization in order to locate a person or two who are sensitive to this subject. The inquirer should begin by reviewing those parts of Chapter 3 that describe many different patterns of management and those parts of Chapter 11 that discuss organizational character so as to be able to ask good, relevant questions when a sensitive respondent is found. The firm's and the industry's growth rates are particularly important; vigorously growing firms are usually more "open" in their managerial relations and they simply have greater opportunity to offer.

Of persons from within the organization, the most valuable are likely to be middle-level managers. First- and second-level supervisors often have little opportunity to see how most of the management structure actually functions. Of persons outside the organization, trained observers (such as consultants, professors, and reporters—even though the latter's writings are usually not useful on this subject) are likely to be the most helpful. Occasionally a businessperson who is a customer to or a supplier of the organization in question can be helpful if assured that all comments will be held in confidence. Although bankers and financial analysts might be expected to know quite a bit about the companies with which they deal, their understanding of the management process, unfortunately, typically leaves much to be desired. Former employees of the firm can be quite helpful; however, one must be cautious in evaluating their views because they may be covering up their own failures.

Complexity of Management

If a person's ambitions are modest, he or she need not be greatly concerned with the complexity of management; probably an undergraduate education, on-job experience, and an occasional seminar (perhaps offered by the trade or professional association in the relevant field) will suffice. If, however, a person's plans call for going far up the management ladder, he or she must become competent in most of the aspects of management set forth in Figures 10–2a and b (one for business, the other for government).

The ambitious young manager faces a formidable task of setting priorities among the many subjects to be learned and of deciding which are to be mastered via formal schooling, which via work experience, which via on-job training, and which via less formal educational programs.

A young manager ideally should come to the first job with at least three skills: (1) a knowledge of the languages of management, accounting and statistics; (2) the ability to produce a logically organized, reasonably clear report; and (3) the capacity to speak well. Formal education in managerial processes (planning, controlling, etc.), concepts (such as strategy, systems theory, etc.), and techniques (simulation, organizational development, etc.) are best approached after at least three years of work experience. The reason for this is that the inexperienced person can grasp these subjects only on a rather meaningless academic level.[3]

The many other career-building decisions that must be faced by an ambitious young manager will be discussed later in connection with scenarios for careers in small-business, large-business, and nonbusiness organizations.

Scenario Planning

A person starting out on a managerial career should attempt to state his or her objectives for about twenty years hence; these should be stated in terms not only of position (a description is more meaningful than a title) but also of the type of work and the types of satisfaction to be achieved. Certainly, it is the rare person who can lay out a set of objectives that will survive unchanged for twenty years; nevertheless, this is the way to start planning because it keeps a person aware of the possible long-range implications of shorter-range plans.

These objectives should then be "stepped back" to ten-year objectives-plans by asking: If I am to achieve such and such in twenty years, what progress (position, type of work, experience, education) must I have achieved in ten years? By a similar process, sets of five-year, three-year, and one-year objectives-plans should be derived. If the first-year objectives-plans are realistically attainable from the starting point and if each step to the next set is realistic for the time allowed, then the plans should be usable. Otherwise they must be reworked until they become usable.

To think through all these steps will, of course, require a great deal of discussion with knowledgeable people both at the start and at periodic review periods. Even with extensive exploration, the early drafts of such scenarios will be sketchy and tentative, but they will become more detailed and firmer with each reworking (perhaps every two years). Plans should never be set in concrete; they are most useful when they serve as flexible guidelines. While the short-range plans will be concerned chiefly with securing education and rounded experience, the longer-range plans will be chiefly concerned with achievement of position and the influence needed to achieve the values set as objectives.

Put into scenario form, a career plan can chart the relationships among how a field (an industry, profession, or type of government activity) is expected to develop, the types of opportunities it offers, the individual's personal development, and the rivalries and competition that may be expected along the way. Thus a scenario should provide specific road markers that serve as the basis for biennial evaluations of actual progress against plans on the following:

1 *Assumptions* about how a field as a whole and the organizations in it will develop as to size, function, and opportunities.

2 *Feasibility of paths* of progression envisioned in the plans. Do they still appear realistic in view of how the field has developed since the plans were formulated?

3 *Progress of the individual* in terms of position, reward, and influence and also in terms of education and experience. These evaluations bring the manager face to face with the hard questions of whether to stay with his or her present organization or to move to another.

4 *Strengths and weaknesses of the individual* relative to achievement of remaining steps toward final objectives. How accurately has the manager anticipated the types of problems, criticisms, and rivalries encountered? Do the remaining plans provide for overcoming these?

5 *Continuing appropriateness of objectives,* that is whether, once one has achieved a more mature understanding of oneself and one's field, the objectives still appear challenging; or should they perhaps be revised to be more ambitious or less so, or to focus on a different type of satisfaction?

Along about the fifteenth year of pursuing such a set of objectives-plans, many individuals should begin planning for a second career—an idea that is becoming increasingly feasible and increasingly popular. Sometimes a second career is appropriate because the manager achieves a top position well ahead of schedule. In such cases, it is not wise to stay in the top position more than ten years. The facts of life are that the great bulk of executives achieve what they are going to achieve in the first ten years in an influential position. After that, chances are that continuation will subtract from, rather than add to, their records. In a second career in a different field that they can enter at the top, such individuals often make significant contributions and are much happier doing it. Sometimes a second career is appropriate when a manager "tops out" short of his or her goal, that is, when it becomes clear that there will be no further advancement. In such cases, a shift to a private venture, to teaching, or to government work can add new interest to life.[4]

SPECIFIC IDEAS FOR CAREER SCENARIOS

A Small Business of Your Own

In recent years, increasing (but still small) numbers of business school graduates have planned to start small businesses of their own, usually in partnership with one or two others or with an investor. There are two big attractions: (1) the possibility of greater long-run gain and (2) the prospect of being one's own boss—free from the restrictions and bureaucracy often found in large organizations. And there are two big drawbacks: owning and managing a small business is tremendously hard work, and the failure rate is high.

Studies of success and failure in small business have established quite clearly that the leading cause of failure is lack of rounded managerial experience in the particular field on the part of the key person(s). This means that the prospective entrepreneur should not be in too great a hurry to start his or her own business; rather, the career plan should provide at least five years for acquiring rounded managerial experience and for learning the particular business while on someone else's payroll. One way of doing this is to go to work for a medium-sized firm that is large enough to have competent managers heading up each major function yet small enough that the prospective business person will be able to see how the general manager pulls all the functions together. Another possibility for gaining this rounded managerial experience is to work for a large firm that distributes through small businesses (such as oil companies and their gas stations) or that supplies small firms (such as a chemical company selling plastic compounds to many small fabricators). In either case, the large firm knows a great deal about how to operate the small firms, often providing management assistance to them.

Kinds of Experience   During the years in which he or she is gaining experience while on someone else's payroll, the prospective entrepreneur's career plan should call for getting experience in a number of departments (especially marketing and operations) and experience (perhaps as an "assistant to" or as a staff member) at the general management level where one can see how all the different specialties are brought together. It is also important to learn finance, especially planning capital needs and cash flow. If all these things cannot be learned on the job, they should be studied in night courses. Some universities offer courses (some credit, some noncredit) in small-business management or in launching a new venture that thoroughly cover not only the financial planning but also how to do the original market research on which a new venture is based. It is particularly important to learn how to plan a competitive strategy. Because they are weak, small firms need to have well-conceived competitive strategies even more than do large firms. If such courses are not available, a course featuring a computerized business game can do a good job of simulating experience at the general management level and of teaching financial planning. For the business owner, graduate degrees are not important; what is important is that these things be learned.

Having completed five years or so of preparation and feeling that the time has come to launch his or her own business, the prospective entrepreneur should schedule a careful check against all the processes and specialties exhibited in Figures 10–2a and b. Inevitably, the inexperienced entrepreneur will be less than fully prepared on some of them; perhaps there are gaps in such areas as employee selection, credits and collections, or management information systems. He or she should then be sure to get help on these activities from consultants, partners, investors, or board members.

Before actually launching the business, the entrepreneur should prepare a complete prospectus that has won the approval of these same persons.

Staffing for Strength   As the firm grows, the small-business head should first hire people whose strengths are in the areas of his or her weaknesses. Another way to get help is to keep a close association with two or three other small-business managers with whom confidences may be exchanged. Each such person will have some experience, some strength different from those possessed by the others.

After the first two or three years of ninety-hour weeks are over and the business is becoming established, the career plan should call for resumption of the lifelong learning policy. Particularly helpful would be a case course in business policy in which the manager analyzes the problems of many different real companies. Such study should help the manager anticipate and solve the developmental and competitive problems of his or her own business. Over the years, the manager should systematically participate in a variety of seminars offered by industry associations, consultants, or universities. Such courses will help a young business person finally acquire competence in each of the many aspects of the complex field of management.

An alternative scenario might call for starting a venture without giving up the job in the large organization until the venture is well enough established to be able to pay a salary. Thus it is sometimes possible to start on a part-time moonlighting basis or with a partner who is on the job full time.

A variation of the part-time approach is to start a number of different ventures that do not involve heavy investment. The basic idea here is that a failure may be washed out quickly with light loss while a success may be expanded and pursued indefinitely. Many light losses may be more than balanced by one growing venture that is successful year after year. One entrepreneur, a professor in his early years, started at least twenty businesses of which only two succeeded; however, one of those has over the years made many millions of dollars and the other returns almost $100,000 per year before taxes. All the failures added up to less than $150,000 in losses.

A Big-Business Career

Many different types of careers, ranging from modest to all-out ambitious, are possible within the big-business setting. The objective may be to reach a comfortable middle-management line position in sales or manufacturing or some other specialty, or to reach a staff position from which the person may influence some particular aspect of the way the firm operates, or to go very high in general management. Because it would take too much space to discuss scenarios for all these possibilities, only the most challenging one—the very ambitious alternative—will be considered.

The first two to three years out of college should be devoted to accomplishing two things: (1) learning everything possible about the department, the company, and the industry and (2) securing, and performing well on, responsible assignments. Although many large firms will place a college graduate in an orientation program involving brief rotations to a number of departments, it is probably better to settle into one spot and aggressively seek responsibility as soon as possible. From any spot within a firm it is possible to learn a great deal about the different departments and about the industry by immersing oneself in trade literature and textbooks, by talking with people from the various departments, and by generally being alert and inquiring.

After two or three years of experience, the novice manager is ready to benefit from graduate education and should proceed to get it. Although some persons are skeptical about the value of formal graduate education in management, in actual practice most large companies give strong preference to M.B.A.'s in recruiting for high-potential appointments. While an M.B.A. certainly is not a guarantee of success, it definitely opens the door to opportunity.

Full-Time Graduate School? A major decision involves whether to get the graduate degree by full-time or part-time study; both approaches can be viable. In many cases there will be no choice, either because the person cannot afford to go to school full time or because no quality part-time program is available. Sometimes the key persons in a firm will strongly favor big-name schools that require attendance on a full-time basis. In such cases, it is wise to study full-time even if this means heavy borrowing. In cases where there is choice, the basic criterion should be whether or not the individual is progressing satisfactorily in the company. If indications are that, during the three years or so of part-time study, he or she will get a promotion and some valuable rotation, the part-time format should be adopted. If, however, indications are that promotion and rotation will be slow in coming, he or she should make the break and go to school full time. After getting the degree, it may be possible to return to the same company on a faster track; if not, it should be possible to locate with a company that does put M.B.A.'s on a fast track.

In the years immediately after graduate school, the emphasis should be on getting assignments of at least two years' duration in each of the major departments. The earlier one can get credentials in finance, the better; but all the major departments are important. It is at this stage that the hard questions about whether or not to change companies must be faced. Clearly, if one cannot get rounded managerial experience fairly rapidly where one is, moving to another organization that does offer such opportunity is indicated. But the new organization must be carefully selected (possibly through a high-level executive recruitment consultant), because too much job hopping can ruin a reputation.[5] One thing to look for is the presence of some in-company executive development program that gives a person a chance to learn and a chance to demonstrate ability on special assignments that will elicit the attention of higher executives.

In this stage of a career it is advisable to find out exactly what the boss and the higher executives are looking for (or, in other words, on what factors they are making their ratings) and aggressively seek those jobs and special assignments that offer a chance to perform on those factors. Usually line jobs have higher visibility than staff jobs. Also, it is advisable to be aggressive about attending outside seminars, not relying on M.B.A. courses but taking a "lifelong learning" attitude.[6] At this stage it is also often wise to ally oneself with a fast-moving higher executive whose work is worthy of sincere admiration; this person may offer valuable advice. Listen to this person and follow his or her advice.

As one nears the top, it is a good idea to gain visibility via industry activities (committees, speaking, writing for journals.) These activities will help both within the company and outside. Getting a chief executive's job often requires changing organizations; waiting for the top spot in a particular organization can be a long and sometimes futile approach. There is only one top spot in a firm; there are many in an industry.

A Government Career

Degrees and other certifications of formal education are highly important to ambitious persons in government service. They help persons to enter at a higher level (by strengthening them for the entrance exam), and this makes a substantial difference because of the requirement of 1 or 1½ years in grade before one is eligible for promotion. For those who cannot get a graduate degree before entering, there are now a large number of internship appointments at federal, state, and local levels that enable one to acquire a graduate degree while working.[7]

In the early years, government career executives should learn all that they can, not only about the business of a particular agency (be it housing, revenue collection, health services, school administration, or whatever) but also about the specialist fields in which they are placed (that is, personnel, budget and finance, organization and methods, etc.). Some federal departments have organized career-development paths and programs within these specialty fields. These kinds of knowledge are needed to do a job—or, more specifically, to understand the objectives of one's unit, to know what the boss wants, and to help the boss to look good. Capability in budget formulation and budget execution is universally appreciated within government service; so, also, is a thorough understanding of the legislative process.

There are two strategies—in addition to plain working and studying hard—for acquiring the basic knowledge that one should acquire during the early years. One is to get into internal audit work with the General Accounting Office or a slot in the Office of Management and Budget—assignments that get a person deep into the workings of many agencies. Another is to get three or four years in fieldwork with an agency; a person with field experience will, on going to headquarters, have an advantage over those who have been at headquarters from the start.

After a few years and some performance accomplishments, the main concern becomes broadening out from the particular specialty and particular agency. This can be done by either outside study, professional association activities, in-government training programs, or a combination of the three. Today there are available many management development programs at various levels within departments and governmentwide; many federal programs have been opened to personnel from state and local governments. Many states have their own programs, and cities have the International City Management Association's program.[8] Also, there is the prestigious White House Fellows program. It pays to be aggressive about finding out what is required to qualify for these programs and about proposing oneself for appointment to them.

There is an active program in the Federal Civil Service and in many other jurisdictions for advancing managers across departmental lines.[9] The individual should find out what specifications are fed into the computer for the next job that he or she wants and then proceed to get those qualifications on record. Also, it is a good idea to locate and become friendly with a person or sponsor who is in a position to make a selection for such a position (since it is possible to select from lists of qualified persons and even to call for new lists). Being active in professional associations is a good way to become acquainted with such a person. Job hopping within the Civil Service does not carry the stigma associated with job hopping in the private sector; in fact, it is often necessary in government because one is more likely to find oneself stymied in a particular organization behind a line of qualified persons.

As one approaches the high levels of government service, one can aim for assignment to the Federal Executive Institute or to various high-level executive development programs offered by universities throughout the country. Also, it is possible to get a year of full-time education while on full salary. At the federal level, there is an organized business-government exchange program. Attendance at such programs plus some writing for government-management journals are excellent means of achieving visibility and opportunities.

NOTES

[1] Help in working out the answers to these and many more "know thyself" questions is given in a manual by Edward L. Adams, Jr., entitled *Career Advancement Guide* (McGraw-Hill Book Company, New York, 1975). For exciting insights into the topic, see Samuel A. Culbert, *The Organization Trap* (Basic Books, Inc., Publishers, New York, 1974), especially chap. 21.

[2] Douglas T. Hall, "Potential for Career Growth," *Personnel Administration,* May–June 1971, pp. 50–52. The present author will be forever indebted to Herbert E. Evans, his first boss, who helped him see the challenge of management.

[3] Accordingly, the author rejects the popular career strategy that calls for taking a graduate degree immediately after college and then going to work as a consultant. Although it is true that consulting work provides valuable experience, so young a consultant will not only be a poor consultant but also will not learn soundly from the experience.

[4] Charles D. Orth, III, "How to Survive the Mid-Career Crisis," *Business Horizons,* October 1974.

[5] One research study shows no significant difference in career success between those M.B.A.'s who stay with one organization and those who make two job changes; however, those who make more than two job changes are generally less successful: C. Randall Powell, "Do MBA's Really Job-Hop?" *Journal of College Placement,* Spring 1975, pp. 67–74. The report on which this article is based is *MBA Career Performance Ten Years after Graduation* (The Midwest College Placement Association, St. Paul, Minn., 1974).

[6] For specific suggestions, see P. T. Crotty, "Continuing Education and the Experienced Executive," *California Management Review,* Fall 1974.

[7] For a collection of articles on many aspects of internships, see Thomas P. Murphy, *Government Management Internships and Executive Development* (Lexington Books, D. C. Heath and Company, Lexington, Mass., 1973). For information on what programs are available where, contact The National Center for Public Service Internship Programs, 1140 Connecticut Ave. N.W., Washington, D.C. See also Frank Logue, *Who Administers?* a 1972 report for the Ford Foundation summarizing a variety of programs at federal, state, and local levels.

[8] Murphy, op. cit., chaps. 3 and 4 for city programs and chaps. 14 to 16 for federal programs.

[9] David Stanley, "Federal Executives and the Systems That Produce Them," *Personnel Administration,* May–June 1969, pp. 29–34.

RECOMMENDED READING

Adams, Edward L., Jr.: *Career Advancement Guide* (McGraw-Hill Book Company, New York, 1975). A manual with forms, guidelines, and ideas for doing a thorough job of self-analysis and career planning.

"Career Problems of Young Managers," Ross A. Webber, *Management* (Richard D. Irwin,

Inc., Homewood, Ill., 1975). A twenty-page chapter focusing heavily on such topics as "loyalty dilemmas," "personal anxiety," and "ethical dilemmas." Also an extensive bibliography.

Culbert, Samuel A.: *The Organization Trap* (Basic Books, Inc., Publishers, New York, 1974). A provocative book, by a man with degrees in industrial engineering and clinical psychology, for persons who are concerned lest the organizations they work for control them rather than vice versa. The author feels that there is much that the individual can do to relieve the problem.

Dible, Donald: *Up Your Own Organization* (Entrepreneur Press, Santa Clara, Calif., 1971). A handbook with many aids for the person planning a small-business career.

Hall, Douglas T.: "Potential for Career Growth," *Personnel Administration,* May–June 1971, pp. 18–30; also reprinted in J. H. Donnelly, Jr., J. L. Gibson, and J. M. Ivancevich (eds.), *Fundamentals of Management* (Business Publications, Inc., Austin, Tex., 1975). Stresses the motivational and attitudinal aspects of career building rather than the skills-acquiring aspects. Bibliography cites considerable research.

Jennings, E. E.: *Routes to the Executive Suite* (McGraw-Hill Book Company, New York, 1971). Much specific advice on career strategy, tactics, and behavior.

Murphy, Thomas P.: *Government Management Internships and Executive Development* (Lexington Books, D. C. Heath and Company, Lexington, Mass., 1973). Twenty-one articles, half by academics from the field of public administration and half by practitioners in public administration. The articles are critical reviews of many issues, but there is also considerable specific information about internship and executive training programs.

"Plotting a Route to the Top," *Business Week,* Oct. 12, 1974. A seven-page supplement to the weekly magazine; contains numerous instructions for career pathing plus brief success stories of named young men in named corporations. There is also a five-item bibliography which is supplemental to this recommended reading list.

Reif, W. A., and John W. Newstrom: "Career Development by Objectives," *Business Horizons,* October 1974. Contains a career-development model based on MBO, contingency planning, force-field analysis, and the psychological contract.

Name Index

Subject Index